D1513134

CORRESPONDING CULTURES

Corresponding Cultures

THE TWO LITERATURES OF WALES

M. Wynn Thomas

UNIVERSITY OF WALES PRESS
CARDIFF
1999

British Library Cataloguing-in-Publication Data.
A catalogue record for this book is available from the British Library.

ISBN 0–7083–1531–3

Published with the financial support of the Arts Council of Wales

THE *A*SSOCIATION FOR
*W*ELSH *W*RITING IN *E*NGLISH
*C*YMDEITHAS *L*ÊN *S*AESNEG *C*YMRU

Typeset by Action Publishing Technology, Gloucester
Printed in Great Britain by Dinefwr Press, Llandybïe

i'r ddwy ferch –

'cynnadl dau anadl, da yw' –

ac i'r hen ddyn

His office was indulgently to fit
Actives to passives. Correspondency
Only his subject was

(John Donne, 'Love's Deity')

'[there is] the second sight that comes from living in two
cultures'

W. E. B. DuBois

Contents

~

Acknowledgements

~

Some of the material in this book has appeared, in an earlier form, in the following publications: *The Swansea Review, Scintilla, Welsh Writing in English: A Yearbook of Critical Essays, The New Welsh Review, Thirteen Ways of Looking at Tony Conran, Trying the Line: A Volume in Tribute to Gillian Clarke, Dangerous Diversity: The Changing Faces of Wales, Poetry in the British Isles: Non-Metropolitan Perspectives*. My thanks are due to the editors for allowing me to reproduce this material, in substantially revised form, in this present study, and to the organizers of the following lectures and conferences at which draft versions of some of these discussions were first presented: the 1992 Conference on the Literature of Region and Nation (Swansea); the 1993 Conference of the European Society for the Study of English (Bordeaux); the 1994 Reichel Lecture, University of Wales, Bangor; the 1994 Conference on the Literature of Region and Nation (Bratislava); the 1995 Conference of the European Society for the Study of English (Glasgow); the 1997 Conference of the Usk Valley Vaughan Association; the 1997 Conference on Wales and America (Swansea, Tŷ Llên, 1997); the 1998 Schick Lectures, University of Indiana (Terre Haute); and the 1998 Conference of the Association for Welsh Writing in English (Gregynog). I am also grateful to friends and colleagues such as Dr Tony Brown, Dr James A. Davies, Professor Dafydd Johnston, Professor Linden Peach and Mr Glyn Pursglove for their responses to some of the following chapters. I am most particularly appreciative of the kindnesses I have received from distinguished writers such as Gillian Clarke, Tony Conran and Menna Elfyn. Once again, the staff of the University of Wales Press, under the direction first of Ned Thomas and then of Susan Jenkins, have more than earned my respect for their patient scrupulousness. But as always the greatest debts of gratitude are the unfathomable and inestimable ones I owe my wife and my daughter, to whom this book is humbly dedicated: 'Y mae pob llenyddiaeth yn gyfrinach y mae'r allwedd iddi dan garreg drws teulu a phentref a bro a gwlad' (Saunders Lewis).

Penyrheol, Gorseinon, 1997
Southgate, Bro Gŵyr, 1998

Introduction

~

Corresponding Cultures: in the present context, the term 'corresponding' is meant principally to denote one valuable way of articulating the subtle nexus of relationships between the Welsh- and the English-language 'discourse communities' of Wales, as inscribed in their respective literary cultures. As such, part of the aptness of the term lies in the range of possible meanings it brings into play, meanings that define the Welsh situation in the very process of repeatedly subjecting it to cross-examination. For instance, by way of defining the word 'correspond', the *Oxford English Dictionary* suggests:

> To answer to something else in the way of fitness; to agree with; be conformable to; be congruous or in harmony with; to answer to in character or function; to be similar to; to respond; to hold communication or intercourse with; to communicate with another by interchange of letters; to answer to.

The chapters that follow likewise attempt to gloss this book's title by implicitly inflecting the term 'corresponding' in many different ways, so as to bring out its barbed character when applied to the Welsh cultural scene. After all, to indicate important instances in which a shared history may, on certain occasions, have resulted in interesting 'congruities' between the two cultures is also, sadly, to highlight, more often than not, the lack of 'harmony' that nevertheless existed between them. Likewise, there is far less evidence of the two cultures 'holding [substantive] communication or intercourse with each other' (whether by 'interchange of letters', so to speak, or not) than there is of their 'responding' to each other in a spirit of mutual suspicion. Corresponding they have been, not least when unconscious of being so: co-responding (in the sense of mutually nurturing, reinforcing and sustaining) they very largely have not. Indeed, this

1

book was written with Roland Mathias's minatory reflections constantly in mind:

> [Wales] is an unlikely beast, a bilingual country with two cultures in correspondence, and it does not yet exist west of Offa's Dyke. There are those who have remained faithful to Welsh: there are those, far more numerous, who – perhaps through no fault of their own – have lost all of Welshness but the accent and possess almost nothing in its place, certainly not a genuinely English culture: and there are a few mourners and stretcher-bearers out in no-man's land. Whatever of grace is to come must depend most of all on the multiplication of this band, on the changing of its garb and function to one which creates life and does justice to it.[1]

A quarter of a century has passed since those words were written, and much has undoubtedly changed, one hopes for the better, in the meantime. Nevertheless, there remain disturbing correspondences between the situation described by Mathias and the present state of affairs.

The basic pattern of this book is so simple as, no doubt, to be self-evident. Beginning by venturing back to the seventeenth century in order to emphasize that a correspondence between the two cultures has long been one of the main constitutive facts of Welsh identity, I next attempt to indicate some of the ways in which such a coexistence has nevertheless taken on a very different complexion, and an incomparably greater complexity, in the twentieth century. The chapters that then follow examine several respects in which the two cultures impinge on each other, interrelate or otherwise correlate, and among the forms of inter-cultural transaction considered are literary translation and cross-cultural literary influence. I also explore the way in which in Wales even the terms in which gender identity is construed may be intimately affected by the bicultural situation.

Finally, I consider the correspondences with America that have been discovered, or rather constructed, by Welsh writers, in both languages – connections that incidentally reveal hidden aspects of the ongoing conversation between the two cultures of Wales itself. One reason for this new 'turn' at the end of the present study is my wish to indicate potentially illuminating modes of correspondence between aspects of the Welsh cultural situation and those of other countries. Sustained exploration of the possibilities opened up by such cultural excursions would, however, require another book, and a different one. But even in writing the present study, I have always been conscious of the inviting parallel cases that exist elsewhere.

Take, for instance, the kind of reading of contemporary Scotland offered by the poet and critic Robert Crawford. In a recent introductory essay, he has drawn attention to the compensatory work done after the failure of the 1979 Devolution programme by Scottish economic, political, social and cultural historians to establish 'what one might see as an intellectual infrastructure for the culture of a future Scotland with democratic control of its own affairs'.[2] In particular, Crawford acknowledges the attempt made by such intellectuals to correct the deficit of knowledge in Scotland of the country's historical achievements. In this connection he implicitly endorses P. H. Scott's observation: 'It is astonishing, but perhaps symptomatic of the effects of denigration, that hardly any attempt has been made before to study Scottish culture as a whole' (*SBC*, 91). It scarcely needs saying that the current situation in Wales remains astonishing in precisely this same lamentable respect.

But although Crawford respects the work of intellectuals who have sought to offer 'substantial overviews of what constitutes a distinctive and continuing Scottish tradition' (*SBC*, 92), he also has reservations about their methods and the assumptions underlying their whole (and holistic) approach. It is his contention that

> it is the job of intellectuals not so much to produce further totalizing views of Scottish culture, not to define Scotland and Scottishness, but to dedefine them ... Scotland needs not the pursuit of some elusive *echt* Scottishness, but requires many reminders of its protean and plural past, present and future. (*SBC*, 92)

And as he elaborates this thesis, his views begin to approximate to (and therefore, broadly speaking, to correspond to) those implicitly advanced both in my present book and in two previous studies.[3] Among his most directly relevant comments are the following:

> In this context, as I have argued elsewhere, the work of Mikhail Bakhtin may be of some use since it allows us to conceive of

3

identity in terms of an ongoing (and, by nature, fluid) dialogue, rather than in terms of a fixed and unchanging monologue. Scotland, then, alters according to its relations with the rest of the world, not least the rest of Britain, changing and being changed by interaction with other cultures and communities. More than that, Scotland itself is dynamic, authored through an internal poly- phonic process. That authoring involves a variety of languages (not least English, Scots and Gaelic) and their attendant trad- itions; it involves an ongoing regional interaction between parts of Scotland as different as Glasgow and the Outer Hebrides, St Andrews and Dundee. Scotland is also a complexly and shiftingly gendered construct. (*SBC*, 92)

Anticipating the objection that this is merely to apply to Scotland the currently trendy tenets of postmodernism, Crawford sensibly counters by arguing that it is, rather, an overdue recognition of the fact that 'Scotland is and has long been a multicultural, multi- lingual society' (*SBC*, 93).

This is a theme that Crawford has also explored to rewarding effect in his poetry. 'Simultaneous Translation' is a poem that wittily draws out the wider implications of noticing that there are nowadays 'Gaels in Glasgow, Bangladeshis in Bradford'.[4] It is, for Crawford, a revelation not only of the polyglot mixture of contemporary Scottish society but also of the range of different discourses constitutive of each and every modern self: 'This is where we all live now,/ Wearing something like a Sony Walkman,// Hearing another voice every time we speak' (*T*, 14). His most inventive, and ambitious, meditation on this subject is the poem in which he camps up the theme of linguistic diversity by making the letter *Z* a suave, gung-ho, secret-agent hero, renowned for his *Boys' Own* undercover exploits in any number of countries, whose cultural alphabets he has infiltrated and whose codes he has thereby cracked: '*Z* quotes a line of Aristophanes/ In several languages, drifting from one to the other/ And feeling each change him, sensing how they all make him up' (*T*, 24). This is consistent with Crawford's belief that, in its 'other tonguedness' or linguistic self-division, Scotland is 'not a peripheral exception to but a model for international writing in the English-speaking world.'[5]

That Wales is a parallel case is certainly true, as it is also true that the country would benefit immensely from viewing itself in

4

the (perhaps flattering) mirror of Crawford's exhilarating affirmations of cultural pluralism. But that Wales is identical to Scotland in this regard is untrue in one crucial respect. Crawford's Z blithely 'whispers a few words of Gaelic/ To save time encoding' (*T*, 22). Scots Gaelic has, indeed, long been merely one of Scotland's languages, the historic reserve of a small, regional, residual subculture that makes a minor, though nevertheless significant, contribution to 'Scottish identity'. (A similar view might be ventured, with equal justice though perhaps with more provocation, of modern Irish.) The contrast with Welsh could therefore hardly be greater, and it helps highlight the dangers, in the present cultural climate, of allowing the status of Welsh to become so depoliticized and normalized that, benignly regarding English as simply their other native tongue, Welsh-speakers will fail to see the threat its incomparably greater socio-political power inherently represents. The truest 'correspondence' here may be not so much between Welsh-speakers and Gaelic-speakers as between Welsh-speakers and the American Blacks and Hispanics, who understandably and wisely view the new multiculturalist ethic of the United States with considerable suspicion, regarding it as tending to result in their assimilation to a pre-existing monocultural norm. As the Wales–Scotland example suggests, correspondences can, like metaphors, quickly become misleading if they are taken too literally, are trusted too far, or are understood in the wrong way. They need always to be handled delicately, with due regard to the way in which they are liable to be no sooner used than abused.

A genuinely fruitful 'correspondence', in the sense of creative co-operation, between the two cultures of Wales seems to me still a very long way away, and conditional upon a radical psycho-cultural restructuring of the country that is likely to involve little less than a revolution in consciousness. I mention this here only because such comments cannot figure prominently in the discussions that follow, whose purpose is not to dictate the terms on which the two cultures *should* correspond but, rather, to establish how in historical reality they have been corresponding for centuries. They have, after all, been sharing this space, co-existing, interacting, influencing each other, consciously and unconsciously, for the best part of the last thousand years; and yet, as the millennium approaches, no substantial study exists of this cultural dynamic – a dynamic which is surely not a mere ancillary fact about Wales but one of the main products and determinants of modern Welsh history. The silence that has reigned on this intimate, culturally procreative experience of cohabitation seems little less than astonishing, until one realizes that this silence is, in itself, eloquently expressive of the terms on which the two cultures have traditionally corresponded. In so far as this book has a hidden prescriptive agenda, as opposed to its openly descriptive methods of analysis, it is this: that before Wales can fully know itself for what it is, it must confront, acknowledge and carefully consider its bilateral character. Robert Crawford has noted that 'as if to emphasize this need for a new pluralism in Scottish Studies, one that gives full range to variety, and little scope for essentialism, the term "Scotlands" is finding increasing favour north of the border' (*SBC*, 93). The trouble with the word 'Wales' (as with Wales) is that it has proved difficult to think of it in the plural.

Yet, even as I write, I am conscious that to give the above points due emphasis is to risk sounding portentous, and even millennialist and apocalyptic. To strike such a note would be particularly inappropriate, since this book is far from being the comprehensive, definitive, agenda-setting study that the 'programme' outlined above would seem to require. What follows is no more than the most modest of beginnings, a collection of chapters indicative, merely, of the work that needs to be done. What heartens me, however, is the signs that, over the last few years, many other writers, critics and scholars – working 'out of' both the major languages of modern Wales – have been proceeding along bipartisan lines broadly corresponding to my own. Between us, I am confident, we can at least begin to make some progress.

1

'*In Occidentem & tenebras*': putting Henry Vaughan on the map of Wales

~

The Mount of Olives: or, Solitary Devotions, the book published by 'Henry Vaughan *Silurist*' in 1652, includes the following passage:

> The Contemplation of *death* is an obscure, melancholy *walk* an Expatiation in *shadows & solitude*, but it leads unto *life*, & he that sets forth at *midnight*, will sooner meet the *Sunne*, then he that sleeps it out betwixt his curtains. Truly, when I consider, how I came first into this world, and in what condition I must once again go out of it, and compare my appointed time here with the *portion* preceding it, and the *eternity* to follow, I can conclude my present *being* or *state* (in respect of the *time*) to be nothing else but an *apparition*. The first man that appeared thus, came from the *East*, and the *breath* of *life* was received there. Though then we travel *Westward*, though we embrace *thornes* and swet for *thistles*, yet the businesse of a *Pilgrim* is to *seek his Countrey*. But the *land* of *darknesse* lies in our way, and how few are they that study this *region*, that like holy *Macarius* walk into the wildernesse, and discourse with the skull of a dead man? We run all after the present world, and the Primitive Angelical life is quite lost. (134)[1]

At present, Vaughan's prose is even more undervalued than his poetry, and so *Mount of Olives* is regrettably little known. And yet it is such a beautiful and revealing devotional text. This passage, for instance, shows us precisely how and where Vaughan chooses to put himself on the map. He is one who chooses to live in the west – the same 'west', of course, as that towards which John Donne journeyed on Good Friday in his celebrated poem, and which in our own belated, and perhaps benighted, time Seamus Heaney has wryly revisited in 'Westering, in California'.[2] This west is the heartland of spiritual paradox: it is at once furthest

7

from and closest to the East, which is the site of both Eden and Calvary, man's source and his salvation.

Vaughan's west is to be cherished precisely because it is neighbour to 'the land of darknesse': that is, because it so powerfully prefigures the physical death that is to come, and is therefore a constant reminder of the urgent need to secure the everlasting light of spiritual life. In working with this trope Vaughan is defiantly affirming his allegiance to a tradition of spiritual discourse that has been violently displaced by the new spiritual discourses and symbolic language of militant Puritanism. But he is doing more than that. He is also giving symbolic expression to the way he is historically circumstanced. He is representing those victorious Puritans as the bringers of darkness to his land, and he is implying that out of such catastrophe unexpected good may yet come, since true believers, forcibly removed from influence in what Vaughan calls 'the present world', will become alienated from it and will instead enter into communion with 'the skull of a dead man' – a phrase which may conveniently refer not only to Golgotha but also to that saintly royal martyr, the late beheaded king.

'Man in Darkness' – the title of this particular section of *Mount of Olives* – is in one important sense Vaughan's term for Anglican man secretly blessed by historical catastrophe. As he writes, in a passage that seems to admit us to the state of mind that produced *Silex Scintillans* (1650 and 1655):

> It is an observation of some *spirits*, that *the night is the mother of thoughts*. And I shall adde, that those thoughts are *Stars*, the *Scintillations* and *lightnings* of the soul strugling with *darknesse*. This *Antipathy* in her is *radical*, for being descended from the *house of light*, she hates a contrary *principle*, and being at that time a prisoner in some measure to an enemy, she becomes pensive, and full of thoughts. (133)

Of course, *Silex Scintillans* is in significant measure a deeply personal, confessional document, born of the darkness of bereavement. It would be interesting, I think, to compare it with *In Memoriam* as an attempt to bring the experience of loss into healing alignment with faith. So, in the second of the two poems about 'Jesus weeping', Vaughan brings the Lord's grief for mankind to bear on his own condition, until he is able to find within himself a new 'grief so bright/ 'Twill make the Land of darkness light' (340). Vaughan is also like Tennyson in that he is all the more vulnerable to loss because he is simultaneously threatened with the destruction of the public world of shared spiritual meanings that alone could enable him to cope with it. *Silex Scintillans* is great partly because it is a salvage operation. Or, to change the metaphor, it is great because Vaughan uses poetry to help him create a micro-climate of faith sufficient for his urgent personal needs. Such a climate is possible only 'in the west'.

When he speaks from the west, then, Vaughan speaks in part of the Puritan darkness that threatens to oppress the whole land. But also, as his adoption of the term 'Silurist' implies, he speaks specifically as a west Briton: that is, as one living where that general encroaching darkness of his period is particularly, palpably dense. The paradoxical corollary is that, in being the region nearest the night, it is also the region nearest the spiritual scintillations and lightnings of the stars, and maybe nearest what Vaughan called 'the Primitive Angelical Life' as well. In using the west in this deliberately equivocating way, Vaughan is typical of those Royalist writers of the Interregnum period whose work Lois Potter has examined in her fascinating study *Secret Rites and Secret Writing: Royalist Literature, 1641–1660*. She demonstrates the many kinds of coded messages ingeniously employed by such politically disempowered and quietly subversive authors, and instances the use they made of retreat literature:

The common theme of withdrawal from an uncongenial world into solitude and darkness – for instance, in Henry Vaughan's poetry – is ... ambiguous; is the world a hostile place simply because it *is* the world, or because its dominant political or religious trends are uncongenial to the writer? Vaughan's parables, unlike Herbert's, do not always make clear which is the plain text and which the coded one. Is the exile of earthly life a purely metaphysical concept in an age when so many royalists were living in exile or had lost part of their estates? The standard metaphors for human existence are almost indistinguishable from the conditions in which writers actually felt themselves to be living; an atmosphere of darkness, imprisonment, isolation, drunkenness, and possession. This atmosphere in turn affects their ability to speak 'as themselves'.[3]

Vaughan's 'west' may therefore be understood to refer not only to a spiritual state of mind but also, in coded terms, to the west of Britain in which he was actually living. To read Vaughan's Welshness in these terms – that is, in terms of both its symbolic and its political geography – is perhaps to begin to understand it better.

* * * *

How Welsh is Henry Vaughan? The question can only be answered, perhaps, by our attempting to understand how Vaughan was historically situated: that is, by understanding Henry Vaughan's Wales. When the eminent American poet Jorie Graham visited Swansea in 1995 she was still in the throes of her excitement at discovering in Vaughan a poet who had antici- pated, by the generous margin of three centuries, the supple variability of cross-line rhythms that characterizes the poetry of her famous compatriots Marianne Moore and Robert Creeley. It is as if, Graham beautifully suggested, Vaughan's writing ebbs and flows in response to the unpredictable gravitational force of a secret, adjacent, invisible world. And yet, until her arrival in Swansea, Graham had not suspected Vaughan of being Welsh. This may be regarded as objective, significant, indeed potentially conclusive, proof that Vaughan's Welshness is in no way inscribed in, or as, poetry. And yet, on discovering Vaughan was in all likelihood a Welsh speaker, Graham (who is herself trilin- gual) felt that here was the explanation for what she called the distinctive 'torque' (i.e. twist or rotary force) of his language.[4] It is a splendid image, all the richer for suggesting that other meaning of *torque* (of which Graham could at best have been only subconsciously aware) identified by the *OED*: 'A collar, necklace, bracelet, or similar ornament, consisting of a twisted narrow band or strip, usually of precious metal, worn especially by ancient Gauls and Britons.' Of course, we need to beware the bewitchment of images, and talk of torque perhaps comes cheap. And yet, bilingual Henry Vaughan, self-styled Silurist – Ancient Briton: it may possibly be by invoking him in those terms, implic- itly identifying in the process the hidden cultural torque in his very signature, that we best prepare ourselves to consider his Welshness.

10

That Vaughan was a Welshman was

> an accident: drawn into the classical English culture of the day,
> breaking up as it may have been, he did not know how to be either
> local or evangelical. If he praised his Wales, it was to prove to
> distant people that the cultured life, in their terms, was possible in
> what they thought of as wilderness. It was to prove that the true
> faith, religious and political, still flourished among the folk of a
> backward tongue. (244)[5]

This is the weighty, and learned, opinion of Roland Mathias, a
distinguished poet who is one of the most impressive men of
letters Wales has produced since the Second World War. Along
with Raymond Garlick, Mathias has been responsible for a
remarkable exercise in cultural archaeology. Together they have
painstakingly unearthed evidence of a continuous record of
English-language writing indigenous to Wales that stretches back
to the Middle Ages. The recovery of such a record has been of
vital importance for their sense of modern Welsh writing in
English (to which they have both made valuable contributions) as
being heir to a centuries-old Welsh 'tradition' of anglophone
writing.[6] Therefore, Mathias's reluctant, honest, conclusion that
Vaughan essentially belongs to *English* culture is a verdict that
carries all the more weight when one realizes it represents the
triumph of scrupulous scholarly conscience over both personal
writerly need and strong patriotic inclination. It must have cost
Mathias dear to reach such a conclusion.

Formidable evidence in support of Mathias's interpretation
can certainly be found in Vaughan's own early poems to the Usk,
'*Ad fluvium Iscam*' and 'To the River *Isca*'. The latter is a dutifully
perfect example of the English topographical poem, deliberately
modelled on, and ostentatiously invoking, classical models.
There are obvious points of resemblance between it and Sir John
Denham's celebrated *Cooper's Hill* (1642). In verse over-
embellished with references to classical culture, both ancient and
'modern', Vaughan presents himself as the Usk's future *genius loci*
– as the poet who, by stooping to write about this previously
obscure landscape, is guaranteeing it a future immortality such
as, for instance, Sir Philip Sidney bestowed upon the Thames.
The poem would, in fact, repay reading as a classic colonial text.
In it, Vaughan is ostentatiously an 'Oggsford' man (to quote the

immortal phrase from *The Great Gatsby*),[7] a native who has returned to the provinces as no mere provincial, but as a cultured scholar. If Vaughan is popularly remembered for his love of his native place, he should also (on the evidence of this poem) be understood as one who felt deeply *anxious* about that place – about how exactly to place it, and himself, on the cultural map. In 'To the River *Isca*' he adopts the role of what V. S. Naipaul would call a 'mimic man', that well-known colonial type. The Welsh-speaking landscape (for the people and place-names of Breconshire were at that time thoroughly Welsh) is, with painful political correctness, rendered acceptable by being translated into almost parodically 'classical' English.[8] Or is it? At the close of the poem, Vaughan, in a vain attempt to draw a charmed circle around his beloved region, to keep the Civil War at bay and make his a 'Land redeem'd from all disorders', writes as follows:

> may those *lowd, anxious Cares*
> For *dead* and *dying things* (the Common *Wares*
> And *showes* of time) ne'er break thy *Peace,* nor make
> Thy *repos'd Armes* to a new warre *awake*! (43)

The reference – and it could be the first in Vaughan's writing – seems to be to those ancient inhabitants of the region, the Silurians, with whom Vaughan was thereafter so conspicuously and pointedly to identify himself. Indeed, he was the originator of the word *Silurist*. It is therefore worth pausing to digest the reference.

As Vaughan well knew, both at firsthand from Tacitus and at second hand through the work of such recent writers as Camden, the Silurians were the most fierce and indomitable of all the opponents the Romans faced while acquiring their great empire. Yet once they were finally overcome, the Silurians became thoroughly and enthusiastically Romanized. By calling himself 'Silurist', Vaughan was therefore providing himself with a highly complex cultural identity, and 'placing' himself in a fascinatingly ambiguous way. To begin with, he was reminding his English friends that his 'classical' credentials were infinitely superior to theirs: his ancient Cambro-British ancestors had, after all, won the respect of Rome itself, being honourably mentioned in Roman dispatches, and they had participated in Roman civilization, whereas the upstart English could at best claim to be heirs of Rome only by virtue of their recent classical education. But there are other implications to Vaughan's choice of the Silurist identity. He was, of course, a thorough-going unionist: that is, both consciously committed to, and the unconscious cultural product of, the fateful 1536 Act of Union of England and Wales. But unionist though he was, he was not English; nor was he simply, unambiguously and uncomplicatedly 'Welsh'. The Act of Union had been conveniently interpreted by the Welsh as the climax of a thousand-year-old struggle to recover their 'lost' British identity.[9] The English were happy enough to play that particular game while it suited them – indeed, it helped them both to establish their own nation-state and to gain their first empire – but they very effectively played the game on their own Anglicizing terms.[10] Vaughan's claim to be a Silurist has behind it, then, the whole tangled, complex history of the conditional, privileged terms on which the Welsh vainly, and with frequently pathetic persistency, claimed to be 'British'. As we shall see, this is a crucial factor in his situation, a prominent feature of the torque. But for the time being it is enough simply to note that by humorously introducing the Silurians into his poem to the Usk, Vaughan may have been signalling his particular Welsh brand of Britishness, thereby inadvertently revealing the unresolved and potentially conflictual elements of his cultural identity. Far from being a fully assimilated Englishman, he remained an uneasily transitional or borderline case. He was indeed one of those who lived on 'the shifting margins of cultural displacement.' He was an inhabitant, in Frantz Fanon's haunting terms, of 'the zone of occult instability where [a colonized people] dwell'.[11]

As has, however, already been noted, the Silurians are primarily mentioned by Vaughan in connection with the war between King and Parliament. 'To the River *Isca*' is a Civil War text, as is *Silex Scintillans*, the great, two-part collection of poetry on which Vaughan's reputation principally depends. Yet, while scholars have amply demonstrated this, they have tended to overlook the extent to which this poetry was intimately marked, and perhaps determined, by the distinctive character of the Puritan 'occupation' of Wales, following the rout of the Royalist armies and the execution of the king (1649).[12] One was the Anglican and Royalist Vaughan; the other was the Puritan mystic, Morgan

Llwyd (1619–59), the finest of Welsh-language prose writers, and one of the greatest of Welsh writers.[13] In 1653 – sandwiched, as it were, between Parts I and II of *Silex Scintillans* (first published in 1650 and 1655 respectively) – Llwyd brought out three devotional masterpieces urging the Welsh reader to discover that 'Lord Jesus is as a golden Mine in our owne fields, under our owne earth, and is in Saints as the soul in the eye, or Sun in the Firmament, or fire in the inward furnace, or inhabitant in a house'.[14]

An immanentist given to inspired use of the language of inward, alchemical, transformation, Llwyd would seem to us to be the natural soul-mate or spiritual twin of the hermetically inclined Vaughan, who detected seeds of light and bright shoots of everlastingness in the whole of creation. Yet in actual historical fact the two were implacable enemies. Indeed, Llwyd was a leading member of the Puritan administration responsible for the forcible ejection of Henry's twin brother, the cleric Thomas Vaughan, from his Welsh incumbency, under the terms of the 1650 Act for the Better Propagation and Preaching of the Gospel in Wales. Historians have described this act as 'the nearest thing Wales ever acquired to Home Rule',[15] on the grounds that it uniquely recognized Wales to be a case separate from that of England. And exactly why Wales was so regarded by Puritans may be understood from the majestic opening of one of Llwyd's intensest works:

> O people of Wales! my voice is directed at you . . . The dawn has broken and the sun has risen on you. The birds are singing; awake (O Welshman), awake; . . . behold, the world and its pillars are shaking. The earth is in turmoil, there is thunder and lightning in the minds of the peoples.[16]

Radical Puritans like Llwyd – and Welsh Puritanism was by and large characterized by its spiritual radicalism – believed the victory of the Parliamentary armies to be a divine sign that God was preparing the way for the Second Coming of Christ. Therefore, in the precious little time that remained, Wales – a notoriously un-Puritan and pro-Royalist country – had to be saved by mass religious conversion. 'The land of our nativitie is asleepe', wrote an anguished Llwyd, 'and the people dreame and talke through their sleepe' (*GMLl2*:252). He dedicated his genius to conducting a spiritual rescue mission, and determined to save his people from imminent perdition. This helps explain the extraordinary vibrancy, urgent originality, and resourceful innovativeness of his prose: after all, circumstances had invested language with a new, awesomely fateful, power. It also helps explain the ferocious energy of his evangelizing and of his political campaigning. It was the millenarians (of whom a disproportionate number were Welsh) that persuaded Cromwell to call the Parliament of Saints in 1653, with a view to its bringing about an apocalyptic transformation of the social, political and religious life of the country. Llwyd's three great prose works of that year were directly inspired by, and intimately connected with, these developments.

Triumphalist Puritanism in Wales tended, then, to be extreme in character and uncompromising in word and in action. Pre-Puritan Wales was regarded as having been virtually religionless, and stigmatized as one of the darkest corners of the land.[17] Such a 'politicized' use of the trope of darkness is well worth recalling in connection both with Vaughan's different use of it in *The Mount of Olives* and with his famous predilection for the contrary imagery of light. Indeed, in representing himself so insistently as an inhabitant of the 'west', Vaughan may have been simultaneously identifying himself as a victim of signally oppressive Welsh Puritanism. It is important that we learn to read Vaughan's religious discourse as a kind of subversive counter-discourse whose terms are significantly related by opposites to the terms of dominant Welsh Puritan discourse. Take the following instance, from the address to the reader which prefaces *Primitive Holiness* (1654): '*I write unto thee out of a land of darkenesse, out of that unfortunate region, where the Inhabitants sit in the shadow of death: where destruction passeth for propagation, and a thick black night for the glorious day-spring*' (162). Not only does this involve a reversal of the Puritan trope of darkness, which is here ironically used to represent what they *bring*, rather than what they dispel; it also includes a saracastic pun on that key term in the Welsh Puritan vocabulary, *propagation*. Now, with this in mind, and recalling that, as the preface to *Silex Scintillans* demonstrates, Vaughan thought of himself as one who redeemed vain wit by employing it for serious, substantial, spiritual purposes, it is tempting to speculate that Vaughan's famously recurrent use, in his writings, of images of natural growth or dissemination ('seeds of light') may secretly represent a luxuriant foliation of that single root pun on 'propagation'! The following example (obviously indebted to the Bible) is taken from *Primitive Holiness* itself: 'The fame of holy men (like the *Kingdome of God*) is a *seed that grows secretly*' (166).

'*I envie not their frequent* Extasies, *and raptures to the third heaven*', writes Vaughan of his Puritan opponents in *Mount of Olives*:

> *I onely wish them real, and that their actions did not tell the world, they are rapt into some other place. Nor should they, who assume to themselves the glorious stile of Saints, be uncharitably moved, if we that are yet in the body, and carry our treasure in earthen vessels, have need of these helps.* (104)

Radical Puritans liked to term themselves 'saints', roughly indicating by it a socially egalitarian but spiritually élite membership of a 'gathered' Church. On both these counts, Vaughan objected to what he clearly felt to be the grotesque abuse of the term. In *The Mount of Olives* he pointedly contrasted 'the *shining* and *fervent piety* of those Saints' – that is, the early Christians – 'with the *painted* and *illuding appearance* of it in *these of our times*' (146). And his sensitivity to the ideological warfare being conducted through the strategic deployment and redefinition of key terms, extended to the generic terms used to identify different kinds of writing. As Nigel Smith has pointed out in his excellent recent book, Vaughan styled the poems in *Silex Scintillans* 'hymns' in pointed defiance of the Puritan decree that versified versions of the Psalms were the only 'sacred poems' acceptable by God.[18] For Smith, this is an instance of the redefinition and internal transformation of established codes of writing that was the 'literary' counterpart of the politico-religious revolution brought about by the Puritans. The total collapse of old forms of thought and expression ushered in a period both of unparalleled experimentation with new kinds of discourse and of radical reformation of inherited genres. The former could even encompass a new visionary stylistics, involving the violent wrenching of conventional vocabulary and grammar in order to accommodate a kind of 'automatic writing', dictated directly by the Spirit.[19] Examples of the latter range from the Christianized epic of Milton to the raw allegories of that uneducated Baptist tinker John Bunyan; and the prose of Morgan Llwyd likewise affords us supreme examples of an inspired improvisation of style, and a striking metamorphosis of forms.[20] Smith has pointed out that Vaughan's 'hymns' are brilliant textual evidence of an *Anglican* sensibility's reaction to the creative licence, or chaotic disorder, of the times. And I would further venture to suggest that, in *Silex Scintillans*, Vaughan was moved by his circumstances to attempt a new kind of spiritual poetry, or poetry of 'retreat'. This is a point to which I hope to return.

Although Vaughan used once to be described as if he were the serene Vermeer of visionary poetry, I find his poetry excitingly edgy, nervously alive with the anxiety of turbulence and disintegration: 'Thy hand alone doth tame/ Those blasts, and knit my frame' (257). It is sometimes as if he were trying to use words and images as personal stabilizers, trying to furnish himself with a safe locale and location, a secluded native landscape which would constitute what a modern psychoanalyst might call 'a holding environment'; a place for admitting yet domesticating psychic and political chaos. What we know of the general turbulence both within him, following his brother's death, and abroad in a political world turned upside-down by Puritanism offers grounds enough for supposing *Silex Scintillans* to be the work of a stressed and distressed soul. But, in addition, it seems worth noting that in Wales Puritanism brought particularly acute turmoil in its train, as the Propagation Act invested immense power in a small cadre of ministers and laymen, the best of whom were almost manically industrious, and the worst of whom were, at least by popular reputation, resourcefully corrupt.

The atmosphere in Puritan-controlled Wales was certainly exceptionally intense, and *Silex Scintillans* intimately exhibits the form and pressure of that particular experience in that particular place. An encounter with a zealously 'pure', extreme form of Puritanism helped turn Vaughan into a soul *in extremis*. Radical Puritanism helped change him into an inventive, innovative reactionary. Militantly evangelizing Puritanism prompted him to turn his poetry into an underground resistance movement. Sectarian Puritanism moved him to bring a whole region, emblematized by its landscape, into the parish of his care. And millenarian

17

Puritanism brought out a corresponding but opposite apocalyptic impulse in Vaughan. Welsh Puritan millenarians included militant Fifth Monarchists, such as the military governor Thomas Harrison and the fiery evangelist Vavasour Powell.[21] Determined to transform society by force, if necessary, they confidently predicted the very date of Christ's return. Llwyd, a prolific writer of millenarian verse, was briefly excited to emulate them: 'fifty goes big, or fifty sixe/ or sixty five some say/ But within mans age, hope to see/ all old things flung away.'[22] In pointed contrast, Vaughan insists that the day of His coming is a mystery God reserves for Himself. This ties in with Vaughan's sense of his distance from God, movingly expressed through his envy of that 'blest believer', Nicodemus, who was able fully to encounter God's majesty while still in the flesh and so 'Did at mid-night speak with the Sun!':

> O who will tell me, where
> He found thee at that dead and silent hour!
> What hallow'd solitary ground did bear
> So rare a flower,
> Within whose sacred leafs did lie
> The fulnes of the Deity. (358)

But Nicodemus lived in those ancient times when intimate intercourse with God was still possible for humans. Vaughan believed strongly that the world was running down as it drew to its close – that it was in a state of physical, moral, and spiritual decay. Hence the nostalgia for the past that permeates his writing:

> Sure, It was so. Man in those early days
> Was not all stone, and Earth,
> He shin'd a little, and by those weak Rays
> Had some glimpse of his birth . . .
> He sigh'd for *Eden*, and would often say
> *Ah! what bright days were those?* (271–2)

By contrast, Llwyd's millenarianism partook of the spiritual enthusiasm of those who were loosely called 'New Lights', because they believed that the Spirit was preparing the way for the Second Coming by an enlarging and transfiguration of consciousness, thus heightening human awareness of the awesome power and mystery of the divine. This belief (articulated in part through correspondence with the great English Puritan Peter Sterry) contributed in Llwyd's case to the development of a new, revelatory, spiritual idiolect.[23] When reading him we become aware of what might be called the apocalyptics of style; whereas in reading Vaughan we become aware that *his* brand of millenarianism (surely reinforced through reaction against the Llwydian variety) resulted in a poetry and poetics of anamnesis – of reactivation of memory and recuperation of lost powers of spiritual understanding.[24]

By Vaughan's standards, radical Puritans, with their emphasis on personal, unmediated encounter with the Holy Spirit, were self-deluded ecstatics who were dangerous anarchists. His quarrel with them was registered not only at the level of doctrine and ideology but also at the level of language and genre. It is worth noting the conservative theology that so often tempers Vaughan's innovative poetics and stylistics. What is at issue between him and the 'schismatics' is the whole question of the origin and nature of authority. He believes that they are far too quick to claim the authority of the Holy Spirit for their merely personal words and deeds. By contrast, when dedicating *Mount of Olives* in 1651 to 'The Truly Noble and Religious Sr. Charles Egerton Knight', he invokes that gentleman as the surrogate of the dead king, who in turn was, of course, God's regent on earth. 'It is no other', he humbly writes, 'but that your *name* (like the *royall stamp*) may make *current* and commend this *poor mite* to posterity' (102–3). The pointedly traditional trope alludes, of course, to the king's image on coins, the seal of approval that can alone make money authentic 'currency'. For Vaughan the author, language already authorized by the established Church carried a strong presumption of spiritual authority. He did not easily believe in unmediated access to spiritual truth. To the radical Puritans who dispensed with symbol, ritual and liturgy and referred individual souls to a naked inward encounter with the indwelling Spirit, Vaughan cautiously replied that he too had undertaken his own explorations of the inner world, and had returned with findings very different from theirs:

> [I] came at last
> To search my selfe, where I did find
> Traces, and sounds of a strange kind.
> Here of this mighty spring, I found some drills,
> With Ecchoes beaten from th'eternall hills;
> Weake beams, and fires flash'd to my sight,
> Like a young East, or Moone-shine night,
> Which shew'd me in a nook cast by
> A peece of much antiquity,
> With Hyerogliphicks quite dismembred,
> And broken letters scarce remembred.
> I took them up, and (much Joy'd,) went about
> T'unite those peeces, hoping to find out
> The mystery; but this neer done,
> That little light I had was gone:
> It griev'd me much. At last, said I,
> *Since in these veyls my Ecclips'd Eye*
> *May not approach thee, (for at night*
> *Who can have commerce with the light?)*
> *I'le disapparell, and to buy*
> *But one half glaunce, most gladly dye.* (249)

So much for the confidence of the radical Puritan belief in new light, in Adamic language, in direct inspiration. Vaughan's use of language in *Silex Scintillans* is often consciously Egertonian: that is, far more devoutly and deliberately authorized by hallowed religious tradition than some of his New Age modern devotees care to admit. And his is also a painstaking act of reconstructing the hieroglyphics of a shattered faith by piecing together 'broken letters scarce remembred' – a feature advertised by the very typographic layout of several of the poems. Even after the 'original' work of such partial restoration, those hieroglyphics remain essentially undecipherable, emblematic of some lost aboriginal purity and of the limitations of fallen man's understanding of spiritual mysteries.

Vaughan's response to the Propagation Act, so zealously enforced by Welsh Puritans, was to strive to recover the spirit of the Primitive Christianity of the early Church. He saw the unordained Puritans as 'Commission'd by a black self-wil' (303), as distinct from the true priests, who were commissioned by divine authority: 'we have seen his Ministers cast out of the Sanctuary, & barbarous persons without *light* or *perfection*, usurping holy offices' (135). Under the Act, unsatisfactory priests were ejected from their churches, but the Puritan Approvers found it extremely difficult to replace them with godly ministers. Hence, many churches remained closed, as Vaughan mournfully noted in a prayer in *The Mount of Olives*:

> The wayes of *Zion* do mourne, our beautiful gates are shut up, and the Comforter that should relieve our souls is gone far from us. Thy Service and thy Sabbaths, thy own sacred Institutions and the pledges of thy love are denied unto us; Thy Ministers are trodden down, and the basest of the people are set up in thy holy place. (131)

The Mount of Olives was itself a collection of prayers, observations and meditations, arranged to bestow spiritual order on the passing of the day and of the year, as substitute for the Book of Common Prayer, of which Vaughan had been deprived by the Puritans. Similarly, *Silex Scintillans* is, in a sense, a substitute for the formal ceremonies and rituals of worship. Taken together, these works represent the secretly improvised sacred texts of the hidden Church in internal exile. And Vaughan was therefore naturally attracted to the story of such early Christian fathers as Paulinus, bishop of Nola, a longtime dweller in remote places (like Vaughan himself), and a churchbuilder mindful always of the Biblical warning 'Unlesse the Lord build the house, wee labour in vaine to build it' (204).

The irony is, of course, that the unchurched and spiritually unhoused Henry Vaughan had been forced by Welsh circumstances not only to build his own inner Church but to adopt the Puritan outlook of every man his own priest. Unordained himself, like those despised 'mechanics' who suddenly experienced spiritual empowerment through the Puritan revolution, he was galvanized into public personal witness, while embarking on the extraordinary mental adventure of mapping the vast *terra incognita* of his own inner being. The result, as with the Puritans, was the emergence of a startlingly new, doubtfully orthodox, spiritual discourse, compounded in part of the free internalizing (like the Puritans') of biblical texts traditionally embedded in doctrine, and in part of hermetic imagery.[25] His renowned interest in the latter parallels Llwyd's profound interest in the extraordinary

21

writings of the maverick German mystic Jakob Böhme.[26] Llwyd and Vaughan both, therefore, turned to more or less esoteric sources of visionary symbolism. They thereby evolved a highly distinctive kind of spiritual discourse tuned not to the routine orthodoxy of the respective faiths they each obediently professed but to the inner music of their own being. And there was, or so I would suggest, a distinctive culture of radicalism in the Wales of the early 1650s that encouraged them to do this – to become pere-grine souls. It is noticeable that, after that period, neither Llwyd nor Vaughan ever wrote with the same intense originality again.

Vaughan's nostalgia for the past has already been mentioned. It now needs to be more fully contextualized. The Welsh were notorious for their obsession with pedigree, their lust for lineage, their superstitious adherence to dubious myths of origin. This was natural since, prevented by conquest from building an actual state, a stateless nation had no other way of constructing a mean-ingful historical identity. Consequently, the *beirdd*, the traditional Welsh poets, were custodians of the sacred stories of descent, both of individual noble families and of the whole 'tribe'. As remembrancers, they drew heavily on such works as Geoffrey of Monmouth's celebrated fabrication *Historia regum Britanniae* (*History of the Kings of Britain*, c.1136).[27] And after the crowning of Henry Tudor (1485) this rich accumulation of 'native' lore proved notoriously useful for an *arriviste* Tudor monarchy intent on providing itself, and the modern English state it sought to establish, with ancient historical legitimacy. Yet, at the very time that Welsh legends were gaining general currency and formidable political clout, they came under sceptical scrutiny. The Humanist scholars of the Renaissance and Reformation were themselves dedicated antiquarians, but their interest in the past was of an embryonically 'modern', historical, kind, and several of them became quickly suspicious of such versions of the past as were peddled by Geoffrey and the *beirdd*. In Wales, an intellectual power struggle developed between the enlightened, progressive, modern scholars and the conservative bardic order, resulting in the eventual dissolution of the latter at virtually the very time that Vaughan was writing.[28]

The myth that matters for our understanding of Vaughan is the myth of the British Church. Derived partly from Geoffrey, it embodied the (historically correct) belief that the ancient Welsh

(Cambro-British) had been Christianized very early, well before Catholic Rome sent missionaries to 'England' to convert the pagan Saxons. According to legend, the aboriginal British Church was established by King Lucius in the second century.[29] It may easily be appreciated how attractive this story was to the founding-fathers of the Anglican Church. It allowed them to score a great propaganda coup by announcing that, far from being a heretical, *nouveau riche*, upstart, the Church of England was the reincarnation of the ancient pre-Catholic British Church. This was the party line eagerly adopted by the Archbishop of Canterbury, Matthew Parker, and popularized by John Foxe's *Actes and Monuments*. During the first half of the seventeenth century, the old myths were debunked by distinguished ecclesiastical scholars such as Ussher and Fuller, but the urge to provide the Church with an apostolic founder remained, and in 1685 Edward Stillingfleet, bishop of Worcester, convincingly argued that it was St Paul, no less, who had established the Church of Britain. For Welsh Anglicans, such hoary founding myths held particular appeal, since these legends endowed them with the glamour and power of being the true originators of the Church of England.[30] Bishop Richard Davies (?1501–81) was the greatest Welsh churchman of the sixteenth century, and co-translator with William Salesbury of the New Testament into Welsh (1567).[31] In the grand *Epistol at y Cembru* (*Address to the Welsh Nation*) that prefaced that historic publication, he made memorable patriotic play with the myth, and this celebrated text, which had a decisive influence on subsequent Welsh historiography, would almost certainly have been known to Vaughan.

Vaughan included a poem entitled 'The British Church' in the first part of *Silex Scintillans* (1650). As scholars have noted, it was in part a way of honouring his great hero George Herbert, who had published a poem with the same title in *The Temple*.[32] But there may be more to it than that. By the 1650s the Puritans in Wales were directly disputing the Anglicans' claim to be the heirs of the Ancient British Church, and insisting instead that the title belonged by rights to them, by virtue of their resumption of the pure practices of the Primitive Christian Church. Llwyd's great work, *Llyfr y Tri Aderyn* (*The Book of the Three Birds*, 1653) incorporates exactly such a Welsh Puritan attempt to appropriate the powerful legendary narrative.[33] So Vaughan's poem could be a contribution to the propaganda war being waged in Wales at the time of its publication. But there may be more again to it than that. By conceiving of his land as the aboriginal landscape of Christianity in Britain, Vaughan (who, after all, pointedly signed himself 'Silurist') would have been imbuing it with a dignity of spiritual ancientness that gave a depth of quiet authority and confidence to his affection for it. Critics have long recognized the unique power of Vaughan's invocation of his native landscape. But what has never been considered is the Welsh myth that may have underwritten that textual power.[34]

The point may most succinctly be made by looking at the beautiful poem 'The Shepheards' (304), in which Vaughan wonders why the birth of Christ was first revealed to such marginal people (like the Welsh?): 'How happend it that in the dead of night/ You only saw true light,/ While *Palestine* was fast a sleep . . .?' He concludes that it may have been because they trod in the footsteps of '*Patriarchs*, Saints, and Kings' who had themselves been shepherds in that land: ''Tis true, [God] loves that Dust whereon they go/ That serve him here below,/ And therefore might for memory of those/ His love there first disclose.' The poem may be interpreted in several ways, but its most important meaning for us is that Vaughan felt himself to be inhabiting an anciently haunted landscape, and was thereby authorized and empowered to turn topography into tropography: that is, to treat the sacred landscape as a fertile source of sacral imagery.

Like the shepherds, Vaughan was – and felt himself to be – a culturally marginal figure; or so I believe. Wales seemed backward and remote when viewed from London, or from Oxford, two 'centres' with which Vaughan was familiar, and whose dim, condescending, view of Wales was regularly communicated to him in the letters of friends forever puzzled as to why he should have chosen to stay there.[35] *Silex Scintillans* is, in a way, his answer to them, in the form of a brilliant, innovative variation on the traditional literature of pastoral 'retreat'. Vaughan's work is full of 'quotations' from that literature which constitute a complex kind of intertextuality. One of his ploys is to interweave the classical with the Christian pastoral mode, by emphasizing that God has always favoured the simple and the humble. But of primary interest to me is what I regard as the *cultural politics* of the retreat poem as written by Vaughan – his version of what

Whitman called 'the politics of nature'; because it seems to me that in his mature work Vaughan, writing as Silurist, and aided by the myth of the British Church, may have been implicitly reversing margin and centre, turning culturally marginalized Wales into the ancient (and modern) centre of spiritual authority. It is another twist in Jorie Graham's torque.

As the foregoing would suggest, no serious attempt has yet been made by scholars to place Vaughan in the context of Welsh-language culture. Yet he was familiar with the traditions, as he showed when explaining to his cousin, John Aubrey, the mysterious craft of the Welsh *beirdd*. They believe in 'Awen' (the muse/inspiration), he says, 'which in their language signifies as much as Raptus, or a poetic furore'. He then proceeds colourfully to recount what happened to a young Breconshire shepherd when he fell asleep while minding his flock:

> he dreamt, that he saw a beautifull young man with a garland of green leafs upon his head, & an hawk upon his fist; with a quiver full of Arrows att his back, coming towards him (whistling several measures or tunes all the way) & att last lett the hawk fly att him, w^ch (he dreamt) gott into his mouth & inward parts, & suddenly awakened in a great fear & consternation; butt possessed with such a vein, or gift of poetrie, that he left the sheep & went about the Countrey, making songs upon all occasions, and came to be the most famous Bard in all the Countrey in his time.[36]

Is Vaughan, the Oxford sophisticate, here mocking the superstitious beliefs of his primitive countrymen? He could well be. But it is equally possible that Vaughan, the dedicated hermeticist and intent listener to the *naturalis musica mundi* (the natural spiritual music of the world), believed that the Welsh *beirdd* had intuited, in an admittedly crude and uncomprehending way, the presence of the *anima mundi* to which he was himself so thrillingly alive:[37]

> heark! In what Rings,
> And *Hymning Circulations* the quick world
> Awakes, and sings;
> The rising winds,
> And falling springs
> Birds, beasts, all things
> Adore him in their kinds.
> Thus all is hurl'd

In secret *Hymnes*, and *Order*. The great *Chime*
And *Symphony* of nature. (255)

Pressed to a decision, I would suggest that in fact Vaughan oscillated, or hesitated, between the two views I have proposed, and that in so doing he precisely registers for us the plight of the educated Welshman of his day, caught in the interstices between two contrasting and competing cultural systems. Such a cultural plight is evident in the writings of the great Welsh-language scholars of that period, with whose work Vaughan was certainly familiar. For instance, he took the shepherd story from the work of Siôn Dafydd Rhys (John Davies of Brecon, 1534–c.1619), a recent neighbour of Vaughan's, and a fellow-Oxonian, whose intellectual and physical adventures probably took him as far as the historic Council of Trent.[38] And Vaughan was familiar enough with the configuration of Welsh scholarship to warn Anthony Wood against mistaking this John Davies (or John David Rees) for *the* John Davies, of Mallwyd (?1567–1644), the multilingual scholar and grammarian whose reputation for prodigious learning has echoed through the centuries right down to our own time.[39]

As well as being exceptionally gifted, the two Davieses were representative figures: they exemplified the massive shift produced in Welsh culture by the combined impact of Renaissance learning and Reformation scholarship. Although continental in scope and using Latin as its international *lingua franca*, this astonishing new world of learning was mediated to a significant degree in Wales by England, via the newly established grammar schools and the University of Oxford.[40] The relationship between the new, Oxford-educated intellectuals (of whom Vaughan, of course, was one) and the old intellectual élite of traditional Welsh culture, the *beirdd* (poets), was an extremely uneasy one.[41] The scholars accused the guild of poets of lying, of egregious flattery, and of jealously protecting their trade secrets – the esoteric rules of *cynghanedd*. They also scorned their ignorant superstition, their reactionary politics and their stagnant art. But at the same time the scholars lovingly anatomized, by the latest 'scientific' methods, the grammar and vocabulary of the vernacular, the Welsh language so richly displayed to advantage by the *beirdd*. Patriots as well as scholars, in the best Reformation tradition, the scholars moreover urged the *beirdd* to share their unique store of lore and craft with the whole wide waiting world of sophisticated Europe. Of course, whether in 'modernizing' Welsh culture such scholars were also unconsciously Anglicizing it is a question that is bound to occur to us today. What is certain is that they helped undermine first the confidence and then the performative power of the *beirdd*, with the consequence that a thousand-year-old tradition unique to Wales came to an end just as Vaughan was writing *Silex Scintillans*. No more poignant example could be adduced of the effects on traditional Wales of the cultural invasion of the foreign, the modern and the new, the irresistible political instrument of which was the Act of Union. And when viewed in this context, Vaughan's great religious poetry is susceptible of being read either as the product of a violently historic cultural rupture or as the unlikely continuation of old habits of belief and expression by radically other, totally unforeseen and ostensibly foreign means. It is worth recalling that Vaughan's family, the Vaughans of Tretower, were *uchelwyr*, the class of minor gentry who maintained the *beirdd* after the defeat of Llywelyn (1282), and whose gradual defection to English culture, markedly accelerated after the Act of Union, was a major contributory factor in the breakdown of the bardic tradition.

Henry Vaughan's twin brother, the irascible and combative visionary hermeticist Thomas Vaughan, bluntly told a distinguished contemporary: 'For my own part, I *professe* I am no *Englishman*, neither would I be *taken* for one such, although I *love* the *nation* aswell as *thy self*.'[42] Henry Vaughan's poetry may come to seem to be echoing these words, if one explores the cultural twist and turn at the very centre of his torqued being. For 'torque' the OED offers the following clarification: 'Twisted or bent into a double curve like the letter S'. When next we read the title-page of *Silex Scintillans* and note the proud identifying signature 'Silurist' (an *enw barddol*/bardic *nom-de-plume*? Or an affirmation of his modern 'classical' identity?), we might profitably remember that haunting definition, and reflect again on the twist of historical fate that produced Wales's Henry Vaughan.

* * * *

27

It is, then, in some such terms as these that I feel Vaughan's greatest writing could be accurately characterized as both 'west' and 'Welsh' in character. But the rest of this chapter will explore his Welshness in a very different fashion, by considering some of the ways in which it has been interpreted, and in the process 'constructed', by several recent English- and Welsh-language writers who have found in Vaughan a means of understanding *themselves* as writers of twentieth-century Wales.

'Readers today may prefer him not as a mystical theologist but as a wonderful poet of pieces: a magician of intervals', declared Dylan Thomas, intuiting what Vaughan himself described as the 'dismembred' character of his writing. 'They remember odd lines', Thomas continued, 'rather than odder poems' (32).[43] These comments form part of an introduction to his broadcast readings of a selection of poems by poets whose 'Welshness' he proceeds to gloss on his own terms. Vigorously distancing himself from those who 'often give the impression that their writing in English is only a condescension to the influence and ubiquity of a tyrannous foreign tongue', Thomas roundly declares 'I do not belong to that number' (31), preferring instead to believe: 'It's the poetry, written in the language which is most natural to the poet, that counts, not his continent, country, island, race, class, or political persuasion' (32).

It would not be all that difficult to show how, in suggesting that the English language is Vaughan's only true native country, Thomas is neatly sawing off the very branch he himself is sitting on. After all, if poets are to be identified only with the language in which they write, then what justification could there be for devoting a radio programme of verse in English to 'Welsh poetry'? However, setting such objections aside, it is worth registering how Thomas proceeds to construct a 'Modernist Vaughan'. In other words, he invents an ancestor in his own image, revealing in the process the distinctively Welsh character and distinctively Welsh provenance of Thomas's own Modernist aesthetic. Very much a poet of the 1930s, he had grown up in a decade of cultural civil war, where Welsh-language poets, many of them increasingly nationalist in outlook, had begun to question the Welsh credentials of Wales's new English-language authors, most of whom were in any case already attracted to various kinds of internationalist ideology. Saunders Lewis, the leading Welsh-language artist and ideologue of his era, brought this issue to a head in 1938 by famously answering in the negative his own question 'Is there an Anglo-Welsh literature?'[44] (In his radio talk, Thomas pointedly dismisses the term 'Anglo-Welsh' as 'an ambiguous compromise', 31). The essence of Lewis's argument was that, since there was no distinctively Welsh form of English, neither could there be a distinctively Welsh kind of literature in English. He contrasted the case of Wales in this respect with that of Ireland, thereby demolishing the grounds for believing that Wales could produce in English the culturally committed kind of Modernist writing he associated with Synge and Yeats. Nevertheless, that still left open the alternative, supranational, brand of Modernism represented by the James Joyce who signed off, at the end of *Portrait of the Artist as a Young Man*, with 'Dublin, 1904: Trieste 1914'.

Somewhat of a Joycean Modernist, at least by choice that in turn owed not a little, as we shall see in a later chapter, to the way he had been culturally circumstanced in 1930s Wales, Dylan Thomas created a Henry Vaughan who paradoxically provided his supranationalist Modernism with a national pedigree. He countered Saunders Lewis's argument that there could be no such oxymoronic thing as a Welsh English poet with the claim 'that Welshmen have written, from time to time, exceedingly good poetry in English. I should like to think that that is because they were, and are, good poets rather than good Welshmen' (32). Vaughan was important to Thomas precisely to the extent that he was a Welshman who had written good poetry that was *not* recognizably Welsh in character. And that sense of deep and fateful personal affinity was for him intensified by the fact that Vaughan had produced poems 'in which the figures of his authentic and intense vision move across a wild, and yet inevitably ordered, sacred landscape' (33). Just as Vaughan has been detached by Thomas from the actual historical Wales of his time, so here he is removed from his actual context in the Anglican community of his day. Instead, he is seen as a lone, idiosyncratic visionary – again not dissimilar, one might suggest, to Dylan Thomas's perception of himself.

As Thomas correctly points out, Vaughan may possibly have known something of Dafydd ap Gwilym, but he opted instead for George Herbert as his poetic master. Obviously, such a 'choice' had profound cultural antecedents and implications, which

Thomas, by 'naturalizing' Vaughan's use of English, 'chooses' to ignore, as did some other Welsh poets and scholars who were roughly of Thomas's generation. My old teacher and sometime colleague, A. J. Smith, a native of the Rhymney valley, was one of the most distinguished of post-war scholars of Metaphysical poetry, and used pardonably to scoff at the very idea that writers such as Donne, Herbert, or even Vaughan could in any meaningful, let alone significant, sense be accounted Welsh. A scrupulous scholar, Jim Smith reached the impeccably informed conclusion that these writers could be properly understood only in terms of the English Anglican or Anglo-Catholic tradition, and in the wider context of a European Baroque tradition of wit. However, when applied to Vaughan, such an assessment does seem to have been generated, at least in part, by the political unconscious of the scholarly argument. There appears to be a desire at work to remove Vaughan entirely from the fraught modern context of debates about permissible definitions of anglophone Welshness.

One student who was contemporary with Jim Smith at Aberystwyth was T. H. Jones, both men having returned from wartime service. Jones was already an emerging poet, whose eventual mysterious death in Australia in 1965 was to be a serious loss to post-war Anglo-Welsh literature. Aspects of his developing concerns as a creative writer are obliquely apparent in the MA thesis he submitted in 1949 on 'The Imagery of the Metaphysical Poetry of the Seventeenth Century'.[45] It shows that he was particularly drawn to Donne, Herbert and Marvell, whom he regarded as the true Metaphysicals. Their work, rather like Jones's own, was 'predominantly psychological, and its expression inhering in terms of contrast and paradox ... Its total meaning is enriched by its internal tension of apparently conflicting possibilities' (183). He then proceeded to trace these features of the writing back to its origins in an 'age of transition', again reminiscent of Jones's own sense of himself as caught in transit between a religious and a secular culture, a Welsh-language and an English-language inheritance, a closed rural society and a cosmopolitan urban milieu.

Chapter 6 of his thesis is devoted to Henry Vaughan, whose exact status as a poet seems to puzzle him. Having himself been raised on an upland farm near Newbridge-on-Wye, virtually next door to Vaughan's own parish, Jones is surprised to note how very few of the features of the actual countryside are recorded in his fellow-countryman's poetry. For him, Vaughan is an otherworldly poet, one 'who succeeded in living as intimately in the 'Countrie/ Far beyond the stars' as in this world' (158). And about the ways in which Vaughan was actually historically and culturally circum-stanced – a 'transitional' figure if ever there was, also living in 'a broken landscape of regrets' (*THJ*, 3) and as such someone decidedly closer to home for Jones than was Donne – the thesis has absolutely nothing to say; as if Harri Jones's Anglocentric education at Builth Wells County School and at the University College of Wales, Aberystwyth, had made that a closed book to him, however well read he may have been in the actual poetry.

But it was that self-same closed book that some of T. Harri Jones's Anglo-Welsh contemporaries grew determined to open. In fact, the interest shown in Vaughan by post-war English-language writers from Wales became a significant by-product of a new phase in their understanding of their 'Anglo-Welshness'. The committed, campaigningly nationalist poets of the 1960s come face-to-face with Vaughan in the rumbustious Harri Webb's quietly respectful, but rueful, 'Harri Webb to Harri Vaughan'.[46] As a non-believer, Webb finds Vaughan's cele-bration of spiritual light unpersuasive, but more important is the conclusion he pointedly draws from this disparity between his outlook and that of Vaughan: 'To you our rivers sang of bliss/ Beyond all mortal pales,/ I ask no other heaven than this,/ My paradise is Wales.' But after going on to imply that Vaughan was thus guilty of a kind of betrayal of Wales by choosing instead to whore after a strange god, Webb concludes the poem on a conciliatory note, extending to Vaughan the hand of friendship in a gesture that seeks to claim the Silurist as, after all and despite himself, a member of the Anglo-Welsh community: 'Yet will I stretch to you a hand/ And look you in the eyes,/ Who share the same enchanted land,/ The same all-healing skies.'

Another poet of the same period was also stretching out his hand to Vaughan, but in the name of a Wales somewhat different from that of Webb. Roland Mathias's private affinities with Vaughan, although never advertised by a scholar morally hostile to self-exposure, have continued to form the armature of his judiciously historical studies. An Oxford graduate in history,

Mathias has been working for many years on a substantial unpublished study of Vaughan as 'Silurist', but in his first essay on the poet, published in 1952, he began by setting Vaughan in, and against, the physical landscape of his native region:

> If you leave the long barns of Newton on your left hand and choose deliberately the path, well-mudded from the yard, that crawls under the railway, now and for long a part of the natural order, the red track by which you climb, at first edged heavily by a line of scrubby trees, finally loses its zeal and plain intent in the thistly field and lopped forest of Allt yr Esgair. Here Henry Vaughan must have often walked when the wood was thick down to the valley bottom, watching the sun touch the topmost leaves with bronze and catching a glimpse down an occasional ride of the light on Tor y Foel or the cottages at Cross Oak. (20)[47]

Vaughan may indeed have walked there, but Mathias's point is that nowhere does the poet, in spite of his reputed love for the country of the Usk, actually detail its unmistakable landscape: 'Whatever else Vaughan was seeing, he was not seeing the life of man against the natural surroundings of Breconshire' (25). Instead, as a pre-Romantic and Metaphysical poet who started out as an Anglophile neoclassical writer, Vaughan uses generalized features of topography to emblematize, and thus to mediate, spiritual truths. Moreover, unlike the other great Metaphysicals, 'he was more committed than free poise would permit to the spiritual realm, and used the material world chiefly as a means of interpretation and analogy for the reader' (30). In this, Mathias suggests, he was unconsciously Welsh, in that his work typified a culture which had traditionally celebrated 'the victory of spirit over eyes and ears' (31). But while thus admiring Vaughan, Mathias is also clearly somewhat discomfited by him. The sheer splendid recalcitrance of physical reality is slighted in his work, its stubborn quiddity treated as malleable by the spirit. This is a metaphysics, or rather a theology, that disconcerts Mathias, a modern Christian struggling to keep faith in the face of the demonstrable intractability both of the hard physics of the universe, and of grimly established human historical fact – in the face, in short, of what Mathias, in his marvellous poem 'Brechfa Chapel', called 'the slimed/ Substantiation of the elements' (46).[48]

But Vaughan's 'cavalier' treatment of natural locality also disturbs Mathias for a different reason. Although Mathias's maternal family home was within the proverbial stone's throw of Vaughan's own 'patch', and although Mathias was born in that area, he spent most of his boyhood, adolescence, and even young manhood outside Wales, as his family moved from place to place in England and Europe wherever the Army posted his chaplain father. When, eventually, Roland Mathias succeeded in making his way back as an 'alien' to his native Wales, he felt himself to be very much an outsider, desperately longing to belong, but able to 'call nothing my own' (*SC*, 17). As he later noted, 'I am sorry in my heart to be shut out, but glad that memory gives me strength to go on knocking. Memory and guilt. For guilt is a knocker too' (163).[49]

On his return, he felt incapable of making real contact with Welsh people. Instead, he gained a kind of admittance to Wales through its landscape and its history, with the former frequently understood by him as incarnating the latter. 'All that man was// In history pictures here', he writes in 'On Llandefalle Hill' (*SC*, 38), and notices 'Reluctant light,/ Parade of a far terror, wind greyhound/ In the mosses':

> Sheep graze, a cart track shows
> Yellower where
> The grass is thin and pressed: habit prescribes
> The way. If God allows
> He spoke once to our fathers, the babes
> Will remember it to the wasted tribes.

Henry Vaughan, so inward with his landscape that he unconsciously reproduces not its over-familiar details but its essential contours, or *Gestalt*, when describing the landscape of the soul, is in this respect Mathias's opposite. Yet he is also his kin, and even perhaps his non-identical twin. Mathias the returnee felt so diffident about presuming to be Welsh that he took up his mental, and indeed his physical, abode in border country – studying the recusants of Herefordshire and Gwent before settling as headmaster in Pembrokeshire, that little England beyond Wales. But soon he came to feel that the majority of the monoglot English-speakers of Wales were also inhabiting a border country, that they were haplessly suspended in limbo between two cultures, and that the patron saint of the writers of this twilight region was Henry Vaughan. Mathias's Vaughan is a writer whose work promotes reflection on the bicultural character of Wales, and who proves that Anglo-Welsh culture – Anglo-Welsh being here an epithet loosely applied to those 'who [elect] to write in English out of a firmly Welsh background' (243)[50] – is many centuries old.

It so happens that Vaughan's geographic and cultural bipolarity matched that of Mathias fairly closely. Both were born in the Brecon area, but both were educated, and thoroughly Englished, at Jesus College, Oxford. Vaughan's presumed background in Welsh-language culture quickly became occluded and has remained irrecoverable: there remains a tantalizing gap in our knowledge, exactly corresponding to the gap between the two cultures Vaughan was heir to. Mathias grew up in a home where his father spoke Welsh but his mother harboured a secret hostility to the language: 'the gap between the two heritages – those of my father and mother – disclosed a darker acre of tension for their eldest son', Mathias has written: 'in it creativity, brought fully awake by age, first pawed and snuffed' (*AW*, 162). Much of his mature work has been concerned with the closing of that 'domestic' gap, with the reconcilement of 'the two heritages', and it is in this connection that the case of Vaughan has continued to fascinate him.

Only 'out of free choice', Mathias has emphasized, 'can there be built a Wales in English which is not England and which is in touch with the living heart of a Wales that beats in Welsh' (*AW*, 168). The example of Vaughan stands in a complex, and indeed ambiguous, relation to this vision. Unknown for so long, even in his native region, he is representative of that of which the Anglo-Welsh are so dangerously ignorant – namely, their own history. To rediscover him, therefore, and to reconnect with him, is vitally necessary for them, since it is an important means by which they can equip and empower themselves to participate 'in the continuum of Wales' (183).[51] But the rediscovered Vaughan proves to be of equivocal significance. The question 'Who did he write for?' produces a painful answer: not for his immediate, Welsh-speaking, community but for the educated English, and for a Welsh anglophone and anglophile élite. Who, then, are modern Anglo-Welsh authors writing for? Is there, indeed, a richly and consciously Welsh readership available to them? These and other disturbing questions are left hanging in the air. And in 1952, Mathias sees a parallel between Vaughan and the Anglo-Welsh poets of Mathias's period:

> [Vaughan] was, in fact, doing what modern Welsh writers in English are accused of doing – writing for an English audience. But unlike some moderns, he was not contorting his country to excite notice. Indeed, his pride consisted in presenting it as normal, healthy and English as possible. (*DL*, 27)

Mathias himself was to devote the following decades to an attempt to cure Anglo-Welsh writing both of its simulated Englishness and of its caricatured Welshness.

But if Vaughan was not speaking to Wales, at least he *was* speaking out of universal spiritual experience, rather than producing a kind of 'confessional poetry, written in the tiresome belief that the poet's experiences are in some ways unique' (*CG*, 184), a trend which Mathias believes is deplorably exemplified in so much Anglo-American poetry. He has deemed Dylan Thomas 'guilty' of just such a poetry, and Mathias shares with Tony Conran and Jeremy Hooker a feeling that writing of that kind is both morally suspect and deeply un-Welsh. Vaughan's poetry is therefore seen as the precursor after all of modern 'communitarian' Welsh writing; and, indeed, his poems show how such a cultural ethos originated in religious belief.

Vaughan is, then, regarded by Mathias as a figure who typifies the fundamentally Christian cast of Welsh culture. But by an irony not lost on Mathias himself, Vaughan was in fact an Anglican persecuted by and fiercely hostile to that mid-seventeenth-century Puritanism from which Mathias's Congregationalism directly derived, as indeed, although more indirectly, did Welsh Nonconformity as a whole. That said, Vaughan becomes a kind of spiritual *alter ego* for Mathias, a figure who allows him to ponder such matters as 'the subject of the poet himself, his place and true function in a God-directed world' (*RW*, 237). Always punishingly strict on himself, and wary of any hint of self-dramatizing self-pity, Mathias is able, without compromising himself morally, to raise through the example of

Vaughan the question of how Christians (and Christian poets) may thrive in adverse times. It is fitting that his early poem 'On the Grave of Henry Vaughan at Llansaintffraed', in the collection coincidentally entitled *The Roses of Tretower*, should be a spiritual meditation:

> Sun at arm's length, infant cajoling ball,
> And stretching finger full of a hale man's blood,
> This is the promise, here the hump and wall
> By which the grave yew ghosts continue longer
> And in their church of damp have hosts.
>
> In this blind parcel is the portion lost,
> The hampered reason, the most potent sin:
> Yet the prostrate endurance of this dust
> Beyond the rain's dearth, into a light season,
> Marks the exacting purpose of this earth.
>
> Man that is God and ghost, fuel and fire,
> Factor and master, ephemeral, crossed
> *Peccator maximus* stirring to desire,
> Dust shall have shape and sing, in the sun faster –
> This hump is Pisgah and each shoulder wing! (25)[52]

Here Mathias follows Vaughan in attempting to redeem 'impious wit', Vaughan having himself famously followed the example of 'the blessed man, Mr *George Herbert*, whose holy *life* and *verse* gained many pious *Converts*, (of whom I am the least) and gave the first check to a most flourishing and admired *wit* of his time' (220). Mathias's fierce 'cross'-examination of language, his self-torturing spiritual inquisition of vocabulary and syntax, is part of his attempt to 'convert' the fallen speech of modern life to spiritual meaning. No wonder he understands Vaughan, and Herbert, so incomparably well. He is of their spiritual kind, and he uses their language because it is second nature to him. So when he writes of the grave that 'In this blind parcel is the portion lost,/ The hampered reason, the most potent sin', he is movingly echoing Vaughan's great words in the Preface to *Silex Scintillans*:

> It was wisely considered, and piously said by one, *That he would read no idle books; both in regard of love to his own soul, and pity unto his that made them, for* (said he) *if I be corrupted by them, their*

Composer is immediatly a cause of my ill: and at the day of reckoning (though now dead) must give an account for it, because I am corrupted by his bad example, which he left behinde him: I will write none, lest I hurt them that come after me; I will read none, lest I augment his punishment that is gone before me. I will neither write, nor read, lest I prove a foe to my own soul: while I live, I sin too much; let me not continue longer in wickedness, then I do in life. It is a sentence of sacred authority, that *he that is dead, is freed from sin*; because he cannot in that *state*, which is without the *body*, sin any more; but he that writes *idle books*, makes for himself another *body*, in which he always *lives*, and *sins* (after *death*) as *fast* and as *foul*, as ever he did in his *life*; which very consideration, deserves to be a sufficient *Antidote* against this evil disease. (219)

Mathias has always been palpably afraid of writing 'idle books' that would have a malign kind of immortality, and it is partly this spiritual dread of his own writerly gifts – a dread which is extremely rare in our day – that has enabled him to understand Vaughan's poetry so profoundly well.

       ★ ★ ★ ★

But Roland Mathias was not the only figure influential in determining the character of what I have called the second, post-war, phase of Anglo-Welsh culture. Tony Conran also came to play a significant part in this development, and in an essay published in 1986 he, too, duly turned his attention to Henry Vaughan. Central to Conran's work as poet and translator has been the belief that classical Welsh-language literature was the product of a high civilization wholly outside the orbit of that Western Christendom within which English culture developed. And a corollary of this is his contention that Anglo-Welsh literature can be distinctively Welsh only in so far as it succeeds in translating into English the values of that civilization, and the literary forms in which they are inscribed. Conran therefore sees his work as translator from the Welsh and as Anglo-Welsh poet simply as two sides of the same coin, and this will become apparent in later chapters of this study.

He also views much of what passes for modern Anglo-Welsh literature as nothing but provincial writing: 'It is part of a process of provincialization, making Wales a province, not indeed of

England, but of something called "Britain"'(9).[53] That process began with the violent accession of the 'Welsh' Tudors to the English throne, and the consequent fabrication of an Anglo-British ideology. For Conran, though, that ideology, in its original form, began to distintegrate in the seventeenth century, as the aristocratic class that had produced it and been supported by it was progressively displaced. With the collapse of the old ideology of Britishness, the Welsh, who had thriven on it for over a century, were left stranded and became marginalized by the emergent order. Thrown back on their own devices, they eventually produced their own peculiar form of Methodist culture, which in due course provided a strong basis for central Welsh participation in the new version of Britishness that evolved in the nineteenth century as Wales and Scotland developed the industrial muscle that England by then so badly needed. For Conran, most of twentieth-century Anglo-Welsh literature is only a belated relic of that now exhausted and anachronistic nineteenth-century 'Bringlish' ideology (to borrow Nigel Jenkins's inspired coinage).

Conran provides an important place for Henry Vaughan in this master narrative of Welsh history, which is also a comprehensive interpretation of Anglo-Welsh literature. He strikingly contrasts Vaughan with Herbert, whose genuine humility does not prevent his poems in *The Temple* from resonating with the unforced authority of one who speaks from and to 'the national church of the whole people' (*YBP*, 13). Vaughan is very different. In *Silex Scintillans*, 'the quietism and the clutter are fruits of obscurity, of a provincialism of a spirit, an isolation from the centres of power where important decisions are made' (*YBP*, 15). In other words, Vaughan is a Welsh provincial Briton. But he is also, Conran continues, 'a Welshman, during one of those periodic lulls in Welsh culture that precede periods of intense activity' (16). In other words, Vaughan is, for Conran, the harbinger of Methodism, and the hitherto unnoticed poetic forebear of William Williams Pantycelyn.

The historical credibility of such a claim is, in the context of the present discussion, less important than is the way it instances the use an important creative writer such as Conran can make of Vaughan to provide his own transcultural practices with historical authority. 'My one piece of evidence for [connecting Vaughan to Williams Pantycelyn] is quite subjective', Conran frankly admits, 'and arose out of my experience as a translator' (*YBP*, 17). While attempting to translate Pantycelyn's hymns for what turned out to be his landmark volume, *The Penguin Book of Welsh Verse*, Conran found that English hymnody could afford him no assistance. Thrown back on his own devices. he found, to his surprise, 'that the idiom I had used was as like Vaughan as I could have made it' (*YBP*, 17):

> The weight of it, the specific gravity, seemed to be like Vaughan. Of course, Pantycelyn is more dynamic. As I say, he was a man of power. He wielded the thunderbolt. But the lyric feeling, the romantic yearning, the eagerness to convey largely private religious sensations; even much of the imagery – these are very reminiscent, certainly in my translations, of the kind of thing that Vaughan does, and other seventeenth century poets do not:

> > I look across the hills
> >   Of my Father's house, and see
> > The sunlight on the ground
> >   Whose grace sets me free . . .

> > The children of the world can know
> >   Nothing of such grace
> > As sucks my liking and intent
> >   Off each created face . . .

or even

> > By cross and grief, by tempest driven,
> > The saints are ripened into heaven.

William Williams, of course, wrote hymns in English as well as Welsh – he was Anglo-Welsh as well as Welsh. And Raymond Garlick, it is interesting to see, quotes a stanza from one of them which he says is 'reminiscent of the world of light and darkness of Henry Vaughan':

> > O let me see those beams of light,
> > Feel that celestial spark
> > That veils the beauties of the world
> > In an eternal dark. (*YBP*, 17–18)

Through the view that Conran takes of his translations of William Williams Pantycelyn, Vaughan's poetry becomes, albeit modestly and passingly, an active element in modern Welsh writing: that is, in modern Welsh writing in English at the precise point where that meets and merges with Welsh writing in Welsh. Given the general thrust of *Corresponding Cultures*, there is something particularly appropriate and satisfying about that, as there is in the interest that has occasionally been shown in Vaughan, over the last few decades, by Welsh-language writers. A notable instance of this is the significant essay, published in 1943 in that landmark Anglo-Welsh periodical *Wales*, by 'Davies Aberpennar', who, as Pennar Davies, went on to become one of the most intellectually audacious of post-war writers in the Welsh language. Davies approvingly noted that Vaughan, though a Christian Platonist, and

in spite of his rapturous self-abandonment to what D. H. Lawrence would have described as 'the drift towards death', nevertheless insisted on the goodness of the body. And yet it is perhaps not so surprising when we remember that he was a physician. He could not conceive of a perfection in which the body was not present and perfect.[54]

In emphasizing this aspect of Vaughan's vision, Davies was implicitly recognizing his own kinship with him. Because although a renowned theologian, and Principal of the Welsh Congregational College, Davies daringly proclaimed, throughout his poetry and fiction, the sanctity of the sensual, sexual human body, revealing himself to be one of the unorthodox ecstatics of Welsh culture. In his novels – one of which will be examined in detail in a later chapter – Davies periodically treated Vaughan as a figure whose belief in 'mankind's primitive blessedness' fascinated twentieth-century neo-romantics who were attracted to a gospel of redemption.[55]

Of modern Welsh-language writers, however, it is the poet Alun Llywelyn-Williams who perhaps used Vaughan to greatest creative effect.[56] On the opening page of his travel book *Crwydro Brycheiniog* (*Wandering through Breconshire*), he mentions Vaughan as one of the great Welsh figures whose statue might have better graced Brecon's main square than that of Wellington which arrogantly occupies the spot – an example, Llywelyn-Williams suggests, of a colonized people's conditioned preference for the heroes of its colonizers. But it is in the chapter on exploring the country between Brecon and Abergavenny that he most fully considers Vaughan as a native of an area now thoroughly anglicized but which had remained extensively Welsh-speaking virtually down to the end of the nineteenth century.[57] Indeed, Llywelyn-Williams consciously writes as a cultural archaeologist, uncovering the rich evidence of that so recently departed and sadly lost 'civilization'. In the process he manifestly identifies with scholars such as Carnhuanawc (1787–1848) who fought to defend the Welshness of the area, and he poignantly recalls his own encounter during the Second World War with the last person in the district whose mother tongue had been Welsh. Blind, and approaching eighty, the old man had at first replied to him in English, so long had it been since he had last conversed in Welsh:

> he seemed unable for some moments to persuade his tongue to utter the sounds that had been alien to him for so long. At last, he turned to speaking slowly and stumblingly in his mother's tongue. And then the dam burst, and I had the opportunity of listening to a flood of the most tuneful Welsh I ever heard. There were tears in the old man's eyes when I had to depart. (56)

Set in this context, Vaughan becomes an enigmatic and ambivalent figure, one who produced great poetry by turning his back on the language and culture both of his own early background and of the region he served so well as doctor and as poet.

In engaging with Vaughan, Llywelyn-Williams is, however, doing more than engaging with a historical 'case'; he is engaging very intimately with his own personal history. As he recalls, he was first entranced by Vaughan's poetry at school in Cardiff, when he was an 'Anglo-Welsh' schoolboy who as yet knew relatively little Welsh. But for the inspiring influence of his history master, R. T. Jenkins (who went on to become one of Wales's greatest historians), Llywelyn-Williams might never have realized that the key to so much of the history of his own country was to be found in the Welsh language of which he knew so little.[58]

Vaughan, therefore, represents the 'Anglo-Welsh' poet Llywelyn-Williams might himself have become, and Vaughan's 'defection' from Welsh (particularly when viewed, with historical hindsight, as prelude to the eventual wholesale Anglicization of Breconshire) becomes the ideologically pointed antithesis of Llywelyn-Williams's conversion to Welsh.

But the matter is not as simple as that; because Llywelyn-Williams is as attracted to Vaughan as he is suspicious of him. Did Vaughan, he wonders, turn to writing poetry in English because classic Welsh-language poetry adhered to a convention of impersonality of utterance that denied his soul distinctive expression? Such a speculation probably reveals more about Llywelyn-Williams himself than it does about Vaughan. Because, although he chose to write poetry in his 'learned' language of Welsh, the young Llywelyn-Williams of the late 1930s felt a much closer affinity to the English-language writers of his time than he did to the great Welsh-language tradition of *barddas*. He therefore knew from personal experience what it was to find anglophone culture troublingly congenial to himself as poet.

What is more, Llywelyn-Williams also knew from personal experience that by the twentieth century English had itself become a Welsh language. Having been raised an essentially English-speaking child in Anglicized Cardiff, Llywelyn-Williams was deeply aware of being an outsider to traditional, rural, Welsh-speaking Wales. If he eventually came to empathize with the plight of the old man from Breconshire, he also remained conscious throughout his life of the differently legitimate Welshness of anglophone Wales; and, while never relaxing his vigilance on behalf of the Welsh language, he steadily tried to foster a better understanding between his country's two linguistic communities. 'Pont y Caniedydd' is the major poem he devoted to this theme, and the figure and country of Henry Vaughan are central to it.

As Llywelyn-Williams explained:

Pont y Caniedydd is a real bridge two or three miles south of Brecon ... I suppose the name means The Singer's Bridge ... and it suited me to take it ambiguously, since 'caniedydd' can mean 'poet', and in the context of the poem it is the poet's desire to be a kind of bridge.[59]

How, though, to bridge past and present (and eventually present and future), particularly given the ruptures in Welsh history: that is the poem's main concern. The actual bridge, where the road dips down to a brook, initially figures for Llywelyn-Williams as 'a yesterday grown strange', inalienably remote as this rural spot seems from the modern, industrialized and urban Wales that is nevertheless near neighbour to it. In addition, Pont y Caniedydd stands for much else that has vanished: the Welsh-language culture of Breconshire, a lost religious faith, a rooted society. And this loss is registered in the poem partly in terms of forgotten historical personages – Howel Harris and his Trefeca Methodist community, the once powerful Vaughan family of Tretower, and its most famous scion, Henry Vaughan. The impotence of the past to reproduce itself, to ensure due entailment and proper transmission of its values, is felt acutely by a Llywelyn-Williams disorientated alike by the wasteland of Berlin in 1945 and by the headlong hedonistic consumerism of post-war Welsh society.

But in the end he characteristically places his cautious, limited faith in the power of art (including his own) to bridge the gaps opened up by history. Art it is that alone seems capable of awakening the echoes of an underlying harmony in human experience from generation to generation; and those are the echoes to be heard at Pont y Caniedydd:

> here is the sonata
> we heard cleansing fear in the sober chamber
> the night before going to the wars;
> here is an undertone of the blessed ring
> of pure eternal light a poet of yesterday
> saw shining overhead. (175)

That 'poet of yesterday' is, clearly, Henry Vaughan. Llywelyn-Williams' bridge to him is, however, the product not of shared Christian faith, but of a 'translation' into modern, secular terms of his famous religious vision of eternity 'like a great *Ring* of pure and endless light,/ All calm, as it was bright' (299). For Llywelyn-Williams the lines define humankind's unchanging condition, by powerfully expressing every age and generation's insignificant place in a sublimely vast and uniformly indifferent universe.

★　★　★　★

So, the poetry of Henry Vaughan continues to speak intimately to several writers of our own time, most particularly those whose Welshness is, for them, too, problematic.[60] '*If, when you please to looke upon these* Collections', Vaughan wrote to his patron, Sir Charles Egerton,

> *you will find them to lead you from the Sun into the* shade, *from the open* Terrace *into a private* grove, & *from the* noyse *and* pompe *of this world into a silent and solitary* Hermitage: *doe not you thinke then, that you have descended (like the* dead) in Occidentem & tenebras, *for in this* withdrawing-roome (*though secret and seldome frequented,) shines that happy* starre, *which will directly lead you to the* King *of* light. (158)

As we began by noting, the Henry Vaughan of *Silex Scintillans* believed himself to be living 'in Occidentem & tenebras': that is, in the west which was the shadowland of gathering darkness; but through his poetry he continues, repeatedly if fitfully, to illumine the culturally divided Wales both of his own time and of ours.

2

Hidden attachments

~

In a recent, subtle book, *The Location of Culture*, Homi K. Bhabha has several thoughtful observations to make about the dynamics of intra- and intercultural relationships:

> The problem is not simply the 'selfhood' of the nation as opposed to the otherness of other nations. We are confronted with the nation split within itself, articulating the heterogeneity of its population. The barred Nation *It/Self*, alienated from its eternal self-generation, becomes a liminal signifying space that is *internally* marked by the discourses of minorities, the heterogeneous histories of contending peoples, antagonist authorities and tense locations of cultural difference.[1]

The deconstruction of the essentialist idea of a nation as simply unitary, as wholesomely 'organic', is of particular significance to those of us who acknowledge the validity of the different kinds of Welshness that are highlighted by (although by no means identical with) the differences between the Welsh-language and the English-language culture of twentieth-century Wales. As Bhabha helpfully notes: 'It is in the emergence of the interstices – the overlap and displacement of domains of difference – that the intersubjective and collective experiences of *nationness*, community interest, or cultural value are negotiated' (*LC*, 2). That word 'negotiated' signifies the tolerant aspects of the complex psychological, social and political manœuvres involved in the never-ending work of maintaining a nation. But, as Bhabha emphasizes, the process also involves

> the competing claims of communities where, despite shared histories of deprivation and discrimination, the exchange of values, meanings and priorities may not always be collaborative and dialogical, but may be profoundly antagonistic, conflictual and even incommensurable. (*LC*, 2)

As is well known, modern Welsh writing in English originated in intense intercultural rivalry between traditional Welsh-speaking west Wales, which was rural and Nonconformist, and new, industrial, south Wales, where the hegemonic power of English was very apparent. From the very beginning, therefore, the two literatures of modern Wales seemed destined, by the very social process and configurations which underwrote them, to be enemies and rivals, since the rise of the society which produced the one seemed predicated on – and even dedicated to – the destruction of the culture sustaining the other. Literary hostilities actually commenced with the publication in 1915 of Caradoc Evans's *My People*, the collection of stories usually taken to mark the appearance of a distinctively Welsh literature in English.[2] Although written by a Welsh-speaker, the stories depicted the inhabitants of west Wales as morally retarded and viciously cretinous. Key to Evans's undoubted success was his ability to create a vividly peculiar English idiolect, the equivalent of redskin-speak in old cowboy films, that made the Welsh-speaking community appear to be condemning itself out of its own mouth.[3]

With *My People*, *Kulturkampf* began in Wales with a vengeance, and for a generation thereafter Anglo-Welsh writing seemed to Welsh-language writers to bear the mark of Caradoc like the Mark of the Beast. Indeed, one has only to examine Dylan Thomas's work with even half a slightly jaundiced eye to see the tell-tale brand for oneself. In the story 'The Peaches', a little boy from Anglicized suburbia is fascinated by the colourful eccentricities of his Welsh-speaking relatives left behind down there on the farm in the Welsh wild west, including those of his cousin Gwilym, who, lashing himself into a preacher's frenzy, reaches a grand climax in his address to God: 'Thou canst see . . . everything, everything; Thou canst see all the time. O God, mun, you're like a bloody cat.'[4] Most interestingly of all, the famous poem 'After the Funeral', written in memory of Thomas's aunt, Ann Jones, is constructed like a cultural rescue mission – with Thomas wrestling verbally with the local Nonconformist preacher for her soul. 'After the funeral, mule praises, brays', Thomas 'stand[s] . . . alone' to build a poem in language which will liberate the spirit in her which had been repressed and crippled by the culture in which she had lived. While her hands '[l]ie with religion in their cramp', Thomas would 'call all/ The seas to service that her wood-tongued virtue/ Babble like a bellbuoy over the hymning heads'.[5] In this way, Thomas in effect reverses Gwilym's practice. Whereas the latter had turned a barn into a sombre chapel, Thomas replies by returning the rural world to nature, and turning nature into an alternative religion: '[I] Bow down the walls of the ferned and foxy woods/ That her love sing and swing through a brown chapel,/ Bless her bent spirit with four, crossing birds.' 'After the Funeral' thus reveals one possible cultural source of that obsession with natural process which characterizes many of Thomas's best poems from 'The force that through the green fuse drives the flower' to 'And death shall have no dominion'. It is the poet's reply to the world-view of the Nonconformist preacher.

Welsh-language writers were understandably alert to what they interpreted as the cultural militancy, so spectacularly instanced in literature by Caradoc Evans, of the expansionist English-language community in south-east Wales. 'Argoed' is a majestic narrative poem published in 1927 by T. Gwynn Jones, a major figure in the modern renaissance of Welsh-language literature. It concerns a tribe in a remote part of ancient Gaul that lives a pacific pastoral life in tune with its ancient traditions. Unknown to the tribesmen, Rome has already conquered the greater part of their country, destroying its language, its customs and its cities. They discover this only when one of their poets is met with ridicule and incomprehension as he tries to sing his traditional songs in another part of Gaul. When the Romans eventually attempt to tax the people of Argoed, the tribe sets fire to the forest rather than submit to foreign rule. The tragic fable beautifully illustrates the main features of an evolving cultural ideology and explains the internal logic of its structure. A threatened language looks to its writers for preservation; they become both the culture's memory-bank and its cutting edge; in turn literature becomes an instrument of cultural politics. It was under these forcing conditions – conditions dramatized by the aggressive appearance of Anglo-Welsh literature – that the greatest Welsh-language writing of this century developed.[6]

Whereas, in 'Argoed', the tone of T. Gwynn Jones's response to the threat of Anglicization was elegiac, there were Welsh-language writers prepared to meet aggression with aggression.

Saunders Lewis, arguably the most impressive intellectual figure in twentieth-century Welsh culture, became notorious during the 1930s for at least two indecent assaults on the Anglo-Welsh. Always inclined to blame the situation in Wales on the industrialization of the south, which had brought Anglicization in its wake, he savagely lampooned that region in his poem 'The Deluge, 1939'. The proletariat was accused of having produced 'a culture of grease', and he put words of terrible self-indictment into their mouths: 'We command no language or dialect, unconscious of insult/ And the masterpiece we gave history is our land's M.P.s' (75).[7] It was this same contempt for southerners, now carefully concealed, that powered his cool, elegant, academic arguments, in a famous lecture of 1938, against there ever being a genuine Welsh literature in English:

> The growth of Anglo-Welsh writing in recent years is the inevitable reflection of the undirected drifting of Welsh national life. It will go on, becoming less and less incompletely English, unless there is a revival of the moral qualities of the Welsh people ... Mr Dylan Thomas is obviously an equipped writer, but there is nothing hyphenated [i.e. Anglo-Welsh] about him. He belongs to the English.[8]

Because, for decades after *My People*, the conflictual aspects of intercultural relations in modern Wales were so prominent, and so historically significant, it is tempting to suppose that they covered the entire case, and thus to consider the relationship of the two literatures throughout that period under a single, simple rubric. In fact, however, the situation was almost dauntingly subtle and fluid, as can be conveniently illustrated by a reconsideration of 'After the Funeral', that very poem by Dylan Thomas so confidently anatomized above. On closer examination, the poem appears to involve not only the central pattern of binary *opposition* that has already been noted (preacher/poet and so on), but also a complex process of cultural *transposition*. Here, perhaps more explicitly than anywhere else in his poetry, Thomas shows himself aware of the Welsh poetic tradition. He does not just talk vaguely about bards; he knows at least that they stood at the hearth, in the midst of the company. He is aware of the bard's social role. It is, indeed, manifestly, a praise poem, not to a great lord but (movingly) to this 'humble' woman. At the same time this bard is not, one feels, speaking 'as part of the community', producing a poem which 'moves as if it [has] the whole community behind it'.[9] He 'stand[s] ... alone', more like a poet in the English, lyric tradition. At this point, therefore, Thomas could be said to be standing on the intercultural boundary, as will be further explored in a later chapter. He knows Wales – and something of the Welsh tradition – from the inside (presumably from Welsh-speaking west Wales) but is also an outsider (by familial class aspirations, by the loss of the language, for example). Expressed in Saunders Lewis's terms, what we find in 'After the Funeral' is evidence that Dylan Thomas *was* a hyphenated Welshman after all.[10]

But the term 'hyphenated' is as much of a hindrance as a help, since it implies a fundamental distinction between true (Welsh) Welshness and mongrel (Anglo-Welsh) Welshness. Much more useful in the Welsh context is the term 'hybrid', in Bhabha's sense of the word:

> When Bhabha insists on speaking of cultural *difference* rather than cultural *diversity*, he is employing [a distinctive] strategy. Where some see a jumble of interacting cultural monads – the contest of a diversity of stable identities – Homi Bhabha sees interacting 'positionalities', constantly reshaped, always in flux. In place of the opposition of Self and Other, the strategy of hybridity proposes, once more, that the Other is already 'within' the Self.[11]

Bhabha's crucial point is that there is no such thing as a 'pure', 'uncontaminated', 'self-sufficient' culture. *All* cultures are unstable compounds. To see this is to hesitate before simply stigmatizing 'After the Funeral' as the confused product of cultural dislocation. It is also to discover interesting new ground *shared* by Welsh-language and English-language writers. For instance, R. Williams Parry's famous poem, 'Y Llwynog' (The Fox), often supposed to be quintessentially Welsh, can be read as a striking example, parallel to 'After the Funeral', of a cross between English Romantic poetry and the indigenous Welsh tradition.[12] The poem turns on an epiphanic moment when the poet, already hesitating on a glorious summer's evening whether to respond to the sombre sabbath bells of his village or to opt rebelliously for the sun-drenched mountains, is granted a revelatory glimpse of the flaring natural beauty of a fox. It can be construed as a moment when English Romanticism puts Welsh Nonconformity to rout, when Williams Parry (like Thomas) consciously places himself at the *margins* of his pious community, and when he worships his fox in much the same spirit of defiant Romantic paganism in which Thomas rapturously hymned 'the walls of the ferned and foxy woods'.

What are needed, therefore, are new, subtle, ways of exploring the fluid relationship between cultures in Wales, with particular reference, for example, to liminal, or boundary states.[13] There is, after all, an important sense in which a great deal of modern Welsh literature has been produced as a kind of rite of passage to mark the cross-over from one language, and culture, to another. If Saunders Lewis (a Wallasey-born, Liverpool-educated graduate in English literature) crossed from English to Welsh, then so, in a way, did Pennar Davies, Waldo Williams, Alun Llywelyn-Williams, and many, many others, including, in their separate and distinctive ways, Emyr Humphreys and R. S. Thomas. And then there is a whole host of examples, to which we were early alerted by Glyn Jones, of a socio-familial move-ment from Welsh to English – examples as varied as those of Idris Davies, Gwyn Thomas, and Gillian Clarke.[14] The facts, in these and in innumerable similar cases, are very well known, but the psycho-cultural significance of such cross-overs has hardly begun to be explored.[15] Modern Welsh literature (in both languages) is rich in examples of what Bhabha has called 'the performance of identity' in order to ensure 'the resettlement of the borderline community of migration' (*LC*, 9).

In Wales we have scarcely begun, then, to examine the ways in which two cultures can be co-operative – can make history and make literature, at the same time and in the same place. And so our understanding of the *modus vivendi* of the two, intermeshing, languages and literatures has so far been elementary, to say the least. The issue is an intellectually demanding one, and even at the most preliminary level, any serious enquiry would have to bear such factors as the following in mind.

1   *Common origins*

To understand how the Welsh-language renaissance and Anglo-Welsh literature actually have a common point of origin involves a revisionist reading of Caradoc Evans. His work needs to be seen not only as the point at which the two cultures diverged into hostility but as the controversial by-product of a period when the two literatures converged – and, indeed, co-operated – to confront a common enemy. That enemy was Welsh Non-conformity, and it was with 'Ymadawiad Arthur' ('The Departure of Arthur'), a poem whose pagan Celtic materials and sensuality of alliterative language scandalized the Nonconformist establishment, that the modern Welsh-language renaissance had begun in 1902. The author, T. Gwynn Jones, was shortly joined by other *enfants terribles* such as W. J. Gruffydd, whose chosen medium was not poetry but drama, so that by the time *My People* was published in 1915 a literary assault on the pieties and sensibilities of the faithful was well under way. In 1913, for example, D. T. Davies's play *Ephraim Harris* caused an outcry among religious conservatives because it centred on a deacon who in his youth had (supposedly) begotten an illegitimate child, and whose (initially unwilling) concealment of that fact for half a lifetime served to intensify his bigoted intolerance of any hint of moral laxity in others. Around the same time, T. Gwynn Jones produced an explosive translation of Ibsen's *Ghosts*, and W. J. Gruffydd, always provocative, caused a stir with *Beddau'r Proffwydi* (*The Tombs of the Prophets*), a play in which Nonconformity was subjected to the bitter gibes, raillery and sarcasm of a very angry young man.

Many of these Welsh-language plays were quickly translated into English and then staged alongside the English-language drama of J. O. Francis, a Welshman whose plays similarly reflect the society's changing attitudes towards religion. His 1914 play, appropriately entitled *Change*, was hailed as a masterpiece in its day – performed both in London and New York, and toured throughout Wales – but his sound claim to be the real originator of an authentically Welsh literature in English has sadly long been lost to sight behind the sensationalist writings of Caradoc Evans. The point is, then, that Evans's work, although audaciously original in character, affords only a brilliantly extreme example of that animus against Nonconformity which animated both the best Welsh-language and the best English-language literature of that period.[16]

2 *Cross-fertilization between the two literary cultures*

A full investigation of the subject would cover translation, bilingual numbers of literary journals, so-called seepage (Conran's phrase) between the two cultures, the intertextuality produced by conscious and unconscious allusion, and so on.[17] Further consideration will be given to these and other matters in later chapters in this study, and so attention is here drawn only to the neglected but highly significant fact that on at least three occasions this century one of the two literary cultures has in crucial respects been permanently changed by the invasion of material from the other. This first happened to Welsh literature, in the late 1930s, through the medium of Alun Llywelyn-Williams. As was noted in the preceding chapter, he was brought up mainly speaking English and so naturally felt a close affinity with the Anglo-Welsh writers of the period. Therefore, when he turned in his early twenties to writing poetry in Welsh he found that the models available to him in that language were foreign and uncongenial. Instead, he forged, partly out of the social realism of the new Anglo-Welsh novel and the slow, meditative manner of the young self-interrogating Anglo-Welsh poet Alun Lewis, a new, quiet-voiced, low-pitched style of writing keyed above all to personal honesty. And with it he unknowingly established a new tradition of writing in English, whose distinguished practitioners in our own time include two of the most interesting of contemporary poets, Gwyn Thomas and R. Gerallt Jones.[18]

Then, after the war, the process was reversed, as Anglo-Welsh literature was transformed under Welsh influence. For both the major figures who then emerged, namely Emyr Humphreys and R. S. Thomas, their writing was an expression of the cultural and political nationalism they had learnt from Saunders Lewis.[19] In addition to being a giant creative talent, Lewis was a founder member of Plaid Cymru, the Welsh Nationalist Party. To this very day, both Humphreys and Thomas continue to be inspired as writers by his example, and in the case of the novelist Humphreys both his stylistics and the subject of his writing have been deeply influenced by Lewis's cultural philosophy. So if the first generaion of Anglo-Welsh writers (Dylan Thomas and his contemporaries, who grew up in the 1930s), are frequently called 'the children of Caradoc', then these and other leading male Anglo-Welsh writers of the post-war period could well be designated the sons of Saunders.

That, of course, is strange indeed, since Lewis had announced in the 1930s that Anglo-Welsh literature did not exist and never could.[20] Equally strange is another example of cultural cross-fertilization. Immediately following Dylan Thomas's death in 1953, a host of young Anglo-Welsh writers strove to emulate his histrionic, hyperbolic style – among them being the young John Ormond, Dannie Abse and Leslie Norris. But with maturity a reaction set in, against Thomas's example and in favour of the diametrically different style of that other Thomas, Edward, who has continued for the last three decades to be the diffident muse of much Anglo-Welsh poetry. But at the very time that Thomas, Dylan, was being jettisoned by the Anglo-Welsh, he was being discovered and adopted by certain Welsh-language writers who in the process caused a scandal and an outcry and a split in Welsh writing by producing a poetry that was condemned by the conservative critics as obscurely Modernist.[21] The best of these iconoclasts, Euros Bowen, found in Thomas a liberating, home-grown example of Symbolist writing, and, accordingly, proceeded to revolutionize *cynghanedd*, or traditional strict-metre writing, carrying his experiments even into the incongruous realms of prose poetry. As can then be seen, it makes no sense whatsoever to treat these two literatures as though each has had a separate history, with a cultural *cordon sanitaire* sealing it off from infection from the other. And yet there has been a stubbornly persistent tendency in Wales to do just that.

Such a failure of cross-cultural imagination has proved particularly harmful to those English-language poets whose very conception of poetry, and of the role of the poet, is modelled, to a significant degree, on that of the *bardd gwlad*:[22] that is, of the poet as serving his/her community, deliberately cultivating versatility, regularly producing what in English high culture tends to be scornfully dismissed as 'occasional' verse (much of it knowingly disposable), even while also capable of functioning at an altogether more 'sophisticated' literary level.[23] Harri Webb, for instance, was a richly cultured man, whose translations of Lorca, Mistral and Glanndour sit, in his *Collected Poems*, alongside the rollicking, rumbustious materials he produced for the poems-and-pints sessions which for him involved poems and (political) points.[24] Jingoistic jingles, carols of carousal, barracking-room ballads at election time (Webb admired Kipling as well as Cynan, A. E. Housman as much as Banjo Patterson), these were all the products of one who sometimes deliberately set out to be a political Max Boyce. And, like the latter's 'Hymns and Arias', a significant number of Webb's poems have been immortalized as folklore, affectionately rendered anonymous by popular acclaim, entering the language in ways, and at a depth, that could yet help alter political discourse in Wales, just as Webb always intended. 'Colli Iaith', 'Our Budgie', 'Ode to the Severn Bridge', 'Dyffryn Woods' – these and many more may well long outlast the ephemeral occasion of their composition. And in writing the marching songs of militant patriotism, in circulating (through his verse) the gossip that binds together a community, Webb was (to paraphrase one of his own lines) a bit like Eisenstein transcribing the *Football Echo*.

It takes a clever man to make history (both ancient and modern) rhyme as comfortably with nationalism as it at least occasionally does in Harri Webb's nation-building work, or to turn wit into the glue of popular political camaraderie. The Webb who could simplify politics into a crusading passion and who excelled at comic burlesque was in fact a complex man. Like Gwyn Thomas, he was that interesting paradox, an Oxford-educated audodidact, one who had had to teach himself everything that really mattered about his place and people. Like Saunders Lewis, he came to nationalism partly by way of a reaction against the alienating example of a 'foreign' war. And Webb's 'Wales', again like that of Lewis, was very much situated on an international map. As his poem to the celebrated French anthropologist Frantz Fanon explicitly shows (*WCP*, 136–7), Webb saw Welsh history as a history of colonial exploitation, and it would be interesting to read his poetry in terms of Fanon's influential account of the different phases of the anti-colonial struggle for national liberation.

Not that Webb's nationalism was the product of intellectual analysis. Rather, it seems to have been the unifying political expression of his divided personal and cultural situation. Estranged from his immediate family, he discovered an extended family in the nationalist movement. As his Anglicanism became residual, he found a new faith in the nationalist cause. A Jack from Anglicized, industrialized Swansea who 'converted' to

Welsh, he embraced a political ideology that sought to create a common front between two oppressed (and overlapping) groups – that of the Welsh-speakers he had joined and that of the Welsh proletariat from which he had derived. And in the figure of that cultural conservationist the *bardd gwlad*, he paradoxically found the prototype of the poet he himself chose to become. Except that whereas the *bardd gwlad* used familiar poetic forms to reinforce existing Welsh-language community and help it reproduce itself into the future, Webb used similarly conventional forms in order to *construct* an 'Anglo-Welsh' community out of the rubble of the smashed, neglected, self-neglectful and self-forgetful industrial culture of south Wales. Whereas the *bardd gwlad* was his people's remembrancer, Webb's task was to remind his people of what they never knew they knew.

One of Webb's most notable heirs in our time is Mike Jenkins, whose important work of cultural reclamation and political rehabilitation in Merthyr – work that has recently involved the literary mining of a Merthyr sociolect that is incomparably rich in social deposits – deserves far greater attention than it has so far received. Jenkins has sometimes very movingly served as *bardd gwlad* to a community that has been left stripped of its memory and its dignity, along with the wealth it at one time so liberally produced for the greedy world to take.[25] Another of Webb's heirs is Nigel Jenkins, whose work, from *Acts of Union* to *Ambush*, has tended to be misread for want of the kind of cross-cultural understanding advocated above.[26] The consensus view has been that his collections include the occasional strong poem but that they are seriously weakened (and the writer's artistic integrity compromised) by the inclusion of trivial occasional and performance pieces, entertaining enough in their way but not really worth recording for posterity.

Such reactions may, though, be somewhat besides the point, since Jenkins sees poetry as a continuum, ranging not only across genres but also (and almost defiantly) from 'poetry' to 'verse'. Its value, both as a personal and a social medium, lies for him in its range and flexibility, exemplified not only by the virtuoso command of a plethora of genres but also by sudden shifts of register, vocabulary or perspective *within* poems. Such an approach undoubtedly owes something to the American poetry in which Jenkins is well versed. But it also owes much to the *bardd gwlad* tradition, of which he is well aware. Like Webb, he too wishes to use poetry to help reconstitute Welsh anglophone community. It is important to bear in mind the politics of his poetics; he is committed to addressing a socially diverse audience, and therefore implicated in his poetry is a vision of the restoration of the collective, the reintegrating of 'classes' and the reconnecting of the present to the forgotten (or deliberately eliminated) past. Indeed, his latest collection, *Ambush*, might equally well have been called either *Remember Tomorrow* (the title of the cassette, issued by Gomer, of Jenkins reading his own poems) or *Past Tense, Future Imperfect*.

But in *Ambush*, Jenkins's poetry acquires a striking new dimension, as the *bardd gwlad* goes cosmic, demonstrating how, in terms of the universe, human life is a merely local event, strictly throwaway and occasional in character; yet, in terms of our planet, all forms of life have virtually become a human dependency, so that only by respecting and cherishing the bio-cultural diversity of one's 'locality' can one ensure the survival of the earth and its human universe. Jenkins therefore sets out to cultivate in his readers an awareness of multifaceted identity involving multiform responsibilities; and promoting such an awareness requires the mobilization, by the poet, of a multiplicity of discourses. So, his poems are by turns (or by turns of phrase, tone and genre) parochial, cosmic, internationalist, bitter, funny, satiric, dismissive, comic, farcical, tragic, off-hand, mocking, blunt, gnomic. It is only in the totality of their effect that the poems reveal themselves to be at once fully local and cosmic in conspectus. After all, our place as human beings on this planet, and the planet's place in the cosmos, can only be appropriately registered through bewildering shifts in scale and in point of view. And if Nigel Jenkins has in part learnt this from post-war American poetry, he has also in part found in the practice of the *bardd gwlad* an important Welsh example of an unpretentious poetry humbly and alertly responding to constantly changing occasion.

3   *The experience of otherness*
One of the main (but unspoken and unacknowledged) ways in which the two cultures have related to each other this century has been by each turning the other into its own sinister opposite, the

dark foil to its own virtues. A recent, highly entertaining example of such manœuvring has been supplied by Marcel Williams in his potboiler of a novel, *Diawl y Wenallt* (The Devil of Milk Wood), where a fictive image of Dylan Thomas is used to probe these hidden aspects of Wales's biculturalism.[27] In style and in spirit (an appropriate expression, as we shall see, in this connection) the novel is a slighly raunchier version of the Carry On films. Williams's 'Carry On Dylan Thomas' is about the way the carryings-on of the 'historical' poet become first a scandal and then an inspiration to the (initially) good folk of Cwmselyn village, who end up enthusiastically carrying on (in every sense of the phrase) the Dylan Thomas tradition of lust and lechery. The novel consists of a series of comic set-pieces, the first of which opens with Gwendolyn Meyrick, MP, unveiling a plaque commemorating Thomas's stay in a cottage in the village. As the curtain is drawn, she discovers, to her dismay, that a lively subtext has been appended (in English) to the official record: 'Tipsy, spineless and sponging he was as usual, a glib, garrulous old goat, all booze and belly, and belching ignorance of everything truly Welsh' (*DW*, 5).

At the beginning of the novel, then, the whole village is united in its disgust at the long-dead Dylan's drunken antics, which included an attempt upon the virtue of Miss Protheroe, now a chapel stalwart but a demure young schoolgirl at the distant time of Thomas's visit. The villagers' self-righteous indignation climaxes in a mock-funeral, designed to lay Thomas to rest once and for all. People come not to praise Dylan but to bury him, and the centre-piece of the ceremony – presided over with elaborate solemnity by the village undertaker – is a substantial coffin on which is painted a scene depicting a Thomas down on all fours, creeping along a floor awash with beer, and with empty bottles and flagons littering the background. This expressive frieze is, however, surpassed by a massive painting, the work of the minister Dafydd Pughe, who denounces Dylan in his sermons as an arch-drunkard, a raving Beelzebub, the enemy of Welsh, and chief of pagans. With the television cameras busily filming, Bronwen Powys (the shapely first female Archdruid of Wales) unveils the painting by plucking a cord and exposing a canvas that depicts not only a physically repulsive and drink-sodden Thomas but also the glorious resurrection of Ann Jones (the old aunt elegized by the poet in 'After the Funeral'). She is shown triumphing over Thomas's verbal attempts to bury her, and is dressed in the traditional Welsh costume of red-and-black dress, quilted under-slip and multi-coloured shawl. Her tall black hat with lace frill has fallen off her head as she struggles to heave Dylan's cruelly heavy foot off her chest. All in all, she nobly portrays the admirable qualities of the traditional Welsh 'mam', so vilely traduced in Thomas's work.

However, it is not Ann Jones but Dylan Thomas himself who comes roaring back from the dead to disturb and excite the villagers in the remainder of the novel, and to seek whom he may devour. He stages a (carnally) rousing come-back in the spirit, appearing first to Miss Protheroe, whom he propositions with all his wonted and undaunted vigour. Although virtuously resisted by her, the old devil takes his revenge on Cwmselyn by arranging that all hell breaks loose in the village. Soon fingers are everywhere reaching parts that other fingers have never reached and couples start living up to the name. Copulation thrives, stimulated by those infusions of Dylan-mania that are supplied by performances of Bronwen Powys's *Beyond Milk Wood*, a play based on the poet's life which considerately provides scope for considerable hanky-panky. One of the highlights of the drama is the scene in which Dylan (enthusiastically played by the Reverend Dafydd Pughe) spends a delightful, suspenseful period with his hand, in full public view, resting titillatingly on the knee of Mrs Wallis Simpson – whom he has met at a dinner-party arranged by her beau, the Prince of Wales.

Eventually life in the village is turned into one long, frank Saturnalia, involving everyone except the glacially virtuous Mrs Melissa Morris. All are relieved that the original libellous painting by the minister has long since been indignantly destroyed, carefully slashed (to avoid mutilating delicate areas of the poet's anatomy) by Hugo Floot, professor of English at a certain University College just along the road from the Mumbles. (Floot, a fervent Dylan-admirer, seems to feel more honoured than distressed at the discovery that his man-eating tiger of a wife, Lavinia, has, before her marriage, had a child after a mere ten-minute encounter with the potent poet.) The Reverend Pughe, now joyously converted from minister to satyr, is anxious to make amends for his original sin in painting such an unfavourable picture of his new hero and so he embarks upon a second attempt. This time Dylan is depicted nailed to a cross, still with a smile on his lips and a fag hanging from the corner of his mouth. Under the painting is the legend 'Forgive them, for they know not what they do.' As the minister explains, he has never been moved by Jacob Epstein's coldly towering statue of Christ in Majesty at Llandaff Cathedral, believing that it would be more appropriately entitled 'Christ Deep-Frozen'. His own painting, he feels, is by comparison the real thing.

Diawl y Wenallt is a calculatedly popular novel – as rollicking, saucy and raunchy as any self-respecting blurb-writer could possibly wish. It is also interesting, though, in a different way. Marcel Williams's cleverness consists in his realization that in the Welsh context 'Dylan Thomas' is more than the sum of his work, being a socially constructed figure that enables two rival cultures to image both themselves and each other. In demonizing him, Welsh-language culture has simultaneously demonized Anglo-Welsh culture and exalted itself, by endowing itself with exaggerated qualities of virtue and piety which, it solemnly implies, have been mocked and traduced by Thomas and his Anglo-Welsh followers. On the other hand, in promoting Dylan, Anglo-Welsh culture has exalted itself and debased Welsh-language culture. The latter, it is claimed, is sexually inhibited and hypocritical, lacking the maturity, sophistication and worldly wisdom of an English-speaking world. In other words, 'Dylan Thomas' is kept in being at the very point where two opposite and equal stereotypes meet – he is held in place, as it were, by the pressure of a cultural need exerted from two opposite directions. In a way, *Diawl y Wenallt* wishes a plague upon both these houses. Or, to put it differently, Williams dialectically exploits each of these stereotypes, recruiting one to mock the other, and producing narrative which brings them into play together only to burlesque them both. Nonconformist Welsh-speaking Wales is certainly not the image of virtue it has sometimes represented itself as being – a point made by the real Dylan Thomas when he followed (much more genially) in the footsteps of Caradoc Evans and reached *Under Milk Wood*. Behind that affectionately debunking radio play lay a whole century's praise, in Welsh, of the virtuous cultivated 'volk' and their incomparable village life.[28] But nor is Nonconformist Wales a hotbed of sexual sin, full of secret *News of the World* frolics, as Anglo-Welsh literature has long tiresomely supposed. And, of course, in addition to all this, Williams makes corned beef of a sacred cow, mincing no words in his attack on the pieties of Dylan-worshippers, those acolytes both scholarly and otherwise who divinize the flawed poet by treating his work as Holy Writ.

Williams's novel is an instance of how each of the two literary cultures of Wales is liable to use the other as the mirror of strangeness which allows it to formulate and support its own favoured self-image. This might be called the mirror-stage of cultural self-definition, and it may be further illustrated by the symbolic geography of Wales as outlined in, and to some extent created by, its two literatures. Anglo-Welsh literature has a long, fascinating history of depicting the western, Welsh-speaking regions in lurid terms that emphasize their insularity and backwardness, thereby either implicitly or explicitly defining the Anglicized eastern regions by contrast as progressive and cosmopolitan. These images of cultural self and other can be traced through the works of Caradoc Evans, Dylan Thomas, Gwyn Thomas, and so on. Theirs, though, was more of a counter-attack than a first strike, because from the late nineteenth-century onwards Welsh-language writers were inclined to depict the industrialized south-east as the Devil's patch, as opposed to God's own country of the pious north and west. Modified versions of this bipolar myth have been significantly operative in the works of important twentieth-century figures as otherwise different from one another as Saunders Lewis and D. J. Williams.

There is, though, another, very different aspect to this process of 'othering', since each of the two linguistic cultures of Wales can, consciously or otherwise, use the presence of the other as source of creative self-estrangement. Bobi Jones, for instance, was raised in a monoglot English home, became entranced by Welsh at school, and went on to become one of the outstanding Welsh-language poets of our time. As has often been remarked, he treats Welsh as if it were a strange paradise of sensuous sounds for his personal delectation.[29] His is an extreme case of the rediscovery of the distinctive creative potential of Welsh as a linguistic medium that the omnipresence of English has made possible for Welsh-language writers. This may even have been an unlikely contributory element in the development of the modern Welsh literary renaissance during the early decades of this century. And to some extent the presence of Welsh has in turn defamiliarized English for Anglo-Welsh writers. Indeed, the use of Welsh as a prism through which to fracture English preparatory to creative reassembly has a long history, extending right back through Dylan Thomas (perhaps), Glyn Jones (certainly), and Caradoc Evans (emphatically) all the way to Gerard Manley Hopkins.[30]

Over the last decade, the kind of linguistic defamiliarization that occurs when language becomes other to its ordinary self – a process which is a by-product of Welsh biculturalism – has been specifically remarked upon, and exploited by, leading Anglo-Welsh poets. In those parts of *Skevington's Daughter* (1985) that relate to his experiences as a Welsh learner, Oliver Reynolds came close to anticipating the heteroglossic carnival that, as I mentioned in my introduction, Robert Crawford nowadays favours.[31] Nothing makes us more aware of how interwoven with consciousness language is than our attempts to learn and use an unfamiliar, and defamiliarizing, language. And this, for Reynolds, is where the usefulness of Welsh to him as a poet really begins. He is made aware, in 'Ch', of the oral, sonant character of language and becomes a fetishist of vocables, nervously appreciative of the musculature of words: '*Chwap*, for instance,/ Takes you from the start./ Lifted swooning, dammed up,/ Your only release/ In the coming vowel' (*SD*, 71). But otherwise how and where does Welsh take you? Does learning it, for example, add or restore a dimension to your Welsh identity? Reynolds prefers simply to bring that possibility into play and leave it there, as when explaining why he and others attended a Welsh class: 'Each has his reason to be here/ Speaking through declenched teeth:/ I'd thought it time to stop/ Welshing on the language/ And learn about roots,/ If only etymological ones' (*SD*, 63). These puns are, evidently, possible only because the Welsh language exists, thus further implying that a Welsh writer may be indebted to it and empowered by it without ever learning it or even committedly acknowledging it.

Welsh is again a liberating influence on his imagination in 'Asgwrn cefn y beic' (*SD*, 67). There his realization that the Welsh term for crossbar is, literally, 'the backbone of the bike', enables him to make a lively conceit out of what to native Welsh speakers is a dead metaphor. But he also shares every learner's frustrated feeling that when one is speaking a foreign language 'Truth waits on vocabulary' (*SD*, 73). However, such frustration can in turn result in an exhilarating reappreciation of the extent of one's command of one's own native tongue – one's own language is as it were restored to one in all its defamiliarized richness in the process of trying to master an 'other' tongue. So Reynolds's exuberantly innovative ways with English in *Skevington's Daughter* are in part the gift of Welsh.

Another writer who relishes living where two languages interface and become estranged from themselves is Peter Finch. In a zany poem called 'Language', he checks off the people who have sat in his guest armchair during the past week: 'Dafydd Wyllt/ Rajiv Gandhi/ The rep from Thames and Hudson/ My mother on a fleeting visit/ George Willoughby/ Cary Archard'.[32] That's the kind of crazy, mixed-up world that contemporary Wales is, and part of Finch loves it, connoisseur that he is of contrasting visual or verbal textures. But if his Welsh Dadaist writing sometimes mimics the phantasmagoric nature of his society, at other times it tries to galvanize a complacent people into awareness of the outrageousness or absurdity of their conduct. The poem 'Language' consists in part of a wildly improbable fantasy about a gang of skinheads turning up at a shop and 'buying/ learn in a day Welsh course.' Finch, pretending alarm, takes emergency action:

> Up onto one
> leg like a golden rooster
> and calmly check
> for swear words
> in the *Collins–Spurrell Modern English–Welsh Dictionary*.
>
> Relief by expletive
> Page 393. *Flip* – verb.
> in welsh – *Fflipio*
>
> Doesn't work. No strength.
> Reality has again been
> tampered with.
> I put the book back
> in the history section.

The cultural joke in this fantasy, as in *Diawl y Wenallt*, cuts both ways: on the one hand it mocks the complacent assumption of monoglot English-speakers in Wales that Welsh cannot ever really be a language fit for the aggro of modern living, and on the other hand it mocks the false gentility of much of contemporary Welsh-language culture.

Like Oliver Reynolds, Finch finds that languages jostling for space excite his creative attention. Take, for instance, his Welsh wordscape, 'South East Wales as characterised by its phone book': 'Abduljabber, P./ Abed, Itadel/ Aberaman Original Band/ Akers, Irving' and so on.[33] This is a stimulus to multiple reflection. What does it mean any longer to speak of 'English', when the very alphabet of the language has become so polyglot? What are the plusses to Wales when Abed, Itadel textually cohabits with Aberaman Original Band? What are the minuses, when for many Welsh people Aberaman is on the way to becoming as undecipherable a name as Abduljabber? Is it appropriate or just plain racist to admit to noticing that that name includes the word 'jabber'? Could it not be that part of Finch's point is the anti-imperialist one: that all languages, including world-conquering English, are alike no more than 'jabber'? This postcolonial point certainly seems to emerge from another Finch poem, 'How to Stop a Duck': 'Hor Kurr Kirra/ gurr up/ ger *back*./ In Welsh this is *bach*/ which means little/ or small/ or dear' (*SP*, 74). This is a classic example of the way in which, in a bicultural situation, one language is constantly 'interfering' with the other, undermining its authority by turning even its most serious words into irrelevant, arbitrary or unseemly puns. Finch's poem proceeds by generating incredulous comedy out of the solemnly authoritative procedures of pedantic dialectology ('Source; *Animal Call Words*'). In one way it is simply an enjoyable *jeu d'esprit*, but in another way its gamesomeness leads us on a wild-goose chase into the labyrinth of language, where we are left stranded to contemplate its bewilderingly mysterious ways. And in a neo-colonialist Wales which is still inclined to take English to be the very language of reality and to dismiss Welsh as an embarrassing anachronism, to confront readers with this experience of the equality, and the equal relativity, of all languages is to commit a liberatingly subversive political and cultural act.

4   *Shared social experience*

At times, scholars of Anglo-Welsh literature seem almost to conspire together with their Welsh-language counterparts to give the impression that the history of modern Wales can be neatly divided between the two literatures, with industrial experience being the monopoly of the Anglo-Welsh, and rural life being the preserve of the Welsh. This allows writers in both camps to preen themselves by claiming to represent the real Wales. The Anglo-Welsh see themselves proudly as participants in what has been sonorously called 'the majority Welsh experience of the past century': namely, the experience of the making and then the unmaking of an industrial society.[34] They accordingly construct a great tradition of industrial writers, beginning with the celebrated generation of the 1930s – the colourful showman Jack Jones, the militant Marxist Lewis Jones, the quietly impassioned Gwyn Jones, and the valleys' very own folk poet, Idris Davies; with Richard Llewellyn's novel *How Green Was My Valley* providing a useful example of how not to do it – unless, that is, you want to end up in Hollywood. Then after the war there is the inventively garrulous Gwyn Thomas, Rhondda's answer to Damon Runyan, with his distinctive brand of quick-witted fiction.

In its turn, Welsh-language society has tended to recycle a whole set of complacent complementary myths about itself, most of which tie it firmly to rural life.[35] And yet, as Tony Conran long ago pointed out, a very significant number of the major Welsh-language writers of this century have come from an industrialized background – albeit, in most cases, from the slate-quarrying townships of north Wales rather than the mining valleys of the south.[36] A failure to act on this perception – a failure exacerbated by the historian's tendency to think a writer is an industrial writer only when (s)he says so, that is when (s)he writes expressly about industrial matters – has resulted hitherto in a very provincial and impoverished treatment of Wales's rich, complex, bicultural industrial literature. Until Caradog Pritchard and Kate Roberts, for example – indisputably two of Wales's greatest fiction writers of this or any other century – are generally, routinely, recognized as major fabricators of industrial fiction, Wales's understanding of its industrial past (given that literature is an important and unique aid to such an understanding) will remain sadly lopsided and incomplete.[37] What is needed is a context in which the work of Tilsli, D. T. Davies, Islwyn Williams, Gwenallt, T. E. Nicholas (Niclas y Glais), Pennar Davies, T. Rowland Hughes, Kitchener Davies (whose play *Cwm Glo* is a key cultural document), Rhydwen Williams, Dyfnallt Morgan, Richard Hughes (Dic Tryfan), Gareth Alban Davies, Robat Powell, Mihangel Morgan and others could be creatively related to that of the English-language writers from the industrial regions of Wales.[38]

It has rarely been noted that two important poets, the Welsh-language poet Euros Bowen and the English-language poet Vernon Watkins, spent much of their childhood in industrial south Wales. The remainder of this chapter will be devoted to an exploration of some of the ways in which the socio-cultural background they therefore in a sense shared may help explain why and how they both developed into the fine, and distinctively Welsh, Symbolist poets they eventually became. It is hoped, in the process, to demonstrate how our understanding of writers in both languages may be significantly altered, and deepened, when we venture to make comparisons across the language divide.

*   *   *   *

When the young Dylan Thomas acted the part of 'the Rimbaud of Cwmdonkin Drive', the humour of the role obviously derived from the incongruous notion of a scandalously bohemian artist lurking in the most primly respectable suburb of a drab Welsh town.[39] Viewed in this light, the phrase 'Welsh Symbolist' would seem to be a cultural oxymoron; a colourful exercise in social surrealism. Yet Thomas was only the most prominent member of a whole generation of Welsh and Anglo-Welsh writers inspired by Symbolism to identify poetry with the mystique of trope and the consciousness-raising powers of rhythm. His friend Vernon Watkins was of that generation, as was the prominent Welsh-language poet Euros Bowen. Ten years Thomas's senior, Bowen included an extravagantly Symbolist elegy for the famous younger poet in his very first volume, published five years after Thomas's death.[40] There Thomas was indeed mourned as a Rimbaud – as one who had ended up dead-drunk after garnering to excess the intoxicating harvest of poesy, and whose passing had made a widow of wine. But what is significant is that this self-consciously Symbolist elegy is written in the unlikely form of an *englyn* – one of the most intricately rule-bound forms of alliterative Welsh poetry in the ancient, strict-metre tradition. This neatly illustrates the central thesis of the following discussion: that leading Welsh poets were moved to absorb, and thus naturalize, Symbolism because they found, in aspects of the Symbolist aesthetic, modes of thinking and of writing that were immensely congenial and serviceable to them as Welsh writers who had to operate in a specific, not to say restrictive, socio-cultural environment. The point is all the more clear when one realizes that the significant *English* writers of the same period (*c.*1935–1965) were not in general interested in Symbolism to anything like the same degree.

The poetry of Watkins and Bowen offers us interesting insights, then, into a creatively enabling process of adaptive importation that was happening, more or less simultaneously, both in the Welsh-language and in the English-language culture of Wales. The very fact that it was, indeed, a bicultural phenomenon suggests, of course, that it was a reaction to a situation shared by the two cultures. And the first point to make is that both cultures had been formed, and continued to be informed, by the values and ideology of Welsh religious Nonconformity. In this connection the personal backgrounds of Watkins and Bowen prove to be well worth investigating. Bowen, the son of a Nonconformist minister, himself spent many years training to enter the ministry before he converted to Anglicanism and became a priest of the Church in Wales instead. His convert's zeal for icon, hieratic ritual, liturgy and the spiritual mystery of sacrament is very evident in the kind of poetry he wrote, as is his dissatisfaction with the anti-aesthetic ethos of the Nonconformity in which he was raised.[41] For him, the commonplaces of Symbolism – the insistence, for instance, on the heuristic power of the image – could still, as late as 1950, be experienced as intimately transformative illuminations.[42] When he came to articulate his poetics, in a series of important essays, he blazoned his defiant belief in the spiritually exalted practice of thinking with tropes and likened his own poetry to a stream of symbols. He contrasted his concept of himself as a poet-priest, mediating spiritual truths through irreducible images, with the rationalist, and Nonconformist, habit of regarding the poet as a preacher with a message to deliver.[43]

His well-known poem to a swan opens with a recapitulation of this poetics, and thus begins by reflecting on its own procedures – 'Gweld argoeli a dirgelwch/ yw celfyddyd encilfa heddiw, –/ gweld lliw a chyhyredd, gweld llacharwyn/ ymwelydd nef rhwng moelydd ein hoes'. ('Seeing signifying and mystery/ is today's art of the hide, –/ seeing colour and musculature, seeing the white/ dazzle of heaven's visitor between the bare slopes of our age.')[44] And the spiritual dynamics of this seeing – the sense that true vision involves an active response in kind to the underlying creative processes of the cosmos – is conveyed by the coupling of verbs where one would normally expect a verb–noun combination: 'Gweld argoeli'/ 'Seeing signifying'. But if Euros Bowen shared the Symbolists' conviction that the higher truths could be incarnated only in symbolical discourse, he refused to believe with them that such a discourse was the preserve of an intellectual élite ostracized and victimized by an uncomprehending society. Indeed, his poem to the swan seems to be in part a reply to Mallarmé's celebrated poem 'Le vierge, le vivace et le bel aujourd'hui', where Mallarmé implicitly likens himself to a magnificent swan, dreaming of flight, but trapped by its wings in the frozen lake of a mundane reality: 'A phantom condemned to this place by his pure brilliance, he stays motionless in the cold dream of scorn worn in his useless exile by the Swan.'[45] When Bowen translated this poem into Welsh, he added an interpretative note, explaining that the swan represented Mallarmé's high-Romantic belief that the true artist was always rejected by his society.[46] Placed in this context, the conclusion to Bowen's own poem to the swan reads like a refutation of Mallarmé's vision in its own symbolical terms: 'He moves shivering his feathers, then waits/ and in the bold blow of a second he breaks from the water;/ slowly he went, then high into the air,/ and pulls a soul from its cold through the fire of his wings.'[47] Here the swan's flight signifies in part the poem's power to communicate its redemptive vision of the world to any and every reader – an egalitarian and communitarian concept of poetry that perhaps distinguishes a Welsh Symbolist from a French Symbolist.

Whereas Bowen's devotion to symbols was related to his reaction against Nonconformity, Vernon Watkins's case was rather different. Both his parents were Nonconformists, but he was raised in an Anglican, and indeed an Anglicized, ethos through being sent at a very young age to an English public school.[48]

In consequence, he came to see Wales – including the Nonconformity that underpinned the country's culture – from the romanticizing perspective of a partial outsider. A key poem in this respect is 'Returning to Goleufryn', based on Watkins's memories, from childhood, of his grandfather James Phillips's home in the distant rural west of Wales. Phillips was a staunch chapel man, and in his gentle poem of nostalgic recollection Watkins sees, in the religious aura of his grandfather's home, shades of an older, mysterious spirituality – the spirituality of the ancient, legendary world of Merlin/Myrddin, in whose reputed town of Caerfyrddin James Phillips lived. As Watkins there walks the path of his childhood along the banks of the River Tywi, he feels himself participating in a *rite de passage* through which he is conducted into age-old truths:

> Sing, little house, clap hands: shut, like a book of the Psalms,
> On the leaves and pressed flowers of a journey. All is sunny
> In the garden behind you. The soil is alive with blind-petalled
> blooms
> Plundered by bees. Gooseberries and currants are gay
> With tranquil, unsettled light.[49]

Watkins believed that poets worked with archetypal symbols that were the mysterious vehicle of a perennial philosophy.[50] And with the eccentricity of genius he saw Nonconformity in 'Returning to Goleufryn' as the modern Welsh avatar of ancient Celtic religion. The figure he particularly associated with the latter was Taliesin, legendary magician, shape-changer and poet. Watkins believed a true poet possessed a Taliesin-like ability to keep track, through metamorphosing symbols, of the steadfast spiritual truths constantly being rearticulated through the manically mutable world of time. This is the credo announced in the poem 'Taliesin in Gower':

> Yet now my task is to weigh the rocks on the level wings of a bird,
> To relate these undulations of time to a kestrel's motionless poise.
> I speak, and the soft-running hour-glass answers; the core of the
> rock is a third:
> Landscape survives, and these holy creatures proclaim their
> regenerate joys.

(*VWCP*, 184)

Watkins elsewhere provided a prose gloss on his poetic vision: 'A supreme work of art', he said, echoing Yeats, 'is able to persuade us that it is drawn from a timeless source, that it has existed forever, and that it is we, who believed in the fugitive nature of time, who were deceived'.[51] This highlights for us another reason why symbols, understood as the form that permanent spiritual truths take in time, were so attractive to these particular Welsh poets. Theirs was a generation living through a period of bewildering social, economic and cultural change, as can be seen from the examples of Bowen and Watkins. Watkins dated his rebirth as a poet to the vision of eternity that came to him during the mental breakdown he suffered shortly after leaving Repton School, where he had been idyllically happy. But it seems likely that the instabilities of his early background had been long preparing the way for his collapse. From earliest childhood he had been effectively prevented from integrating himself into any dependable, nurturing community. His father, a bank-manager, moved the family from place to place to keep pace with promotion; the young Watkins was thus prevented, both by his superior class background and by his status as perpetual newcomer, from forming any close attachments to the various industrial communities in which he lived. At the same time, his Welsh-speaking parents' decision not to pass the language on to their son meant that he was cut off from the chapel life that sustained them. He was miserably unhappy at the first English public school to which he was sent, at the age of ten. Only upon reaching Repton did he find himself in genuinely congenial company. No wonder that his departure from there precipitated a crisis in the form of a nightmare vision of temporal chaos. And it is this vision that forms the dark lining of the silver affirmations of his mature poetry: 'The perfect into night must fly;/ On this the winds agree./ How could a blind rock satisfy/ The hungers of the sea?' (*VWCP*, 121).

Euros Bowen grew up, like Vernon Watkins, in the turbulent industrial townships of south Wales, during a time of great economic hardship and socio-political tension. But he was the Welsh-speaking son of the manse, and so was protected by chapel culture from the cruellest pressures of that time. Maybe it was this early foundation in security, an experience denied to Watkins, that later enabled Bowen the poet to be such a confident and convinced celebrant of a metamorphosing world. Theirs are strikingly contrasting cases: whereas Vernon Watkins sought through timeless symbols a spiritual refuge beyond the flux of things, Bowen used symbols to indicate the spiritual dimensions of all the phenomena in a constantly changing world. As he frequently stressed, his was at bottom a sacramental vision.

The difference between the two is apparent in the poems they respectively addressed to Nefertiti. Bowen was holidaying in Moscow when, to his astonishment, he saw a young girl whose lissom beauty reminded him of the refined features of the Egyptian queen:

> But the authority of her beauty lay not in a slim throat,
> Such as Pharaoh's bedfellow once possessed,
> But in her nose, straight as a dye, and her forehead,
> And the nose's ivory, and her perpendicular brow.
> And the high crown of smooth, dark auburn hair.[52]

And all this is set off by the fashionableness of her white blouse, black skirt and nylons. His wondering appreciation of her is heightened by his surprise that an unmistakably modern beauty of such ancient, classical proportions can exist within a policeman's whistle-blast of the red towers of the totalitarian Kremlin. It is a striking vindication of his faith in values that seem to thrive on change, that are constantly renewing themselves in the changing image of their times.

Vernon Watkins's version of Nefertiti is very different. It centres on the awed response to the image carved on her sarcophagus:

> The features rarified, through tenderest darkness seen,
> Thrust forward, lifted out of life, the hair caught back,
> Unsheathed in true perfection, flashed forth like a queen.
>
> (*VWCP* 157)

This perfectly moulded mask of Nefertiti is the eternal purity of form that is left after all that was perishable has been refined away. It was created by toiling craftsmen, 'each beating out in gold the sacred from the crude'. And 'the calm, stylistic face' seems to be 'cover[ed] with cold fire'. Breathless as an acolyte, Watkins beseeches us not to disturb the perfect repose of this figure:

Break not for love of death the vigil of that queen.
Who could translate her stillness to a waking world,
A room by daylight changed, yet where a god has been?
Dust falls, time's atom falls, into a portent whirled
Of luminous, killing language where men lack the key;
Yet she, she clasps with folded hands her hidden scroll,
Her eyes being set in death, being taught with joy to see
That radiant Master guard the stations of her soul.

For Watkins the artifice of eternity stands revealed in the image of Nefertiti, and his response to it is full of his adoration of symbols mysteriously rooted in an unchanging reality that transcends time.

The interest Watkins and Bowen showed in the Egyptian queen Nefertiti brings us to the third, and last, way in which their Welshness had a bearing on their passion for Symbolism. Both were convinced cosmopolitans. They believed that Symbolism was the universal language of the spirit, spoken by all great art regardless of the culture from which it immediately derived. Though a Welsh-language poet, and therefore seemingly a marginal or provincial figure, Bowen felt himself to be directly connected, through his use of symbolism, with mainstream European culture. As an artist, he very much regarded himself as a Welsh European. Watkins once famously described himself as 'a Welsh man, but an English poet', by virtue of the fact that he wrote in English only.[53] But he, too, found release from that Englishness by making contact, through the symbolism of his poetry, with a great European tradition that included, in his eyes, Hölderlin, Heine, Novalis, the French Symbolists, George and Rilke. He communed with them most intimately, he felt, by translating their work. 'The approach of scholarship appears to stop at the original poet's written text', he wrote, 'but the translator who is a poet is concerned with the whole orbit of the poet's thought during the period of composition; the written text is the track of a secret and more elaborate movement to which he alone, through an affinity of mind, has the key'.[54]

The intensity of his own identification with another poet's vision is evident in his translation of Rilke's sonnet on the broken sculpture of Apollo:

We did not know his unfamiliar head
Where hung the ripening apples of his eyes,
But still his torso candelabra-wise
Glows, where his gazing, screwed back from the dead,

Holds itself back and gleams. The bow of the breast
Could not else blind you, nor in subtle turning
Of loins could a smile break that goes there yearning
To that mid-place which held the seeds at rest.

Else would this stone short and disfigured cower
Under the shoulders' dropped, transparent power
Nor shine like sparkling skins of beasts of prey

And would not from all contours of the knife
Break starlike out: for there is no place, nay,
Which does not see you. You must change your life.[55]

The English sonnet conveys Watkins's thrill of recognition – his intuitive understanding of what the torso of Apollo *symbolized* for Rilke: namely, the unconfinable power of a spiritual radiance.

Euros Bowen was also a noted translator into Welsh of poetry from Greek, Latin and French. In addition he travelled very widely – to Scandinavia, Russia, Australia, Morocco, Israel, Greece, France, Germany, Italy – and he incorporated his experience of the high art of these countries into his poetry. It became natural for him to see himself, as a Welsh poet, as the modern heir of an ancient European culture the highest values of which had been incorporated in symbols that had accumulated a great wealth of significance by being used repeatedly over the centuries by so many great artists. This is the vision to which he gives expression in the poem 'Carrara Marble'.[56] There he remembers his visit to the quarries that had provided Michelangelo with his marble. The green slopes, he recollects, were covered with the white snow of marble-dust that extended right down to the nearby river. Later, on his return home to Wales, he was walking in winter along the snow-covered banks of his local river, when it seemed to him that he saw an image rising radiantly from the water, the image of a youthful David as famously depicted by Michelangelo. The implications of this are clear. All artists, be they Italian sculptors or Welsh poets, are visionaries who share a language – the language of the spiritual inner meaning of things, the international language of symbols.

Some years after Dylan Thomas's death, Bowen commented that Thomas was not, as was commonly supposed, a Welsh poet writing in an English tradition but, rather, a Welsh poet whose work was European in character.[57] What Bowen probably had in mind was the Symbolist basis both of Thomas's poetics and of his actual praxis. The leading *English* poets of Thomas's generation had, after all, proved very largely indifferent to the Symbolist movement, since both its aesthetic philosophy and its methods seemed to them essentially foreign to the temper of their native culture. Those Modernist poets writing in English who *were* clearly indebted to Symbolism tended to come from countries other than England, as Edmund Wilson noted in his celebrated study *Axel's Castle*, first published in 1931. He there argued that 'the literary history of our time is to a great extent that of the development of Symbolism'. But this crucial fact had, he added, been overlooked by English critics, 'because the work of [Modernist] writers is the result of a literary revolution which occurred outside English literature'. It had, therefore, he concluded, 'been particularly easy for certain of the leaders of contemporary English literature – that is, of the literature since the War – to profit by the example of Paris, because they have themselves not been English'.[58] By way of example he mentioned Yeats, Joyce, Eliot and Stein. To these can now be added the less brilliant but none the less interesting cases of Vernon Watkins, Euros Bowen and, indeed, Dylan Thomas – poets who were in a sense Symbolists because they were Welsh, and who were therefore truly the Rimbauds that their Cwmdonkin Drives had produced.

*　*　*　*

To study Euros Bowen and Vernon Watkins in tandem, then, is to begin to see what, in practice, it means to think in those cross-cultural terms advocated at the beginning of this chapter: to think, for instance, of writers in the two languages of twentieth-century Wales as deriving from a common cultural source and as sharing social experiences. To think in these terms may be beneficial to our apprehension and appreciation of particular writers, and it should sharpen our sense of the magnitude and hospitable capaciousness of modern Welsh literary culture. But, above all else, to think in these terms is to begin the process of making connections, finding associations, across the cultural divide that has been both the making and the undoing of modern Wales. It is to begin the delicate work of stitching Wales together again, of producing an image not of a simple monolithic entity but of a remarkable profusion of significant differences, creative hostilities, silent interconnections and hidden attachments. Relevant here are the words of Susan Bassnett in her recent work on *Comparative Literature*:

> Coming to terms with the past means facing the ambiguities of a plural history . . . There can be no clearly-defined point of origin, no exact source, and as a result no polarization between binary oppositions. What remains is the need to recognize the complexities of the historical processes that have resulted in such pluralism.[59]

As the twentieth century draws rapidly to a close, it is surely high time we begin seriously to explore the recent 'plural history' of our Welsh present, and attempt a proper audit of Welsh culture, in order that we might more fully know who we are, and where we are, as another century begins.

Portraits of the artist as a young Welshman

~

Anxious to deny that his collection of stories *Portrait of the Artist as a Young Dog* was substantially indebted to Joyce's classic of autobiographical fiction, *Portrait of the Artist as a Young Man*, Dylan Thomas claimed that his title implied, rather, only a playful glance at his age's general preoccupation with artistic self-portraits,[1] a preoccupation cultural historians have subsequently treated as a definitive characteristic of Euro-American Modernism:

> *À la Recherche du Temps Perdu* is both a portrait of the artist and a discovery of the aesthetic by which the portrait is painted; clearly, a Modernist aesthetic. The theme of the portrayed artist is a recurrent one in the Modernist novel, and one of the means by which the aesthetic self-consciousness of the species develops through the great classics of Modernism. Proust's Marcel, Mann's Tonio Kröger, Joyce's Stephen Dedalus, Gide's Édouard are all 'portraits of the artist'; and nearly all are parts of plots that take us toward the centre of symbolist possibility for art. The modern artist, often an exile, takes on shape as a spirit; a voyager into the unknown arts, and an embodiment of the difficulties in the form which surrounds him, taking his place in the complex perspectives of the writing itself.[2]

Itself a collection of stories about story-telling, Thomas's *Portrait* is ingeniously written in a style in which a colourful populist realism becomes the vehicle for self-reflexive exploration of the forms of writing. This hybrid approach, mixing 'high' culture with 'low' life and popular appeal, is nicely suggested in the casual, throwaway title of the book. It combines a teasing reference to Joyce, a mockery of the high solemnity of Modernism's sanctification of 'the artist', a knowingly modish narcissism (an artistic portrait of the artist), a promise of tasty 'laddishness' ('young dog' being, of course, period cant like 'young blade'), and a hint of that underworld of fantastic metamorphosis (comical, farcical, plangent and Circean-sinister by turns) into which the stories lead us, and where, at the very end, they disturbingly abandon us.[3]

Portrait of the Artist as a Young Dog could, in fact, be subtitled 'A Guide to Modernist Art', since it self-consciously features so many of the classic themes and practices of literary Modernism, all emerging from an overall design 'that takes us toward the centre of a symbolist possibility for art.' In tracing the artist's growth from childhood through adolescence, that design further typifies Modernist fiction in the new inflexion it gives both to the genre of the *Bildungsroman* and to the traditional quest-narrative, as the latter has been conveniently summarized by Richard Kearney:

> This [narrative] structure takes the form of an individual's search for value in a degraded world. Hence the conventional pattern of the novel is that of a journey from meaninglessness to meaning, from the insufficiency of the surrounding environment to some new vision or value. This quest structure is characterised by an experience of fundamental rupture between the creative imagination of the hero (the subjective term) and the reality (objective term) which he or she is trying to explore, cultivate and valorize. It goes hand-in-hand with a psychological preoccupation with the hero's solitary ego as it struggles with an alien world.[4]

Kearney recognizes that Joyce's *Portrait of the Artist as a Young Man* 'remains a traditional [quest] novel to the extent that it is a story of desire and journeying. Stephen's pretensions to transmute the world into art are treated ironically by Joyce himself.' So, too, are the narrator's pretensions viewed with a degree of irony by Thomas in his *Portrait*. However, Kearney adds, Joyce's work breaks with tradition, and becomes innovative in a distinctively Modernist fashion, to the extent that it renders the traditional quest-structure self-conscious:

> As the title itself testifies, Joyce intends to make art objective to itself; Joyce the artist-author writes about himself as the artist-hero, Stephen, who in turn writes about himself as the artist-*manqué* ... In the *Portrait* the novel as artistic product has already begun to mirror its condition of possibility as artistic process, it already tends towards self-representation. (*CB*, 391)

This is also true (although perhaps after a somewhat different fashion) of Thomas's *Portrait of the Artist as a Young Dog*, coming to the fore at such moments as when, in 'Old Garbo', the young reporter, surveying the colourful crowd thronging Swansea's High Street, silently registers his intention: 'I'll put you all in a story by and by.'[5] However, when, at story's end, he publicly announces that seemingly same intention to the seedy, worldly-wise senior reporter Mr Farr, the identical words take on an entirely different meaning. The Modernist artist's secret vow to be faithful to his arcane art is changed into the journalist's promise to deliver good popular 'copy'. Appropriately enough, Thomas was to refer to his *Portrait* as 'illuminated reporting' (*CL*, 333*)*. In the tension between these two contrasting versions of 'writing' (useful, popular writing versus the 'fancy' writing of poems and stories), and between the two related views of the writer (serviceable 'reporter' as opposed to avant-garde 'artist') there undoubtedly lies a key to Thomas's own development as a writer, and perhaps an insight into his situation as a writer from Wales: a specifically *Welsh* Modernist. Modestly limited explor-ation of Thomas in these localized terms would certainly be very much in line with current Joyce scholarship,[6] and it might usefully begin by noting the way *Portrait of the Artist as a Young Dog* opens and ends. 'The Peaches' deals with the mingled bewil-derment and excitement of a little boy from the Anglicized middle-class Uplands of urban Swansea lost in rural, Welsh-speaking Carmarthenshire. 'One Warm Saturday' ends with a romantic adolescent lost near the Strand, inter-war Swansea's notorious red-light district, and feeling that his provincial town itself is way out on the dreary, lost, decaying margins of the modern world: 'The light of the one weak lamp in a rusty circle fell across the brick-heaps and the broken wood and the dust that had been houses once, where the small and hardly known and never-to-be forgotten people of the dirty town had lived and loved and died and, always, lost' (*PYD*, 128). In both cases, Thomas represents his development as an artist (a development mainly figured in terms of the growth of imagination) as very significantly conditioned, if not determined, by how and where he is physically and culturally *placed*. His Anglicized, provincial Swansea (actually described, in 'Old Garbo', as 'Tawe, South Wales, England' – a classic instance of colonial disorientation) exists interstitially, as Homi Bhabha would say,[7] occupying an amorphous place (uneasy yet stimulating) between the Welsh-language culture of the past and of the West and the big, wide, sophisticated contemporary world.

It is in such a twilight region that Thomas's imagination grows, fostered alike by wonder and by fear, and vividly marked by the curiously kindred experiences of location and of dislocation. He is at home yet homeless, like the Tom and Walter who, in 'Just Like Little Dogs', spend their desolate evenings huddled in the no man's land between town and sands in the darkness under the Brynmill railway arch. Uncomfortable place though it be, it is also a magical, womb-like cave for confessional story-telling, as is the appropriately named 'Warmley'; and as is the Gorsehill 'jungle' where, 'playing Indians in the evening, I was aware of me myself in the exact middle of a living story, and my body was my adventure and my name' (*PYD*, 18). By turning the Welsh west of rural Gorsehill into the Wild West of Hollywood films, using his imagination to broker a creative relationship between two equally strange realms, the boy turns his estrangement to potent advantage. The adult Dylan Thomas was himself to do likewise, even as he learned to mock his own self-aggrandizing and self-pitying stance as the artist-outsider: 'He thought: Poets live and walk with their poems; a man with visions needs no other company; Saturday is a crude day; I must go home and sit in my bedroom by the boiler' (*PYD*, 110).

'The Peaches' also suggests other ways in which Thomas the Modernist was consciously a Welsh artist. The boy's yokel cousin, Gwilym, clearly represents the decaying Welsh Non-conformist tradition that tries to imprison the fledgeling artist within its own narratives. Aware of the 'senior' native tradition of histrionic preachers, Thomas regards them as rival story-tellers, so that his younger self's struggle with the would-be-spellbinding Gwilym and his god, in 'The Peaches', seems like a witty reversal of Elijah's contest with the prophets of Baal! Similarly, the semi-autobiographical genre of 'portrait' is what Thomas has to offer in place of his religious culture's 'genre' of public confession, traditionally instanced in the Methodist *seiat* (fellowship meeting) and comically parodied in 'The Peaches': '"Now I take confessions," said Gwilym from the cart' (*PYD*, 19). (Gwilym Marles was, of course, the bardic name of William Thomas, the prominent Unitarian minister who was the uncle of Dylan Thomas's father, and after whom Thomas himself was named Marlais.) Thomas cannot prosper as a secularized modern artist, then, until he has thus first successfully defied chapel culture; nor can he see Welsh society for what it is until he has cleared the air with his own breath – just as, in his Aunt Annie's mausoleum of a parlour, the boy in 'The Peaches' has to clear the dust off the family photographs before he can see what they contained: 'I blew on the glass to see the pictures. Gwilym and castles and cattle' (*PYD*, 15).

But in 'The Peaches' Thomas's relationship to that rural, religious, Welsh-speaking culture from which his parents had 'escaped' is, in fact, emotionally complex. If he finds it at once threateningly and comically strange, he is also intuitively attached to it. Delighted at first to make common cause against his weird relatives with his friend Jack, down on a visit from Swansea, the boy ends by implicitly valuing the rough warmth of his Aunt Annie's hospitality – 'She forgave me when I drank tea from the saucer' (*PYD*, 21) – above the middle-class treachery of tell-tale Jack and his snobbish mother. Such ambiguities of tone, richly expressive of Thomas's own equivocal cultural position (scornful of a society to which he was nevertheless intimately attached), are of the essence in *Portrait of the Artist as a Young Dog*, and are noticeable whenever he deals with the character of art, particularly when he does so via the synecdoche of 'story'.

Writ large throughout the collection is the question – clearly deriving from Welsh Nonconformist culture – of the truthfulness of fiction, and of the imagination from which fiction derives. The telling of 'whoppers' – whether in the form of outright lies ('Patricia, Edith, and Arnold'), tall tales ('Extraordinary Little Cough'), dreams ('A Visit to Grandpa's'), collective fantasies ('Where Tawe Flows'), private melodramas ('Who Do You Wish Was With Us?'), or busy, damaging gossip ('Old Garbo') – is a central trope in a collection in which the stories themselves are often so very highly coloured as to constitute a heightened, or hyperbolical, realism. Licensed so to write though he conveniently was by his very subject – the differently fantasticating states of mind of childhood, adolescence, and 'the artist' – Thomas may also have had other reasons for relishing such an opportunity. In 'The Fight' the narrator wonders why he is so attracted to lying, and decides: 'It was exciting to have to keep wary all the time in case I contradicted myself, to make up the story of a film I pretended to have seen and put Jack Holt in Richard Dix's place' (*PYD*, 47–8). Setting aside the light this may throw on the well-attested delight Dylan Thomas (like William Faulkner and many another fiction-writer) took in the brinkmanship of actual fibbing, the remark is certainly consistent with the exuberant spirit and style of some of the rampant, self-conscious fictionalizing in *Portrait of the Artist as a Young Dog*. Just as the influence of Nonconformity is very evident in the guilty, 'sweets of sin', approach to sexuality and the flesh in those stories, so is that influence also manifest in the collection's fascination with the duplicity of fiction, whether in life or in art. In other words, Thomas's approach to 'making art objective to itself', that distinctively Modernist strategy, is via his experience of Welsh Nonconformity's mistrustful highlighting of the artfulness of art.

However, that culture's mistrust took the form not only of a warning to readers and listeners against succumbing to the seductive falsehoods of others' beguiling fictions, but also of a stress on the dangers of the unregulated imagination to the actual possessor of it. So, in 'The Peaches', the little boy's terror at being left alone outside a pub in Carmarthen square is in part an experience of falling victim to his own fearsome and fearful imagination: 'A story I had made in the warm, safe island of my bed, with sleepy midnight Swansea flowing and rolling round outside the house, came blowing down to me then with a noise on the cobbles' (*PYD*, 8). This awareness of the sinister uncontrollable potency of the imagination recurs throughout the *Portrait* and is revealed as a significant element in Dylan Thomas's conception of the artist. Once the genie is let out of the bottle, there's no getting it back in. 'I knew what was going to happen', the narrator recalls in 'Who Do You Wish Was With Us?', just as his friend Ray begins to sink into melancholy recollection of the many ugly deaths in his family: 'Nothing could stop him now' (*PYD*, 90). Underneath the conspicuous display of fictive mastery in the stories in *Portrait of the Artist as a Young Dog* there runs a dark fear of loss of control over both the inner mental and the outer social world. No wonder that in 'One Warm Saturday' the artistic young man finds, in the ordinary rumpus of Bank Holiday Swansea, a temporary refuge from the threat posed by his own solitary mind: 'He had no need of the dark interior world when Tawe pressed in upon him and the eccentric ordinary people came bursting and crawling, with noise and colours, out of their houses ... out of the common, wild intelligence of the town' (*PYD*, 114).

In all these ways, then, *Portrait of the Artist as a Young Dog* (1940) is specifically a portrait of a writer born of, and not merely into, the Wales of the inter-war years. Indeed, the stories show how the radical displacements that had occurred in Welsh society before and during Dylan Thomas's day (the language shift; the decline of Nonconformity; the move from rural to urban; the oscillation between a residual awareness of Wales's cultural distinctiveness and an emergent sense of its English provincialism) could develop in a writer not only a heightened consciousness but also a heightened consciousness of himself as a writer. Under such circumstances, art naturally turned self-reflexive, as writers were left feeling they did not quite know their place, in more senses than one. They consequently felt liberated, empowered, restlessly alive to kaleidoscopic possibilities, and yet bewildered and anxious – exactly the potent mixture of feelings registered in *Portrait of the Artist as a Young Dog*.

Given these general socio-cultural circumstances, it follows that Thomas would hardly be the only Welsh writer of the time to make art and the artist the very subject of his art. Two others of Thomas's generation who did likewise – publishing their novels considerably later than Thomas did his stories but setting them in periods overlapping with that covered in *Portrait of the Artist as a Young Dog* – were Glyn Jones (1905–95) and Pennar Davies (1911–97). The former's *The Valley, the City, the Village* (1956) and the latter's *Meibion Darogan* (1968) both deal centrally with artists, and between them furnish evidence that the role of the artist and the character of art were newly problematized subjects that were of pressing interest to both the linguistic cultures of Wales at this time – a striking instance of how the shared historical experience mentioned in my preceding chapter could produce cognate artistic results in two cultures that were not only fundamentally different but even often directly and bitterly opposed.

*   *   *   *

There was much, in any case, that Pennar Davies and Glyn Jones had personally in common.[8] Both were natives of the industrial valleys of south Wales, the former coming from Mountain Ash (Aberpennar in Welsh), the latter from the other side of the mountain, in Merthyr. Although Welsh was spoken in their respective childhood homes, neither of them grew up speaking the language,[9] yet both acquired a complete mastery of it in adulthood – Davies by learning it from scratch at school and at university, Jones by applying himself as a young man to improving his rudimentary grasp of his parents' tongue. And although Davies went on to become an important Welsh-language author while Jones chose to write creatively only in English, their committed bilingualism meant that each not only could respect but also would intermittently contribute to the literature of the other, and that both believed in fostering closer relations between Welsh-language and 'Anglo-Welsh' writers. Having been raised nominally Nonconformist, both experienced in young adulthood a 'conversion' to a fully believing, active Nonconformist faith, with very important consequences for their art. Davies was ordained as a Welsh Congregationalist minister (Annibynwyr), while Jones eventually served as a long-standing deacon in a Welsh Congregationalist church, and their radical Christianity made convinced and suffering pacifists of them both during the Second World War. Such iron devotion to principle was, in both their cases, startlingly at odds with their exceptional mildness of manner and sweetness of spirit.

When, in the early 1940s, *Wales* organized a writers' questionnaire – a development indicative of a new self-consciousness amongst Welsh artists – the replies of Davies and Jones appeared on the same page of the 1946 issue, addressing such questions as 'For whom do you write?' and 'What is your opinion of the relationship between Literature and Society?'[10] Their coappearance on this occasion, and in Keidrych Rhys's *Modern Welsh Poetry* (1944),[11] followed a six-year period when there had been an interesting degree of overlap in their publishing careers. Just as Davies (under his original *nom de plume* of 'Davies Aberpennar') had contributed occasional poems and reviews to the seminal English-language journal *Wales*, in which Jones's work was regularly and prominently featured, so too Jones was an occasional contributor to *Wales*'s Welsh-language counterpart, *Tir Newydd*, with which Davies was closely associated. The intense interest shown by Jones in the startlingly original poetry and prose of his friend Dylan Thomas was to an appreciable degree matched by Davies's fascination with the same writings, and their common devotion to such literary experimention found neatly parallel expression in their reviews of *The Map of Love*, with Jones's review appearing in the *Welsh Review* and that of Davies being carried by *Wales*.[12]

Wales, *Tir Newydd* (*New Ground*), the *Welsh Review*: these – along with *Heddiw* (*Today*), a politico-cultural periodical to which Davies also contributed – were the laboratory texts of the period 1935–45, little magazines in which young writers in both languages experimented with new styles and new ideas. And the sudden, coincidental sprouting of such a rich crop of new literary magazines evidences the extent to which the cultural soil and the political climate of that period in Wales were exceptionally conducive to a radical reassessment by emerging artists of their role and *modus operandi*. Editors and contributors alike evinced a crisis mentality, and a brief survey of their recorded attitudes allows us better to understand the general conditions that could give rise to the kind of intense self-examination by writers that in the case of Davies and of Jones (as of Thomas) was to find expression in, or as, portraits of the artist.

'As I walked through the wilderness of this world, as I walked through the wilderness, as I walked through the city with the loud electric faces and the crowded petrols of the wind dazzling and drowning me that winter night before the West died':[13] It was with these words from Dylan Thomas's appropriately entitled *Prologue to an Adventure* that the first number of *Wales* dramatic- ally opened in the summer of 1937. Apocalyptically Spenglerian in tone, the whole piece was a kind of secularized rewriting of Bunyan's visit to the City of Destruction, a phantasmagoric account of the narrator's alienating experience of the nightmare socio-political cityscape of the 1930s. And it is the socio- economic catastrophe of the same period that is ultimately the subject of 'Scene', the poem by Glyn Jones that was printed immediately following *Prologue*. After surveying the landscapes of the north and west of Wales, Jones ends by identifying himself as a man not of those attractive rural parts but of the suffering communities of 'the crooked coalfields':

Standing now where that birth-star was eloquent
I see my bitter county dawn between
My hands. I grieve above five valleys leaning
Suppliant against my unstruck rock. (*W*, 8)

In so far as these contributions by Thomas and by Jones were knowingly infected by an international malaise, they were, of course, representative not only of the Welsh but of the wider European scene in that period. But while implicitly recognizing this by noting in his second number that 'We've been accused of trying to be "European"' (*W*, 35), and by passing mention of the Spanish Civil War (*W*, 35), *Wales*'s brash founder-editor, Keidrych Rhys, nevertheless insisted on the specific Welshness of the writing: 'The present-day problems of the real Welsh writer are many, varying tremendously from those of others writing across our frontier' (*W*, 35). His contributors, he exuberantly claimed, '[show] the new interest of the Celt in the social scene' (*W*, 35). Then, unabashed as always by self-contradiction, he added that 'Welsh poets from the *Gogynfeirdd* [twelfth to fourteenth century] onwards have always possessed a Sense of their Own Age' (*W*, 36).

Ever the flamboyant impresario, Rhys cunningly represented the writers for *Wales* as the young shock troops of a militantly oppositional alternative culture, out to raze the establishment to the ground. And in his lively knockabout terms 'the establishment' could variously mean the closed shop of literary London ('the English Literary Map of log-rolling, cocktail parties, book clubs, knighthoods, O.M.'s, and superannuated effeminacy in Bloomsbury editorial chairs') (*W*, 37), the sclerotic National Eisteddfod, the capitalist press, and the deferential Welsh service of the BBC. Adopting a Poundean abruptness of manner and striking a streetwise attitude hardboiled as that of Chandler's Philip Marlow, Rhys made his editorials sound like the fighting talk of an impatient young generation contemptuous of its escapist elders' addiction to euphemism. The self-dramatizing Rhys found it easy to associate the defiant pride he wrung from an economically depressed and culturally oppressed Wales with Saunders Lewis's controversial action in setting fire to the 'English' bombing-school at Penyberth, a year before the founding of *Wales*. In 'The Fire-Sermon or Bureaucracy Burned',

printed in the second issue of *Wales*, he described that action as
'a poet's story cut by the strong/ Magic of a dominant land'
(*W*, 69), and wrote a praise-poem in honour of 'a hero with a
drastic programme' (*W*, 69). Then in the fourth issue, as if to
make amends for the anti-climactic bombast of this verse, Rhys
printed Gwenallt's taut Welsh-language tribute to Saunders
Lewis, with its rasping opening: 'And for the sake of Wales you
acted the fool/ A fool like all the martyrs of Christ and Mary'
(*W*, 141; my translation).

As Rhys acknowledged, Gwenallt's poem had first appeared in
Heddiw, the politico-cultural magazine begun in 1936. One of its
two founding editors was Aneirin Talfan Davies, who later
became one of Dylan Thomas's most significant Welsh mentors
and one of the great architects of a BBC service in post-war
Wales that was to transform Welsh culture in both languages.[14]
(Dylan Thomas, Pennar Davies and Glyn Jones were all to have
important work commissioned and broadcast by this service.)
The action of Lewis and his colleagues in setting fire to the
bombing-school had, in fact, been one of the factors that had
prompted Davies and his associates to launch their challenging
new journal, and its very title accordingly announced its intention
to address contemporary issues. As is clear from *Heddiw*'s first
editorial, the action at Penyberth was taken as a symbol of
cultural reinvigoration and as an indication that Welsh Wales
(and perhaps Wales as a whole) was at long last shedding that
docile passivity which Davies and his contemporaries believed
had been inscribed in the nostalgic writings of the previous
generation.[15] That generation was seen as having initiated a glorious twentieth-century renaissance of Welsh-language literature,
before subsiding into moribund conventionality, and Davies
saw a parallel decline in Welsh Nonconformity. Son of a
Nonconformist minister, he was eventually to convert to the
Anglican faith, but as co-editor of *Heddiw* he opened its pages to
contributors searching for ways of making Welsh Nonconformity
genuinely current – a search that was deeply to concern both
Pennar Davies and Glyn Jones, not only as private individuals but
also as questing artists.

Heddiw's conscious attempts to mediate its age took many
different forms. In the early issues a pan-Europeanism was vigorously advocated (as it was implicitly in *Wales*); attention was

drawn to the ever-increasing cultural power of the 'new' media of cinema and radio, with Aneirin Talfan Davies himself contributing a lively review of Chaplin's *Modern Times*; and eisteddfodic culture was blisteringly attacked by none other than the redoubtable Kate Roberts, who also warned that unless Welsh-language writers and intellectuals bestirred themselves, the BBC, and with it the commanding heights of modern Welsh culture, would be controlled entirely by the Anglo-Welsh! Her worries were echoed in different terms by Aneirin Talfan Davies in his important review (1939) of Dylan Thomas's *The Map of Love* (1939). Having first identified that work as the product of the kind of adventurous Anglo-Welsh poetics advocated in *Wales* (to which he paid cautious tribute), Davies went on to regret the thorough Englishness of the tradition to which Thomas nevertheless seemed fundamentally to belong. The unmistakable genius of the writing posed a particular problem, since where in contemporary Welsh-language culture, Davies wondered, could an original talent be found to counter Thomas's genius for English? 'Unless Welsh can attract the loyalty of young men of the unmistakable gifts and talent of Dylan Thomas', Davies warned, 'then the death of the language cannot be long delayed.'[16]

Davies's comment brings us to an important neglected subject: the tension between the Welsh-language and the English-language culture of Wales that was such a vital part of the extraordinary dynamic of the literary culture of this period. It is a subject as complex as it is sensitive, and as such must not be simplified, on pain of considerable damage to our understanding both of the Wales of that past and of the Wales of our present. During the 1930s the language issue constituted the 'dark matter' of the Welsh case, as it may still do today. Just as this mysterious 'dark matter', invisibly filling the cosmos, determines (through its gravitational pull) the actual disposition of the visible universe, so too in Wales the language issue is liable never to be more influential than when it seems least evidently present.

The Welsh-speaking Rhys's attacks on eisteddfodic literature, purportedly Bible-black with ministers of religion and funded by moneys that would have been better used to support the anglophone writing he himself championed, were in part intended to bait respectable Welsh-language culture. But they were also very much in line with the thinking of young Welsh-language writers themselves, as were his dismissive references to 'a bran-dip in the hip-bath of Arthuriana and *Oesau Canol*' (*W*, 36). And another of the paradoxes of Rhys's provocative approach to Wales's two languages was that, even as his *Wales* was stridently proclaiming English-language writing to be the one most excitingly attuned to the contemporary Welsh situation, he continued to include in the periodical's pages Welsh-language poems of a quality that called such a claim into question. As his example therefore suggests, the heightened awareness each of the two linguistic cultures had of the challenging presence of the other at this time resulted in a spectrum of responses (ranging from outright mutual hostility through to mutual admiration and emulation) that had far-reaching creative consequences. So, for instance, Glyn Jones's discovery, during the 1930s, of *hen benillion* and of the strict-metre poetry of the golden age fed directly into the development of his own distinctively Welsh brand of anglophone Modernist writing. Conversely, the awareness by Kate Roberts and Aneirin Talfan Davies of the progressivist character of Anglo-Welsh writing led to a radical restructuring of style not only by them but also by many another writer of the emerging generation, including Pennar Davies and Alun Llywelyn-Williams.

The inclusion of a Welsh-language poem by Llywelyn-Williams in the Summer 1938 issue of *Wales* (*W*, 172) was perfectly appropriate. In *Tir Newydd*, the little magazine of which he was the founding editor, Llywelyn-Williams had repeatedly expressed his admiration for the exciting generation of Anglo-Welsh authors whose work seemed to him possessed of a vibrant contemporaneity missing from the Welsh-language literary scene. By the 'new ground' (or 'new territory') to which the title of his journal referred, Llywelyn-Williams meant both these important regions of 1930s experience on which, he felt, Welsh-language writers had been reluctant to tread and the industrialized, Anglicized, regions of south Wales on which they had effectively turned their backs. Llywelyn-Williams was a young student at University College, Cardiff when he started *Tir Newydd*, and he drew heavily on the talents of his fellow-students, most of whom were either from that city or from the surrounding industrial regions. One of his periodical's main aims was to address the changing role of all the arts in view of the turbulent social, economic and political life of the pre-war decade.[17]

An essay on 'The Welsh Definition of an Artist' appeared in the very first number,[18] and thereafter the editor himself wrote several challenging pieces on the same subject. In an essay on 'The Welsh Language and City Life' he lambasted the leading artists and intellectuals of the day for 'refusing to face the artistic problems of our industrial regions (and indeed their other problems), and [for] trying to escape from them by treating them as unWelsh phenomena'.[19] By contrast, Rhys Davies and Jack Jones were commended for being alive to the transformative energies in urban-industrial culture that were busily fashioning the future even as Welsh-language writers complacently slept the present away and dreamed of a departed rural paradise. Llywelyn-Williams renewed his charge in a later essay, offering 'Some Observations on the Contemporary Poetry of Wales'. The main burden of his argument was that the giants of the Welsh-language literary renaissance at the beginning of the century (W. J. Gruffydd, R. Williams Parry, T. Gwynn Jones) were now a spent force. Awed by their example, however, Welsh poets continued to practise an outmoded poetry, blind to the gathering catastrophe it was their responsibility to confront:

> The whole civilization and culture of Europe is in dire danger; man's morality is aghast at the powers of his science; the standards and power of religion, especially those of the Christian faith, need to be considered anew; all social arrangements, in the fields of trade and industry and international politics, are hastening towards disaster, and crying out for reform.[20]

Wanting *Tir Newydd* to take account of the many, often radical, ways in which the contemporary arts registered the crises of the period, Llywelyn-Williams invited Glyn Jones to submit an essay on Surrealism.[21] His pioneering study conscientiously traced the European history and somewhat muddled philosophy of the movement, whilst rather sceptically noting the Communist sympathies of such leading figures as Aragon, Herbert Read, David Gascoyne and Paul Nash. Jones ended by suggesting that Surrealism was more likely to act as a valuable transient stimulus than to be of long-standing significance. This conclusion rested partly on the belief – so revealing of Jones's own grounding in the Welsh tradition of literary craftsmanship – that total trust in the unconscious was inherently incompatible with high artistic achievement.

During the immediate pre-war period, the simultaneous appearance of several lively new journals such as *Wales*, the *Welsh Review*, *Tir Newydd* and *Heddiw*, was, then, symptomatic of the feeling amongst young Welsh authors, on both sides of the cultural divide, that the activity of writing needed to be radically re-examined in the light of the convulsive social, economic and political changes of the 1930s. Wrenching times – in Wales and in Europe alike – could be adequately inscribed only through a dislocation of established styles and conventions. Literature had somehow to register the shock of unprecedented events – the belated impact of international Modernism, the collapse of Welsh industrial society, the challenge of Marxism, the threat of Fascism. Aware that alert young English writers were already regrouping around such innovative journals as *New Verse*, Welsh writers both in English and in Welsh were galvanized into instigating or supporting corresponding developments in Wales.

The little journals that resulted were attempts to combat that sense of helpless isolation mentioned in an important letter published in *Tir Newydd* in August 1939.[22] The author was Pennar Davies, newly returned home after a brilliant career as scholar at Balliol College, Oxford and at Yale, an experience that had confirmed him in his cosmopolitan outlook. Davies argued that Wales lacked the concentration of intellectual and artistic talent that had enabled the great cities of modern Europe (Paris, Rome, Vienna, London) to generate literature of revolutionary character and power. Welsh literature tended therefore to be conservative in style and provincial in standard. Whilst praising the periodical *Wales* for providing a forum for intellectual exchange – acting as a kind of metropolis for the intellect, where the liveliest creative imaginations could intermingle and cross-fertilize – Davies argued that neither it nor its Welsh-language counterpart, *Tir Newydd*, could ever provide a sufficiently rich, catholic, cultural milieu for Welsh writers. What was badly needed, he urged, was a Literary Society embracing both the languages and literatures of Wales. In addition to promoting dynamic interaction between the two native languages, such a society would actively seek to make contact with the diverse cultures of contemporary Europe – a step that particularly appealed to Davies, who was a sophisticated Europhile and a gifted linguist.

Keidrych Rhys shared Davies's dream of a bicultural Literary Society, but reflecting in 1971 on the pre-war situation, Pennar Davies felt their project never really stood a chance:

> Even if the war had not wrecked our literary society of the 'New Wales' I doubt whether there would have been enough good will at that time to bridge the linguistic divide. Some of those intending members who used the national language looked askance at the sons of Caradoc and nearly all inclined towards some form of the doctrine that art is propaganda, while some of the prominent among the Anglo-Welsh, like Dylan Thomas and Vernon Watkins, were suspicious of any act of commitment to Wales or to anything except their poetic craft.[23]

The same year (1939) as Pennar Davies's letter appeared in *Tir Newydd*, Glyn Jones appended a 'Sketch of the Author' to the Fortune Press edition of his *Poems*, and gave alternative expression to the sense of isolation mentioned by Davies. Once he had begun to mature as a writer, Jones explained, his ambition had been 'to achieve a body of workers' poetry' – not the modish kind of 'public-school communist verse' then appearing in England but 'poems which the workers themselves could read, understand and appreciate'. However, having experimented for some time with poems modelled on Welsh folk poetry, he came to realize that 'the workers work eight hours, have had a three R's education, and care nothing for poetry'. At the same time he met Dylan Thomas, whose 'difficult, and even perverse' poems he enormously admired. Finding in Thomas a like-minded experimentalist, with strong avant-garde interests, Jones abandoned his vision of providing the masses with reading material, and felt 'relief at escaping their cramping invigilation'. Proceeding to set aside all concerns about an audience for his poetry, he became resolutely 'content to communicate with myself, to indulge my love of those words and phrases which I had suppressed to a large extent before the scrutiny of my workers'.[24]

These convergent statements by Jones and Davies highlight the ambiguous position of young Welsh artists a bare month before the outbreak of war. On the one hand they felt marginalized – by the brutal demonstration, in the social, economic and political fields, of the impotence and irrelevance of art; by an awareness of being remote from the significant sources of new artistic creativity; by the absence of a supportive artistic community, apart from a coterie of like-minded writers of their own generation; and by their avid commitment to forms of writing that appealed neither to society at large nor to the senior figures in Welsh literary culture. On the other hand, their sense of marginalization made them cleave all the more fiercely to their medium and exploit its potential, caused them to bond closely with their own kind, and focused their attention on the problematical character of art.

Dylan Thomas gave precocious intuitive expression to this complex of circumstances in some of his early atmospheric stories, where the figure of the artist recurs in connection with Thomas's exploration of dream states. The air in these 1930s stories, many of them vaguely set in the fantastical 'Jarvis country', is almost stiflingly thick with the anxieties about sexuality and death that agitated an adolescent imagination which had fed on gothic images garnered from horror films and vampire stories. But mixed in with these symptoms of psychic disturbance are signs of socio-cultural pathology, as is particularly evident in 'The Orchards'. This oneiric fantasia features a young man, Marlais, who dreams of a woman seen against the sexually suggestive background of a hundred orchards breaking into flame. Waking, he goes in search of her by employing words in an attempt to realize his vision, only to experience defeat:

> He struggled with his words like a man with the sun, and the sun stood victoriously at high noon over the dead story ... The word is too much with us. He raised his pencil so that its shadow fell, a tower of wood and lead, on the clean paper ... The tower fell, down fell the city of words, the walls of a poem, the symmetrical letters.[25]

In desperation, he takes to the housetops, clambering along in pursuit of his dream, high above the town, 'brave in his desolation' (*ML*, 107); but to no avail. And so he comes down to earth instead, takes to the road, and eventually battles his way to his dream destination. It is the difficult terrain he traverses *en route*, however, that is so revealing, suggestive as it is of the way the young Thomas viewed his Swansea. Picturesquely perched by the edge of the sea, with beautiful Gower stretching to the west, it was nevertheless encroached upon from the north and the east by a sinister industrial wasteland – the lower Swansea Valley devastated by copper smelting, the huddled industrial townships that produced coal and tinplate, the gloomy south Wales valleys dark in their cramp.[26]

Thomas had first adumbrated this geo-cultural vision at the age of 18 in a series of articles he wrote for the *Herald of Wales* on 'The Poets of Swansea'. 'Only a great writer', he there concluded, 'can give this absurd country [of Wales], full of green fields and chimney stacks, beauty and disease, the loveliness of the villages and the smoke-ridden horror of the towns, its full value and recognition' (*EPW*, 120). In 'The Orchards', Marlais loses his 'virginity' and enters the world of adult experience he must suffer in order to be an artist by making his way through just such an 'absurd', Munch-like landscape. It includes

> the rim of Whippet valley where the trees, for ever twisted between smoke and slag, tore at the sky and the black ground . . . But Whippet's trees were the long dead of the stacked south of the country; who had vanished under the hacked land pointed, thumb-to-hill, these black leaf-nailed and warning fingers. Death in Wales had twisted the Welsh dead into those valley cripples. (*ML*, 110–11)

Such descriptions conflate Thomas's fear of industrial culture with his fear of the undead, the Nonconformist forefathers in their 'ancestral valley' (*ML*, 111) who threaten to blight his imagination. His Marlais, a modern, pagan counterpart of Bunyan's pilgrims, can reach his goal, as person and as artist, only by overcoming the greatest psychic threat of all, which in his case (as in Thomas's) is represented by sombre Welsh chapel culture:

> By midnight two more valleys lay beneath him, dark with their two towns in the palms of the mined mountains; a valley, by one in the morning, held Aberbabel in its fist beneath him. He was a young man no longer but a legendary walker, a folk-man walking, with a cricket for a heart; he walked by Aberbabel's chapel, cut through the graveyard over the unstill headstones, spied a red-cheeked man in a nightshirt two foot above ground. (*ML*, 112–13)

In representing Marlais as 'a legendary walker, a folk-man walking', Thomas may well be viewing him as a figure from pre-Nonconformist, 'Celtic' Wales, the Wales he had himself invoked in 'The Poets of Swansea' when regretting that W. H. Davies, and other Anglo-Welsh writers, had not taken advantage of 'the wonders of Celtic mythology':

> He could have recreated the fantastic world of the Mabinogion, surrounded the folk lore with his own fancies, and made his poetry a stepping place for the poor children of darkness to reach a saner world where the cancer of our warped generation is no more than a pleasant itch. (*EPW*, 118)

In choosing the title, 'The Orchards', Thomas may well have had in mind the Welsh 'Afallon' (*anglice*, Avilion), the place of apples. And, like Rhys Davies,[27] Thomas associated this 'pagan' and sexually uninhibited Wales with the eccentric, nineteenth-century figure of Dr William Price, Llantrisant, upon whose life he loosely based his own 1936 story 'The Burning Baby' (*EPW*, 22–8). In a review for *Adelphi* (1934), Thomas broadened this vision of a new, post-industrial and triumphantly post-Nonconformist Wales into the belligerently phrased concept of a pan-Celtic literary revival: 'Wales, Ireland, and, in particular, Scotland, are building up, from a tradition of ballad, folk song, the pawky obscenities of Robert Burns, whom MacDiarmid calls the Poet Intestinal, and a whimsical Victorian banality (the Celtic Twilight), a poetry that is . . . serious' (*EPW*, 165–6). 'The Poet Intestinal' would neatly describe the young Dylan Thomas, while his early prose works hark back to a supposedly 'mythopoeic', pre-Christian, Welsh folk tradition.

'The Orchards' is, then, a story powerfully expressive of Thomas's cultural, as well as sexual, preoccupations. It shows him to be a writer caught between fear of the old Wales and hope of the new, experiencing both the trauma of disorientation and the exhilaration of adventure, dreaming of a revolution that will overthrow the established and traditional in the name of innovations that will be at once modern and autochthonous. The ground note of his early writing, however, is that of a writer 'brave in his desolation', like his young contemporaries Glyn Jones and Pennar Daves. Finding raw, instinctive, expression in the Surrealist stories of the 1930s, this climate of feeling was later to be articulated much more subtly in the equivocal comedy of

Portrait of the Artist as a Young Dog, the 1940 collection of Welsh stories in which the mature Thomas chose to tell about how he had come to be a Welsh story-teller. Other, corresponding, fictional portraits of a Welsh artist's life in this period were, however, to take appreciably longer to appear.

★   ★   ★   ★

By the time his novel *Meibion Darogan* was published in 1968, Pennar Davies had already become a distinguished figure in post-war Welsh culture.[28] His exceptional learning – comfortably embracing ancient civilizations, classical culture, a wide range of European literatures and the whole spectrum of Christian theology – had won him the awed respect of his peers. Appointed Professor of Church History at the Welsh Independents' theological college at a young age, he had soon gone on to become its reverend Principal. At the same time he was active in politics with Plaid Cymru, and the author not only of many impressive theological and devotional works but also of several unorthodox volumes of poetry and creative prose.

However, in *Meibion Darogan* Davies reverted to a period in his life before he had come to public eminence. The novel is loosely based on his wartime experience as a member of Cylch Cadwgan – the circle of young Welsh-language writers and intellectuals, most of them pacifists or conscientious objectors, who used to meet during the war years in 'Cadwgan', the home of J. Gwyn Griffiths in Pentre, Rhondda. Like Davies himself, several of the group went on to distinguished careers as authors or academics after the war, and its role as a ginger group in Welsh literature was later confirmed by the publication of *Cerddi Cadwgan,* a groundbreaking volume of poems by members and sympathizers.[29] Important works of fiction were also produced by the Cadwgan circle. The earliest of these were two proto-feminist texts – the first of their kind to appear in Welsh – by Kate Bosse-Griffiths, a brilliant German academic who was an outstanding scholar of the cultures of the ancient world.[30] The influential presence in the group of Bosse-Griffiths (the wife of J. Gwyn Griffiths, who was himself to become a classicist and Egyptologist of international reputation) and of Rosemarie Wolff (a German refugee who was to become Pennar Davies's wife) was symptomatic of the cosmopolitan outlook that Cylch Cadwgan consciously sought to foster. This was one way in which the members, most of whom were radical Christians, aimed to bring an enlivening sophistication into Nonconformist culture. Other ways they favoured included provocatively emphasizing the ludic quality of literature and flaunting their uncompromising intellectuality in the face of both the aggressive anti-intellectualism of proletarian valleys society and the middlebrow character of ageing establishment Nonconformity.[31]

Such a collection of seeming oddballs and exotics aroused considerable hostility in wartime Rhondda, committed as valleys people patriotically were to the British war effort. Indeed, the persecution some members of the Cadwgan circle had to suffer for their pacifism is one of the subjects of *Adar y Gwanwyn* (*The Birds of Spring*) (1972), an entertaining novel written by Rhydwen Williams, one of the most *louche* and lovable members of the group.[32] *Meibion Darogan*, however, concentrates with mingled sympathy and amusement on other aspects of the group's situation – its almost incestuous coterie character; its exhilarating yet arrogant intellectualism; the heady, hothouse atmosphere in which sexual and creative desires mingled and ambiguously throve; and the general atmosphere of permissiveness that helped young talents break free of stiflingly respectable social and cultural conventions. And central to the work, as it was central to the discussions of the Cadwgan circle, is the problematical nature of art, an issue explored through a fourfold portrait of the artist – as actor (Eurof Powell), as musician (Edryd Simon), as novelist (Neddwyn Lewis) and as female dramatist (Senena Francis).

Like all Pennar Davies's unconventional fiction, *Meibion Darogan* is a work of indeterminate genre and of enigmatic character.[33] In his prefatory note, for instance, Davies himself draws attention to its relationship (merely tangential, it is claimed) to the Cadwgan circle, but suggests that his ostensibly realist fiction may be better understood as a dramatization of a wartime dialogue the author had been conducting with himself. This objective/subjective split is, in fact, only one of the many sets of dualisms between which the novel seems to be tantalizingly suspended, all of which are subsumed within the comedy that is the novel's presiding manner but which itself in turn varies considerably in tone and import. And there are other textual

complications. For instance, the novel is conscious of its confus-
ingly mixed ancestry – of its descent from the confessional mode
of Augustine and Rousseau to which Dostoevsky gave a dizzying
fictional twist; from the novel of ideas of Thomas Mann, and the
drama of ideas of George Bernard Shaw; from cartographies of
the soul, beginning with Dante's *Divine Comedy* and ending with
Goethe's *Faust*; and from the turbid records of the psycho-sexual
life, including the novels of de Sade, the poetry of the Decadents,
and the pseudo-scientific studies of Freud. The novel's self-
conscious relation to these and many other paradigms may be
fairly taken as evidence that it is the work of a European intellectual in search of a Welsh intelligentsia. But it may also be
understood as a sign that, like his characters, Pennar Davies is
concerned to explore the extremely complicated provenance of
the medium he is using.

The role of the young Christian artist in conservatively
Nonconformist Wales is of consuming concern in *Meibion
Darogan*, and, in addition to addressing the issue at the level of
subject-matter, Davies actually inscribes it in his textual practices
and hermeneutic strategies. So, for instance, the text's ironic
refusal to allow the reader ready means of self-orientation –
baffling him/her with its cool web of discourse, its tonal indeter-
minacy and its calmly alienating procedures – is Davies's way of
breaking with the concept of fiction as a means of comfortably
reinforcing familiar moral assumptions. His text is designed on
the maieutic model advocated not only by Socrates but by many
Christian mages (not to mention modern psychotherapists and
literary Modernists), the aim being to bring the reader to the
simultaneity of a revelatory new understanding of text and of self
through the shock of defamiliarization. The act of reading consequently becomes reintegrated with wider life-experience in a way
that Davies's reading in Christian existentialism had caused him
to value highly. Fiction thus practised becomes a form of spiritual
obstetrics, helping not only the reader's mind but his/her deeper
being to overcome its innate resistance to disturbingly naked
knowledge of the personal – and more generally human – self.

The knowledge that *Meibion Darogan* has to offer, as we are
coolly insinuated into the slippery innards of the text and of its
characters, is that human psychology is not only labyrinthine
but metamorphic, so that its complexities are ubiquitously

self-altering and so endlessly elusive. The challenge which, as a Christian, Davies attempts to accept is that of confronting this reality without either defensively retreating to simplistic ethical distinctions or capitulating to *laissez-faire* moral relativism. The former he, of course, sees as the failure of Welsh establishment Nonconformity; the latter he regards as the failure of the modern secular world.

Kierkegaard regarded Socrates' maieutic method as the negative way, which could produce the psychological conditions for an authentically positive way of engaging with difficult truths.[34] Pennar Davies's non-committal textual method of teasing us into thought in *Meibion Darogan* was itself complemented later in his career by the more direct, but none the less complex, approach he adopted in his intellectually adventurous trilogy of novels.[35] As gradually became clear, these constitute a kind of twentieth-century version of *Imitatio Christi*, since they offer an account of a remarkable modern individual whose life seems naturally and uncannily to resemble, both in narrative outline and in spiritual import, the earthly career of Christ himself. And it is through the life and person of Arthur, who is represented as something of a maieutic artist, that many of the questions deliberately left open in *Meibion Darogan* are brought to a kind of positive resolution. These include such problems as the mingled foulness and sacredness of the flesh, the unstable moral potential of sexuality, the self-serving aspects of spiritual confession, the narcissistic aspects of one's relationship to others, the competing claims of the active and the contemplative life, the value of self-possession as opposed to transgressive but self-augmenting rapture, and – a fundamental issue which is, for Davies, internally connected to all of these – the power, at once uniquely valuable and questionable, that art so troublingly possesses.

In *Meibion Darogan* the characters tangle with each other and with their own desires whilst the author looks on with amusement and some sympathetic bemusement. No wonder the novel at one point toys with an image of God as a divine humorist! The work traces the changing relationships between a Cadwgan-like circle of young artists, ministers and intellectuals, and a family of four women sharing a house in the locality. Martha, a care-worn matriarch and a typical product of rural Welsh Nonconformity (as her biblical name suggests), has many years previously moved her family to the foreign valleys of south Wales in order to avoid scandal. Her wilful and passionate daughter, Nest, has borne an illegitimate child by a lover who had originally been the fiancé of her sister, Senena – both sisters being fatefully named, thanks to a local doctor, after tempestuous characters in Welsh history. To conceal the birth, Martha has moved home with Senena and brought little Lea up as her own child. Years later, Martha and the teenage Lea share the home with a now mysteriously bed-bound Senena, who has developed into a famous dramatist, and with an unrepentant and untamed Nest, who smoulderingly tolerates her mother's biting reproaches.

Not surprisingly, such a mysterious *ménage à quatre* attracts the attention of the neighbouring young 'Llety Rhys' set, whose leading members, already intoxicated by dreams of moral and artistic daring, first begin to speculate feverishly about the psycho-drama being acted out within the family, and then proceed to become infatuated with the three 'sisters'. And into the complications that ensue Davies weaves intricate reflections on the nature of art. For instance, Edryd Simon is an aspiring young composer who secretly hopes to compose a messianic work that will save Wales from extinction. He also believes passionately in the *élan vital* that pulses through Beethoven's music and that is pent up, awaiting creative release, in all human beings. He is therefore readily persuaded by Neddwyn Lewis, a young trainee minister and would-be writer, that Senena is a kind of Elizabeth Barrett Browning, giving vent in her plays to repressed desires (including lesbianism), while awaiting liberation. Lewis, in turn, is a connoisseur of psychic extremity, holding to a kind of pseudo-Baudelairean or sub-Dostoevskyan belief that man becomes spiritually alive only in those strange twilight regions where extreme evil can unexpectedly reverse itself into saintly good. For him, great writers are the great transgressives who dare to explore these regions in their works, oftentimes (like Senena) at the expense of their lives. Eurof Powell, the minister who is the third in this trio of friends, is a talented actor in life as on the stage and in the pulpit. He is tortured by the ease with which he can deceive others, and himself, but clings to the hope that by persisting in acting the good man he may eventually truly grow into the part. Meanwhile, he is left agonizing over the ambiva-lences of his 'art'.

It is these three characters who, so Davies explained, represent three aspects of his own nature during the 'Cadwgan' period. As such, *Meibion Darogan* may usefully be described as a portrait of the artist as a subversively unorthodox young Welsh Nonconformist minister. The coolness of the comedy implies that the middle-aged Davies sees in these avatars of his confusedly divided young self an embarrassing Romantic naivety and ignorant spiritual presumptions. Nevertheless, he is clearly still proud to own as his the psycho-spiritual daring that made these three young artists genuine explorers (however callow and misguided) of the complex mysteries of moral, psychological and spiritual life. As such, they represent one of his settled views of the modern Welsh artist's duty – to act as missionary to those modern lukewarm Laodiceans, the self-satisfied, hypocritical, blinkered members of Nonconformist society.

Another of Davies's perspectives on the genuine Welsh artist was that (s)he was the descendant of the Old Testament figure, Bezaleel, 'the chief maker of a Tabernacle that never quite was', and a true artist who, as his name indicates, 'worked in the shadow of El [the Almighty]' (*AW*, 120).[36] And in being condemned to work in modern Wales, Davies believed, such an artist was condemned to work in 'Babylon': that is, in the world of that mass, secular, techno-industrial and consumerist society to which Davies gave the name Anglosacsonia because he associated it primarily with the destructive, hegemonic culture of Anglo-American capitalism. In Davies's terms, the Second World War had been essentially fought between 'Babylon' and the murderously totalitarian cultures of 'Cain'. *Meibion Darogan*, therefore, partly celebrates, albeit in equivocating comedic terms that highlight the flaws in the very thing that is being celebrated, a world of somewhat confused intellectual and erotic permissiveness asserting itself in the teeth of the monstrous regimentations of the era.

There is, though, another aspect to the case. The main action in *Meibion Darogan* is bracketed within two references to Stanley Coslett, an ordinary local lad who is away serving in the wartime navy. The reference in the novel's opening pages highlights the difficulty both Eurof Powell and young Lea have in relating to someone of Stanley's class and humble background, and in feeling concern for his fate. And the mention in the novel's concluding pages of his probable death at sea casts a quizzical light on the blithe emotional cavortings of the self-absorbed main characters. In other words, what has avant-garde art, however variously conceived by Eurof, Edryd, Neddwyn and Senena (and, of course, by their creator) to say to a character such as Stanley? And if it has nothing to do with him, then what can it possibly have to say for itself?

In many respects, Pennar Davies's development as a writer (and as a minister), from the wartime period in which *Meibion Darogan* is set to the later period when it was actually written, involved an attempt to answer these questions, and to close the gap between himself and Stanley. Part of the poignancy of this situation was that that gap was also the gap between Davies and his own working-class background.[37] Moreover, this same gap (experienced by many as a wound) troubled the minds and the work of most of the leading south Wales writers of Davies's day, including Idris Davies, Alun Lewis, Gwyn Thomas – and Glyn Jones.[38]

* * * *

In *The Valley, the City, the Village*, young Trystan Morgan, the central character, who is growing up to be an artist, notices his beloved grandmother's hands, 'red and rugged, the hands of a labourer, their knotted erubescence evidenced familiarity with the roughest work'.[39] These contrast, to his shame, with 'my own painter's hand, culpable, indulged, and epicene, as it moved adroitly in the perfect glove of its skin' (*VCV*, 10). And as he grows into adolescence and young manhood, his devout grand- mother confronts him with a view of art as profane, sensual and frivolously impractical. Although he eventually comes to resist her insistent wish that he become a missionary, Trystan finds that her frank hostility to art lives on within him in the form of a range of misgivings about the artist's role that he has somehow got to come to terms with. It means that he, and the novel as a whole, becomes almost obsessively preoccupied with conflicting accounts of art and its purpose.

Trystan Morgan/ Morgan Glyn Jones: in thus transposing his own first name to produce Trystan's surname Glyn Jones may have been registering the paradoxical relationship between himself and the subject of his novel. Whereas Trystan's grandmother resisted his becoming a painter, Jones's mother resisted his becoming a writer but actively encouraged him to develop his talents for painting instead. However, these two ostensibly opposite reactions amount in fact to much the same thing. Just as Trystan's grandmother believed painters to be dissolute and irreligious, so, too, was Jones's mother convinced (on the basis of her own family history) that writers were immoral and wholly irresponsible. By making Trystan a painter, though, Jones was doing more than adopting a strategy for overcoming inner resistance on his own part to confronting memories of his mother's hurtfully fierce disapproval. He was highlighting objections, not only by his mother but by much of the Welsh society which he knew and for which he cared, to the particular kind of writer he had chosen to be.

In *The Valley, the City, the Village*, Jones lovingly (but not uncritically) limns the Nonconformist, proletarian and rural peasant aspects of Welsh society. The industrial valley in which Trystan grows up is obviously a locale where chapel culture and working-class culture are very closely meshed, whereas the west Wales village where he spends his holidays and to which he eventually turns for psychological healing is a place where chapel values permeate rural culture. Moreover, a certain kind of respect for the writer is implicit in these societies' reverence for words: that is, for story-telling, songs, political oratory and preaching. 'In the austere theology of her faith', Trystan notes of his grandmother, 'music and poetry, traditionally employed by hymnist and sacred composer, had received, as surely as Magi gift or pascal offering, the divine approbation' (*VCV*, 75–6). But what there is no real place for, or comprehension of, is the kind of writer Jones himself was: that is, an unconventional, challenging and innovative literary artist. And in the figure of a young visual artist Jones finds an eloquent trope for those features of his writing that his society found unacceptable. After all, as Trystan understands from the outset, neither the little south Wales valleys township of Ystrad nor the farming village of Llansant has anything to say to that most exotic of creatures, a painter: 'painting, an idolatrous art, appeared by its nature to fall under the Mosaic ban. Furthermore, how was the dedication of an entire life to the vain pursuit of worldly fame, through the application of colours to paper or canvas, to be justified?' (*VCV*, 76).

Yet that painter stubbornly refuses to give up on his society. This is the real crux of the matter in *The Valley, the City, the Village*. Even though he is attracted to some of the assumptions and practices of Modernism, Trystan Morgan, like his creator Glyn Jones, refuses to become the alienated, deracinated, anti-democratic artist figure that European Modernism sometimes seemed to entail. In its turn, such a refusal entails reservations about those of Modernism's artistic styles that aimed to deconstruct the consensus view of human qualities. Hence in part, no doubt, those deep misgivings about Surrealism that Jones voiced in *Tir Newydd*. And hence, too, Trystan Morgan's swingeing, if callow, attack on Abstract art: 'Could the abstractionist cry to me through his picture, his patchwork of gay rods, spanglings, and cuboid purples, "I love, I love!"? Could he, before his *lobscows* colours and amorphous forms, arrest me with his soul's cry of horror?' (*VCV*, 155).

Proscribed, too – by Trystan and by Jones – is that nihilistic vision embraced in the novel by another artist figure, Gwydion:

> 'To what shall you be likened,', Dion said, when she had closed the door behind her, 'half cart-horse and half bird? Your beak to the hook of the duke-nosed condor or the rough-legged kite, your protrusive muzzle to some bladdery horse-mouth, you seem equine, runtish and knacker-bound.' (*VCV*, 189)

And yet, there is a striking similarity between this cruel lampoon and Trystan's (implicitly endorsed) ways of looking at people as if his eye were 'a high-powered microscope':

> Her bony ice-cold hands, heavily ringed, were the large and masterful graspers of a wicket-keeper, they had flat nails, and an intricate system of blue pipes tunnelling the skin of the shiny backs. The thin skin of these hands and of her face seemed to give off in that dim room a silvery, phosphorescent sheen. (*VCV*, 101)

The resemblance between these two passages is a sharp reminder that, in engaging in this novel with myriad 'false' concepts of art, Glyn Jones is not infrequently struggling to master strong attractions in his own nature towards those concepts. In this particular case, what seems to surface from the juxtaposing of the two passages is Jones's own fearful fascination – disturbingly evident, or so I would argue, throughout his long lifetime as a writer – with the horror that seemed always darkly to shadow, and to threaten to subvert, the wonder of things.[40] In *The Valley, the City, the Village* this horror seems to present itself most strongly wherever experience is sexualized and wherever there is the whiff of violence. For instance, the two earliest events to scar Trystan's boyhood imagination are rumours about a neighbour who 'pulled a baby out of his wife with a iron hook and she bled to death' (*VCV*, 23) and the sight of a blackleg miner being dragged by his furious workmates through the coal-black water of a river (*VCV*, 23). Indeed, the whole novel – like Trystan's own life – pivots around that moment when, as the degree exams approach, he simultaneously discovers that Lisbeth, the girl he has worshipped from afar, is nothing better than 'an English whore', and hears from a young medical student the story of two teenage girls who had been made pregnant by their own brother. Traumatized by this culminating experience of the urban nightmare, Trystan withdraws to rural Llansant to recuperate both as man and as artist. It is as if Jones himself were admitting that the rawness of modern city life (by which he had himself been almost psychically destroyed, first as a young student at Cheltenham and later as a young teacher in the Cardiff slums) was just too much for him to process directly into affirmative art.[41] That urban milieu, which had, of course, been the preferred milieu of so many Modernist artists in Europe and America, was, for Glyn Jones, profoundly disorientating – indeed his Dinas (named after the Welsh for *city*) is a place of cynicism, sterility, arid intellectuality and conventionality, and above all of deracination, where Wales loses touch with itself to catastrophic effect.

The Valley, the City, the Village is, in fact, centrally about the search, under the conditions of the modern and Modernist period, for a distinctively Welsh form of art. It is also, very much in line with the developments already discussed in this chapter, about the emergence out of radically changing socio-cultural circumstances of a different kind of Welsh artist. Indeed, in *The Dragon Has Two Tongues* (1968), his classic study of the Anglo-Welsh writers of his own generation, Glyn Jones himself anatomized these circumstances, particularly emphasizing Anglo-Welsh writers' background in Welsh-speaking radical Nonconformity and the ways in which the cultural values nurtured appeared in their writing in different forms, having been refracted by an Anglicizing system of education, the new 'foreign' milieu of industrial society, and the socio-cultural upheaval attendant upon the change from Welsh to English.[42]

One familiar reflex reaction to change is nostalgia for what has gone, and this feeling is certainly very strong in *The Valley*. It is most simply evident, perhaps, in Trystan's yearning memory of his grandmother as a 'warm and visionary being':

> Sometimes, the whole sky ablaze, and the crimson sunball dissolving hot as rosin upon the hill-top, a tall black figure seemed to float out of that bonfire as though riding a raft of illumination. Her heavy progress was laborious, her shoulders rose and fell against the dazzling hump of hill-crest radiance with the rock of a scalebeam. She shepherded her rolling shadow down the slope; returning from the prayer-meeting she wore over her vast flesh her long black boat-cloak, with the brass buttons like a dramatic row of drawer-knobs down the front of her. (*VCV*, 12)

This is, however, more than a yielding to the self-indulgence of memory. It is obviously a formal composition, that could be variously described as a praise poem or as a verbal approximation to the ecstatic aggrandizements of a painting by such as Van Gogh, Gauguin, or perhaps (given the profound spiritual charge) Rouault. In Welsh terms, it is very reminiscent of Josef Herman's paintings of Ystradgynlais miners, of Will Roberts's pictures of the Welsh peasant, or of Nicholas Evans's sombre meditations on the Welsh miner. It is, therefore, a formal, self-consciously artistic portrait in which Welsh artistic tradition is crossed with Romantic Modernism. Moreover, it is a composition in which the biblical language of the grandmother's own Nonconformist culture is taken up yet transformed by being embedded in what for her would have been a suspiciously foreign sophisticated discourse. In short, the dynamism of this portrait comes from its being, quite consciously, a culturally hybrid composition; and as such it is a synecdoche of the novel itself. Because if there is in *The Valley* a nostalgia for what is lost, there is also evidence everywhere of excited creative exploitation of the by-products of change. Indeed, the litany of Trystan's schoolmates in Pencwm grammar school reads like Jones's own tribute to the racially hybrid Merthyr in which he himself grew up: 'Carlos San Martin, our little Basque; Sammy Evans, cutter-off of window-straps, now regenerate; Evan Williams; Dicky Adler; fat, spectacled Aby Bernstein, who claimed his father's business had only two branches, one in Pencwm and the other in Jerusalem' (*VCV*, 82). But if life in the cosmopolitan industrial valley is, in part, a rich meld of peoples – a society where discourses mix (Welsh, Welsh–English, educated (grammar-school) English, working-class slang, popular Welsh-language stories and songs, materials from both the proletarian and the mass popular culture of England) in ways that Trystan/Glyn Jones avidly capitalizes on – life in the city seems very largely to illustrate the nightmare of purely destructive change.

In fact, in Dinas relatively homogeneous Welsh society seems to self-destruct, producing class-divisions along English lines. The resulting middle class either adopts a conspicuously Anglicized lifestyle, or else (like Trystan's friends Gwydion and Mabli) turns to a nationalist politics based on the fetishization of Welsh-language culture. Either way, the middle class turns its back both on the *gwerin* society of Nonconformist rural Wales and on the proletarian culture of the industrial valleys. In its turn, that proletarian culture becomes horribly debased, under urban slum conditions, and it is to the resulting underclass that the brother and sisters belong whose incestuous conduct so horrifies Trystan. As for such of the *gwerin* as end up living in the city, their likely fate seems illustrated by Trystan's friend Nico. Hairy and powerful of body, but virtually bereft of mind, let alone sensibility, simian Nico knows next to nothing about the rich past of his own people. This, so Jones seems to imply, is what passes for 'education' in the city university from which Trystan feels so thoroughly alienated. The raucous saturnalia celebrated by the drunken members of the undergradute Calliper Club turns, under Trystan's disapproving eyes, into an orgy of nihilism that seems to expose the city's true character, as the seat of misrule.

In this context, art, too, becomes a parody of its true self, variously assuming the distorted form of Mabli's genteel watercolours, of cynically fastidious Gwydion's mandarin Modernism, or of his belief that art exists only 'to give us the thrill of non-recognition' (*VCV*, 170). But unacceptable though these forms and practices finally are to Glyn Jones, they nevertheless do represent – in exaggerated form – aspects of art he himself found compelling. Above all, they stand for his own bewildered, anguished quest as a young artist for forms of artistic expression more fulfilling than those his own respected society could offer, countenance or comprehend. It is therefore something of Jones's own ambivalent feelings that is, perhaps, captured in the comic scene where Trystan, illicitly attending a drawing-class, is sent by satyr-like Mr Leyshon to return a 'chipped and dirty cast of an enormous foot' to the design-room (*VCV*, 160–3). Arriving there thus encumbered, he finds he has to run the gauntlet of mockery by two pretty girls, who tease him mercilessly. The scene brands itself into his memory, and it also serves to symbolize several aspects of art – its risk of seeming (and indeed being) sheer lunacy, its unnerving subterranean connections with sexuality, and its crazy impracticality!

That Monty Pythonesque sketch, complete with surreally monstrous foot, is also suggestive of the process of psychic dismemberment that Trystan undergoes in Dinas. That foot is the negative corollary of the kind of art he himself was producing at that time; 'paintings in minute detail of very small areas of landscape, say a few square feet of some Ystrad tip with a patch of thin grass on it, or a small rock-pool under a film of coal-dust, or the naked roots of a tree growing out of the earth of the river bank' (*VCV*, 148). These miniatures seem to represent Trystan's inner plight. If they are touching little mementoes and keepsakes that allow him to carry a bit of Ystrad with him into the alien city, they are also timidly snatched portraits of a society which did not care for such art at all, unless it took the form of proletarian realism or straightforward religious affirmation. And the scale of his paintings eloquently suggests an imagination so intimidated by life at large that it desperately retreats to manageable detail. Yet, in spite of its obvious neurotic aspects, this art – with its potential for defamiliarizing a landscape and for rendering the insignificant numinous – does point the way forward for Trystan and does seem to mark a stage in Glyn Jones's own early development into a writer.

As those little miniatures further indicate, Trystan is destined not to make a religion of art (in the approved Modernist manner) but, rather, to become (like Glyn Jones) a religious artist. For him, the way forward is the way back, as he gradually finds the means of recovering, from the wreck of Nonconformity, something of the spirit that characterized it in its prime. The love of creation naturally generates praise, and praise in turn magnifies the beauty of creation – this is the virtuous circle that Trystan's maturing art promises to describe in the concluding section of *The Valley*, which means that the predominant tone of the prose is that of benediction via celebration. Although Dylan Thomas, too, clearly found this tone attractive, he was typical of most of the Anglo-Welsh writers of his generation in that he associated it with a rejection of a Nonconformity he regarded as Calvinistically gloomy. Therefore, in emphasizing a continuity between his affirmative art and Nonconformity, Glyn Jones is close not so much to the English-language writers of Wales as to the Welsh-language writers of the post-war generation. His next of kin, so to speak, are Waldo Williams, Euros Bowen, Bobi Jones – and Pennar Davies.[43]

Jones was also like them in being fully conscious of writing in a tradition of praise that had reached its apogee in the great strict-metre poetry of the golden age of Welsh-language culture, the later Middle Ages. As a prose writer, he was further deeply interested in that other great Welsh classic of medieval times, the *Mabinogion*, a magical work whose cast of shape-changers and whose mesmeric fluidity of design profoundly influenced the writing of *The Valley, the City, the Village*. Indeed, in this novel Jones attempted to create a distinctively Welsh kind of modern fiction out of the daring hybridization of several traditional elements. For instance, Trystan's own pictures, as a boy, veer in style between the kind of puritan-straight realism he practises when sitting on the gallery and surreptitiously sketching the chapel elders (*VCV*, 78), and the very different kind of design with which he compulsively decorates his school exercise-books:

> I surrounded the prim logics of congruency and parallelism with borders of starry blossomed bushes or pinioned helmets, or amputated limbs; I threw about them bunches of poppies, lilies, and balloons and hung them with sagging festoons of Chinese lanterns. (*VCV*, 76)

These school books are transformed into the modern equivalent of the Book of Kells, adorned 'with dewy threads and delicate nets of cobwebs like the interweavings of a Celtic spider'.

Nonconformist realism and exuberant, transformative Celtic fantasy – Trystan (like Jones) strives to bring them both into creative relation. Likewise, the two trees that Trystan mentally juxtaposes. On the wall of his grandmother's house hangs a picture of a gnarled oak-tree growing out of the leaves of the Bible, and among the branches are inserted pictures of the great ministers of her chapel (*VCV*, 40). By contrast, once his Uncle Gomer is embarked on one of his prolix, complex, endlessly digressive stories, Trystan is irresistibly reminded of a very different tree: 'His talk rose like some magical and glittering tree expanding into the dimensions of a grove before one's eyes and heaving itself visibly bough by bough towards the heavens. But he never lost his way in the bewildering webwork of his narratives' (*VCV*, 60).

However, the metaphor of organic growth which is implicit in such images is not really applicable to *The Valley, the City, the Village*. In being the self-portrait of an artist, in its constant reflections on its own medium and methodology, and in its preoccupations with the conditions of its own making, the novel is a thoroughly Modernist fiction. It is aware of itself as a peculiar fabrication of words, as rum an assemblage as Uncle Gomer's (postmodern!) interiors – those bizarre rooms stuffed full of ill-assorted furniture bought second-hand: 'all the clocks, mirrors, ornaments, curtain-poles, spittoons, and picture-frames had come in incomplete and defective lots, through the sale-room, from decayed mansions, taken-over hotels, and steam-ship companies in liquidation' (*VCV*, 58).

In one sense, Uncle Gomer's rooms are, for Jones, true to life itself – a strange yet wonderful farrago of materials. In another sense, they represent the work of the artist – and most particularly, the modern Welsh artist.[44] From one perspective (s)he, too, inhabits a milieu cluttered with the detritus of the past (the decay of the Welsh language, rural culture, Nonconformity, industrial society, etc.), and when that milieu does not seem oppressive or depressing it may easily come to seem as chaotic as the 'boiling deluge of English and Welsh' of Anna Ninety-houses's manic monologues:

without precursory interchange, [she] disembogued her spectacular floods and thaw-waters upon us, she deluged the whole room, the whole valley, the drowning universe, she rode the lawless torrents of reminiscence, intention, and parenthetic exposition, she gambolled and wallowed in the explosive and hurly-burly oceans of her own eloquence, she was riotous Leviathan, unrestrained by mandibular cord or iron hook. (*VCV*, 50)

Images of Bedlam disorder recur throughout *The Valley* and express Trystan's constant terror of psychic annihilation by an unintelligible, mentally uncontrollable world. But the other side of this anarchic vision is the creative possibilities that emerge out of the breakdown of inherited order; and it is these – variously expressed as carnival, metamorphosis, the comic grotesque – that triumph in the end. Yet that victory remains a precarious one; hence the threatening similarity, already noted, between the nihilistically decreative vision of Gwydion – 'the didymist who sees loveliness nowhere' (*VCV*, 302) – and the praise poetry of the groteseque that is eventually developed by Trystan (and Jones). Profound though it may be, the difference between them, in the end, is primarily one of tone and of conviction.

By putting his ear against his Uncle Hughie's soft stomach, the boy Trystan 'heard the sounds that went on inside him, the hinge-whine, the gravel-trickle, the rock-roll, the bowler-plap, and sometimes a strange grinding noise as of someone chewing gristle' (*VCV*, 44). Thus, too, is Jones's imagination the digestive system, so to speak, of his intelligence during that time of immense change in Welsh experience that also gripped Dylan Thomas and Pennar Davies, and that found bewildered and excited expression in their portraits of the artist. All three writers tried to use the turbulence to good innovative effect, but when it came to exploiting the new dynamics of Wales's biculturalism, Jones was easily the most resourceful of the three. And one of the high points of his experimentation in this regard is the conclusion of *The Valley, the City, the Village*, which is a laminate composed of international Modernism, the 'great tradition' of Welsh-language literature, the spunky demotic of proletarian, Anglo-Welsh culture and the earthiness of the rural west. Here the Vision of Judgement, in the form of Goronwy Owen's eighteenth-century classic 'Cywydd y Farn Fawr' (Cywydd of the Great Judgement), blurs into the Circe episode from Joyce's *Ulysses* and Dai's boast from David Jones's *In Parenthesis* (which is itself, of course, consciously Taliesinic), while the dignity of the whole procedure is constantly being subjected to the raucous barracking from the people's gallery! The whole outrageous episode consciously verges on camp, as Jones manages to imply that modern Welsh life – like life itself – seems gloriously to function on terms so inherently improbable, so heedless of 'taste', and so vulgarly spendthrift that the only adequate artistic response to it is a hybrid of burlesque and praise.

4

The good thieves? Translating Welsh literature into English

~

> To translate a poem
> Is to say, look.
> To translate a poem
> Is a *Stabat Mater*.
> You watch as it cries out.
> You hang with it, like the good thief.

This is a stanza from a poem in Tony Conran's *Castles* sequence, a poem that originally figured in a friendly exchange between him and me about the nature of translation.[1] In a review of an augmented edition of Conran's major volume of Welsh–English translations, *Welsh Verse*, I had quoted George Steiner to the effect that there is 'in every act of translation – and specially where it succeeds – a touch of treason. Hoarded dreams, patterns of life are being taken across the frontier.' To this I had added my own gloss, suggesting: 'Given the parlous state of the Welsh language, a volume . . . of successful translations may assume . . . the grim aspect of a veritable series of Welsh poets' heads triumphantly mounted, like Llywelyn's, on the victorious towers of English culture.'[2] Conran's response took the original, and highly appropriate, form of a poem affirming his own belief that translation 'is a yearning thing, an act of faith, an attention to something outside yourself. It is compared here to the good thief hanging with the Word on the cross, saying "Remember me when you come into your kingdom", and waiting for the otherness of the poem to welcome him into its paradise.'[3]

What I was trying to emphasise was that every translation, regardless of how it may be conceived (in more than one sense) by the individual practitioner, is actually born, willy-nilly, into (and in a sense of) a specific politico-cultural situation, a significant aspect of which is the equality, or inequality, of power between the source language (for example, Welsh) and the target language (for example, English). As Susan Bassnett and André Lefevere have pointed out, in order to understand the implications of any given instance of translation we need 'to go into the vagaries and vicissitudes of the exercise of power in a society, and what the exercise of power means in terms of the production of culture, of which the production of translation is a part'.[4] Whereas many had been interested in translating as a particular kind, and indeed a particular quality, of imaginative and linguistic activity, I was wondering what kind of cultural transaction it was, particularly in a Welsh context. Implicit in my comments was the view that translation in this sense was always bound to change its very meaning according to the politico-cultural context in which the transaction was taking place.

This particular exchange is cited only by way of attempting to indicate what an awesome spaghetti junction of a subject 'translation' is – how many dozen different kinds of discourse, each representing vastly different, sometimes mutually suspicious, modes of approach, converge here and variously merge, intersect, or merely cross indifferently over one another. The recent development of 'Translation Studies' as an acknowledged academic discipline marks an attempt to produce a road map of this area.[5] But if in one sense this spaghetti junction appears wherever translation is practised, in another it is a snarl-up of discourses the precise configuration of which is always specific to particular intercultural situations. The discussion, and indeed the practice, of translation is particularly liable to lead to the intellectual equivalent of road rage wherever different linguistic communities uneasily coexist within a given, limited, culturally congested and contested area. In such cases, a road map of the local spaghetti junction is likely to be as interesting as it is certain to be useful.

That modern Wales, with its two languages and two cultures, is one such area is surely obvious to all. And yet next to nothing has so far been done to map translation activity at this location. The difference in this regard, as in so many others, from the situation in neighbouring Ireland is painful to contemplate. There the implications of translation have been subtly and extensively considered, in ways ranging from Seamus Heaney's brilliant essay on translating *Buile Suibhne/Sweeney Astray* to Michael Cronin's impressive academic survey of over a thousand years of *Translating*

Ireland.[6] To turn to those two examples alone is to unearth comments that cry out for application in the Welsh context. For instance, Heaney's wry reflections on the implications, for him, of rendering an Old Irish poem into Modern English: 'a canonical literature in English creates the acoustic within which the translation is to be heard; an overarching old colonial roof inscribed "The land was ours before we were the land's" is made to echo with some such retort as "You don't say!"' (*AT*, 14). Or Cronin's impassioned suggestion that coexistence 'implies translating the cultural, political, religious, emotional language of the other into a language and culture that is strengthened by the presence of the other. The alternative to translation is the muteness of fear.' Would, in a way, that such peaceful coexistence, promoted through translation, were readily possible in Wales.

But it would be a mistake to think that the Welsh case in any way closely resembles that of Ireland. Rather, it is *sui generis* to a highly significant degree. And the peculiarities of the Welsh situation were borne in on Dr Thomas Clancy and myself when we were invited to submit an entry each on Welsh–English translation for *The Oxford Encyclopaedia of Literature in English Translation.* His entry covered all translations of pre-seventeenth century literature, and mine all translations of literature thereafter. What quickly struck me was, first, the extraordinary volume of the translation activity we uncovered; and then – to my initial disbelief – the lack of any scholarly inventory of that prolific activity.[7] And just as there exists no bibliography, however basic, of Welsh–English translation, so has there been next to no substantial discussion of either the history or the cultural implications of this long-established practice. Such limited discussion as does exist has tended to be along the familiar lines that, as one recent commentator (recalling Marvell) entertainingly put it, translation, 'like other loves, seems to be begotten by Despair upon Impossibility' (*AT*, 47).

If at first glance this relative disregard, by the Welsh, of their own significant and distinguished history of Welsh–English translation seems merely exasperatingly peculiar, a moment's reflection will quickly persuade one otherwise. It is surely rather the case that this act of cultural denial, or repression, is symptomatic of the periodically fraught state of intercultural relations in twentieth-century Wales. Deep anxieties about Welsh–English translation have repeatedly arisen from a situation in which the relationship between Welsh and English is such that each language is weak precisely where the other is strong. Welsh is unique amongst the old Celtic languages in having been strong enough throughout this century to sustain an extraordinarily vigorous, rich and varied literary and artistic culture. A currently striking instance of this is the creative synergy between ancient forms unique to the culture (most notably the *canu caeth*) and a variety of internationalist forms of contemporary cultural expression (from free verse to pop to popular cinema). As a result, Welsh-language culture has continued to seem both the senior culture of Wales and indigenous, or autochthonous, in ways an anglophone culture could never be. Consequently, it has appeared (at least in its own eyes) to be the *sine qua non* not only of Welsh cultural distinctiveness but also of the very existence of Wales as a nation. Yet, at the very time that Welsh-language culture was producing a literature unrivalled in quality since the Middle Ages, English was rapidly establishing itself as the language of four-fifths of the Welsh population; a supposedly 'Anglicized' industrial South Wales (where this population was concentrated) was developing forms of social organization increasingly seen by the outside world as definitively Welsh; and an anglophone Welsh literature of striking quality was emerging out of powerful new cultural formations.

Under such circumstances *both* linguistic communities had reason to mistrust Welsh–English translation. Welsh speakers could naturally see in it a strategy of colonial appropriation, a means of bankrupting the language of its assets prior to liquidating its entire culture. English-speakers could suspect that such translation implied a condescending attempt to remedy the shortcomings of an anglophone culture deemed deficient in Welshness. This fear becomes apparent in the form of literary rhetoric Conran uses in the skilfully conciliatory Preface to his *Welsh Verse*, where his aim in part is to lessen his Anglo-Welsh readers' resentment at being seemingly expected, by his translations, to defer to a Welshness in Welsh-language culture that is more 'authentic' than their own:

> On the whole the English-speakers of Wales are hostile to the
> Welsh language and all its works. I suggest that this hostility is

based on a quite unreal fear. Our attitude to the Welsh language should be predatory. We should take from it everything we can get, and two things in particular: a knowledge of the chosen ways that have led to what we call our Welshness; and a weapon, the jawbone of an ass, against our Englishness.[8]

The result of the mutual suspicion between the two cultures as outlined above has been that Welsh–English translation has been implicitly or explicitly construed in terms of a tension of alternative tropes – colonization or freedom struggle; selling out or buying in; cultural betrayal or an honourable ambassadorial service; linguistic aggression or the healing suture of a linguistically divided nation. No wonder, therefore, that a decent silence has been preferred, as a *modus vivendi*, to the public rehearsing of such heated arguments.

But the gain in civility has meant a commensurate loss in self-understanding. One of the hidden cultural resources of Wales is its tradition of Welsh–English translation, a tradition that is at least as old as the eighteenth century and that includes evidence which would surely be invaluable to any serious historian of modern Welsh culture. The tradition also has other aspects. It offers important instances of the way in which Welsh Wales has been mediated to the vast anglophone world – think of Lady Guest's translation of *The Mabinogion*, of George Borrow's excursions into Welsh poetry, of Rolfe Humphries's Americanization of Dafydd ap Gwilym (with musical settings by Johnny Mercer!).[9] And it means that Wales has as much to contribute to as to gain from the increasingly important and sophisticated postcolonial symposia that are run under the auspices of Translation Studies. Given, for instance, the way that translators from the Welsh have been especially sensitized, by their milieu, to the dangers of Welsh–English translation as a form of assimilation by a hegemonic language and an imperialist anglophone culture, they should find many aspects of current debate very pertinent. After all, one of the key contemporary issues is whether translation should aim at the hospitable normalization and domestication of the original text, or whether it should register – in the form of a conspicuous reformation of the receptor language – resistance on the part of the source text to easy linguistic transfer. In support of the latter, Rosanna Warren has pointed out: 'We grow by welcoming difference, not by assimilating it entirely to ourselves. Many of the essays [in her book], accordingly, emphasize "resistance" in one way or another . . . In a fine recent essay, Antoine Berman defines translation as "the finding-and-seeking of the break in the rule [the unruly, *le non-normé*] in the maternal language, so as to insert there the foreign language and its pattern of speech [*son dire*]"' (*AT*, 5). This strategy, famously exemplified in the last century by Hölderlin's translations from the Greek and in this by Ezra Pound's *Homage to Sextus Propertius*, is one that has to a degree been adopted by Conran when translating Welsh *barddas* (strict-metre poetry), as is suggested in the following chapter.

The present chapter will avail itself of the *modus operandi* of Translation Studies in order to explore Welsh–English translation, not least as a practice that illuminates important aspects of intercultural relations in modern Wales. To facilitate such an approach, value judgements on the 'literary worth' of the translations will by and large be avoided. The following discussion therefore lays no claim to being comprehensive, and anyone wishing instead for a summary history of Welsh–English translation is referred to the entries in the forthcoming *Oxford Encyclopaedia* mentioned above.

* * * *

Something of the range of interests covered by Translation Studies is suggested by Susan Bassnett's listing of the representative questions that are asked within the discipline:

> Why do some cultures translate more and some less? What kind of texts get translated? What is the status of those texts in the target system and how does it compare to the status of the texts in the source system? What do we know about translation conventions and norms at given moments, and how do we assess translation as an innovatory force? What is the relationship in literary history between extensive translation as an activity and the production of texts claimed as canonical? What image do translators have of their work and how has that image been expressed figuratively? These and countless other questions testify to the great shift in perception which has taken place, in which far from being a secondary,

marginal activity, translation could be considered as a primary shaping force within literary history. (*TS*, 142)

A similar, potentially inexhaustible, series of questions could be formulated with the Welsh situation specifically in mind. How relevant would it be to consider the personal cultural circumstances of the translators? For whom are translations intended? How significant is the historical moment in which the translation is produced? How far is politics and/or cultural politics inscribed in the translation? Where is the translation published? Which authors and texts are chosen for translation and why? Is the history of the critical reception of the translation known? Did the author translate herself/himself? Was the translation the work of a single author or by several hands? What is the nature, or status, of a bilingual edition? What view of the receiving culture is implied by the translation? What view of the source culture? How far should one locate a translation in the context of the styles of writing and/or translation available in the receptor culture at the time? How does a translator deal with a situation where the source culture and the target culture are out of phase with each other? What happens when there is a significant sociological mismatch between the source and target cultures? Could the works *not* translated be as significant an aspect of translation history as are those that *are* translated? Is the gender of the translator and/or the gender of the person whose work is translated at all material to the case? How far can a translation become active as a literary influence on the target culture?

It should be emphasized that this is not just a list of 'academic' questions; nor has it been assembled merely as an ingenious exercise in theorizing the activity of translation. Rather, these are questions that readily present themselves once one begins seriously to concern oneself with the history of Welsh–English translation. Moreover, all of them have the potential to yield illuminating, and perhaps original, insights not only into that history but into the very infrastructure of Welsh culture. However, it goes without saying that very few of these questions can be meaningfully pursued within the confines of a single chapter.

From the very beginning, Welsh–English translation has been embedded in the nexus of ideologies associated with the relationship between Wales and England. Indeed, 'Welsh-language literature' itself could in one important sense be said to have first appeared in English translation. Or, to put it less provocatively, Wales was in part awakened to the national distinctiveness of its ancient literary culture partly by viewing it through the eyes of England. It is, of course, a classic colonial situation. The heroic salvage mission of Evan Evans (Ieuan Brydydd Hir), who indefatigably tramped Wales in search of the great body of poetry buried in medieval manuscripts, was undertaken with the encouragement both of those greatest of patrons of Welsh scholarship, the London–Welsh Morris brothers, who were natives of Anglesey, and of English poets and scholars, including Thomas Gray and Thomas Percy. His historic volume *Some Specimens of the Poetry of the Antient Bards* (1764) was, as Prys Morgan has pointed out, 'in part a book for the English market'.[10] Accordingly, the contribution of Evans's English versions of early Welsh poetry to the development of late eighteenth-century Celticism has already been thoroughly examined by literary historians.[11] His English texts, however, remain to be closely studied both in themselves and in the context of our new understanding of the way a British ideology was being constructed during this period, the equivocating Welsh response to which was typified by Evans's translations.[12] There was on the one hand the reassertion, in defiance of English prejudice, of a pride in Welsh history and culture, resulting in a carefully depoliticized cultural nationalism. When Lewis Morris and Evans first unearthed the manuscript of the *Gododdin*, the former rejoiced that here at last old Wales had an epic to rival *Paradise Lost* (as well as the *Iliad* and the *Aeneid).*[13] Altogether more pointed, though, was the maverick, mythopoeic introduction provided, probably by Iolo Morganwg, to William Owen Pughe's edition of *The Heroic Elegies and other poems of Llywarch Hen* (1792).[14] Yet, exercises in nation-building though these works consciously were, hidden in such scholarly researches was a commitment to contributionism: in other words, a dutiful emphasis on what Wales could offer Britain.[15]

The bipartisan ideology underpinning Evans's translations, and inscribed therein, has been the dominant ideology of Welsh–English translation virtually ever since. It is evident in John Humffreys Parry's *The Cambro-Briton and General Celtic Repository* (1819–22), as well as in *The Cambrian Register* (1795,

1796, 1818) edited by William Owen Pughe, who was at the same time attempting to demonstrate, in keeping with the wilder fancies of late seventeenth- and eighteenth-century philology, that Welsh (unlike mongrel English) was a pure vernacular directly descended from the ur-language of humankind.[16] During the nineteenth century, this kind of theory of language became unpleasantly entangled with the influential, and unsavoury, pseudo-scientific practice of classifying nations, and cultures, according to racial (and racist) stereotypes. In this context the supposed 'Celticism' of the Welsh was evaluated in highly ambiguous terms, as appears in the introduction by John Jenkins to his *The Poetry of Wales* (1873). The volume, he explained, was produced at the explicit prompting of English friends, who desired to be better acquainted with the literature of 'the aborigines of this country, with whom we have so much in common'.[17]

Jenkins's version of Welsh literary history is a fascinating period piece, replete with cloyingly loyal British sentiments: 'Within living memory royalty has graced this national gathering of the ancient British race [the Eisteddfod]' (13). In short, the book is very much a product of a period so well described by Hywel Teifi Edwards and other scholars; the period following the publication of the noxious Blue Books Report on the moral state of the nation, when Wales's anxiety about its perceived cultural backwardness found obsessive expression in the promoting of itself as a musical nation;[18] the period when Matthew Arnold was willing to admire Welsh literary culture strictly on condition that it regard itself as a merely antiquarian phenomenon, to be investigated by the scholars who would occupy the proposed Oxford Chair in Celtic Studies; the period when Arnold sidelined the Welsh by praising them as too sensitive ('Celtic') for the harsh modern world of science and power politics;[19] and the period when the Welsh were becoming increasingly anxious to dissociate themselves both from their own reputation as trouble-makers (the Merthyr Rising, the Rebecca Riots, Chartism, a turbulent industrial proletariat) and from the violent nationalist extremism of their fellow-Celts in Fenian Ireland. All these factors are clearly inscribed in Jenkins's book of translation, evidenced alike in the choice of contents, in the conciliatory (not to say ingratiating) style of the preface, in the politely anglicized translations (by various hands) – a fine example of translation as 'the mimicry of the dominant discourse [i.e. the discourse of the colonizer]' (*THC*, 6) – in the internal patterning (or Victorian packaging) of the volume ('the sublime', 'the beautiful', 'the patriotic', 'the sentimental', etc.) and in Jenkins's own ineffable comments. 'While the English crowded to look at the horse race or prize fight', he writes in Arnoldian vein, 'the Cymry met peaceably in the recesses of their beautiful valleys and mountains to rehearse the praises of religion and virtue' (14). This is not the last time that Welsh literature in translation will be offered to English readers as a tasteful refuge from vulgar English mass culture – an offer that will duly influence both the style of translation and the selection of materials. And the racist tinge of such comments is confirmed by Jenkins's claim, following Owen Pughe: 'The Cymric is unquestionably an original language, and possesses a force and expression entirely unknown to any of the derivative tongues' (16). Such a theory conveniently helped strengthen the myth, growing in importance at that very time, of the Welsh as a uniquely religious people that enjoyed a special affinity with the godly 'patriarchs' of the Bible. It is fair to add, however, that in advancing such outrageous racial myths Jenkins was only getting his retaliation in first. At that time the most influential racial theories, developed to reflect and legitimize the imperial power structures of the day, condescendingly viewed the Celts as primitives – a term that ever since the Romantic period had carried a deeply ambiguous charge.[20]

The anxious Britophilia of the Welsh was nowhere more evident than in the National Eisteddfod of Wales – at that time an institution that was proudly Anglophile – which for many decades included a translation from Welsh into English in its programme of competitions.[21] The context for such an arrangement is best exposed in the poem chosen for the English-Welsh translation competition by the Committee of the 1912 Eisteddfod, which was held at Wrexham. It was William Watson's nauseating 'Wales: A Greeting', a poem that began with a stanza praising the Welsh as 'A people caring for old dreams and deeds,/ Heroic story, and far-descended song', before turning in the second stanza to the real meat of the message. The Welsh, it trumpets, are so wedded to the English that they

Will feel no separate heartbeats from our own,
Nor aught but oneness with this mighty Power,
This Empire, that despite her faults and sins
Loves justice, and loves mercy, and loves truth,
When truly she beholds them; and who thus
Helps to speed on, through dark and difficult ways,
The ever-climbing footsteps of the world.[22]

It exults that the staunch Welsh will ever be devotedly at the side of the English, however fierce the storm. These were the sentiments that helped send Welsh youngsters in such horrifying numbers to the trenches two years later; and it was William Watson who, in 1918, acted as National Eisteddfod adjudicator of the best English-language poem written in praise of the contribution made by Welsh soldiers to the war effort.[23]

The antiquarian and scholarly approach to Welsh literature which had first given rise to Welsh–English translation (and to which Arnold had simply given a sinister new political inflexion) was exemplified at the turn of the century by the work of A. P. Graves, Robert Graves's father.[24] But at much the same time H. Idris Bell, himself a distinguished scholar, deliberately set out to introduce English readers to a Welsh poetry that was vigorously contemporary in spirit and in idiom. In his introduction to *Poems from the Welsh* (1913) Bell 'insisted . . . that the poetry of today is part of a long development, and is neither, on the one hand, the mere relic of an expiring tradition, nor, on the other, an antiquarian revival'.[25] He accordingly paid particular attention to the work of the new, university-educated, poets whose work was appearing at that very time, and he consciously presented his work as evidence – not only for the English but for the Welsh themselves, who had for a generation been persuaded otherwise – that, far from being outmoded and moribund, the Welsh language was capable of sustaining a literature of real modernity, the product of 'a distinctive culture which, in these days of colourless cosmopolitanism, is of inestimable value' (*PW*, Intro.). Bell, therefore, deliberately conceived of his translations as a riposte to the Anglocentric and imperialist Arnoldian version of British contributionism.

Bell's second volume, *Welsh Poems of the Twentieth Century* (1925) was an even more important publication, and continues to seem an impressive demonstration of how abreast he was of the most excitingly innovative developments in contemporary Welsh culture.[26] Bell showed, in his ground-breaking introductory essay on 'The Development of Welsh Poetry', how completely this poetry gave the lie to the Arnoldian concept of the 'natural magic' of Celtic poetry, a concept that in Victorian England had proved as tenacious as it was pernicious, thanks in part to its appeal to writers from Tennyson and the Pre-Raphaelities to those of the Celtic Twilight generation. Realizing that there was a negative gender ascription hidden in such a concept ('the feminine delicacy' of Celtic genius), Bell countered by emphasizing the 'virility' of the new Welsh poetry, and did so partly by featuring the manly Welsh poems of the First World War. Bell also demonstrated to advantage his sound and sensible, if rudimentary, grasp of the distinctive kinds of social structure produced by Welsh history. Rather than explain Welsh melancholy by reference to dubious theories of racial character, it was better, he suggested, to recall the condition of chronic uncertainty in which the impoverished mass of Welsh people had actually lived. And he ended by inviting his readers, both English and Welsh, to find in his translations evidence of a refinement in modern Welsh culture that was absent from an English culture which was becoming rapidly vulgarized by 'the language of the *Daily Mail* . . . the faded inanities of the London music-halls . . . the brainless, heartless, hopeless vanity of English suburbia' (*WPEV*, 139). At this point, Bell's introduction inadvertently reminds us of its contemporaneity with Eliot's anti-populist *The Waste Land*, and his translations suddenly appear to be part of that reaction by Modernist English writers and intellectuals against mass democratic society that John Carey has anatomized and anathematized.[27] The anti-industrialism of Saunders Lewis was an instance of the same phenomenon, and Bell's account of Welsh literature and society, published the year previous to the Great Strike of 1926, is itself notable for lacking any reference to Welsh industrial society. To notice such things is to realize how often translation from the Welsh has, during this century, carried within it a hidden ideological agenda; how it has tacitly constituted a conservative critique of contemporary English (or American) society.

Translation may usefully be considered as an attempt to mediate one culture to another, and Welsh–English translation has involved several interesting strategies in this regard. Bell's introduction to *Poems from the Welsh*, for instance, includes a dedicatory poem 'To Winifred', who thus comes to personify the imagined (or 'constructed') English reader and acts as a kind of muse of the translator's poetry of mediation. Bell also advertises the fact that he is an Englishman who learnt Welsh as an adult, thus clearly establishing his credentials as a go-between in terms with which an English readership, as well as a Welsh-speaking one, could identify.

This dual function of Welsh–English translation (as needing to carry conviction with bilingual Welsh writers and readers while reassuringly speaking the language of monoglot English readers) becomes particularly evident when the two functions become clearly distinguished. Thus, in the 1946 collection of Kate Roberts stories published under the title *A Summer Day*, the names of the actual translators (Dafydd Jenkins, Walter Dowding and Wyn Griffith) are only modestly recorded.[28] What is featured instead is the Introduction by Storm Jameson, who was at that time a respected and high-profile popular author. In this sympathetic essay Roberts is presented as a product of a foreign culture, which Jameson vividly renders by sketches of the Welsh social and physical landscape. Her spinal argument is that 'Wales is easy to reach and not easy to know . . . inland, in the valleys, especially of the north, we are in Wales, that is, abroad . . . In the end it is better to admit that here, sharing with us a small island, is a country as alien as Slovakia' (*SD*, 7, 9).

In responding in this way, Jameson was very much speaking for and from the England of that particular time. 'For six years', she remarks in her opening sentence, 'English people in love with a foreign country have been growling in their cage. I do not know how many of these have discovered that we have a land frontier with a foreign country, to be approached with the curiosity and humility proper to travellers abroad' (*SD*, 7). For six years, the Continent had been out of bounds to the English, who instead found both a wartime refuge and the best available substitute for exotic experience in neighbouring Wales. During the war, Wales became suddenly and briefly attractive, not least to the bevy of writers and artists, many with neo-Romantic tendencies, who congregated in west and north Wales for this brief period. Jameson's comment reminds us of such as Dylan Thomas,

Keidrych Rhys, Lynette Roberts, Ceri Richards, Graham Sutherland, John Minton and John Craxton, and of the temporary glamorizing of Wales and its writers at this time by wartime English periodicals, notably Cyril Connolly's *Horizon*.[29] And in reminding us of this, Jameson also reminds us of more: of how important it is when considering a translation to consider its precise historical moment, to identify the social, political, cultural and economic circumstances of its production. After all, Jameson's preface is also, self-evidently, the kind of marketing ploy to which Welsh–English translation must resort, when it is not benefiting from state subsidy.

The timing of a translation carries with it complex implications entailing not just marketing considerations, but a whole 'reading' of both the source and the target culture. Such an assessment can directly affect the choice of author, the choice of material by that author, the terms in which the translation is packaged, even the terms in which a translation is actually written. The post-war period that saw the appearance of *A Summer Day* also encouraged the production of other Welsh–English translations. In publishing *The Gorse Glen* (1948), a translation of *Cwm Eithin*, Hugh Evans's delicately nostalgic recollections of life in a disappeared rural culture, E. Morgan Humphreys was clearly appealing to post-war English longings for lost stabilities.[30] T. Rowland Hughes's *O Law i Law* (*From Hand to Hand*) is a novel in which the main character relives and reconstitutes a vanished, communal past as he is forced to dispose, one by one, of all the objects from his beloved family home. When it appeared in a 1950 English translation by Richard Ruck, the novel was obviously calculated, by its London publisher, to appeal to an English generation that had suffered the loss of homes and known the shattering of pre-war certainties. Significantly, it was the only one of Hughes's novels – all of which were to be translated by Ruck over the following decades – to 'enjoy' a London publisher.[31] In due course, London did, though, venture to sponsor another translation by Ruck. In the aftermath of the *Lady Chatterley's Lover* trials, during the heady days of the sexually liberated 1960s, John Rowlands's mildly explicit novel *Ieuenctid yw 'Mhechod* (*Youth is my Sin*), was strangely marketed under the markedly less titillating title *A Taste of Apples*.[32]

The Rowlands novel was a rare example of an attempt to image

Wales, through translation, in other than staid, not to say conservative, terms. Jameson's comments on Kate Roberts's stories are memorable and intermittently striking, but, for her, part of the appeal of their world is that it is full of 'the presence of a living culture which is not that of the elsewhere triumphant machine age' (*SD*, 7–8). Welsh translators readily connived at reinforcing this impression. A celebrated case is that of the translation by Waldo Williams of D. J. Williams's notably idyllic memoir of turn-of-the-century life in rural west Wales, *Hen Dŷ Ffarm*. Waldo's *The Old Farmhouse* (1961) was the work commissioned as 'the sixth in the series of translations published under the auspices of the Council of Europe in order to make available to a wider public literary masterpieces written in the lesser-known European languages'.[33] Waldo fervently identified with the rural communitarianism that was so persuasively advocated in *Hen Dŷ Ffarm* by means of a humorously affectionate portrait of the *gwerin*/folk. And *The Old Farmhouse* is thus significant as an instance of how a major poet (and Waldo was unquestionably that) could find in translation a rich, alternative means of advancing his own particular vision. But it is also significant as an instance of how translation can be used to promote a specific ideology. When Sir Ben Bowen Thomas chose this memoir to represent Wales to Europe, not only was he thereby choosing to image 'Welsh' Wales in a highly selective (and, of course, dated) manner; he was also implicitly offering war-ravaged Europe a particular kind of image of itself as a Europe of the traditional, rural peoples.

This choice of text was consistent with the view, already noted as being influential and persistent in Welsh–English translation, of Welsh-language culture as a kind of counter-culture offering an 'alternative' to modern mass, consumer society. That this view is still current appears from a recent selection of Euros Bowen's poetry, translated both by the author himself and by Cynthia Saunders Davies. In his Foreword to the volume, Rowan Williams, the bishop of Monmouth, argues: 'All of the major poets of twentieth-century Wales . . . have been deeply preoccupied with Christian themes.' And in the Introduction, Canon A. M. Allchin places Bowen's poetry in the context of current interests in ecology, creation-centred spirituality, and Celtic spirituality.[34]

A very different 'sales pitch' for translations from the Welsh was offered by Emlyn Williams back in 1950. He had been invited to contribute an 'Introduction' to Ruck's *From Hand to Hand,* and he did so *con brio.* Indeed, his colourful manner of approach is such as to provoke reflections on the nature of both 'Introduction' and 'translation', and on the relation between the two. In one sense, Williams seems almost to parody the convention, formerly observed in polite English society, that a person should not be properly acknowledged until (s)he had been 'introduced.' In other words, Williams elaborately 'vouches' for the author, T. Rowland Hughes, and does so in a way that seems implicitly to mock traditional English suspicion of the rather forward Welsh. But at the same time Williams exploits his own reputation as an actor of famously histrionic tendencies to 'introduce' Hughes in much the same way as performers used to be 'introduced', or 'featured', in old-time theatre and music-hall. By thus framing the translation within the verbal equivalent of the proscenium arch, Williams implies that *From Hand to Hand* is a performance guaranteed to provide top-class entertainment. Implicit here is the reputation of the Welsh for being theatrical, a reputation mainly associated, in 1950, with Anglicized industrial south Wales, but which Emlyn Williams deliberately claims for the Welsh-language culture of the west and, of course, his native north.

In fact, in his Foreword Williams repeatedly attacks Anglo-Welsh literature as a sham, contrasting it with the authentic representation of contemporary Wales to be found in Hughes's Welsh-language novel. Williams's phrasing is such as to suggest that he has in mind a number of different Anglo-Welsh targets, including the enormously popular *How Green Was My Valley* of Richard Llewellyn, the colourful industrial romances of Jack Jones, and the 'self-consciously psychological probings by earnest young moderns who are neither Welsh, English, nor anything else, but the rag-doll offspring of Tchekov and D. H. Lawrence' (*FHH,* Foreword; no pagination).

Williams's outburst is a reminder of how complex and emotionally charged a part Welsh–English translation has played in the development of relations between the two linguistic cultures of Wales in the present century. This is in fact a subject that could scarcely be exhausted in a book-length study, but it may be considered here only briefly.

*   *   *   *

Although Welsh–English translation was originally, as has been shown, an aspect of Wales's relationship to England, it eventually developed into an aspect of Wales's relationship to itself. During the last third of the nineteenth century, the massive industrialization of south Wales resulted in an ethnically mixed population that found its *lingua franca* in English. And as that population was gradually consolidated into an anglophone culture that was nevertheless in significant respects Welsh, so too English became a Welsh language that threatened to replace the Welsh language itself. Under such circumstances, it is not surprising that one of the earliest instances of Welsh–English literary translation specifically intended for the monoglot English population of Wales is provided by the educational system that was, by the turn of the century, cautiously attempting to weld the new anglophone culture of coalfield society to the traditional Welsh-language culture of the rural west and north. The establishing of a separate Welsh Board of Education in 1907 assisted this work.

Cambrian Lyrics for the Use of Schools belonged to the series of New Historical Readers for Welsh Schools, also known as the Anglo-Welsh Historical Series. The selection of poems, mostly by such nineteenth-century worthies as Alun, Ceiriog, and Eifion Wyn, who were the idols of Welsh Victorian Nonconformity, was prefaced by the editor's remarks. 'This small collection', he explained,

> is dedicated to 'Young Wales'. While it provides for the needs of Welsh boys and girls, at the same time it caters for the 'strangers within our gates'. Welsh history teaches us that the young Normans who established themselves in the fertile plains of Gwent and Morgannwg nearly nine hundred years ago grew up in their adopted country to be more patriotic than the natives themselves, and in manhood became the lovers and liberal patrons of Welsh literature.[35]

Intended, then, as an instrument of cultural assimilation, the selection, with its emphasis on the sentimental pieties of a rural culture, was unfortunately all too evidently the product of a society remote from that of the industrial valleys. Moreover, the selection was redolent of that Liberal Wales whose political hegemony an increasingly unionized coalfield proletariat was at that very time militantly challenging. A few years later, and with that Liberal ascendancy now well and truly defeated in anglophone industrial Wales, the Liberal MP Francis Edwards brought out his own privately printed book of translations from the Welsh, again featuring the likes of Ceiriog, Islwyn, Eifion Wyn, Elfed, and John Morris-Jones. Taking their defiant, yet ultimately elegiac, epitaph from Ceiriog's sentimental dirge 'Alun Mabon' (*Y mae'r heniaith yn y Tir/ A'r Alawon hen yn fyw*: 'the old tongue persists in the land/ And the old melodies yet live on'), Edwards's genteel translations sound like the English swan-song of a dying Welsh cultural and political breed.[36]

The *Cambrian Lyrics*'s programme of cultural integration (and, implicitly, of political *rapprochement* between residual Liberal and emergent Labour Wales) was vigorously carried forward by *The Welsh Outlook*, the important monthly journal established in 1914. From the beginning, its attempt to promote a bicultural Wales involved both the publication of Welsh-language poetry (the whole of T. Gwynn Jones's *awdl* 'Tir na n-Óg' was printed in the March 1916 issue) and the occasional inclusion of Welsh–English translations.[37] A similar cross-cultural sympathy was manifest in A. G. Prys-Jones's anthology of *Welsh Poets*, published in 1917.[38] However, the bitter power struggle between the two politico-cultural factions had already found explosive expression in Caradoc Evans's collection of short stories *My People* (1915).[39] Evans's inspired caricature of a morally verminous Welsh-speaking society in the rural, pious west resulted in a rupture between 'Welsh' and 'Anglo-Welsh' literary culture that lasted for more than a quarter of a century. The situation was worsened by the turn towards centralist Socialism taken by many of the inter-war generation of Anglo-Welsh writers even as their Welsh-language contemporaries were being attracted away from British Unionism towards a Plaid Cymru that advocated a sharply politicized form of cultural nationalism at the core of which lay a militant commitment to the Welsh language. An Englishman such as Idris Bell could, of course, rush into this situation where natives understandably feared to tread. Hence, in part, his domination of Welsh–English translation during a period when the inactivity of the Welsh themselves in this field was highly indicative of the tense state of cultural affairs.[40]

As has been suggested in Chapter 3, the situation improved in the late 1930s, when a number of young Welsh-language writers (e.g. Alun Llywelyn-Williams, Pennar Davies, Aneirin Talfan Davies), themselves of urban-industrial background, formed a kind of common front with some members of the new, high-profile, 'Dylan Thomas' generation of the Anglo-Welsh. They were joined in an enthusiasm for avant-garde Modernist writing and in revolt against both the London and the conservative Welsh-language establishment. Keidrych Rhys, who acted as the movement's unofficial impresario, accommodated several Welsh-language poems in his provocative journal of innovative writing, *Wales*. At the same time Gwyn Jones, editor of the more sober *Welsh Review*, adopted an English-only rule for this rival journal while advertising its solidarity with Welsh-language culture by printing samples of its literature in English translation. Jones, himself a noted short-story writer, may well have been the first to encourage translations of that genre. Examples of the work of Kate Roberts and E. Tegla Davies appeared in the *Welsh Review*, as well as folk verses (*penillion*), epigrammatic *englynion*, and strict-metre poetry (translated by Gwyn Williams and by the Bells, father and son).[41]

In thus consistently printing translations from the Welsh along-side important new work in English, Gwyn Jones was doing more than simply establishing new editorial practice or devising a new kind of literary journal. He was in effect hazarding a new, inclusive vision of Wales as a bilingual, bicultural, nation – a vision embodied in the magnificent translation of the *Mabinogion* (1948; Everyman, 1949) jointly prepared by Thomas Jones and himself.[42] Thomas Jones was Professor of Welsh at University College, Aberystwyth, where Gwyn Jones was Professor of English. But if, thanks to his pioneering example, the literary journal was shown to be a genre hospitable to such a vision, then over the following decades it was the anthology that came to perform the same significant office. From D. Myrddin Lloyd's *A Book of Wales* (1953) to Meic Stephens's book of the same title (1987), and to James A. Davies's *The Heart of Wales* (1994), the anthology acted as a means of constructing a unified view of a deeply divided nation by including substantial material trans-lated from the Welsh.[43] Equally significant were anthologies that effectively challenged ruling assumptions about the cultural character of a particular location. So, for instance, the bicultural character of experience in industrial south Wales was demonstrated, against the grain of the politically biased assumption that life there was an English-language preserve, in the *Valleys* anthology edited by John Davies and Mike Jenkins (1984). Meic Stephens's Cardiff anthology revealed the unexpectedly rich Welsh-language life of Dannie Abse's city, and James A. Davies's anthology of Swansea underlined the fact that it had long been the site of cultural exchange with its Welsh-speaking industrial hinterland.[44]

Beginning with the Faber selection of 1937, the many anthologies of Welsh short stories performed the same integrating function as the general anthologies, and their editorial introductions afforded such staunchly Anglophile writers as Alun Richards a rare opportunity of relating to Welsh-language literature on terms that seemed to them reassuringly fair. Particularly even-handed – and as such a notable contribution to the development of an appropriately inclusive discourse of nationhood – was Gwyn Jones's introduction to the 1971 Oxford University Press volume of *Twenty-Five Welsh Short Stories* that he coedited with the Welsh-language author Islwyn Ffowc Elis. The editors specifically regarded theirs as remedial work in the culture. Reviewing the space allowed to translated work in the five previous anthologies of Welsh short stories, Jones justifiably claimed his and Elis's to be the first fully to represent the bicultural character of Wales. He tellingly added that the deficiencies of previous editions in this respect reflected not only 'the strain and misunderstanding' that had bedevilled relations between the two literatures, but also the relative paucity of Welsh-language fiction available in translation.[45]

Jones's remarks highlight other important features of any translation situation, including the fact that, by and large, poetry takes less time and effort to translate than fiction (a significant factor wherever there is an absence of a professionalized culture of translation), and the dependence of any ambitious translation programme on a supportive, and best of all sponsoring, social, economic and political substructure. The latter appeared in Wales only in the 1960s, as a direct result of a politically inspired shift in ideological outlook, to which translation had contributed, in which it participated, and from which it benefited – as Gwyn

Jones indicated in thanking the recently established (1967) Welsh Arts Council Literature Department for grants towards the commissioning of new translations for *Twenty-Five Welsh Short Stories*.

That complex 1960s phenomenon, to which such inadequate yet useful labels as 'a national rewakening' and 'the second flowering' have been attached, radically changed both the practical and the ideological conditions under which Welsh–English translation had been produced. Something of the longer-term consequences became apparent in Gwyn Jones's 1977 volume, *The Oxford Book of Welsh Verse in English*, a publication of multiple significance.[46] Jones found that alongside the work of a long-standing tradition of older, 'pioneering' translations, there existed a body of more recent work on which he could profitably draw. As Anglo-Welsh writer, editor, academic, and influential manager of key cultural institutions, Jones had himself been one of those who had variously helped engineer such developments, not least by creating an enabling institutional structure. And as credulous intellectuals supposed at the time that Wales was preparing to embrace such limited self-determination as was on offer in the 1979 Devolution proposals, Jones's volume used translation as a means of signifying mutual commitment by Wales's two linguistic communities to a new, culturally inclusive and mutually appreciative sense of common nationhood. In the event, the rejection of Devolution in the 1979 referendum signified a rejection of 'translation', in this broader sense, and a reaffirmation of the apartheid policy of separate development (effectively ghettoization) of the two linguistic cultures.

Writers upon whose translations Jones drew very heavily in compiling his anthology included Gwyn Williams and Tony Conran, two important translators who may conveniently be taken to represent the difference in style and social orientation between two different decades. Published by Editions Poetry London in 1950, Williams's *The Rent That's Due to Love* was a striking new departure in the mode of translating traditional Welsh poetry. In his attractive Introduction, Williams emphasized two things: that his was a strictly personal selection, exemplifying in part a reaction against 'the religious blight' that had afflicted Welsh culture since the eighteenth-century Methodist revival; and that, in addition, his anthology was a response to contemporary English interest in Anglo-Welsh literature:

> Welshmen in English have recently attracted a good deal of attention and their work is generally felt to be different from that of English writers. In these translations I may have done something to indicate the nature of a vast body of poetry which, whether they are aware of it or not, embodies the source upon which they draw.[47]

His comments are an important reminder of the many 'invisible' contexts that inescapably determine the production and reception of Welsh–English translation. For instance, there is the 'internal politics' of the relationship – sometimes resembling a civil war – between the two modern Welsh cultures to be considered; and there is also the external consideration of how at any given time England 'perceives' Wales – a perception that, in the literary realm, may be significantly influenced by the current standing in England of Anglo-Welsh literature.

In 1966 Gwyn Williams followed his pioneering 1950 volume with the important anthology of translations from classic strictmetre Welsh poetry, *The Burning Tree*; and in between he produced *Presenting Welsh Poetry* (1959), a collection of translations, by various hands, of Welsh poetry from the sixth century to the twentieth.[48] He persuaded a distinguished public figure of the time, Sir Ben Bowen Thomas, to provide a suave and diplomatic Introduction, designed to conciliate Welsh and English readers alike. Acknowledging that 'some Welshmen will not like to see English translations' (*PWP*, 5–6), Thomas went on to characterize the book as the product of an age of worldwide *rapprochement*. 'On the world scale, UNESCO is now urging its Member States to busy themselves with a major project for the appreciation of the cultural values of East and West' (*PWP*, 6), Thomas reminded readers, before wittily adding: 'In a sense this anthology is a kind of minor project within the United Kingdom, designed to help the majority to know something of the poetry of the minority in the West, who for generations have enjoyed the freedom of the East' (*PWP*, 6). In his own Introduction, Williams too concentrated on the prospects for cross-cultural reconciliation, but this time in a sense specific to Wales, when he noted that 'with the present tendency, and this is new in the history of the country, to parallel development in life, thought and education in the two languages, it is possible to foresee a growing together in the nature of Welsh writing in English and in Welsh' (*PWP*, 15).

Whereas Williams's entrepreneurial work was buccaneering in spirit, the calculatedly engaging products of a period when market-orientated Welsh–English translators had to chart their own risky course, that of Tony Conran, almost a decade later, was somewhat different. Published in 1967, *The Penguin Book of Welsh Verse* was prefaced by a brilliant survey of Welsh-language poetry, a dense and lengthy essay that began as uncompromisingly as it meant to continue: 'In the first instance I think it is wiser to treat Welsh poetry as something *sui generis*, a product of a civilization alien to our own. Otherwise, you may find in Old Welsh a somewhat bloodless version of Anglo-Saxon'.[49] Encoded in this assertion, as Conran pointed out almost twenty years later in his Preface to the second, augmented edition, published as *Welsh Verse*, were three of his main aims as translator: 'First, the political. My English-speaking countrymen in Wales were being treated as if they were immigrants in their own country, potential Englishmen and women' (*WV*, 13). Secondly, Conran wanted to make Welsh-language materials poetically available to the English-language poets of Wales: 'Culturally, therefore, I hoped my book would accomplish for us something of what the great translators from Irish . . . did for the Irish renaissance' (*WV*, 14). And, thirdly, he wanted to alert Anglo-Welsh poets to the fact that, as the Welsh-language poetic tradition showed, Welshness was not a matter of subject-matter or style but, rather, 'a matter of what poetry is expected to do'. Unlike English poetry, Welsh poetry, so Conran argued, 'gives one a criterion of whole speaking, of making poetry as a private person, a social being and an objective observer – all at once' (*WV*, 16).

To the extent that these assumptions were the genetic code, as it were, determining the growth of all his translations, Conran's incomparable volume constituted a radical comment on the social character of his time. As such it belonged to a distinguished tradition of translation as cultural critique – think, for instance, of Pound's use of *Homage to Sextus Propertius* as an instrument for attacking the militarist imperialism of his own period. Conran's

targets included the individualist spirit of 1960s England, manifested not only in the popular and consumer cultures of the day
but equally in the styles of poetry favoured by Larkin and his
acolytes and epigones. The obverse of this was that Conran's
work also implicitly endorsed the various forms of collective
action on behalf of Welsh cultural separatism that energized the
1960s. This ranged from the extensive civil disobedience
campaigns of Cymdeithas yr Iaith Gymraeg (the Welsh Language
Society), to the political movements opposing first the drowning
of Cwm Celyn, in the early 1960s, and then the Investiture of the
Prince of Wales at the end of the decade. And a natural accom-
paniment to these organized protests was the poems-and-pints
sessions designed to mobilize the political will of the Welsh
people.

Harri Webb, a conspicuous contributor of lively agitprop
pieces to such events, whose work was discussed in chapter 2,
would occasionally use translation as a telling weapon in his political armoury. His 'The Woods of Cynon' is a splendid rendering
of a seventeenth-century Welsh poem cursing the English iron-
masters for felling the forest.[50] Poets such as R. S. Thomas and
Emyr Humphreys had already deliberately included translations
in their work, partly to signify their solidarity with the political
nationalism and the cultural militancy of Welsh-language poets
of the generation that looked to Saunders Lewis, and Plaid
Cymru, for leadership.[51] Webb, however, used translation in a
less symbolic and more practical fashion, so that the immediacy
of his politically activist approach complemented Conran's
contrasting programme of using translation to effect a gradual
alteration of the deep structure of Welsh consciousness.

Recognizing in such practices a political agenda to which they
were unsympathetic, if not downright hostile, other Anglo-Welsh
writers of the 1960s intermittently used translation for other
purposes, sometimes implying a counter-politics. John Ormond's
free adaptation *The Hall of Cynddylan* is really an instance of a
modern elegiac poet finding in Llywarch Hen's ninth-century
poem a lament for all social decay, including the decay of the
largely Anglicized south Wales industrial society of which
Ormond was a native, and whose passing he bitterly regretted.[52]
The liberties that Leslie Norris took in his poem 'The Dead',
after Gwenallt's celebrated 'Y Meirwon', are especially revealing.

For Gwenallt's insistence on the iron ropes that hold a middle-aged man fast to the particular people and specific place that had moulded him, Norris, characteristically shying away from what he would feel to be the nationalist chauvinism incipient in the original, substitutes sentiments which are altogether more diffuse:

> Reaching fifty, a man has time to recognize
> His ordinary humanity, the common echoes
> In his own voice.[53]

Norris's emollient version contrasts with the edgy harshness that makes Gwenallt's poem so electrifying, and that alteration of tone through translation was also an implicit political statement, since Norris particularly objected to the uncompromising combativeness of Welsh nationalist politics in the 1960s. His alternative discourse of civility is again clearly to be heard in the concluding lines of his translation. Gwenallt's poem of fierce indignation closes by turning away from the unconvincing abstractions of socialism's vaguely internationalist utopia (literally, of course, no-place) and reaffirming identity with 'family and neighbourhood, man's sacrifice and suffering'. The lines implicitly root *his* internationalism in the specifics, and *in extremis*, of his Welsh experience. Norris, instead, eliminates that contrast, and speaks at the end 'as one who knows/ Nothing certain, nothing; unless it is/ My own small place and people, agony and sacrifice'. A modest localism, which in more than one sense 'knows its place', has been substituted for Gwenallt's ringing endorsement of national localities. And this conversation carried on by translation between two poets with contrasting politics is further complicated by the fact that Norris was a native of that industrial Merthyr (from the Welsh for 'martyr') which memorably enters Gwenallt's poem as the place from which those neighbours of his came in whose hacking silicotic coughs, shooting over the garden hedge, he had first heard the harrowing accents of his society's suffering. Norris's reworking of 'Y Meirwon', therefore, consists partly of rewriting it in his own version of the Merthyr accent, as it were. By moderating its tone and stance, and by omitting its concluding disillusionment with the kind of radical socialist politics for which Merthyr was famous, Norris aimed to make of

'Y Meirwon' a poem, now shorn of the militant version of Welshness he found so disturbing in the 1960s, that could speak for a whole wide world of suffering, whether it be in the Swansea Valley, the south Wales valleys, or wherever.

Alongside his Gwenallt translation, Norris also produced versions of several of Dafydd ap Gwilym's poems, partly as exercises instancing the importance for him as an anglophone Welsh poet of the subtle modulations and violent dynamics of sound in which *cynghanedd* (strict-metre) poetry had its very being. Norris's friend and fellow-Merthyrite, Glyn Jones, had been fascinated by the same phenomenon as early as the 1930s, when, as was implied in the preceding chapter, he discovered in medieval Welsh poetry a kind of Welsh Modernism *avant la lettre*. Deeply interested at that time in the European, as well as the Anglo-American, avant-garde, Jones – a friend of Dylan Thomas's – also had radical left-wing sympathies. And it was as a would-be mobilizer of the proletariat that he became fascinated by Welsh folk poetry, *hen benillion*: 'when I became ambitious to write poetry for the workers I began to use these as a sort of pasturage. I argued that this was the anonymous poetry of the workers of the past, produced and kept alive by the workers themselves, therefore the workers of today would welcome poetry written in the same tradition.'[54]

Jones retained, throughout his life, a fascination with the great poetry of the Welsh Middle Ages which had so excited him as a young man, and translation continued for him to be intimately connected to creation. In 1955 he collaborated with the Welsh scholar T. J. Morgan on a translation of *The Saga of Llywarch Hen*, the famous sequence of poems dealing, among other things, with the bleak experience of ageing;[55] and having himself entered his eighties, Jones adopted the persona of a latter-day Llywarch to voice an impassioned, clear-sighted lament for the grotesqueness of outliving one's physical and mental resources:

> Ach, I am old, bewildered.
> I hide my head.
> My cracked
> Brow looks high, my tall face towering
> Sheer as a cliff of beef. (*CP*, 127)

Jones's Shader, an ageing painter 'lament[ing] his age, like Llywarch Hen, as night comes on', is as uninhibited and unillusioned in his assessments of others as he is of himself:

> My helmet, high felt crown and narrow brim,
> Looks slimy, speckled as a thrush's skintight
> Troutskin chest, in shape, the iron millinery
> My ancestors, those military Celts, wore
> To protect their highly unstable brains.
>
> I am not nice, always lone – also false,
> My mind a ruin in a shirt of roses. (*CP*, 128)

As one who had in complex ways been raised uncomfortably straddling two languages, Glyn Jones obviously found in translation a means of expression, and indeed fulfilment, of an otherwise buried part of himself. And this imperative – of self-completion through self-discovery and self-realization – is one of the most important, and neglected, motives for translating. It was evidently a factor in the case of Idris Bell, an Englishman whose mother had been Welsh. For him, Welsh–English translation must have had a deeply personal, and perhaps largely unconscious, significance. It certainly chimed very resonantly with his own psycho-cultural situation.

T. S. Eliot, who had succinctly explored this dimension of translation in his introduction to Ezra Pound's *Selected Poems*, again phrased it pungently in conversation with Gwyn Williams about Welsh–English translation.[56] Any writer turning to a language other than his/her own, he explained, 'was exploring an aspect of himself which could not readily be reached, or perhaps could not exist, in the medium of his own language' (*PWP*, 13). A clear instance of this would be Joseph Clancy, who for three decades has been, along with Conran, the major translator of Welsh literature into English.[57] A New Yorker and a Catholic, Clancy has found in the literature of his adopted culture those very qualities – of religious faith, of peaceable nationalism, of a civil communitarianism – the lack of which he deplores in the contemporary culture of the United States. His writing of Welsh–English translation has therefore involved a 'reading' of both American and Welsh-language cultures, and to some extent both his style of translation and his selection of material have been influenced by his particular angle of approach. So, for instance, in introducing his excellent translations of Bobi Jones's poetry Clancy is able to draw his readers' attention to his subject's '"will to believe" . . . particularly to counter the will to believe that Wales is simply one region of England that has been turning possibility into actuality since the Act of Union in 1536, and especially in the present century.'[58]

Clancy may usefully be regarded as belonging to the distinguished modern American tradition of cultural migrants: that is, of American writers, many of them expatriate as Clancy now is, who refashioned themselves into Europeans or (frequently) into the most fervent of Britons. However, whereas such notables as Henry James and T. S. Eliot would deign to identify only with cultures they regarded as major and central, Clancy belongs to the dissenting branch of the tradition typified by the Pound who was passionate for obscure Provençal! This is a writer-translator lineage to which Clancy knowingly belongs, as he recently revealed:

> what I have been doing is typically, even traditionally, American. Longfellow translated Dante and used the verse-pattern of the Finnish *Kalevala* for his American Indian epic of *Hiawatha*, Ezra Pound translated and adapted Provençal and Chinese poetry, and since the 1950s it has been a very American thing to be a poet-translator, to understand, as a recent anthologist noted, 'translations of poetry from other languages . . . as an important part of [one's] own work'. Witness Horace Gregory, Robert Fitzgerald, Richard Wilbur, W. S. Merwin, Robert Bly, and others, including the Welsh-American Rolfe Humphries.[59]

The relationship of his translations to his 'original' work is as vital an aspect of Clancy's case as it is of Conran's: 'It let me discover and exercise other muscles, so to speak, enabled me to "breathe" differently in verse, and so provided a way of exploring and expressing other kinds of experience' (*TWTG*, 38).[60] Translation as a means to eventual self-realization as an 'original' artist has been a powerful incentive to many a writer, and in Clancy's case it seems to have an intimate bearing on his two outstanding features as a translator: namely, his quite extraordinary range, and his concern to balance his majestic 'overviews' of two millennia of Welsh poetic tradition with a devotion to

particular poets, whose individual work he has extensively represented in English.

A different kind of personal cultural transaction has, however,
been enacted by those Welsh–English translators who have been
natives of Wales. As early as 1896, Edmund O. Jones prefaced his
selection of *Welsh Lyrics of the Nineteenth Century* with a poetic
envoy representing his translations as cultural ambassadors,
mediators of his own culture to his mother's England. His dedicatory verse opens on a nervously jocular note, vibrant with the
tension at the core of Jones's being:

> They flout me as half-English – a disgrace
>   For which scarce all your virtues can atone,
> Mother, in whom I find no flaw but one,
> That you are Saxon! – but this fault of race
>   Fell not on me nor yet, I fear, your grace
>   Of English speech.[61]

As the short poem develops into a presentation of his (sadly
conventional) translations as an invitation to his mother to join
him in his 'native land', Jones in effect adopts an old convention
in Welsh culture, converting his translations into a *llatai*: that is,
a messenger (usually in the form of a bird) from lover to beloved.
Translation as *llatai*: the image is both poignant and potent in the
context of Welsh–English translation by natives. In this context,
translation can function as a means of producing a healing
psycho-cultural reintegration. An obvious case in point is that of
Tony Conran, who has reflected in prose and in poetry on his
own complex, 'hybrid' cultural parentage. For him, translation is
in part a means to fuller self-understanding, enabling him to
compound his self-definition.[62]

The same would be true of Ernest Rhys, a translator (or
perhaps adapter) of Welsh poetry, whom Conran himself has
acknowledged as an important precursor. Conran well understands how Rhys was one of the few, before David Jones, to intuit
the potential for an original Welsh anglophone poetry in the
ancient *barddas* which was the repository of the values of a
remarkable 'civilization'. 'He is', suggests Conran,' the only
Anglo-Welsh poet of his time who was conscious of the greatness
of his task, even if he failed to live up to it' (*FAWP*, 71). Hence,
in part, his genuinely creative, rather than merely antiquarian,

interest in rendering Welsh poetry into English. And, as Rhys himself was very aware, this kind of translation arose not from mere artistic opportunism, or dilettante interest, but from deep psychic need: 'Wales England wed, so I was bred', he famously wrote.[63] Born in Islington to a Welsh father and an English mother, he was raised in Carmarthen until he was six, when the family moved to Newcastle. In adult life he lived in Hampstead and divided his time between the fashionable London literary scene and the London Welsh society. His *Welsh Ballads* (1898), which contained many translations from the Welsh, was prefaced by a dedication where he actually signed himself ER/Rhys Goch Dyved. In it he consciously adopted the Celtic Twilight language of his day in referring to 'the sorrowful music of Llywarch Hen, or . . . the tune the wind sang to Taliesin'. But he simultaneously admitted that a Welsh-speaking reader of his work would 'hesitate and ask awkward questions'. In other words, Rhys was very aware of the problem of marrying the discourses of two such very different cultures.[64]

If 'Wales England wed' is the motto of Rhys's translations, then 'Wales-bred, England-educated' could have been adopted by R. Gerallt Jones as the epigraph for his *Poetry of Wales 1930–70* (1974). A bilingual text, with the English proffered as essentially a crib for those struggling to comprehend the original Welsh, the volume was intended to demonstrate the 'modernity' of a poetic culture still largely perceived by anglophone readers as conservative to the point of seeming antiquarian. But the volume was also produced by a Welsh-language writer with an established reputation for generous bicultural sympathies and for political non-alignment. Although raised on the Llŷn peninsula, and as such endowed with the richness of vernacular and culture characteristic of that most Welsh-speaking of localities, Jones had been sent away, at a relatively young age, to that most quintessentially English of institutions, Shrewsbury public school. The initial cultural trauma and the subsequent experience of successful adaptation played a formative role in Jones's development. Consequently, his volume may be seen as possessing a ritual, or symbolic, aspect: that is, as a kind of reversal of that journey to Shrewsbury, this time with Jones hospitably inviting the English language to adapt itself to the *mores* of a 'foreign' culture. But the scrupulously bilingual text seems to indicate the protocols that must then apply. Knowing, no doubt in part from bitter personal experience, how mismatched the two languages essentially are in terms of economic, political and cultural power, Jones constructs a bilingual text that signifies only mutual interest and peaceful coexistence. And translation representing itself as functional 'crib' (implying the culturally courteous subordination of English to Welsh in this context) is therefore the 'figure' appropriate for this kind of cultural exchange.[65]

*　*　*　*

Jones's volume was published 'with the support of the Welsh Arts Council', the familiar legend that has appeared on almost all the works of Welsh–English translation published over the last three decades. Such support, albeit reactive rather than proactive, has changed the whole pattern of publication in this field in incalculable ways, not least in that, for better or for worse, it has made mass (that is, English) market appeal a secondary consideration for the translators and publishers involved. So, for instance, when Penguin, the book's original, and of course commercial, publishers refused to reprint Conran's *Penguin Book of Welsh Verse*, it was reissued instead, in augmented form, by the Welsh Arts Council-sponsored Poetry Wales Press (later Seren Books). The reverse happened in the case of the translation by John Idris Jones of Kate Roberts's majestic novel *Traed Mewn Cyffion* (*Feet in Chains*).[66] Originally published by the Gomerian Press with the assistance of a Welsh Arts Council grant, it was snapped up by Corgi Books and marketed (in appropriately garish 'airport' covers) as a popular classic of mass appeal.

By the early 1990s, the advent of desktop publishing was beginning to revolutionize every aspect of book production. Dafydd Johnston's *Canu Maswedd yr Oesoedd Canol* (*Medieval Welsh Erotic Poetry*, 1991) was probably the first volume of Welsh–English translation to be produced partly by these means, and two years later the Welsh Arts Council subsidized the printing of its companion volume, *Galar y Beirdd* (*Poets' Grief*).[67] Johnston's enterprising volumes were also important in other respects. While in one way valuable additions to the distinguished twentieth-century tradition of scholarly editions of Welsh–English translations, these books also typified a new adventurous

141

spirit in such scholarship, resulting from the influence upon it of a whole range of new critical discourses, particularly those of feminist criticism and cultural studies.[68] Helen Fulton's *Dafydd ap Gwilym Apocrypha* (1997) was a scholarly bilingual text of a similarly unorthodox kind. It employed sceptical theories about the ideological nature of canon-formation and the construction of tradition to re-evaluate, and effectively deconstruct, Thomas Parry's 'definitive' 1952 edition of Dafydd ap Gwilym's poems.[69]

Dafydd Johnston is a Yorkshireman who not only transformed himself into a Welsh scholar of sufficient distinction to be appointed Professor of Welsh at University College, Swansea, but whose change of name (David – Dafydd), although never formally intended, signifies his re-baptism, as it were, as a Welshman. His translations are therefore obviously in part a complex manifestation of his elective bicultural character and dual nationality. And as such they are expressive, too, of the endlessly changing relationship of Welsh to English in the cultural kaleidoscope that is contemporary Wales. English 'immigrants' such as Johnston may become more inward with Wales, its language, history and culture than most of the natives. In turn, a significant number of the 'natives' themselves are bilingual in ways significantly different from any previous generation. They feel that English is their native tongue, and that it is as intimate a part of their very Welshness, indeed, as is the Welsh language itself. And, conversely, there are Welsh natives whose mother tongue is English but who feel that the Welsh language they speak only imperfectly, if at all, is nevertheless part of the very marrow of their being. Moreover, the profile of Welsh-language culture has been radically altered by such important post-war phenomena as the mass migration of Welsh-speakers from the traditional rural heartlands of the culture into a predominantly anglophone urban milieu. This move has been both cause and effect of the probably irreversible decline of a homogeneous, rural, overwhelmingly Welsh-speaking culture which has been partly offset by the growth of a different, 'networking' culture of Welsh-speakers living in the urban and previously Anglicized areas of the south. Such a development, accompanied by an explosion of bilingual schools partly catering for this new cultural 'constituency', but ever-increasingly serving to educate children from non-Welsh-speaking homes in the medium of Welsh, has revolutionized the language situation in Wales. Meanwhile, some anglophone immigrants into what were previously the heartlands of Welsh-language culture have admirably attempted to assimilate by learning Welsh or ensuring that their children do so. In such a fluid context, Welsh–English translation perforce takes on a radically different, not to say irreducibly complex, significance and character, reflecting the innumerable ways people are now positioned along and across the language lines.

The working-out of this cultural situation through translation activity is far too multifaceted to be considered here, save by concentrating on one indicative case. (Some of the ways in which this same situation is reflected in recent Welsh writing in English are considered, albeit in passing, in Chapters 2 and 7 of the present study, with reference to such writers as Oliver Reynolds, John Davies and Gwyneth Lewis.) Menna Elfyn's bilingual editions of her own poetry have attracted particular controversy in Welsh-language circles because she was a prominent member of Cymdeithas yr Iaith Gymraeg in previous decades, when her militant activism led to periods of imprisonment. In fact, though, her first volume, *Eucalyptus* (1995), was a continuation of a well-established practice, dating back to the early 1970s, for Welsh-language poets occasionally to venture to produce a bilingual volume. Euros Bowen's *Poems* (1974) and Gwyn Thomas's *Living a Life* (1982), which included translations by the author himself and by Joseph Clancy, were both examples of this; and *Living a Life*, published in the Netherlands, was also an experiment in using English as a language through which Welsh poetry might reach beyond England itself to a Continental readership.[70]

Nevertheless, Elfyn's *Eucalyptus* did remain different in certain respects, some of which reflected a change in the politics of language during the 1980s. The defeat of the Devolution proposals in 1979 revealed how riven, not least by language, the Welsh population still was. It emerged that the Welsh-language heartland of Gwynedd, which had routinely returned a Nationalist MP to Parliament, had voted even more heavily against the proposed Welsh Assembly than had the supposedly Anglicized and British Unionist valleys of south Wales. It became obvious that part of the reason for the widespread opposition to Devolution from both north and south was the opposition of north to south, and vice versa, due to the language divide. And since language was a key, if (ironically) unspoken, issue of the Devolution debate, it was appropriate that the most powerful expression by writers and intellectuals of their desolation at what appeared to them at the time to be a catastrophic decision was a unique work of 'translation'.

Cerddi Ianws Poems, jointly published by T. James Jones and Jon Dressel was a bilingual text which had also been jointly 'authored' by them.[71] Dressel, a Welsh American who divided his time between his native Saint Louis, Missouri, and Carmarthen in his ancestral Wales, sent his friend and colleague Jim Jones an English text fiercely elegizing the Devolution Bill. In response, Jones proceeded to produce, on the basis of Dressel's first draft, a corresponding Welsh-language text which in turn influenced Dressel's completion of the English poem. Hence the Janus face of the title, which identifies a crux specifically alluded to by Dressel in his Preface:

> To what extent the reader of the Welsh and English versions of these poems will be able to ascertain that they are the result of a full-blooded collaboration, rather than a process of simple translation (insofar as translation is ever simple) from English to Welsh I do not know ... The truth of it seems to me to be this: in our feeling for Wales and our concern over the future of the Welsh language and nation Jim Jones and I are virtually identical twins, and there is a very real sense in which these poems are the work of one personality.

Dressel concluded by emphasizing that the poems 'may prophesy ill for Wales, but remember this: though the prophet speaks what he feels to be true, his hope is that his utterance will change the hearts of men'. In retrospect, the *Ianws* translation/collaboration may seem prophetic in quite another sense, appearing to prefigure, in its very form if not in actual intent, a period of rebuilding alliances between the two linguistic cultures of Wales. This was a painful process but it effected a gradual change in the political climate that found important expression in the new Welsh Language Act of 1993. It is out of this politico-cultural background that Elfyn's translations may be said to have eventually come.

Behind these volumes of hers, in fact, lies a vast invisible constellation of politico-cultural circumstances that have made

Welsh–English translation in the 1990s a very different kind of 'statement' from that which it had ever previously been. Two of these circumstances are indicated by the dedication of *Eucalyptus* 'to the new Welsh speakers', and by the recommendation from the Anglo-Welsh poet Nigel Jenkins on the back cover: 'A book like this builds bridges at a time when in national let alone world terms new connections and solidarities are urgently required.' Elfyn's dedication reflects her own personal experience, as a west Wales resident, of the very considerable number of monoglot English 'immigrants' into this Welsh-speaking area who have made impressive efforts to learn the language and to assimilate to the local culture. One such, after an unusual fashion, is the major poet Gillian Clarke. She is a close personal friend of Elfyn's, with whom she has collaborated on various creative writing programmes, and consideration will be given to the work of both in Chapter 6.

Elfyn's close personal and working relationship with both Welsh- and English-language writers is evidenced by the number of poets from both cultures who contributed translations to *Eucalyptus*, and to *Cell Angel*, a volume notable for pioneering, in Wales, the practice of publishing a new, 'original' book of Welsh-language poetry in a bilingual edition. This (controversial) practice undoubtedly owes something to the successful use by Gaelic writers such as Nuala Ní Dhomhnaill of high-profile Irish poets (including the likes of Seamus Heaney, Paul Muldoon, Ciaran Carson, Medbh McGuckian and John Montague) to translate their work and thereby attract world-wide attention not only to the poetry but also to the vibrant contemporaneity of Gaelic culture itself.[72] Elfyn's move, with *Cell Angel*, from Gomer to Bloodaxe Books represented a further step in that strategy. And the sensitivity to world-wide developments that such a strategy reflects is also manifest in other aspects of Elfyn's translation practice. A Welsh feminist, whose sense of herself as being thus doubly marginalized will be explored in Chapter 6, she has realized that by identifying herself, through translation, with a women's movement that has developed a powerful international and internationalist discourse, she is able both to overcome prejudices about the supposed 'narrowness' and 'backwardness' of Welsh-language culture, and to render that culture potently current.

145

Moreover, her experience of creative collaboration with Clarke, itself an instance of the emphasis in women's writing on a co-operative approach, has led to her experiments with translations as a collaborative enterprise. As such, her volumes have some affinity with the experimental work in 'interactive' or 'transactional' translation activity that is taking place in bicultural Quebec. In this connection, Susan Bassnett has pointed out:

> The old binary notion of translation saw original and translated texts as two poles. Feminist translation theory focuses on the interactive space between the two poles, and notes that those poles have long been interpreted in terms of masculine and feminine . . . by celebrating the in-betweenness, [this new theory] reconstructs the space in which the translation takes place as bi-sexual, belonging neither to one nor to the other.[73]

Although the translators in *Cell Angel* in no way seek consciously to conform to any such programme, the corruscating comments by several of them that significantly preface the volume include a number of revealingly gendered tropes for translation. Thus Gillian Clarke emphasizes: 'Translation should not be linguistic or academic work but an act of poem-making. Each word is an old moon with the new moon in its arms. A poet-translator must make a new poem in the shell of another, holding the poet's pen, thinking her thoughts.' While Elin ap Hywel notes that 'when I translate her work I feel like some cut-price Herod. I mourn for the still-born, barely-formed other meanings in a Welsh work which I have had to pin down to one thing or another.' Female-orientated as such tropes are, however, Menna Elfyn implicitly questions traditional gender distinctions by utilizing both male and female translators. Hence men and women alike give (English) voice to experiences, such as menstruation and childbirth, traditionally regarded as an exclusively female preserve.

A very significant feature of Elfyn's case is that translation has provided her with an incentive to develop her own Welsh-language poetry in striking new directions. Her awareness of a wider readership, and a different one, has had a liberating effect on her as a poet, a reaction that comes from her realization that an English-language audience has long since ceased to mean an English-only audience. Over the last two decades, this realization has made an important difference to Welsh–English translation.

As early as 1976, the periodical *Poetry Wales* brought out a special translation issue, in which English was used as a go-between for poetry from Wales, Sweden and Greece, so that the concluding comment in Harri Webb's survey essay on 'The Historical Context of Welsh Translation' seemed appropriate: 'Today, in Wales, there are more translations, and by better poets, than ever before, with more responsibilities, both to Wales and to England and to a wider world whose attitude to "minority" languages is rapidly changing for the better.'[74]

Nor have Welsh–English translators thought exclusively in terms of using English to bring Welsh poetry to a Continental readership. It has become apparent to them that English is no longer the native language of England alone, and that non-English anglophone cultures not only extend across the world from Australia to Canada but also include the United States, a country which, until fairly recently, Welsh-language culture had been inclined to demonize by treating it solely as part of that sinister two-headed monster, Anglo-Americanism. (See the discussion in the concluding chapter of this study.) A sensitivity to this attitude is apparent in the very first paragraph of Joseph Clancy's introduction to *The Earliest Welsh Poetry* (1970): 'As an American amateur attempting to translate some of the finest poetry of the Middle Ages into English, I feel very much an invader. But I am a defender as well: the quality of medieval Welsh poetry is not yet realised by many people outside Wales itself' (*EWP*, 1). Later in his career Clancy exchanged such tropes for the metaphor of 'foreign correspondent', and saw his role in part as that of sending home a regular 'letter from Wales', thus acting as the American equivalent of Alastair Cook. Several of his translations – perhaps most notably the four-volume edition of Saunders Lewis's plays – were specifically produced with an American audience in mind. Clancy's comprehensive collection of Kate Roberts stories was likewise published in the United States, where the book appeared as part of the series Border Lines: Works in Translation, run by the Creative Writing Programme at Temple University, Philadelphia. Such an initiative is itself evidence of the truth of the observation made by no less a figure than Czeslaw Milosz, 'The art of translation has become in this century an important activity for American poets.'[75]

Other translators have followed Clancy's example. Harri Pritchard Jones, a practising Catholic particularly aware of the sizeable Catholic population of the United States, designed his interesting selection of Saunders Lewis's work with that specific constituency in mind. His *Saunders Lewis: A Presentation of His Work* (1990), published in 1990 by Templegate Publishers, Illinois, therefore affords an instructive contrast to the influential volume *Presenting Saunders Lewis* that Alun R. Jones and Gwyn Thomas had coedited in 1973. That work, the product of a conference held in 1968, had been assembled at a time when Lewis was very much the inspiration of young Welsh-language activists. It was therefore natural for the editors to present him as a controversial figure of great contemporary significance not only as artist but also as political thinker and activist. On the other hand, Harri Pritchard Jones's later volume chose to stress Lewis's acknowledged stature as 'a man of ideas, as a fine writer, and, supremely, as a great Christian poet'.[76]

The two editions of Lewis's work, published only twenty years apart, exemplify the truism that every age requires its own translation. This, as Roy Harris has reminded us, is because 'all translations are readings as much as writings. They are analytical readings of a text and are therefore as provisional as any reading must be (cf. photograph, portrait, or any "take" of a subject)'.[77] The present age's particular passion for texts capable of being read in a postmodernist fashion helps explain the kinds of Welsh-language novels that have been rendered into English of late. Contrasting though they are, Wiliam Owen Roberts's Marxist deconstruction of the Middle Ages, *Y Pla* (*Pestilence*, 1992), and Robin Llywelyn's *O'r Harbwr Gwag i'r Cefnfor Gwyn* (*From Empty Harbour to White Ocean*, 1996), a fantastical fiction aptly described by John Rowlands as composed of elements 'fitting together like a jigsaw made of quicksilver', both meet this fashionable bill.[78] And, as also generally happens, a period's passion for a particular style results in the rediscovery, and enthusiastic revaluation, of earlier works that in selective retrospect seem to have prefigured it. One great Welsh-language novel to have benefited from this process is Caradog Pritchard's *Un Nos Ola Leuad*. A vivid version of the text by Menna Gallie was published in 1973 under the title *Full Moon*. But, in keeping with the 1990s taste for jagged, surreal and uncompromising writing, a new translation by

Philip Mitchell was published by the Scottish publishers Canongate in 1995.[79]

In addition to commercial considerations, such as those identified above, there are other interesting factors that have affected the translation of Welsh novels into English. Take the case of the 1963 translation of Daniel Owen's final, and great, novel *Gwen Tomos* (1894). The co-production of a headmaster and a county librarian, the book was partly intended 'to find its way into the schools of Wales' and there help bridge the gap 'that exists ... between those of us who speak Welsh and those who, through past negligence and lack of foresight on the part of others have had no real opportunity to acquire a knowledge of their national language', as Jac L. Williams, himself a professor of education, put it in his Preface.[80] Implicit in his comments was, of course, a reading of Welsh history that most of the English-speaking population of Wales would probably query. Indeed, written into many translations of literature from Welsh into English – most particularly the novel – are arguments about the national history of Wales. If there is a sense in which all history – regardless of what form it may take – involves a struggle by various factions in the present to take possession of the past, or to translate it into the discourse of some current ideology, then this is particularly evident in the case of Welsh fiction. Welsh-language culture tends strongly to assume that many of the key events of Welsh history are, so to speak, in the keeping of the language, which thereby becomes the custodian of that past which alone may help the nation make full sense of its present. Hence the perceived importance, for instance, of making available in English such novels as Marion Eames's popular classic about the seventeenth century Dolgellau Quakers who went on to make such a notable contribution to the development of Pennsylvania (including the establishing of the famous Bryn Mawr College); or of that powerful novel about the nineteenth-century Tithe Wars, E. Tegla Davies's *Gŵr Pen y Bryn* (*The Master of Pen y Bryn*).[81]

One of the problems of Welsh history, and therefore of Welsh-language literature, from today's militantly secular point of view, is that it has been so heavily marked, not to say 'stained' and 'disfigured', by religious zeal. Consequently, many of the greatest Welsh-language texts are religious classics which would be unpalatable to most English-language readers. However, with the recent development of niche marketing, through the kind of rest-less change that is an intrinsic feature of consumerist culture – a development facilitated by the new desktop technology – such organizations as the Evangelical Press at Bridgend have been encouraged to produce texts for an international readership of evangelical Christians. This has brought classics such as William Williams's *Theomemphus* into English translation (under the title of *Pursued by God*).[82]

Another, and very different, contemporary change in the configuration of 'reader-culture' is particularly apparent in the academic field. 'British Cultural Studies' is beginning to adopt a multi-ethnic approach, inspired in equal part by the fashion for postcolonial studies and by current American emphasis on ethnic diversity. Accordingly, the indigenous non-English cultures of the British Isles are beginning to receive attention alongside this century's 'immigrant' cultures that have themselves by now modified, and been modified by, 'Britishness'. One very signifi-cant instance of this radical shift is the inclusion of substantial material translated from the Welsh in *The School Bag*, the import-ant new anthology for schools edited by Seamus Heaney and Ted Hughes as a companion volume to their bestselling *The Rattle Bag*.[83]

The character of the change that has happened in Britain over the last few years is very well explored by Daniel Weissbort in his address 'To the Reader' at the beginning of the special Welsh issue of *Modern Poetry in Translation* (Spring, 1995).[84] Weissbort opens by recalling that there had been a half-hearted, if well-meant, effort to bring out such an issue thirty years earlier, but that some resistance had been enountered from the Welsh side, which Weissbort can now better understand. To Welsh scholars at that earlier time, there seemed a hint of condescension about the interest shown, as if Welsh literature were being treated as a mere novelty. And there was also the fear that Welsh–English translation could only represent a threat to the distinctiveness of Welsh culture: that, in effect, it was 'a kind of second or third invasion, a mopping-up operation'.

Weissbort has, however, been much heartened by the positive, not to say enthusiastic, response forthcoming from the Welsh collaborators this second time around. Noting that the initiative was in part inspired by Swansea's having been chosen to host the

UK Year of Literature in 1995, Weissbort goes on to make several observations that are of the first importance for our understanding of the encouragingly altered climate in which Welsh–English translation currently finds itself operating:

> In the interim between our first thoughts on the subject and the present reality, the effort of decentralization, of regionalization – though I suppose even the term 'region' is too loaded for this purpose! – has perhaps made collections like the present one more feasible or at least acceptable, less implicitly imperialistic. After all, there is now even an academic programme, at the Centre for British and Comparative Cultural Studies at Warwick University, which extends the notion of Comparative Literature and treats the British Isles culturally as a conglomerate, not a single entity with a canon of universally approved artefacts. (Significantly, the director of this programme is herself a translator and translation theorist, as well as comparatist.)
>
> It is hoped that the present issue will be the first in a series that looks at the indigenous, non-English literatures of these isles, as well as at the non-English writings of more recent arrivals from the subcontinent and other parts of the world. We should like, in short, to investigate the evolution of non-English literatures in this country, their impact on what preceded them – or on what followed or paralleled them, as is the case of the Celtic literatures. The effects of these long-term linguistic and cultural encounters or interactions are of concern to us all and, clearly, must also influence the evolution of translation theory and practice. (*MPT*, 5)

★　★　★　★

Offering as it does substantial examples of the work of virtually all the leading poets of contemporary Welsh-language culture, and including in addition seminal reflections on Welsh–English translation by the two major modern exponents of the art, Joseph Clancy and Tony Conran, this issue may safely be said to be one of the landmark documents in the history of Welsh–English translation. And the leading contributors, many of whom are practising poets, naturally touch on several of the central issues that have been overlooked in the present chapter. One interesting problem is identified by Dannie Abse, writing as a sympathetic 'consumer' of translations from Welsh into English. While recording his indebtedness, as a poet, to the classic *barddas* tradition, he goes on to add: 'As for the poems of the Welsh-language

151

20th-century poets ... I despair when I discover not a few of them to be pre-modern, leaning too often on the themes and strategy of 19th-century Romanticism' (*MPT*, 219). It is a reminder of how complex is the issue of the relationship between any two cultures; an instance of how we should not assume historical synchronicity, but might need to consider the possibility of the two being 'out of phase' with each other. As Abse acutely notes, this is a particular problem for translators, and readers, of twentieth-century Welsh-language poetry.

Another vexed issue not considered here but, properly, addressed in *Modern Poetry in Translation*, is that of the 'translatability' of poetry, particularly of Welsh poetry written in the strict metres. Such a crux, and the practical means of addressing it, is bound to feature prominently whenever two or three sensitive practitioners of translation are gathered together, not least because of their having constantly proved, on their very nerves, the truth of Seamus Heaney's observation, 'Literary translation – or version making or imitation or refraction or whatever one should call the linguistic carry-over that is mediated through a crib – is still an aesthetic activity. It has to do with form feeling as much as with sense giving' (*AT*, 20). Translators with real form feeling are, of course, extremely rare, but Welsh literature has been fortunate in being served by one or two such in the modern period.

This chapter's failure to address either the question of 'synchronicity' or that of 'form feeling' (alias the translator's struggle to find in the target language 'linguistic conditions of meaning' in some way equivalent to those that made the work so potent in the source language) may stand for all the other important aspects of translation that have been omitted from this discussion.[85] And these omissions may, in turn, be construed as adding weight to the suggestion, made at the very outset, that Welsh–English literary translation needs, deserves, and is certain amply to repay, serious, extended attention – the kind and quality of attention that have already been given, for instance, to translation from Irish into English. There has as yet been no book about the culturally illuminating history of Wales 'translating itself to itself and to the outside world'.[86] There has certainly been nothing to compare with Michael Cronin's *Translating Ireland* or Robert Welch's *Changing States*. Yet such a study is by now urgently needed, not least because, as Cronin has stated, 'the history of translation ... is a history of encounters' (*TI*, 1). Indeed, in the history of Welsh–English translation may be found a history of those cultural encounters in which modern Welshness actually consists.

As for translators, they are apostrophized by Cronin in heroic terms: 'Architects of literatures and languages, channels of influence, ambassadors for the Other, they embody at the same time many of the painful dilemmas of Ireland's troubled history' (*TI*, 1). And if shades of the Welsh scene seem to haunt that particular assertion, then so is a way forward for Wales poignantly adumbrated in another of Cronin's observations: 'Thus, translation is not only an act of reconciliation between countries but also within a country ... The cultural ecumenism of translation offers the possibility of a common ground that often proves elusive in a divided society' (*TI*, 200).

And yet, sympathetic though I am to such pleas, there are certain reservations, I feel, that must be uttered, certain caveats that must be entered, and these, too, have been eloquently registered by Cronin himself. Being not only an interlingual but also, inescapably, an intercultural transaction, translation varies endlessly in status and in significance depending on the cultural context within which it is practised and/or experienced. That is why it is misleading, and may even be dangerous, to speak of 'translation' *per se* as distinct from, say, translation from Welsh into English at a specific period. So much depends, for one thing, on the relative status of the two languages concerned: to translate from one 'major', unassailable, language into another (English into German, say), is quite different in implication and consequence from translating from the language of the Navahos into English, say, or – to take an analogous case, where the overwhelming strength of the target language is a threat to the very existence of the source language – from Welsh into English. Moreover, the ramifications of translation are, in such cases of radical cultural asymmetry, totally beyond the control of even the best-intentioned translator. So strong, for instance, is present-day anglophone culture world-wide that many of the millions of monoglot readers 'naturally' assume that an English translation of a 'foreign' work is as good as the original/as good as original; thus also assuming that the translation is a totally adequate replacement for the original text, which is thereby effectively declared superfluous and rendered invisible.[87] In such cultural circumstances as these, translation may come to function, however unintentionally, not as a form of creative encounter with the Other (as Conran sensitively wishes, in the poem quoted at the beginning of this chapter) but, rather, as a means of eliminating the Otherness which is inscribed in/as a different language.[88]

I mention this *not* in order to condemn Welsh–English translation but, rather, in an attempt to ensure that such translation take place within the proper context of a vigorous programme to nurture the development of a genuinely diglossic, bicultural Wales. This will have to involve the abandonment by Welsh people of the remnants of a colonial mentality, otherwise Welsh–English translation is likely to serve, as it did in late-nineteenth-century Ireland, only to increase the marginalization and to hasten the disappearance of Welsh. Cronin summarizes this syndrome succinctly: 'Eric Chafitz argues that "at the heart of every imperial fiction (the heart of darkness) there is a fiction of translation". The colonial Other is translated into terms of the imperial Self, with the net result of alienation for the colonised and a fiction of understanding for the coloniser' (*TI*, 92).

Nor is this issue merely to be understood as involving the relationship of a 'minor' culture to a 'major' one. It was W. H. Auden who wisely observed: 'Due to the Curse of Babel, poetry is the most provincial of the arts, but today, when civilization is becoming monotonously the same all the world over, one feels inclined to regard this as a blessing rather than a curse.'[89] The survival of Welsh, and its literature, needs constantly to be put in this international context, and when viewed in such a light Welsh–English translation is seen to be an inherently equivocal, double-edged activity. Under such circumstances, translators properly intent upon being culture-brokers are sadly all too liable to find themselves suborned into acting as culture-breakers. The best they can themselves do is act on the understanding that they may best function as good thieves when they continue to affirm the blessings of Babel even as they strive to overcome its curse. Heaney it was who noted that, as translator of *Buile Suibhne*, he had to progress through two stages. First, he 'cuffed the original with a brusqueness and familiarity that was not earned but that gave me an immense satisfaction. I was using *Buile Suibhne* as a trampoline: I should have been showing it off, but instead it was being pressed into service to show me off' (*AT*, 18). Much later, he came to maturity as a translator: 'only after the translation had been completed for the second time and I had earned that familiarity which I had originally arrogated – it was only then that the work truly yielded itself over' (*AT*, 20). The sentiments echo Tony Conran's words with which this chapter opened: 'Translation is a yearning thing, an act of faith, an attention to something outside yourself. It is compared here to the good thief hanging with the Word on the cross, saying "Remember me when you come into your kingdom", and waiting for the otherness of the poem to welcome him into its paradise.' In the next chapter I shall be considering how this recognition of Otherness informs Conran's own poetry and his whole poetics.

5

'Shaman of shifting form':
Tony Conran and Welsh *barddas*[1]

~

For almost forty years, Tony Conran has consistently been one of
the most impressively singular of the English-language writers of
Wales. Much of what he has published, during a distinguished
career as translator, critic and poet, has borne the authoritative
stamp of a consciousness whose character is out of the ordinary,
and he has always had the confidence to obey the imperatives of
his own imagination, to write out of his own distinctive convic-
tions. This has tended to set him apart from other Welsh writers,
since Welsh-language and Anglo-Welsh culture share, to some
extent, an ethos which emphasizes collective experience and
values representative witness. The paradox, in a way, is that
Conran is himself the most persuasive ideologue of this communal culture and has fashioned his own work partly in accordance
with his idealized conception of it. But in practice he seems
significantly less close to the traditional *bardd gwlad* (community
poet) or court poet, than he is to Modernist grandees such as
Eliot, Pound, Bunting and David Jones, strong-minded individu-
alists all, who professed their undying love for 'established'
traditions that, on closer inspection, proved conspicuously of
their own making. In Conran's case, this 'making' partly involved
a refashioning of Wales in terms that allowed him to consolidate
his originally tenuous grasp on his own Welshness. Very imperfectly introduced, at Colwyn Bay Grammar School, to his own
country's history, he later came to realize that 'if I was to be taken
seriously in Wales, for my soul's sake I had to justify myself as a
Welshman. Welsh culture had to be my culture, Welsh standards
my standards: otherwise I was nothing but a charlatan.'
Accordingly he came eventually to nurture his own '*muthos*, the
myth by which I was able to reconcile this colourful Wales of the
[medieval Welsh] poets with the rather drab and "uninteresting"
Wales I had been brought up to ignore'. Only gradually did he

begin to refine that *muthos*, extending it to embrace the very Wales it had originally been devised to exclude.[2]

Something of a cult has been made in modern Wales of the culture of belonging, with appreciative emphasis being placed upon the supposed rootedness of the *gwerin* and the proletariat. And yet some of the best writing about Wales this century, in each of the country's two main languages, has come from the peregrine imaginations of migrants – individuals who sought out or stumbled upon, who 'discovered' and/or constructed, a culture more spiritually congenial than the one to which they were actually native. A list of the most prominent examples would certainly feature Saunders Lewis, R. S. Thomas, David Jones, Emyr Humphreys, Alun Llywelyn-Williams, Bobi Jones, Pennar Davies, Roland Mathias, Raymond Garlick and Jan Morris, and might profitably be extended to include Tony Conran. Here the facts of his upbringing may be treated as useful cultural co-ordinates. On his father's side, he is descended from 'a military family that left being wealthy Dublin burghers in the second half of the eighteenth century, to find fortune in the wake of British colonial expansion in India, Ceylon, Gibraltar and the West Indies' (*AW*, 112). Conran was himself born in India, but was raised by his maternal grandparents in Liverpool and Colwyn Bay. Although he attended university at Bangor, his real awakening to Wales happened only when he became a postgraduate, and was precipitated by two complementary events: the death of Dylan Thomas, and Conran's discovery of translations of medieval poetry by Gwyn Williams, from whom he borrowed the *muthos* mentioned above. For the past forty years he has passionately committed himself to the working-out, through both his poetry and his poetics, of the implications of those transformative cultural experiences. The result has been a remarkable body of work which is only beginning to be properly assessed.

Perhaps Conran's single most impressive achievement as a poet is *Castles* (1993), a striking work consisting of 'variations on a theme' in the form of thirty-six poems that intricately follow on, one from another.[3] Here the local rhetorical device of *dyfalu* (definition of an object by a tangled skein of fanciful figures), so integral to the *barddas* of Welsh antiquity, is changed into an elaborate structural principle. Conran's father (commemorated in a fine elegy) was an engineer, and his presumable skills at fabricating massively effective structures have, in a sense, been recognizably inherited by his son. The 'built voice' in this work links together vast tracts of personal and historical experience, just as the railways his father constructed for the Bengal and Nagpur Railway networked a subcontinent. That heroic labour was undertaken in the service of empire, and so Conran's own family history supplies him with insights into the cultural and moral complexities of the imperial process. Having been deprived by the colonizing English of their ancestral lands, the Irish Catholic Ó'Conaráin family 'chang[ed] to prods', themselves becoming progressively Anglicized as they 'found fortune and Englishness in hot places – Clive's India, Ceylon, Jamaica' (*C*, 62).

The author's branch of the family eventually fetched up in Denbigh, living (when on leave) in the shadow of one of those Norman castles that Conran, thanks to his family background, is able to view with the eyes both of the colonizers and of the colonized, of the rooted and of the deracinated. It is in this double perspective that he views the complex, intercultural transactions that have constituted Welsh history, and the castles of Wales, here pointedly rescued from the Welsh Tourist Board, are used to figure and to fix the subtle dynamics of national development. Beginning as a stark icon of conquest, as the Norman lord's brutally simple assertion in stone that 'I keep this land' (*C*, 9), the castle gradually acquired meanings almost as numerous as the slabs of which it was built. In the hands of the Welsh it took the form of defence and defiance, but this only provoked the English into the first unmistakable signs of empire-building, still visible in 'eagled Caernarfon's loosed *imperium*' (*C*, 77); ' – Such walls, such towers/ Curtain under the eagles/ Byzantium the Second Rome . . .' (*C*, 59). Those allusions back are a pointed reminder of the dreams of empire nurtured more than once by the Welsh themselves, originating with their earliest hopes of inheriting the mantle of imperial civilization from Rome, and continuing through Wales's passionate identification with the several British Empires, beginning with that of the Tudors. So much for any simple, absolute distinction between peoples that are colonized/ oppressed and peoples that are colonizers/oppressors.

Equally significant was the foreign castle's expanding sphere of influence, the invisible domain of a growing cultural and linguistic hegemony. At Kidwelly there are everywhere signs, in the substantial ruins, of the castles having become domiciles, of a land no longer occupied but comfortably settled. The native Welsh tried to assimilate these assimilators by reconstituting political history as myth. Drawing upon the old legend of the giant heroic leader Brân (literally 'Crow'), they headed (via Bosworth) for London, which they claimed, in the name of Brân's head buried in the mound under the White Tower, as the ancient capital of the Britons. Meanwhile in Wales the abandoned castles collapsed into ruins, helped by the counter-attacks upon their walls by locals, scavenging stone for farms and outhouses. So the dominant, invasive culture was to some extent modified through its interaction with the local.

Castles are revealed by Conran's poems to be significant sites as well as impressive sights. They are places that represent not only the colonial conquest but also the slow, equivocal process of cultural cross-fertilization that produced the hybrid culture of modern Wales. Conran is well situated to appreciate this, given his family's ambidextrous history. By the same token, he is well placed to see Welsh history as the synecdoche of British imperial history from Ireland to India. But in *Castles* these panoramic perceptions, which provide the segmented poem with its impressive socio-political scope, originate in intimate psycho-history: that is, they are inseparable from the configurations of Conran's relationships with his father, his mother and his friends. The first of these relationships was particularly formative, as Conran reveals in a series of almost baldly frank poems about his father. Linked in with these is a series of self-portraits, explanations and amplifications of that sardonic snapshot of his physically ungainly spastic self, posed against a castle's gracefully ruined arch, that occurs earlier in the sequence: 'Shapeless,/ Lopsided, bald, my trousers/ Sagging, like a dodo/ Trying to fly' (*C*, 15). Unfitted for a life of action by the cerebral palsy which afflicted him at birth, Conran grew up doubly removed – geographically and psychologically – from his father's world. *Castles* is a complex exploration, by way of crossings and criss-crossings, of this psycho-social space, just as Conran's own development as an artist was at once the antithesis of, and parallel to, his father's career. Like empire-builders and engineers, each artist places his proud signature, the imprint of his ideology, on the world, as Conran ruefully shows by contrasting the paintings by

Richard Wilson and J. M. W. Turner of Dolbadarn Castle. This is one of those many effective moments in the poem when Conran exposes his own artifice, drawing attention to his chosen medium of representation and thereby admitting that he is himself implicated in the power-nexus that he is examining.

An early cosseting that never compensated for a resentful sense of having been abandoned, a tenuous relationship to place that did not begin to alleviate the gut feeling of deracination – these, on the evidence of *Castles*, were important experiences for Conran in childhood and youth, and they clearly help to explain the value he eventually came to place both on the discovered/imagined community of Wales, and on the elective affinities of friendship. Virtually from the beginning, many of his poems were conceived as gestures of imaginative solidarity with others: gift poems, epithalamiums – and elegies. *Castles* is itself a set of six elegies, including one each for his father and five of Conran's friends, and it is by recalling, and reconstituting, the condition of their lives and the manner of their dying that he summons ever deeper constellations of meaning out of his central trope. As the work progresses, so the claims of intense religious experience are almost reluctantly conceded, until the writing resonates with a felt tension between the claims of the tump of Golgotha on the one hand and, on the other, the imperious secular authority of 'Dai Pont the Procurator'. As Hazlitt famously remarked, 'the language of poetry naturally falls in with the language of power'.[4] Conran is secretly fascinated by the decisive display of power – 'the achieve of, the mastery of the thing'[5] – that he finds in castle-building and figuratively related acts of ruthlessly creative self-assertion. But his imagination then recoils into sympathy with what, in his prefatory Note, he identifies as 'the non-assertive, the inhuman [i.e. non-human], the subconscious – death, trees, fear, religion, what might have been'. This dimension of existence – which this chapter will later consider under the rubric of 'otherness' – is explored in *Castles* by means of a poetry that can be as fluid, in its transitions, as dream. There are passages that remind one of those colourfully phantasmagoric Ceri Richards paintings based on Dylan Thomas's poems, and one of Conran's favourite tropes for writing here is that of art ('collage', 'landscape', 'triptych').

Conran's wide-ranging explorations are sponsored by, and

realized through, the variety of forms he uses. His multi-part poem is a rich amalgam of different modes, genres, discourses and registers. Verse loosely based on blank verse ('So that his teen-age son could dress himself', *C*, 63) is used to trace out his relationships to his father and family; the sestina form that concludes each section is turned into an ingenious *double sestina* at the end of section IV; passages of imagistic sharpness ('Cashel or rath, hillforts of/ Dry stone or earth ramparts', *C*, 20) contrast with deliberately mannered writing that verges on the Welsh baroque ('*On the spry thyme, saffron-heeled Hymen . . .*', *C*, 53); poetry relaxed enough to accommodate prose coexists with tightly patterned discourses of vision, ritual and liturgy ('Elen of the roads,/ *Have mercy,*/ Of the raised clay and the cleared cut,/ *Have mercy*', *C*, 60); a proudly resonant poem in defence of translation ('The Good Thief', *C*, 46) gives way to a quiet narrative of reminiscence ('Sandwiches', *C*, 47–8); a Dante-esque passage at the end of 'Father and Son (cont/d)' (*C*, 66–8), followed by savagely childish verses of self-mockery ('And wasn't I the Wise Man/ At the end of it all?', *C*, 69). All this amounts to much more than a formidable belated Modernist display of technical virtuosity. It is these shifts in style and tone that allow Conran to honour the multiformity of historical experience and to deal with the laminates of personal consciousness.

With the end of the century rapidly approaching, we can now conclude with some authority that the poetic sequence has been one of the most important literary forms of the past hundred years. Moreover, from Hart Crane's *The Bridge* to Geoffrey Hill's *Mercian Hymns*, from Hugh MacDiarmid's *A Drunk Man Looks at the Thistle* to John Montague's *The Rough Field* and Gillian Clarke's *Cofiant*, and from Idris Davies's *Gwalia Deserta* to Emyr Humphreys's *Ancestor Worship*, the sequence has repeatedly demonstrated its ability to accommodate material both sociopolitical and personal: it has the capacity to bring the one realm of experience into suggestive relationship with the other. It is to this versatile genre, with its spirit of consortium and its noncoercive power of conspectus, that Conran's *Castles* in some ways belongs, although, as its author stresses, it is actually a single work. Its segmented structure seems particularly suited to a contemporary Welsh consumer society increasingly inclined to retreat from history, and from communal experience, into the supposed sufficiency of a reductively conceived selfhood. For Conran, poetry is a multiple social transaction of a kind to which Welsh *barddas* made him privy when, as a young developing poet, he first approached it with his eye on translation.

★ ★ ★ ★

From the very beginning, Tony Conran's translation of Welsh poetry was an integral aspect of his own development as a poet, so that throughout his career there has been a symbiotic relationship between the two activities. One way he himself has offered of accounting for this is to see it as characteristic of his generation. According to Conran, the English-language writers emerging in Wales during the 1950s were culturally disorientated:

> Like many Anglo-Welsh poets of the second generation – John Tripp, myself, Meic Stephens, Gillian Clarke – [Bobi Jones's] adult experience was of post-Depression Wales. For older people, and poets among them, it had often seemed that the only thing to do with Wales was to leave it . . . But now a new generation was coming to be aware of what we had lost. For most of us, Wales was a journey into an exile we were born with. We were heirs to a richness we could only apprehend as memories of childhood. We were third-generation immigrants into our own land, easier with English people, very often, than with our own still Welsh-speaking compatriots. Threatened by both the ruling-class English intelligentsia we were trained to serve, and by the native Welsh culture that we felt had the birthright, we tried to make room for ourselves. We wrote elegies for lost Wales. We proclaimed that the Dragon has two tongues. We translated Welsh poetry.[6]

In this passage many of Conran's leading themes and preoccupations are brought together to form a highly suggestive profile of the circumstances underlying important features of his poetic practice. The condition of exile is touched upon in all its complexity – if early exile in England helped Conran rediscover and focus his Welshness, then the returnee's experience of a second exile, this time in his very 'own' country, helps us to see his poetry 'from the Welsh' (in several senses of that phrase) as a second kind of homecoming, a journey out of the exile he was born into. This 'journey' may, in turn, be alternatively imaged as anamnesis, a restoration of lost memory. In a recent review,

Conran chided Leslie Norris for his insouciant discarding of the historical ties that result in social commitments, and referred with approval to a famous contrasting Irish case: '[Patrick] Kavanagh did take responsibility for his past, as far as lay in him as a poet. "The Great Hunger" alters the way we look at people now, not simply laments what has passed.'[7]

So, really 'to take responsibility for [the] past' means 'an alter[ation] in the way we look at people now'. 'If one can really penetrate the life of another age', T. S. Eliot approvingly observed of Pound the translator, 'one is penetrating the life of one's own.'[8] Such perceptions go to the very heart of Conran's practice: they alert us to the politics of Conran's poetics of translation and help us see how his own English-language poetry uses a new counter-cultural syntax, and a grammar of alternative social relationship, derived, courtesy of Welsh-language poetry, from his country's past. Indeed, it could be said that in Welsh-language poetry Conran found a 'form' of social vision that, by precisely focusing his own radical dissatisfactions with the contemporary world, progressively saved him, as a poet, from dissipating such feelings in mere romantic nostalgia ('the Fifties were not much,/ Lacked the collective point of a great epoch'), and crudely dissenting anti-capitalist polemic.[9]

Judging by his work, this was a very real temptation. The opening poem of his early collection *Spirit Level* depicts a world degenerated into violence and madness but finds comfort in a Wagnerian image of a resolute dwarf, hidden in the crannies of a rock, hammering a sabre blade, and 'wait[ing] his hero, unmindful all is lost'.[10] The image, like many another in Conran's early writing, owes not a little to the poetry of Robert Graves. Later, in *Life Fund*, Conran's response to the (probable) suicide in 1971 of his friend, the painter Brenda Chamberlain, finds expression in awkward political terms: 'Brenda, this death of yours,/ This acquiescence in the laws of the market/ – How could you do it?'[11] Such recurring false notes – of sentimentally grandiose heroicism and of bewildered shrillness – are poignant indications of the difficulty Conran may initially have experienced in addressing his own times. In the characteristically honest poem 'No!' he confessed (although he would doubtless hate the term) that regret is 'an old friend on my doorstep', spoke of 'Nostalgia/ For the hand-made, the times before the last,/ Where every decorative thing had patina', admitted how easy it was to hate modern 'domesticated vistas', and noted how 'Paranoia/ For the thousandth time/ Threatens to kidnap me'. The poem ends, however, on a courageous note of self-confrontation that seems also to mark the site of his best poetry: 'No, I have to say,/ This is my century./ I shall not be abducted' (*LF*, 117). Paradoxically, his English-language modernization of ancient Welsh-language poetry has been one of the crucial socio-poetic strategies that have saved him from being abducted by the past.

'We tried to make room for ourselves', wrote Conran of his generation in the passage quoted above, and much of his energy as a poetic *makker* has been invested in that undertaking. Even had the young Conran seriously wished to find room in 'English' literature, it would have been denied him following the death in 1953 of Dylan Thomas, the 'Don Quixote of the vaunted phrase' (*FP*, 42), since an anti-Welsh reaction ensued that succoured the anti-bardic wryness of such Sancho Panzas as the 'prosemen' John Betjeman, Philip Larkin and the Movement poets. 'It was no time to inaugurate thought', he remarked in the Audenesque epitaph for the 1950s written in 1958, 'Only to entrench ambiguous positions,/ Afraid of feeling, afraid also of not feeling' (*FP*, 24). In the elegy that effectively marked Conran's poetic début, Thomas was praised for establishing 'A territory kept apart/ With cunning phrases' (*FP*, 42); but already the young poet knew better than to attempt to move into that newly vacated territory. An elegy, the older Conran was shrewdly to note, can be a way of drawing a line under a life, indicating the finality of closure.

Two years later, in 1955, he elegized a very different cultural figure, the Welsh poet R. Williams Parry, adopting (and adapting) for his purpose the mixed metres of the *awdl* form, so utterly foreign to English poetry, that had first brought Williams Parry his eisteddfodic fame. Ostensibly, Conran pays him the tribute of deference, in that the whole poem is organized around the trope of a difficult pilgrimage ('plodding where you were speedy') into the very heartland of Williams Parry's imagination: 'For his love it was, we'd argue,/ This wistful, antiquated wood/ Where all visions end/ And the hurt stabs out/ No more with vivid/ And desperate drums' (*FP*, 8). The Welsh poetry becomes a means whereby English-speakers may re-map their culture through recognizing their own land anew: 'And your wounds glinting/

Like frosty rivers/ That we always knew/ Ran through our land'
(*FP*, 8). But coexisting with this genuine sense of indebtedness to
Williams Parry (and therefore to the Welsh language and its
literature) is the unspoken counterweight of pride in having
wrought in English a distinctive form answerable to indigenous
Welsh experience, the pleasure of having found in Welsh a mode
of writing that licences and underwrites an extravagance of
language of a kind the English tradition (recoiling from Dylan
Thomas) is busily deploring, and the triumph of having successfully engineered in English a 'journey' into the very interior of
Welsh literature, to claim what had seemed to be the exclusive
'birthright' of 'native Welsh culture'. In other words, this Trojan
Horse of an elegy is an important example of Conran making
room for himself, as English-language writer, both 'within' and
'against' the Welsh-language tradition.

Of his generation of Welsh writers brought up in English,
Conran finally reports: 'We wrote elegies for lost Wales. We
proclaimed that the Dragon has two tongues. We translated
Welsh poetry.' But one member of that generation, and one only,
learnt and internalized the Welsh language so completely that he
became not only a distinguished Welsh scholar but also one of the
leading Welsh-language poets of the post-war period. Bobi
Jones's extraordinary achievement continues to fascinate Conran,
who has accounted for it in terms that reveal him to be Jones's
alter ego:

> If you want to be culturally born again, writing in what is not, for
> you, a wholly established language has a lot to recommend it . . .
> The wastage is likely to be enormous . . . But the possibility is
> there. What you lose in stylistic sureness you can gain in energy
> and innocence. From Dylan Thomas to Allen Ginsberg, from Idris
> Davies to Bobi Jones, this is the Devil's bargain that poets have
> been forced or delighted to strike. (*BJ*, 69).

There are 'striking' parallels here with Conran's own situation.
Although he has, of course, continued to write in English, he has
deliberately used his limited mastery of Welsh (a reading knowledge, but no oral fluency), and his qualified familiarity with
Welsh-language literature (he reputedly works as much from
cribs supplied by others as by laboriously deciphering frequently
difficult texts) to defamiliarize and destabilize the inherited

norms of English expression. In that sense, and by those means, English has ceased to be for him 'a wholly established language', his use of it having been informed, and re-formed, by his translating experience. His, too, has been a Devil's bargain – the voluntary relinquishing of 'stylistic sureness' for the uncertain promise of innovation – and for the first two decades or so Conran's consistently adventurous poetry was accordingly of 'strikingly' uneven quality. A constant throughout this impressive career in experimentation has been his interest in the combined ethical and creative power of otherness, and it is, perhaps, under this rubric that his dealings, as poet-translator, with Welsh poetry may be most rewardingly studied.

★ ★ ★ ★

The need to nurture a care for, in the form of attention to, the other is the single most abiding feature of Conran's imagination. A failure to do so may result either in the solipsism he effectively portrays in his poem 'Prospero's Dream' (*SL*, 72), or in the imperial, Urizenic, imagination whose appropriative gestures he dramatizes through the arrangement of arrogant capital letters in 'Space':

CLOCKWORK ETERNITIES UNWIND AS I PENETRATE.
I HAVE REACHED DEAD NEBULAE TO REASON WITH
    THIS KITTEN.
I TAME TO EQUABLE TEMPERAMENT THE MELISMA
    OF STARS.

> but the kitten in its own
> becoming space watches the sun
> sparkle, the leaf turn in the
> light air, leaves it turn,
> attends to the speckled light
> of its own otherwise space, cat
> in the green sunshine, its own
> becoming grace (*SL*, 78–9)[12]

At his best, Conran shows an ability, equal to his unremitting concern, to acknowledge the 'own otherwise space' of animals, people – and cultures. How to relate to otherness without reducing it to sameness is a problem with which he can already be seen to be struggling in his earliest poetry. 'I would have each act/ Definitive as an equation,/ Solved into mystery/ By an awareness of persons', he writes in 'The Swan', as he courts a girl, in the persona of an anti-Lear, by respecting her freedom: 'I would have you speak, Cordelia,/ Such love as you think fit/ Under no pressure of my pride/ Or your too covetous duty' (*SL*, 23). And in 'Four Personae' – one of the earliest examples of his turn to Welsh poetry – he describes the poet Llywarch Hen's assumption of the voice of Heledd, to speak the great lines of mourning for the fall of the princely house of Cynddylan: 'I/ Wondered if it was I that made them/ Or she for whom they were made./ . . . Oddly surprised by the hallucination,/ That it was she, incarnate sorrow,/ That made the lamentings I made/ To mourn Cynddylan, her dead lord' (*FP*, 14). This sense of poetry as transactional, as a form of communication along the 'axis' of I and Thou, and therefore as existing in a space between self and other, is, of course, one that Conran claims to have derived initially from Welsh poetry of the archaic period. In a poem of the sixties he was asserting that 'the poetry of personal/ definition is as obsolete as Napoleon's battles' (*SL*, 77), and in his verse 'Ars Poetica' he further asserted: 'A third person poetry can no longer enact a civilization. The/ poet cannot stabilize his art/ in the tarnishing medium of I and IT' (*SL*, 80)

It is precisely this kind of concern with alterity that lies, or so Wolfgang Iser has recently argued, at the heart of the best kind of translation:

> In this respect a foreign culture is not simply subsumed under one's own frame of reference; instead, the very frame is subjected to alterations in order to accommodate what does not fit. Such changes run counter to the idea of one culture being superior to another, and hence translatability emerges as a counter-concept to cultural hegemony . . . Translation of otherness is primarily concerned with giving it its due without subsuming it under preconceived notions . . . Translatability, however, requires a discourse that allows the transposition of a foreign culture into one's own. Such a discourse has to negotiate the space between foreignness and familiarity[.][13]

A comment Conran made in an interview provides an interesting gloss on Iser's passage:

I translate for a wide variety of reasons, one being that I like making verses, and the technical problem involved in making English poems in so very unEnglish a way. And for a disabled person like myself, who has lived so much through other people's experience, to put such poetic expertise as I have at the service of other poets is not so strange.[14]

The arresting insights into Welsh poetry that have found expression through both Conran's translations and his commentaries may be seen as deriving precisely from the poetry's inalienable otherness, the way in which it continues, in his experience, to occupy a space 'between foreignness and familiarity'. In the interview cited above, for instance, he distinguished between his own versions of Welsh poetry and those of Gwyn Williams, whose *The Rent That's Due to Love* had first awakened his interest in translation:

why Gwyn's [versions] were complaisant about being used as cribs and mine are not may have been something to do with the fact that as a Welsh-speaker the originals were present to him in all their complexity and beauty before, during, and after the translating process, whereas to me they are discovered only in that process, and then dimly remembered afterwards. (12)

As he further remarked, 'I cannot see what is good in a Welsh poem until I have translated it into my own verse. My Welsh is so abysmally poor. I have to wrestle with a Welsh poem to see why it is a poem at all' (12). The point is surely crucial, since it helps explain why, as critic and translator, he is such a startlingly good inquisitor of structures (in Wallace Stevens's phrase), and why, as a poet, he is such a correspondingly good artificer of structures. Rather like the magician Gwydion, as depicted in his recent verse drama *Blodeuwedd*, Conran is an inspired detective of mutating patterns and patterns of mutation, a 'shaman of shifting form,/ Huntsman of nuance and trickery'.[15] His unerring eye for where the power of a poem really lies finds metaphoric expression in the poem 'Wild Form', where he sets aside the hydrangea's 'florets' in order to uncover 'the peppercorn buds [that] mean business – /The real flowers,/ Symmetrically accurate/ Jabs of power' (*B*, 12).

His best-known insights relate to his view that Welsh-language poetry of the great ages articulates, at the level of style, poetic convention and syntax, the deep structure of a form of 'civilization' (no less) that is wholly 'other' than that of England. A full consideration of this complex subject would no doubt involve a comparison of Conran with the many other modern poets of radically conservative persuasion whose anti-capitalist animus has led them to romanticize past times (Eliot's 'dissociation of sensibility'; Yeats's Cuchulainn; Pound's Confucius; Olson's Mayan civilization; Saunders Lewis's Catholic Europe of the Middle Ages; T. Gwynn Jones's Penmon). But as Conran's ideological reading of traditional Welsh praise (or boast) poetry, and the 'gift' poems that reading underpins, have been impressively explored elsewhere, it seems sensible to note some of the additional ways in which Conran the poet has profited from the insights of Conran the translator.[16] For instance, he realized as early as his first reading of Welsh poetry in translation, in *The Rent That's Due to Love*, that, whereas in English poetry it was the vowel that coloured and energized saying, in Welsh the consonant was supreme. Thirty years later, in an essay on Gerard Manley Hopkins, he drew a fascinating distinction between *cynghanedd* poetry as practised by the *gogynfeirdd* (the poets of the princes) and by the later *cywyddwyr* (the poets of the gentry). In the former case, he argued, consonantal repetition is primarily used 'to decorate and pick out the stresses in the body of the line, before you get to the main rhyme . . . It helps to isolate the stressed words.'[17] The volume *Blodeuwedd*, that Conran published more or less contemporaneously with the Hopkins essay (1988), contains several examples of how he as poet had by then thoroughly internalized the lesson learnt from the Welsh:

> The snow's gone, the green sinews
> Of the world stretch in the woods.
> Feeders of light come mewing.
> Leaf puts its key to the lock. (*B*, 18)

It is a fine example of the analytical, critical intelligence at work in Conran's mature poetry. Instead of attempting to reproduce in English the precise patterns of Welsh *cynghanedd*, he has penetrated to the very *raison d'être* of the early Welsh practice (alliteration as reinforcing stress) and has thus been able to

169

make appropriately modified, powerfully functional, use of it in English.

In its own way, such a passage signifies a kind of otherness, since it occupies in English a space between 'foreignness and familiarity'. The same could be said about 'Girl Pregnant':

> Another being is at her gravity.
> She is pulled to its purposes
> Like a continent. Slowly, her flesh drifts.
>
> Crops are re-distributed
> As she passes through new climates.
> Around her contours vineyards are turreted.
>
> Sleepy volcanoes crouch in the haze of her.
> She is well-watered. To the South
> Deserts recede into mirage. (*B*, 16)

Such writing is vividly reminiscent of Alan Llwyd's Welsh-language poems to his pregnant wife, or those of Bobi Jones on much the same subject:

> Today she parades her shape like swellings of song,
> The wings that free her, her throne, her tower.
> She bursts the land with her being, her objective,
>   her blossom,
> Her passion's lofty monument, her belly's dance.[18]

In Conran's terms, such writing is 'Platonic' poetry; that is, praise poetry in celebration of the ideal concept (and spiritual mystery) of 'fertility' (pregnancy being simply the *human* form of that phenomenon). His poem is a ritual of language in honour of that concept, a verbal fertility rite, and the point of ritual (as Conran has remarked) is that it is repeated because it has already been proved to be efficacious. In other words, like any ritual, this poem is in its very *modus operandi* a self-conscious quotation of previous performances – ranging from Welsh praise poetry to the Song of Solomon. Conran is himself rightly fond of bringing an anthropologist's eye to bear on traditional Welsh practices, linking praise poetry, for instance, to the boast poetry of the Bahima of Ankole in Uganda.[19] 'Girl Pregnant' is, therefore, partly the result of reading Welsh praise poetry in the light of analogous practices in other cultures – including the love poetry and religious poetry of the English Metaphysicals. Conran has used this comparison to bring out the element of high-spirited outrageousness in the way conceits are used in the Welsh tradition. In discussing Dafydd Nanmor's poem 'Praise of Rhys ap Maredudd', for instance, he draws particular attention to 'the "play", the fantasy, the serious wit, carried always through the imagery and the closely woven rhythms'.[20]

Such wit is present in 'Girl Pregnant' not only through the mythopoeic conceits but also in the very ambiguity of the title, which is then amplified in the poem by means of what Conran, in his discussion of the Welsh *cywyddwyr*, called a structural pattern of 'counterpoint' (*WV*, 57). 'Girl Pregnant' is a descriptive phrase different in implication from 'Pregnant Girl', since the latter roughly translates as 'girl who is pregnant', whereas the former signifies 'girl being pregnant', thus implying that the girl both is and is not to be identified with her pregnancy. The poem is mainly concerned with dramatizing the girl's helplessness before the 'alien' life force that is transforming her. But then in the last stanza there is reversal of perspective: 'She crowds into a destiny/ That is not hers, though the bow of her/ Slices the covering wave towards her child.' Here what was reluctant acquiescence before the inexorable changes into an eagerly incisive act of motherly volition – and these two aspects of her condition are beautifully captured in the pun on 'bow'. Originally the swollen curve of her belly was seen as her body's response to the pull of alien gravity; but now that curve is re-viewed as the bow of the girl's body-ship headed towards birth and towards fulfilment in accomplished motherhood.

In this respect, there is an important connection between Conran's 'Girl Pregnant' and the second of Bobi Jones's poems about pregnancy, 'Pregnant Woman (in Bed)'. There the gargantuan female figure, engorged with 'alien' life, is likened to 'mother-earth, with your other, set in place/ With its swellings for a day of harvest' (*SP*, 90). The woman is seen as rapt in a mystical self-absorption; entranced by the presence within her of that being other than herself that makes her other to herself – that makes her [m]other:

>   I catch you,
> Locked away in island introversion, conversing
> Without a mouth, connecting with no-one, listening intently
>   at times
> To a distant voice in an existence that makes no utterance.
> Another world is near by: you know it
> For its own sake, the separate one, the besides of the self
> In a secret dungeon you carry. (*SP*, 90)

In such a view of pregnancy – shared by Jones and Conran – there lurks also a trope for the essence of poetry, as they conceive of it. 'Pregnant Woman' and 'Girl Pregnant' are poems in which pregnancy becomes a metaphor for the way in which, in the kind of poetry favoured and practised by Jones and Conran, language is awakened to the undeveloped life that stirs within it, and thus comes to function in a way that makes it other to its customary, self-possessed self. Ceasing to be that modestly utilitarian medium that conscientiously serves, reflects and generally underwrites the modern world of 'common sense' (which is also, for Jones and Conran, the world of consumer capitalism), it becomes extra-ordinary, other-directed, attuned instead to an entirely different order, or level, of existence. It discovers a mirror for itself in the sheer extravagance, the superabundance of life, grotesquely disproportionate to the self-serving economy of human needs; and this it is that is mediated in Welsh poetic tradition through the disciplined exuberance of *gorhoffedd*, the poetry of inventive boast and ingenious conceit to which both Bobi Jones and Tony Conran are addicted.

In this context, it is useful to recall Conran's attraction to Catholicism, and in particular his respect for David Jones, whose creative appropriations of classic Welsh poetry anticipated and paralleled his own in many very significant respects. Conran has described Jones as being 'like one of those one-man renaissances – Iolo Morganwg is the most famous in Wales – who from time to time revive or even reinvent worlds that to all appearances have been moribund for centuries'.[21] In Jones's case, the world miraculously revived in his poetry is, for Conran, the world of 'Welsh civilization': that is, the largely medieval world of the Welsh poetic *traddodiad* ('the praise poetry, music and story telling of the bardic order', *FP*, 66). Conran sees that *traddodiad* as paradoxically originating (in post-Celtic Britain) as an antiquarian tradition concerned, like the poetry of David Jones, to honour and protect a buried cultural treasure.

In his seminal essay 'Art and Sacrament' (which should be read in conjunction with his essay on 'The Utile'), Jones makes much of 'the intransitivity and gratuitousness in man's art that is the sign of man's uniqueness'.[22] He goes on:

> it is here supposed that man is a creature whose end is extra-mundane and whose nature is to make things and that the things made are not only things of mundane requirement but are of necessity the signs of something other. Further, that an element of the gratuitous adheres to this making. (*EA*, 150)

So, too, is a pregnant woman, as represented by Tony Conran, removed from the realm of 'mundane requirement' because both to herself and to others her swollen body becomes 'the sign of something other'. Jones then develops his point in another important way:

> With regard to the gratuitous quality which is said to adhere to Ars it is well to remember that theologians say that the creation of the world was not a necessary, but a gratuitous, act. There is a sense in which this gratuitousness in the operations of the Creator is reflected in the art of the creature. It has become a modern English usage to speak of such and such as being 'for fun'; and when a painter, referring to a work, uses some such expression as, 'That's real fun' we all know that he is not referring to anything funny. On the contrary he is referring to a felicitous quality in the painting. It is a serious matter. We can better appreciate the nature of this kind of 'fun' or 'play' when it is Holy Wisdom herself who says *ludo*. In the famous passage in the Book of Proverbs she is made to say *ludens in orbe terrarum*. She was with the Logos when all things were formed, 'playing before him at all times' and as the Knox translation puts it: 'I made play in this world of dust, with the sons of Adam for my play-fellows.' (*EA*, 153–4)

It is in the context of this religious poetics that Jones, intensely alive to the ludic *ars* of Welsh poetry of the great periods, can, for instance, appreciate the 'hard, vivid and clamorous *Gorhoffedd*' of Gwalchmai's poetry (*EA*, 58). And it is in the context of a similar, seriously playful poetics that Conran's 'Girl Pregnant' needs to be read.

In his discussion of Dafydd Nanmor, Conran mocks Welsh scholars' genteel aversion to finding vulgarly jarring puns in classic Welsh poetry: 'Scholars will probably throw their hands up in despair; but this kind of thing happens in other poetry, so why not in Welsh?' (*WV*, 56) There is perhaps more to this remark than meets the eye. Conran himself thrives on the mixed, the impure, the hybrid, revelling in yoking heterogeneous elements together, even if he has to have recourse to a kind of creative violence. This, too, is an aspect of his operating in that space 'between foreignness and familiarity.' Isn't there a kind of audacious wit involved in his every attempt to 'English' peculiarly Welsh forms of poetry or to 'Welshify' English poetic usage? One of the most delightfully witty examples in his work of successful cultural cross-fertilization is 'Thirteen Ways of Looking at a Hoover' (*B*, 7–11), which consists of thirteen ingenious 'descriptions' of a Hoover that between them convey a Cubist sense of regarding an object from several different perspectives simultaneously:

> iv
> The difficult slow ease of scything hay –
> It is comparable
> To her adroitness with its wheels and flex.

> x
> Its noise is more sensitive than you'd imagine.
> It marks the difference between dusts.

This superb piece can therefore be read either as Wallace Stevens reinterpreted in the light of the classic Welsh poetic practice of *dyfalu* (a riddling definition of a person or an object by stringing together a sequence of outrageous tropes), or as *dyfalu* refracted through the poetry of Wallace Stevens ('Thirteen Ways of Looking at a Blackbird').[23] In other words, it can be understood as a translation either of Welsh into American, or of American into Welsh. And the whole point of the poem (as any one of the great *cywyddwyr* would surely have recognized) is that it is an intercultural tour de force both of craft and of fantastication.

★   ★   ★   ★

The emphasis in the foregoing has been on the way in which Tony Conran's encounters, as translator, with Welsh-language literature have significantly altered his relationship, as poet, to the English language and its poetry. As Wolfgang Iser has noted, 'reflecting oneself in the other entails heightened self-awareness, which leads to self-confrontation' (*WI*, 32). After a fashion, Conran's poetry involves making English-language poetry a stranger to its customary self – a creative strategy of linguistic self-estrangement that may, perhaps, be seen as not untypical either of Modernist literature or of that important species of so-called postmodernist writing that is closely associated with postcolonial experience. It would, indeed, be possible to argue a case for regarding aspects of Conran's poetry as consciously post-colonial, since one of its aims is to expose the fact that the English language, as used in classic English literature, is not culturally neutral but heavily complicit in the work of 'Anglicization': that is, in conserving and advancing the ideology of Englishness. He also deliberately resists the homogenizing influence of 'inter-national forms' of English, mistrusting it as, in 'A Milk Toast', he mistrusts sterilized milk: 'sterilized/ Friesian stuff,/ A lingua franca of dairies/ Minimal enough!' (*B*, 29) His own poetry is dedicated to the subverting of insipidly international English as the *lingua franca* of the modern world; instead, it promotes the idea of many different versions of English, each inflected according to the culture it serves.

As has already been suggested, in his mature work Conran's indebtedness to the Welsh is not always clearly signalled or fore-grounded. It may simply register initially as a powerful 'peculiarity' of style or an arresting oddity of genre. Yet at least some of his best poetry has continued to depend on the creation of a singular kind of English verse that is specifically advertised as being closely modelled on Welsh strict-metre poetry. His experimentations in this manner date right back to his first discovery of Welsh poetry and constitute attempts to 'translate' not poems but little less than a whole poetics. One of the earliest examples is his imitation of the syllabic pattern (but not the *cynghanedd* or rhyme-scheme) of the staple Welsh englyn form, the *englyn unodl union*, in 'For the Marriage of Heulwen Evans':

For you, I invoke old names – Taliesin,
　　With light in his forelocks,
　　That changed before the Huntress
　　To very weft of the wind;

Gwydion, diviner and poet – who gave
　　A girl's lilt to a rose;
　　For all who'd celebrate love
　　To your love shall be summoned. (*FP*, 5)

This conforms to the requirement that in an *englyn* there must be four lines of ten, six, seven and seven syllables, with the first line being subdivided into a seven-syllable unit before the break (dash/*gwant*), followed by a three-syllable unit (*gair cyrch*) to complete the line. And although no attempt is made here to reproduce the *englyn* rhyme-scheme that would require each 'stanza' to end with a couplet, Conran does at least keep to the rule that of these two lines one must end on a stressed syllable ('wind', 'love') and the other on an unstressed syllable ('Huntress', 'summoned'). But the overall effect of all this is anticlimactic: a case, perhaps of old wine in new bottles. The problem is that although Conran has indeed made an attempt (of however rudimentary a kind, judged by his later standards) to emulate the *englyn* form, the actual content of the expression is more Celtic Twilight than Welsh. Before the poem ends there is mention of 'the sea dusted with dawn', of 'love ... gentle as a moth stroking/ The moon upon rushes', and of 'the calm lake of your Welsh truth'. Even allowing for the fact that the rhetoric governing the poem cunningly turns on the claim that this poetry is mere 'tatters' compared to the 'traditional, intricate praises' of genuine Welsh *barddas*, and that it concludes with the wish that Heulwen Evans' children may 'ma[ke] whole/ All fragmentary generations' (such as Conran's own, capable at best of producing only an imperfect, incomplete *englyn*), the impression left by the poetry is of a form of writing being skeletally adopted without any real understanding being manifested of the experiential life of that form in its authentic cultural context. It is almost as if Conran had unconsciously effected a reverse translation – as if, in attempting to 'translate' an *englyn* into English, he had instead turned the *englyn* into a vehicle for expressing an essentially unmodified English sensibility.

Conran also experimented very early on with another staple form of strict-metre poetry, the *cywydd* metre. Again, he sensibly ignored the challenge of *cynghanedd*, and, as with the *englyn*, his efforts to reproduce only the syllabic measure and distinctive rhythmic profile of the verse met with patchy success. Knowing that Dafydd ap Gwilym has traditionally been credited with introducing the *cywydd* into *cynghanedd* poetry, Conran resourcefully turned to this form when imagining how Dafydd might press his courtship of a young maiden:

> Here, they say, are new-fangled
> Metres, new trash ousting old.
> They cast doubts upon my talent,
> Even they say, that poor fool!
> He thinks, by taking a common
> Minstrel rhyme, to revive Welsh.
> He thinks too much on women
> (And in particular one girl,
> Her long hair falling, a shimmer
> Of red gold from the broom tree). (*FP*, 16)

Years later, Conran was to observe that 'the *cywydd* imposes itself on the phraseology and the syntax of language. It is almost as easily recognizable in translation as Hebrew parallelism.'[24] Even in this early example one can see what he means. Nevertheless, this passage is almost as reminiscent of Browning as it is of Dafydd ap Gwilym, and there is about it a slightly bookish air of pastiche.

But these early experimentations, however flawed and unsatisfactory, were to pay rich dividends in due course. As T. S. Eliot (whose work as poet and critic has strongly influenced Conran) once usefully remarked, by 'conscious and continuous effort in technical excellence' a poet 'is continually developing his medium for the moment when he really has something to say' (*EP*, 17). Conran's elegy for one of the greatest scholars of classic strict-metre poetry, Sir Ifor Williams, is itself one of the classic texts of English-language poetry in modern Wales. It is also a virtuoso technical performance, since it consists of a series of English *englynion* that conform in every particular (including *cynghanedd*) to the demanding rules governing the original Welsh:

At a loss is Taliesin – the Black Book
Is bleak, and Aneirin;
On a bed where learning's been
The ravens take their ravin.

Sea-eagles feed at midday;
Too soon they peck at sinew;
Kite, crow and hawk make outcry;
Claws upon red flesh they cloy. (*SL*, 97)

The first of these is an *englyn unodl union*, some of the features of which have already been identified above. What additionally needs to be appreciated is that the unit (*gair cyrch*) following the dash in line 1 should be considered in effect as part of line 2. Once it is thus treated, it will be seen that in fact all four lines rhyme ('Taliesin', 'Aneirin', 'been', 'ravin'). Furthermore, each is a line of *canu caeth* (strict-metre poetry), and is thus divided into two parts, with the consonants of the second half mirroring those of the first to produce one or other kind of *cynghanedd*, as follows: 'A*t* a *loss/* is *T*a*l*iesin' (*draws anghytbwys ddisgynedig*); 'the *Bl*ack *B*ook/ is *bl*eak' (a mere approximation to *cynghanedd draws*); 'On a *b*ed/ Where learning's *b*een' (*draws gytbwys acennog – 'n' wreiddgoll*); '*Th*e *r*avens/ take *th*eir *r*avin' (*draws gytbwys ddiacen*).[25]

The second 'stanza' is an *englyn lleddfbroest*, a variant of the *englyn proest* whose features have been well summarized by Conran in *Welsh Verse*: 'Four lines of seven syllables each, using a peculiar kind of rhyming (called *proest*) in which the final vowels must differ (though not in quantity) while the final consonant remains the same: for example *den*, *ton*, *fin*, and *ran* form *proest*-rhyme in English' (*WV*, 320).

In the 'Elegy for Sir Ifor Williams' Conran succeeds in communicating a strong sense of the 'otherness' of the poetry of the Welsh heroic age to the study of which the scholar had devoted so much of his life. And he does so by constructing what Michael Alexander, commenting on Pound's famous version of the great Anglo-Saxon poem 'The Seafarer', called a kind of 'phonetic simulacrum'.[26] Just as Pound, T. S. Eliot acutely noted, 'is often most "original" in the right sense, when he is most "archaeological" in the ordinary sense' (*EP*, 11), so Conran shows here an extraordinary ability to produce a new mode of writing in English by faithfully reproducing not merely the phonemic patterning but the very grammar and syntax of experience found in the *canu caeth* when it functions as vehicle for a praise tradition, of which elegy is, of course, an important part.

'Throughout the work of Pound', wrote Eliot, 'there is what might be called a steady effort towards the synthetic construction of a style of speech. In each of the elements or strands there is something of Pound and something of some other, not further analysable' (*EP*, 12). Pound's work as translator, he added, contributed substantially to the development of Pound as a poet, since 'good translation . . . is not merely translation, for the translator is giving the original through himself, and finding himself through the original'. These observations apply almost equally well to the work and poetic career of Tony Conran. As he matured in his craft as translator, so did he take unto and into himself as poet not just the intricate technicalities of the *canu caeth* but the modes of sensibility of a whole 'other' culture. According to Raymond Williams's useful formulation, structures of form are also structures of feeling. Conran has made his own way to such an insight, not by slowly assimilating Welsh poetry in some mystically organicist fashion but by methodically analysing the deep structure of its foreign forms so that he is able, when he wishes, to engineer in English a feeling of cultural 'otherness' without imitating Welsh forms as minutely as he did in the 'Elegy for Sir Ifor Williams'. After all, that was appropriately and necessarily an 'occasional' poem: to have repeated such a feat would have been to condemn himself to a kind of ultimately crippling literalness of the imagination.

* * * *

Conran's greatest success in this 'freer' mode, and in 'the synthetic construction of a style of speech', is probably his elegy (or synthetic *awdl*) for the Welsh soldiers who died at Bluff Cove during the Falklands/Malvinas war:

> Men went to Catraeth. The luxury liner
> For three weeks feasted them.
> They remembered easy ovations,
> Our boys, splendid in courage.

For three weeks the albatross roads,
Passwords of dolphin and petrel,
Practised their obedience
Where the killer whales gathered,
Where the monotonous seas yelped.
Though they went to church with their standards
Raw death has them garnished. (*B*, 14)

In this opening passage, and throughout the poem, Conran's seriously playful wit is much in evidence. The first line deliberately isolates an absurd anachronism for our puzzled attention ('Men went to Catraeth. The luxury liner'), and by the second line the clash of archaic and modern registers of speech has already been jarringly established ('The luxury liner/ . . . feasted them'). As the ritualistic pattern of the verse itself suggests ('For three weeks . . . For three weeks'; 'Passwords . . . Practised'; 'Where the . . . Where the'), this is to be a poem *about* parallelisms (between present and past) which are both symmetric and asymmetric, comforting and disquieting, heroic and ironic. It is out of the interplay between such fearful symmetries that the tragic vision of the poem is to emerge.

Of late, Conran has increasingly insisted on describing himself as a writer of tragedy and has expressed an intense interest in older forms of tragedy, wherein the plight of an individual focuses the plight of a whole society.[27] 'Elegy for the Welsh Dead in the Falkland Islands, 1982' is itself tragedy in that mode, the tragedy of a Wales that is lost in history because it has lost sight of its own history, the 'otherness' of which is felt to haunt this poem by virtue of the felt foreignness of both the ancient references and the strange 'body language' of the verse. That history, of which the young soldiers are as unaware as they are of Aneirin's *Gododdin* (the sixth-century poem in which 'Men went to Catraeth' to be slaughtered), is the hidden cruelty of fate that is so destructively at work in and upon their lives:

With the dawn men went. Those forty-three,
Gentlemen all, from the streets and byways of Wales,
Dragons of Aberdare, Denbigh and Neath –
Figment of empire, whore's honour, held them.
Forty-three at Catraeth for our dregs.

The Welsh are appropriately among the last to fall victim to that vision of British Empire to which they have so eagerly subscribed ever since Tudor times, suppressing in the process all memory of their own separate history, which stretches back to the period of the *Gododdin*. As Conran has noted,

> Tragedy is about now, but its method of dealing with it is metaphorical. The tragic world, like a miracle play, is fundamentally anachronistic. It may claim to be about the remote past, but actually, like a symphony, like a great ballet, it lives in its own time, tangential to all our worlds. (*BM*, 15)

His unremittingly dark elegy brings Aneirin's ancient poem tangentially to bear on the Welsh present, to powerfully tragic effect. The young soldiers (addressed as 'Gentlemen all', in a quintessentially English turn of phrase used here with a combination of irony and sincerity) are represented as the victims not only of Margaret Thatcher's aggressive chauvinism but also of a Welsh 'nation' culpably besotted with a Britishness that has left it economically devastated ('Aberdare, Denbigh and Neath'), fertile ground only for military recruitment.

A similar vision of Wales and its history informs *Castles*, a sequence, as we have seen, that is a complex composite of materials at once personal and public, historical and mythic, political and psychological. Contributing to its rich texture is an elegy for Linda Noyau into which Conran poignantly weaves the poem he had originally written for her wedding decades earlier:

> *On the spry thyme, saffron-heeled Hymen*
> *would once (in weaving torchlit dances*
> *appropriate to a great god's greeting)*
> *have given these leave to live as lovers –*
> * they who marry this blithe morrow, and now*
> * their doom doubt, prow out over wild waters.*

> You re-make poems every time they're read –
> Nothing strange in that. Marriage and funeral
> Are metaphors, one of another. And for Linda
> In whom light was alive, it would not demean
> Her death, dressing her in the white brocade of a wedding.[28]

As Conran goes on to recall, the prothalamion was 'Arnaut's

sestina under-read/ With *cynghanedd* plucked for their wedding/ From Dafydd Nanmor's *gwawdodyn*'. And as he now re-reads that poem, its metaphors begin to resonate with different implications, born of new contexts of meaning: 'metaphors in the poem/ Make their circumference the occasions where it's read'. It is a significant moment, not least because it makes explicit what is usually left implicit: namely, the way a poet continues to develop by re-reading himself: that is, he grows by reinterpreting, and re-wording, his central preoccupations in the light of changing circumstances. Moreover, there is a sense in which his 'recycling' of his prothalamion offers a paradigm for understanding the way in which Conran's interest in Welsh-language poetry has served him well as a poet in his own right. As he says, 'You re-make poems every time they're read.' His reading of Welsh-language poetry has indeed involved a complex (and still ongoing) process of re-making, in which the past, as inscribed in Welsh-language texts, and the present, which Conran seeks to address in his own poetry, have come to function (in part through the very otherness of their inalienable difference) as 'metaphors, one of another'.

Conran has always emphasized that to translate is very hard work:

> So hard – the hazard is huge
> I deal against a deluge
> While a dotty world yet wags
> Trumps from a thousand handbags! (*SL*, 96)

In this English *cywydd* about the near-impossibility of writing an English *cywydd*, Conran goes on to characterize his efforts as 'Heart's clamour, labour of lathe'. These are also the skills and energies (of intensely committed heart and cool head) he has needed in order to be able to translate translation into original poetry. This brings to mind Eliot's wise words about the work of his old friend Pound:

> To consider Pound's original work and his translation separately would be a mistake, a mistake which implies a greater mistake about the nature of translation ... If Pound had not been a translator, his reputation as an 'original' poet would be higher; if he had not been an original poet, his reputation as a 'translator' would be higher; and this is all irrelevant. (*EP*, 15)

Like Pound (and indeed like many contemporary writers, such as Tony Harrison, W. S. Merwin and Thomas Kinsella), Tony Conran is a fine poet because he is a fine translator, and is likewise a fine translator because he is a fine poet. Any further attempts to explain his impressive case would be 'all irrelevant'. After all, both poetry and translation are naturally complementary modes of creative expression for one who is, above everything and in everything he does, a 'shaman of shifting form'.

★   ★   ★   ★

A shaman traditionally acquires his power by leaving his tribe for a period of self-sequestration, during which he is initiated into a vision of his people's place in the world so that he may return empowered to communicate that vision when he enters the trance of 'composition'. Conran's initiation into the Welsh poetic tradition, which seriously began, as was noted at the beginning of this chapter, during his lonely residence in England, may usefully be thought of as resembling, in certain key respects, the shaman's *rite de passage*. His consequent transformation from 'outsider' to 'insider' was in some ways strikingly convincing, yet his assimilation into Welsh-language culture had to remain essentially incomplete if he was to act successfully as a mediator of it to the anglophone population of modern Wales.

One of Conran's most powerful accounts of his dependent and petitionary relationship, as translator and as poet, to Welsh-language culture takes the form of an elegy to Bedwyr Lewis Jones, who was, until his untimely death in 1992, professor of Welsh at University College, Bangor, and a distinguished scholar on whom Conran relied for guidance and support. In 'Sending a Harrier to Llaneilian' – Bedwyr's native village and his final resting-place – Conran beautifully utilizes several of the key conventions of *barddas* (the use of bird as *envoi*; the hyperbolic elegizing of a dead patron; the associating of that patron with the quintessential values of a whole culture; the fashioning of a gift-poem to acknowledge gifts) to convey his disorientating sense of loss, not only as a friend but also as an artist who was intimately dependent upon the guidance Bedwyr had to offer. In some ways, the hawk whom Conran urges to fly to Llaneilian represents those qualities of painstakingly meticulous scholarship associated with the dead man: 'Flap to regain/ Inertia ... Your problems/ Are those of scholarship,// The aeronautics of slowness/ In a feature-less/ Terrain.'[29] Thereby, Conran implicitly confesses that he, as creative artist, has been heavily and humbly dependent upon the frequently ungainly and unglamorous work of the Welsh-language scholar. What has therefore been lost with him is a key:

> A key to priest-lofts,
> To glory-holes,
> Civilization
> In brown almanacs.
>
> I've lost a protector.
> A key to the wardship
> Of Wales, a hearth
> Open as day.

It is in search of that key that the harrier is sent on an errand by Conran to the medieval Church of Llaneilian, named for a Celtic saint, which, with its ornately carved rood-loft and its display of craftsmanship, seems to epitomize the intricate civilization to which Bedwyr was heir, and in which he was expert:

> Musics of the tongue,
> Of plucked strings,
> Of chiselled wood.
>
> Tracery of words, phonemes, syllables.
> Tracery of pitch, tone-lengths, rhythm.
> Tracery of uprights, curves, vineleaves.

But even as Conran is moved to celebrate its richness, the Church refuses him consoling access to the secret, the key, for which he is searching. It is as if the removal of Bedwyr has made Conran newly aware of the dark, tragic side of his own positive achievements as poet and as translator; aware of the fact that his genius for mediation is dependent on his living permanently in limbo, on his never being fully native to either of the two cultures he serves. There is, in the end, something poignantly expressive of Conran's own condition in his apostrophe to the harrier:

> You're a dragon now,
> Rummaging Wales
> For a home, a courage,
> A hospitality.

6

The place of gender in the poetry of
Gillian Clarke and Menna Elfyn

~

In 1971, Anne Sexton published *Transformations*, a collection of
poetry in which she retold several of Grimms' fairy-tales, recast-
ing them so as to reveal the hidden agenda of their sexual
politics.[1] One of her most striking successes was 'Snow White
and the Seven Dwarfs', a story which Disney had turned into an
immensely popular post-war 'American classic'. From one point
of view, Sexton appears to stick quite closely to the original
version of the story, except that she translates it into the
American tough-guy vernacular immortalized (and in a sense
invented) by writers such as Raymond Chandler: 'The dwarfs,
those little hot dogs,/ walked three times around Snow White,/
. . . She was as full of life as soda pop' (271). But this streetwise
idiom signifies Sexton's sardonic view of the way in which the
original story sentimentalizes the reality of gender relationships.
By means of this retaliatory and revelatory discourse – which
thereby seems closer to the style of Mae West or Bette Midler
than of Chandler – she exposes the anti-feminine and covertly
macho ideology inscribed in the original 'fairy-story'. In Sexton's
redaction, Snow White becomes a sinister social icon of the feminine, like Marilyn Monroe, or a Barbie doll:

> No matter what life you lead
> the virgin is a lovely number:
> cheeks as fragile as cigarette paper,
> arms and legs made of Limoges,
> lips like Vin du Rhône,
> rolling her china-blue doll eyes
> open and shut.
> Open to say,
> Good Day Mama,
> and shut for the thrust
> of the unicorn.

> She is unsoiled.
> She is as white as a bonefish. (269)

After her cruel stepmother's every attempt to kill her, Snow White is invariably revived from her swoon and restored to her original oppressive state of 'virginal' purity. And when one recalls Sexton's own numerous attempts on her own life, one realizes that she has in this poem created an allegory not only of woman's social plight, as she sees it, but of her own personal condition.

Sexton's *Transformations* is a notable instance of an important trend in women's writing in the United States over the last thirty years, trenchantly characterized by Alicia Ostriker in her essay 'The Thieves of Language: Women Poets and Revisionist Mythmaking.'[2] Drawing upon the feminist theory that represents 'normal' social discourse as silently saturated and secretly structured by patriarchal values, Ostriker distinguishes two strategies adopted by women to begin the work of remedying this situation. On the one hand, there is the search for an *écriture feminine*, a distinctively gynocentric mode of writing emerging from an exclusive *langage des femmes*; on the other, there is 'the vigorous and various invasion', by women, 'of the sanctuaries of existing language, the treasuries where our meanings for "male" and "female" are themselves preserved' (315). This latter strategy, involving the appropriation of established styles and genres for altered ends, is strikingly exemplified, for Ostriker, in the revisionist use made of myth by women writers who implicitly take as their motto Adrienne Rich's observation, in 'Diving into the Wreck', that she carries with her a 'book of myths/ in which/ our names do not appear'. Rich's rewriting of that book of myths to include the female is therefore the representative action of a whole group of modern women writers.

Although the beginnings of this enterprise could be traced at least as far back as the work of Laura Riding in the 1930s, with a high-point reached early in H.D.'s post-war *Helen in Egypt*, Ostriker concentrates on the dozen or more 'major works (poem-sequences, long poems, or whole books) of revisionist myth published by American women' between the early 1960s and the early 1980s (317). These writers include Sylvia Plath, Kate Ellis, Sharon Baba, Rachel DuPlessis, Adrienne Rich, Denise Levertov, Anne Sexton, Ann Stanford and Susan Griffin.

Ostriker ends her survey by noting features that such poets have in common when dealing with mythic material. She sees their poetry as 'enactments of feminist anti-authoritarianism opposed to the patriarchal praxis of reifying texts'; as involving radical revaluations of traditional occidental social, political and philosophical values; as ridding myth of the nostalgia which attaches to it when used by men; and as correlating revisionism with formal experimentation, including the destabilizing of the 'I' which confidently presides over masculine discourse (330–1).

Ostriker also notes that 'revisionist mythmaking' by women is by no means confined either to poetry or to the United States. Margaret Atwood and Angela Carter are clearly major figures in this new 'tradition', which includes a whole host of writers who have appeared since Ostriker published her essay in 1981. Among these may be counted several writers from Wales, as critics such as Delyth George and, most recently, Jane Aaron have pointed out.[3] Both draw attention to the fascination the story of Blodeuwedd holds for women writers, a fascination due not only to the resonant configuration of elements in the original legend but also to the 'strong' masculine reading of the whole offered by Saunders Lewis in his *Blodeuwedd*, one of the classic Welsh-language plays of this century. Implicit in most, if not all, feminine retellings of the Blodeuwedd story is a radical revisionist impulse to steal the story back from Lewis, to reclaim it for women by rearranging its constituent elements.

As Aaron shows, Blodeuwedd's appeal crosses the linguistic divide, eliciting a powerful interpretative response from both Welsh-language writers (Angharad Jones, Elin Llwyd Morgan) and English-language writers (Gillian Clarke, Hilary Llewellyn-Williams). That response may, Aaron argues, be crudely divided into two. For Welsh women writers, Blodeuwedd tends either to represent the loneliness and guilt that accrues to women excommunicated from society for transgressing the moral code, or to stand for the rebelliousness of those who set established, male-dominated society at defiance (193–4). The latter view usually involves seeing Blodeuwedd as instancing natural female energies –and energies linking woman to nature – that have been oppressed and distorted by the dominant, repressive social order established and jealously patrolled by men.

Suggestive though this *schema* is, it understandably gains its clarity somewhat at the expense of the valuable nuances and ambiguities of the actual texts, one of the best of which is undoubtedly Gillian Clarke's poem. One of the most striking, and significant, features of her 'Blodeuwedd' is that in no way does it refer to the fateful part played by no fewer than three men (Gwydion, Llew and Gronw) in Blodeuwedd's tragic story.[4] It could, perhaps, be argued, that this is so integral to the original legend that it is bound to be implicit in any version of it that is told. But to insist on that too much and too soon would be to risk missing the point of Clarke's poem – a point which is made through the omission of the men. A key strategy in her telling of the story is the turning of the legend into one told by women, among women and for women. And a key device is that of establishing, in and through language, binary oppositions which are then deliberately deconstructed. Blodeuwedd is at first colourless, but then her feathers are also 'cream as meadowsweet/ and oakflowers'; 'soundless' she may be, contrasted to the chattering women from whose company she is forever excluded, and yet 'her night lament/ beyond conversation' is 'Blodeuwedd's ballad'; her association with nature signifies both barrenness ('condemned/ to the night, to lie alone/ with her sin') and a habitat of fecundity ('Her white face rose/ out of darkness/ in a buttercup field'); the indoor life of the women is both restrictively decorous and yet primitively ritualistic and productive of a fertile kind of sociability – 'moving in kitchens/ among cups, cloths and running/ water while they talk'; the women themselves are at once nourished and confined by the domestic routine of their 'comfortable sisterhood' – a phrase that just hints at smugness and self-satisfaction, as does mention of how they 'recall/ the day's work, our own fidelities'.[5]

The whole point of Clarke's poem is that it, and its power, derives directly from a radical division of mind, and corresponding sharing of sympathy, between 'freedom' and 'domesticity', 'nature' and 'society', the individual and the collective. The attempts made, at the level of language, to make these distinctions absolutely clear and decisive repeatedly fail because Clarke's language is so beautifully responsive to her fluctuations of feeling and judgement. This dwelling in uncertainty is, for her, the very essence of being a woman, and as an artist she refuses to simplify it by resorting to obvious ways of resolving the matter –

for example by representing female domesticity as merely the internalization of male requirements. The men are kept firmly out of the picture, not because Clarke is unaware of their crucial influence on the roles women play and the lives they lead, as is evident from the Blodeuwedd story, but because she does not believe that the plight of women can be attributed fully, or essentially, to 'patriarchal' influence.

Compared to Saunders Lewis's play, her reading of the Blodeuwedd story certainly involves a revision of the myth in that she reclaims it as a story centrally for women and about women.[6] Accordingly her feeling for Blodeuwedd is challengingly different in kind from that of Saunders Lewis – there is no hint in her poem of that visceral fear of the otherness of the female which is such a memorable element in his otherwise highly intellectual drama. But in so far as Lewis, too, refuses to structure his play along the lines of clear-cut gender difference, opting stubbornly instead for ambiguities of judgement and presentation that much more broadly 'humanize' the story, Clarke's poem may usefully be regarded as complementing, as much as confronting, his play.[7] And it is precisely this incorrigible impulse in her – when dealing with myth, both to give it a feminine inflexion *and* to subsume gender difference within what, for her, remains the overriding, primary category of the undifferentiatedly 'human' – that is worth considering further.

* * * *

'Adrian Henri once said to me: "You're in two political situations, being both Welsh and a woman poet."'[8] Thus Gillian Clarke began her contribution in 1986 to a symposium on gender in poetry. It was natural that she should be invited to contribute, since several of her innovative long poems, beginning with *Letter from a Far Country* (1982), have been lineations of female lineage, feminized genealogies in which the traditional Welsh obsession with male ancestor-worship has metamorphosed into Clarke's very differently motivated and very differently orientated search for her distinctive antecedents as a woman.[9]

The latest, and perhaps the best, of these long poems is 'The King of Britain's Daughter' (1993), an autobiographical sequence that uses myth as a sort of sonic-scan, allowing Clarke to explore the gestation of her own imagination.[10] This work is central to my concerns, but first it is worth considering another, earlier, poem that could also have been entitled 'The King of Britain's Daughter', a short poem in which Clarke again constructs a modern myth of personal origin out of the materials of an authentic Celtic myth. Entitled 'Llŷr', this poem begins with her recollections of a school outing when she was a child:

> Ten years old, at my first Stratford play:
> The river and the king with their Welsh names
> Bore in the darkness of a summer night
> Through interval and act and interval.
> Swans moved double through glossy water
> Gleaming with imponderable meanings. (*SP*, 79–80)

Behind Lear, Clarke glimpses his prototype Llŷr, the Celtic (Welsh) king of ancient Britain. And in the name of the River Avon she sees its antecedent, *afon*, the Welsh word for river. No wonder, then, that the swans move double through this water. Here at Stratford, Clarke sensed the enticing duplicities of language and excitedly listened to the Chinese whisper of words. But her awakening to the resonances of English was coincidental with, and even perhaps internally connected to, her realization that she, as a Welsh girl, stood in a very ambiguous relation to the English language. On the one hand, 'Lear' and 'Avon' demonstrated how English could distort Wales in the very act of reflecting it, just as Welsh culture had for centuries been destructively changed in being subordinated to the socio-political power of England. On the other hand, she felt very much at home, in her element as it were, watching *King Lear* at Stratford-upon-Avon; in this sense, English was after all her native medium, her mother tongue. Her beginnings as a Welsh poet writing in English can, then, be traced back to that originating moment when she saw, and became, that swan '[moving] double through glossy water/ Gleaming with imponderable meanings' (79).

But in Stratford the play's the thing, and it is indeed the part that *King Lear* itself played in the making of her as a poet that Clarke next considers: 'All. Nothing. Fond. Ingratitude. Words/ To keep me scared, awake at night. That old/ Man's vanity and a daughter's "Nothing",/ Ran like a nursery rhythm in my head'

(79). Years later, 'on the cliffs of Llŷn', that Welsh peninsula whose name uncannily chimes with Llŷr/Lear, she broods on the oppressively patriarchal character of her ancient native Celtic landscape:

> The landscape's marked with figures of old men:
> The bearded sea; thin-boned, wind-bent trees;
> Shepherd and labourer and night-fisherman.
> Here and there among the crumbling farms
> Are lit kitchen windows on distant hills
> And guilty daughters longing to be gone. (*SP*, 79)

She readily sympathizes – identifies indeed – with the women of a decaying country who are quietly desperate to escape from the unbending masculinity of so much of the history of Wales – 'Land of my fathers' as the Welsh national anthem proudly hymns it. This putative female rebellion is conceived of partly in terms of a recuperation of sensitivities despised alike by the desiccated Puritan culture of rural areas and the macho proletarian culture of the old industrial regions. So, in gently appreciative lines, in which a filigree of sounds suggests an intimate structure of interrelationships, Clarke registers the intricate, delicate, inner beauty of the new feminized land of Llŷn:

> The turf is stitched with tormentil and thrift,
> Blue squill and bird bones, tiny shells, heartsease.
> Yellowhammers sing like sparks in the gorse. (79)

But in this poem, and in Clarke's poetry as a whole, female rebellion takes another form as well – takes, indeed, the line that she learnt at Stratford from Cordelia: 'That old/ Man's vanity and a daughter's "Nothing",/ Ran like a nursery rhythm in my head.' Cordelia's 'Nothing' is the *Ursprache*, the originating, primal sound of a distinctively female idiom. But it is, nevertheless, not only on her own behalf as a woman but in the name of, and for the sake of, a genuine love of her *father* that Cordelia utters that 'Nothing'. And an important defining characteristic of Clarke's poem 'Llŷr' is the sympathy evinced in it for the haughty old royal reprobate, Lear. Indeed, by the poem's close the 'Nothing' that Cordelia utters has been blended to such an extent with the tragedy it helped precipitate that gender differences have faded away and all that is left is a sense of the sadness inherent in the human condition itself, regardless of gender; the sadness that cries out for, and through, the articulations of poetry: 'When I was ten a fool and a king sang/ Rhymes about sorrow, and there I heard/ That nothing is until it has a word' (80).

Feminist poets and myth-makers of the kind mentioned by Ostriker might well condemn Clarke's poem as a cop-out, since, instead of holding the line between male and female, it ends up by blurring it. But since I am not here concerned with ideological purity, I want simply to try to understand the reasons why Clarke proceeds as she does and to consider, in a pragmatic way, the advantages and disadvantages that accrue to her poetry. There seem to me to be two main, and closely interconnected, reasons why she raises gender issues in terms that allow them to be ultimately subsumed within an all-embracing concept of the human. The first reason concerns her relationship with her father; the second relates to Wales, and the implications of both become richly apparent in that long sequence, 'The King of Britain's Daughter'. This sequence involves the counterpointing of two sorts of narrative, each of which dominates in turn, and each of which can be interpreted as a version of the other. One narrative is autobiographical, involving the recollection of experiences from Clarke's childhood, and the other narrative is mythic, drawing its material from the great stories of the *Mabinogion*.

Clarke's father died very suddenly when she was a rebellious teenager, leaving her unable for forty years to express a grief compounded in no small part of guilt, resentment and anger. 'The King of Britain's Daughter' is one of the poems in which at long last she succeeded in breaking silence, putting words to that 'Nothing' with which she had greeted his death. The sequence is largely set in the far west of Wales, her father's native region, and the heartland of an ancient Welsh-language culture. Over millennia, the rural landscape had been imbued with legendary racial meanings to which Clarke's wondering mind was opened as a child when she was taken from urban Anglicized Cardiff to stay with her grandmother for the summer.[11] That ritual car-journey, magically transporting her from one world to another, is wistfully recalled in the sequence: 'Then rocked to sleep in the dark for a hundred miles,/ my face in his coat, soft growl/ of the Austin in my dreaming bones' (*KBD*, 2). Here, as throughout the sequence, her father is a patient, caring, nurturing, 'maternal' presence. By contrast, her briefly mentioned mother seems cold and unfeeling: witness the way she disposes of her husband's beloved old hat:

> When she gave it away . . .
>
> she gave away mornings of forage,
> beachcombings, blackberries, pebbles, eggs,
> field-mushrooms with pleated linings,
>
> his fist working it to a form
> for the leveret that quivered under my hand
> before it died. (*KBD*, 5)

Amplitude, hospitality, fecundity, delicacy, generosity, mercy – these are the attributes associated with that old hat, the *masculine* womb that gave birth to Clarke's imagination. Moreover, it was her father who gave Clarke the freedom of a countryside, rich in legend, which was commensurate with her innate capacity for wonder. If he electrified her imagination by telling her stories that metamorphosed familiar features into fantastic strangeness, he also safely earthed her imagination in the beautiful landscape of west Wales. By these means, and in a reversal of the gender roles that have conventionally been associated with poetic creation, he acted as her muse, in the sense that he empowered her mind to recognize the generous, inviting malleability of the world. Clarke's poem 'Giants' is therefore at once about the stories he told her, about the liberating scale of his imagination, and about her own resulting conception of her powers as a poet:

> Giants
>
> turn boulders into grains of sand,
> a brimming horizon to a goblet,
> capstone and orthostats of the cromlech,
> a milking stool set aslant
> on the hill's shoulder. (*KBD*, 9)

Though giants are male, Clarke came to associate these kinds of change of scale with female experience. Required to divide their time, and their very selves, between so many radically different environments, women have constantly to be changing perspective and readjusting their sights.[12]

In 'The King of Britain's Daughter', Clarke's father is more like Prospero than Lear, nowhere more so than when his modern skills as a radio engineer are mythically celebrated as the means whereby the modern world was mediated to her in homely terms: the ionosphere reflected her father's 'long wave signals back to earth,// light bending in water./ But things get tight and close,/ words, music, languages/ all breathing together under that old carthen' (*KBD*, 11). (*Carthen* is the homely Welsh word for a thick woollen blanket.) This childhood idyll (Clarke's reworking, perhaps, of her compatriot Dylan Thomas's 'Fern Hill') is, however, destroyed, when the world turns nasty. The outbreak of the Second World War is the point in the poem where the myth of the king of Britain's daughter, hitherto mostly subordinated to the recreation of actual personal memories, really comes into its own. It is therefore useful to bear in mind Clarke's own summary of that famous story from the *Mabinogion*:

> The giant Bendigeidfran, also known as Brân, son of Llŷr, was king of the island of Britain. Matholwch, king of Ireland, married Branwen, daughter of Llŷr. For a year she was happy, until the Irish Court became troubled by an old grievance against Wales. Matholwch's brothers demanded vengeance and Branwen was driven from the King's chamber to work in the kitchens. There she reared a starling and taught it to speak her name, and it flew to Wales to find her brother. When he knew of her sorrow, Bendigeidfran set off in rage across the Irish Sea with a fleet of ships. In the ensuing battle all but seven men were killed. Branwen was brought home to Wales, where she died of grief. (*KBD*, 1)

Intermittently, throughout the sequence, Clarke has evoked the presence of the mighty Brân. But it is only at this turning-point, when the world erupts into violence, that she chooses to enter wholly into the realms of Welsh myth, speaking by turns with the voices of Brân and of Branwen. Branwen, bereft of child, husband and privileged queenly status, mourns all she has lost, and dreams of being rescued through the mighty, elemental powers of her giant brother. He, Brân, in his turn, exults in his spectacular cosmic strength and is roused by anger at his sister's plight to use a language of exultant hyperbole: '*My ships are gull feathers/ towed over the drowned rocks of my rage*' (*KBD*, 15).

Myth is irreducibly multiform in structure and meaning, and is employed by Clarke at this point precisely because she wants to explore, in the very act of expressing, an intricate nexus of experiences. Obviously, the poem is in part an elegy for her father and in part an oblique meditation on war; in addition, Clarke has herself drawn attention to the way it touches upon her parents' often troubled marriage; it may also and simultaneously be about growing up into sexuality and about Clarke's ultimately unsatisfactory relationship with her first husband.[13] However, I want to concentrate simply on the way this poem is a development of a theme central to the whole sequence – the theme of the androgynous imagination: of the girl Gillian/Branwen who has been taught by her father to exult in her giant, Brân-like strength. As an earlier poem in the sequence put it, 'Giants . . . are the metaphors that shift the world,/ make delta, Gulf Stream, sea-road/ from a stream spilt on the beach' (*KBD*, 9). Her father had taught her to acknowledge *both* the delicacy *and* the convulsiveness of her own mind, to image herself in *both* conventionally female *and* conventionally male terms. Experience subsequently taught her that disaster resulted when Brân was separated from Branwen: the latter dwindles from a proud queen into an exploited drudge; the former turns hubristically violent, maddened into creating carnage by an excess of testosterone. It is significant that this mythic interlude at the imaginative centre of 'The King of Britain's Daughter' ends with an elegiac tribute to her father in the form of a beautiful epithalamium celebrating the reunion of male and female, Brân and Branwen:

> When he hears my name
> he comes as a black crow,
> blessed and iridescent
> in the rising sun,
> giant striding the sea,
> prince with his fleet of ships,
> brother with a starling
> cupped in his nesting hands. (*KBD*, 16)

From Clarke's relationship with her father, then, came her abiding impulse to temper her awareness of the important social history and pathology of gender-difference with a reluctance to draw a hard-and-fast distinction between the sexes. Hence, for

instance, her unwillingness to use the Blodeuwedd story as a way
of indicting men, and her retelling it in a way that allowed her to
separate out the various strands or issues, so that she could
concentrate on those that specifically concerned women without
thereby either completely excluding or immediately implicating
men. Hence, too, her characteristic comments such as the following about a supposed new group of poets:

> It is the naturalness of the tone of this school of writers, most of
> them women, which is radically different from the voice of the old
> order. It springs too from the fact that most girl-children speak
> sooner and read sooner than boys, and have earlier memories.
> Words that come early are rooted deeply in sensuous experience
> and can thereafter never lose their primitive force.[14]

This is a woman poet's working theory of language that is at once
explored and consciously instanced in 'The King of Britain's
Daughter'. But Clarke has not yet finished. She concludes by
saying: 'These are, of course, only tendencies. Not all women's
poetry could be identified in this way, and many men possess
these characteristics.' One of the men she clearly has in mind is
Seamus Heaney, a poet by whom she has been greatly influenced, and who has himself memorably identified the 'feminine'
aspects of his own sensibility in essays such as 'Feeling into
Words' and 'The Fire i' the Flint', collected in the volume entitled *Preoccupations*. In another essay from the same collection
he has (skirting stereotype) described his poetry as 'a somnam-
bulist encounter between masculine will and intelligence and
feminine clusters of image and emotion'.[15]

Interestingly enough, this concept of the androgynous imagination, so influentially formulated by the Romantics, seems implicit
in the celebrated treatment of the Branwen story earlier in this
century by the important Welsh-language poet R. Williams Parry.
In 'Drudwy Branwen' ('Branwen's Starling') the intrepidly voyag-
ing, masculine starling, who obviously symbolizes the poet, is
partially feminized not only through close association with the
suffering Branwen but also by being represented as a creature of
sensibility, 'the birds of the world's buffoon', mocked by the
callously jocular sailors.[16] Carrying the message for Brân that the
melancholy Branwen has secured by skilful stitches to his body,

and taught by her to 'speak' the sounds of a desperate human plea for help, he journeys heroically across the ocean from Ireland to Wales, where 'he seeks a single one, –/ The soul that is set apart,/ The god in the form of man' (51). Here, too, in this image of Brân, is a suggestion of the androgynous completeness of a Christ-like redeemer, a man of sorrows yet of prodigious physical strength. Williams Parry's treatment of Branwen contrasts strikingly with, for instance, the use made of her in Harri Webb's 'A Crown for Branwen'. There she becomes the female symbol of Wales, and Webb, as self-styled representative of the newly nationalist 'Anglo-Welsh poets' of the 1960s, designates himself her devoted knight-protector – a clear instance of masculine appropriation of the legend, with conventional emphasis being placed on the help-less passivity of the stereotypically feminine Branwen.[17]

What is clear is that, partly because of her father, Clarke regards the landscape, and the culture, of Welsh-speaking west Wales as fundamentally hospitable to both 'feminine' and 'feminized' experience. This is apparent in details, such as the harmonious blending of male and female in her vision at Ystrad Fflur of 'a river blossoming on stone', or the suggestively bisexual character of her response to the grave of Dewi Emrys, that beloved vagabond of a Welsh poet:

> This roughest stone of all, a sand-stone pod
> Bursting with words, is Dewi Emrys's grave.
> And all around the living corn concedes
> Fecundity to him. (*SP*, 27)

This is not, however, to overlook her more assertive attempts to claim a place in the male-voice chorus of Welsh poetry. In 'Dyddgu Replies to Dafydd' she enables the mute object of the praise of Wales's greatest poet to become a speaking subject, and she thus empowers a woman to speak her own differently erotic love poem; to yearn for 'when the wind whitens the tender/ underbelly of the March grass/ thick as pillows under the oaks' (*SP*, 23). And in the companion poem 'At Ystrad Fflur', Clarke quietly claims, in the name of her female self, not only the place where Dafydd ap Gwilym is buried but also the traditions of praise poetry and *canu bro* (poetry of place), which had previously been virtually a Welsh male preserve. In her poem, the landscape becomes vividly female in body, culminating in a sensation of how 'desire runs// Like sparks in stubble through the memory/ of the place, and a yellow mustard field/ is a sheet of flame in the heart' (*SP*, 24). It is almost as if it has taken a woman to recognize, and in that sense fully to awaken, the riotous 'desire' that is pent up in this location, that latent passion which is the true legacy of Dafydd ap Gwilym and which is the hidden blazon of puritanically and politically oppressed Wales.

It is also the landscape of the west that enables her gradually to dissolve the tension between her parents which had been symbolized, as she has put it, by their quarrels over the Welsh language (to which her mother had been implacably hostile). In 'Blaen Cwrt', her poem about making her home in Dyfed, the restoration of the old farmhouse becomes the ground of reconciliation, of a new order of relating. It is a 'relationship' poem, beginning as it does by addressing an interlocutor: 'You ask how it is. I will tell you' (*SP*, 10). This is a place that exists only in Clarke's relating to it, which in turn is inscribed in her relating of it, which consists of her sense of it as a complex structure of interrelating. It exists only as a place held in common – the stress throughout is on the first person plural; the language is one of encounter ('Holding a thick root/ I press my bucket through the surface/ Of the water'); the similes are social connectives ('Our fingers curl on/ Enamel mugs of tea, like ploughmen'); the syntax is a homogenizing device ('All is ochre and earth and cloud-green/ Nettles'); and everywhere there is the semiotics of coexistence ('Some of the smoke/ Rises against the ploughed, brown field/ As a sign to our neighbours in the/ Four folds of the valley that we are in'). Integration of the self, and simultaneous integration into a community of people and nature, are the poem's implicit themes, made explicit in the concluding lines:

> It has all the first
> Necessities for a high standard
> Of civilised living: silence inside
> A circle of sound, water and fire,
> Light on uncountable miles of mountain
> From a big, unpredictable sky,
> Two rooms, waking and sleeping,
> Two languages, two centuries of past
> To ponder on, and the basic need
> To work hard in order to survive. (*SP*, 10)

These lines seek to contain and pacify instability ('a big, unpredictable sky'), and their resemblance to an epithalamium – a
celebration of the marriage between Wales's two cultures –
acquires a poignancy when read in the light of the tensions in
Clarke's early family background.

By so clearly emphasizing at the outset her intention to 'tell'
her reader/ listener not about Blaen Cwrt but literally 'how it is',
Clarke is demonstrating the power of language, and the authority
to be a poet that is vested in her by this place. In this respect, the
poem is her signature text as a writer, and specifically as a woman
writer, because the kind of sensuous immersion in, and receptive
submission to, the ancient particularities of this landscape in the
very heartland of Welsh-language culture is here associated in
Clarke's mind with a 'feminine' sensibility which (as has already
been noted) is nevertheless not the unique preserve of the female
sex. Thus the poem may be read as a celebration of a feminized
– and, indeed, feminizing – landscape, centring on the implicit
demonstration that Clarke's way of moving in and setting up
home is not the conventionally masculine way of taking possession of a property. Rather, she tentatively feels her way, adapting
herself gently to what is there, taking new shape from it, just as
'Some of the smoke seeps through the stones/ Into the barn where
it curls like fern/ On the walls'.

＊　　＊　　＊　　＊

There remains a second aspect to, and reason for, Gillian
Clarke's refusal to polarize the sexes and to promote gender
conflict, and it is again because she relates to Wales on terms that
are connected to her relationship with her father. Both he and her
mother were Welsh-speakers, who raised their children to speak
only English. Her mother viewed Welsh as an obstacle to social
advancement and so disapproved of any interest shown in the
language by her daughter. The attitude of Clarke's father,
though, was much more mixed. As 'The King of Britain's
Daughter' shows, he surreptitiously encouraged, and fed, her
interest in Welsh legend. He developed in her a kind of racial
memory, making her aware of her inheritance, of being heiress to
a rich, ancient culture wholly unrelated to that of England.
Consequently, when Clarke broke with her husband in the 1970s,

she migrated back to her father's native region of west Wales, settling in Blaen Cwrt. There she learnt sufficient Welsh to enable her to integrate with the ancient indigenous culture of that area. But during the very years of her resettlement, the Welsh culture of west Wales was being seriously threatened by non-Welsh-speaking immigrants, drawn to the area by its great natural beauty, and able to settle there because of the relative cheapness of local housing. It is, perhaps, the decay of a very old, quintessentially Welsh, way of life that is in part being mourned in the concluding parts of 'The King of Britain's Daughter', where Clarke notes that Brân's stone, that had 'balanced its mass so delicately,/ four thousand years withstanding weather/ like a dozing horse' (*KBD*, 20), has now toppled into the sea:

> Today I swim beyond the empty headland
> in search of the giant's stone.
> Do I see it through green translucent water,
> shadow of a wreck, a drowned man's shoulder,
> a clavicle huge as a ship's keel
> wedged between rocks? (*KBD*,18)

Clarke has come to realize that to belong to a Welsh-speaking community is to belong to a permanently beleaguered remnant. This has made her aware of other ways, too, in which Welsh identity is in a precarious condition. Infusing her writing, therefore, is a sense of the tenacious spirit of community (characteristic alike of rural Welsh-speaking Wales and of industrial English-speaking Wales), which has hitherto made possible the survival of a small nation. Solidarity is a feature of the Welsh past which is more than ever a necessity in the Welsh present if there is to be a Welsh future. Under such socio-cultural circumstances, the issue of gender-conflict takes on a very different complexion. Clarke's poetry consistently tries to redress the balance – of the historical record, in social arrangements, of cultural life – in favour of previously slighted female experience.[18] But it attempts to do so *without* destroying the fragile integrity of her people by setting male against female. Hence, for example, *Letter from a Far Country* tries gently, rather than militantly, to make visible the contribution of women to Welsh society past and present; and 'The King of Britain's Daughter' pointedly claims that modern

Welsh woman is the legitimate heiress of the original Celtic inhabitants of Britain.

In many respects, Clarke shares the plight of women in other marginalized cultures, as illuminatingly described by Marilyn Reizbaum in her recent essay on Scottish and Irish Women's writing.[19] 'When a culture has been marginalized', notes Reizbaum, 'its impulse toward national legitimization tends to dominate in all spheres and forms of cultural realization', so that women have inescapably to address the problematical 'relationship between their national and sexual identities'. Consequently, 'women have found themselves in a peculiar predicament, compelled to realize or challenge the demands of the nationalist imperative in order to clarify the terms of their own oppression' by the very culture that has itself been oppressed. In such circumstances, women have to 'reinterpret nationalism and to establish a role for themselves as feminists within it'; and for an example of this work of radical readjustment Reizbaum turns to the poetry of Eavan Boland, a contemporary Irish poet particularly admired by Clarke.[20]

'I felt it vital', Boland has written, 'that women poets such as myself should establish a discourse with the idea of a nation, should bring to it a sense of the emblematic relationship between the feminine experience and a national past.'[21] Clarke has consistently used her poetry to fashion just such a discourse, challenging the patriarchal terms which have dominated the self-descriptions of Welsh culture. However, she has also established her own rules of engagement, which take her own personal experience and local Welsh cultural conditions into account.

*   *   *   *

Eavan Boland has similarly refused to equate her poetry in any simple, unequivocal way with gender identity, and she has talked memorably about the double bind of her relationship, as a woman, to her country's heavily masculine literary tradition:

As I read the poems of the tradition, it could often seem to me that I was entering a beautiful and perilous world filled with my own silence, where I was accorded the unfree status of an object. And yet there was a paradox. As I struggled to become my own subject

– in poems I could hardly write and in a literary tradition which blurred the feminine and the national – these poems were enabling and illuminating. As a woman I felt some mute and anxious kinship with those erotic subjects which were appropriated; as a poet I felt confirmed by the very powers of expression which appropriated them.[22]

These, and other, comments by Boland voice the feelings not only of Gillian Clarke but also of her close friend and near-neighbour, Menna Elfyn, whose Welsh-language poetry Clarke has translated and with whom she has occasionally collaborated. The ambiguous relationship in which Elfyn's work stands to that of the overwhelmingly male traditional literary culture of Wales – a masculinity particularly evident in the classic strict-metre poetry that is at its core – has been evidenced both in her writing and in the reactions to it. Particularly noteworthy, perhaps, is the feeling in some quarters that her poetry was slow to receive the official recognition it deserved (from the National Eisteddfod as from influential anthologists) because, in significant part, of its heterodox, feminine character.

Throughout her career, Elfyn has certainly felt the need, as part of what Boland called 'the struggle to become my own subject', to recast hallowed poetic forms in her own female image. The elegy, for instance, assumes a new, feminine form in such poems as 'Broits' ('Brooch'), which speaks of how 'it's from the soft inner depth/ we work the brooch of our lives'.[23] As well as quietly revaluing an object traditionally stigmatized as a mere piece of female frippery, the poem bodies forth woman's experience of the generative processes secretly proceeding within the concavities of her body and mind. Also – like the poem 'Amber' – it gently subverts the binary (and frequently gendered) opposition between soft and hard, since what is here revealed is how each of these qualities can, in psychic and moral terms, be regarded as an aspect of the other. So, too, in another feminized elegy, this time for a woman who died in the anti-nuclear demonstrations at Greenham Common, heroism is recognized as involving hard moral resolve, appear though it may in 'soft', unfamiliar, female guise: 'And soberly these sisters from Wales/ went – not a bit like Catraeth boyos'.[24]

Praise poetry is similarly changed to arresting effect by Elfyn when, for instance, she devotes a whole sequence to sensual celebration of woman's hair, the display of which has (in line with Pauline teaching) been traditionally censured by the patriarchal chapels, whereas it had been lustily lauded by Dafydd ap Gwilym and his kind who made women the objects of their passion. It is her own passion, however, that is the frank subject of Elfyn's poetry. She it is who assumes the role of sexual petitioner and practitioner, producing thereby a love poetry suffused with the ecstasy of female eroticism. And in thus invading and appropriating a male genre, she makes inventive play with several of its key conventions, including that of the *llatai*, or love messenger. After her husband has been imprisoned for his lawbreaking activities in defence of the Welsh language, Elfyn sends him Basildon Bond messages couched in a hyperbolic language of longing that captures the anguished comedy of despair: 'While you were in prison/ the banks of the Teifi froze/ in civil disobedience,/ and the salmon died/ of broken hearts!' (*E*, 83).

But although instances of Elfyn's fruitful practice of refashioning Welsh genres could easily be multiplied, ultimately more important may be the way she has altered the deep structure of Welsh prosody. This may best be appreciated if one views aspects of her style as simultaneously moving towards *cynghanedd* and departing from it in a silent contrapuntal dance which constitutes a poetic conversation between the masculine and feminine genders. Elfyn's writing abounds in the kinds of sonic and rhythmic devices that characterize *cynghanedd*, but it never quite submits to the strict discipline that governs strict-metre poetry. Implicit in that discipline is an appreciation, by the poets, of what Gerard Manley Hopkins, that celebrated English beneficiary of *cynghanedd*, called 'the achieve of, the mastery of the thing'.[25] And much of what Seamus Heaney has to say about Hopkins in 'The Fire i' the Flint' seems also to illuminate the prosodic practices of Welsh *barddas*:

> The Hopkins poem is fretted rather than fecund . . . The words are crafted together more than they are coaxed out of one another . . . Hopkins's consonants alliterate to maintain a design whereas Keats's release a flow . . . Keats woos us to receive, Hopkins alerts us to perceive . . . There is a conscious push of the deliberating intelligence, a siring strain rather than a birth-push in his poetic act . . . As opposed to the symbolist poetic, it is concerned with statement instead of states of feeling. Indeed, at this point it is

> interesting to recall Ben Jonson's strictures on the Shakesperian
> fluency, rejecting linguist mothering in favour of rhetorical
> mastery . . . [Jonson] values control, rule, revision, how things are
> fit, how they are fitted . . . [Like Jonson, Hopkins] valued what he
> called 'the masculine powers' in poetry, the presence of 'powerful
> and active thought' – it was typical that when he realized his 'new
> rhythm' he had to schematize it into a metric. (*P*, 84, 85, 86)

Thus subtly made, the point may help us understand both Elfyn's
reluctance to identify her (female) self with authentic *cynghanedd*,
and the difficulties the purists of *barddas* have, in turn, sometimes
experienced in trying to appreciate her work.

Another way of understanding this situation would be via a
distinction between a poetry of 'closure' and a poetics of openness. Openness is a state of being, and a poetic stance, fearfully
celebrated in Elfyn's writing. For her, the concept is cognate with
ideas of (ad)venturing, of risk, of vulnerability, of exposure, of
psychic excursion, of acknowledging otherness – all of which
relate in their turn to the way she apprehends her Welshness, her
religious faith, and her womanliness. Menna Elfyn instinctively
recognizes that this nexus of preoccupations is constitutive of her
very being as a person and as a poet, and her poetry is accordingly
full of motifs and images that take her, and us, to the very nub of
this truth. Most obviously, she is fascinated by boundaries, limits,
liminal situations, neighbourliness ('Who is my neighbour?').
Moreover, inscribed in the very rhythms of her writing are the
motions of a spirit at once ardent to press on (daring transgres-
sion) and yet still (cautiously? obediently?) inclined to hang back
('Will the ladies please stay behind?'):

> A headful of hair was a girl's crowning glory,
> It made her hair stand on end
> to see the paradise of it fan over her nape,
> a stubborn standard waving on the wind. (*CA*, 59)

Muted though this passage has been by translation, it is still
possible to hear Elfyn's characteristic hesitant–bold rushes into
speech, and to understand why she favours short spurts of
impetuous expression.

One of her most powerful meditations on openness takes the
form of a 'Psalm to the Little Gap in the Cell Door'. By

contemplating this crack, this peephole, this chink, she is able to organize a series of variations on what is, for her, a seminal theme, before concluding with a tribute to 'Dark-eyed Gaia,/ Namaskara, I greet the divine in you/ which out of my being makes an open door' (*CA*, 25). By thus feminizing the divinity of earth, Elfyn turns the openness that woman is fated to, not least by the definitive character of her genitalia, from a female curse into a physical, psychological and spiritual blessing. But the serenity of this conclusion is far from being the dominant tone of her writing. Rather, she is more likely to be troubled by a turbulent sense of the ambivalence of woman's exposed condition. As she puts it in her elegy for Sylvia Plath and Anne Sexton, 'For a poet who's a mother/ there's no safety-pins for life,/ no prior understanding/ between bottles for baby/ and the paradise of language' (*E*, 81).

'No prior understanding' is a suggestive phrase that opens windows on to Elfyn's poetry. Viewed in these terms, *cynghanedd* can be regarded as a mode of proceeding which presumes a 'prior understanding' of set rules and which therefore honours a standing agreement, a set protocol; whereas, by contrast, Elfyn's feminine poetics favours the constant chancy improvisation of harmonies and meanings. This mode of proceeding is instanced and emblematized in the very title of her elegy for Plath and Sexton: 'Byw, benywod, byw' ('Live, sisters, live'). While very much in the spirit of *cynghanedd*, the buried internal rhyme ('*Byw*, ben*yw*od, *byw*') conforms to none of *cynghanedd*'s many, invariably precise rules. Its inexactitude is, however, part of Elfyn's point. Unlike men, women are unable to live within a social order already so well adjusted to their several needs that it seems 'naturally' to correspond to them. Instead, they live an experientially dispersed existence and learn constantly to improvise a rough, approximate coherence out of it all – rather like the broken, unorthodox harmony of 'Byw, benywod, byw'. For the authoritativeness and finality of *cynghanedd*, Elfyn substitutes the lability of heuristic expression. Such an approach is implicit in the view she takes of Wales in 'The Shapes She Makes' ('Siapiau o Gymru'), a poem that explores the many pictures that may be discerned in any outline map of the country, before concluding that Wales is 'polysyllabled pictures' and that, truly seen, she is 'comically scattered' (*E*, 99).

Obviously, Elfyn's whole outlook, although mediated by her own highly original and unmistakably Welsh sensibility, is derived from the international women's movement, in whose literature she is very well read. In her important essay in *Sglefrio ar Eiriau* (*Skating on Words*), for instance, she demonstrates her extensive knowledge of feminist theory from prominent British, French and American sources, and identifies several key concepts, including phallogocentrism, man-made language, *l'écriture feminine*, the wild zone, body language and gynocriticism. Her readiness to use such concepts as a stimulus for her own writing is, however, more than outweighed by her determination not to identify wholeheartedly with any of them; and such wariness is due in no small part to the sense, stemming directly from her Welsh experience, that gender is by no means the sole determinant of personal identity.

'In order to open up new territory for considering every aspect of the place, feelings and desire of woman', Elfyn has written, 'it isn't sensible to treat gender every time as the *sine qua non* of her presiding passion, because other factors may be equally important and relevant – such factors as class and nationality, to say nothing of those experiences that relate only to intimate personal experience'.[26] As we have seen, this is a view shared by Gillian Clarke and Eavan Boland, and in each case it is rooted in a sense of belonging to a vulnerably small national community – a cultural collective that might not survive a deep split along gender lines. Hence a poem such as that which opens Elfyn's first bilingual volume, *Eucalyptus*: 'The Year of the Bat, 1986', tells of the occasion when the poet responded to a plea, by a panicky woman from the holiday home next door, to rescue her from a bat that had got trapped in her living-room. Releasing it, Elfyn suddenly saw in the creature an image of her Welsh-speaking self as seen by this invasive stranger from England – a threateningly wild thing, to be tolerated only when safely disposed of. In this instance, then, it is not gender but shared language (and therefore culture and nationality) that defines kinship.

By turning the story about the bat into a parable of Welsh culture, Elfyn fashions a self-image for a community that finds no corroborating reflection of itself in 'mainstream' British culture. Like women, Welsh Wales can rely on no 'prior understanding', no established system of signs that acknowledges and serves its needs. And as for the Welsh woman poet, her situation is analogous to that of her Irish counterpart, as summarized by Boland: 'her sense of power inside the poem must be flawed and tempered not just by a perception of powerlessness outside it but also by the memory of her traditional and objectified silence within it' (OL, 186). As poet, Elfyn has therefore to perform much the same service for Wales (and her own Welshness) as she does for women (and her own womanliness); she has somehow to evolve a language that will speak to and for her identity as a Welsh woman. In her effort so to do, she learns of her consequent partial affinity with disinherited peoples of many countries and conditions – the Blacks of South Africa, the Vietnamese, the Bosnians, the Mexican street children – and through her poetry she endeavours to allow their dumb voices to speak.

The two interactive poles of Elfyn's personal world – her strong identification with her own sex, and her ungendered awareness of her Welshness – are illustrated respectively in the poems mourning the child she lost through miscarriage, and the elegiac sequence in memory of the charismatic historian and 'people's remembrancer' Gwyn A. Williams. The former series profoundly alters the *barddas* convention of *marwnadu* (grieving for the dead and memorializing them) by using that ancient genre, for the first time, to express a mother's anguish at losing a physical and psychological part of her very self; the foetus that failed to become a 'child'. Difficult problems therefore immediately arise. How is such an indeterminate 'being' to be addressed ('The lump of life's failed, what can I say', E, 23)? How exactly can such a loss be characterized? How may such a uniquely private anguish be shared with others? How is it possible to honour the passing of a living 'thing' that was also a nascent person, a creaturely object that defied ordinary classification? 'Your coffin was a plastic bag/ like the see-through gizzard/ from a chicken's gut' (E, 21). If this is, for a woman, a lonely and agonizing personal dilemma, then it is also a related torment for a woman poet, because the vocabulary and conventions of traditional elegy are of so little immediate use or comfort to her.

New psycho-poetic strategies have to be developed for dealing with such a crisis. Elfyn finds, for instance, that botanic and biological metaphors 'naturally' present themselves under circumstances where an attachment to an organism has made her sharply aware of the metabolism of her own being: 'A part of me is gone for ever./ Pollen is lost from the mother-cell,/ the petal of the ardent rose/ with its blushes is raped' (*E*, 23). Implicit in this is the difference between a woman's view of the female form and that of a man, with Elfyn turning the male's celebrated cliché that his love is like a red, red rose into a functional view of young female beauty as containing the potential for fecundity. Man's image of willowy young womanhood is given a similar dislocating twist towards a sobering truth in the opening lines of 'Y Gneuen Wag'/ 'The empty shell':

> Though my body was not ripe-shelled
> or brown like the fine hazel,
> still, as a young tree I wanted
> to cast nuts for humanity –
> the bite of them hard and true,
> strength the character in their shells. (*E*, 23)

Through these lines there speaks the culture of service in which Elfyn, the daughter of a Nonconformist minister, was raised. In fact, any full exploration of her sense of herself as a woman would have to take careful account of the ambivalent relationship to that Nonconformist culture which is apparent in all her writing.

It is perhaps most movingly apparent in a passage in which Elfyn touches on the umbilical cord between her elegizing and her ambiguous status as a 'mother':

> No one sang a hymn
> or spread prayers over you.
> You had no praise.
> No one hugged you
> except the black doctor in his fist.
>
> But I, I shall unwrap a song
> for that solitary exequy
> in the busy toing and froing of sickness
> over the hospital's aggressive lights;
> I'll reach to the very last solemn thought
> before I'll let go my elegy for you. (*E*, 21)

The shift to formal poetic syntax and vocabulary in that last stanza ('But I, I shall unwrap a song') marks the point at which

209

Elfyn directly claims from the male elegists the right to honour her own dead, just as the lines that follow mark the point where she snatches her baby back, in imagination, from the depersonalizing milieu of the heavily masculinized world of modern medicine. These verbal gestures are the counter-attack of one who feels, as woman and as poet, that her utterance, like her uterus, has been contemptuously disregarded. And what moves her to such aggression is, of course, a mother's instinct to protect her offspring. These lines of poetry are a protective, belated, verbal embrace, which is also the soft shawl of a winding-sheet. The words are lapped gently around the foetus in order to ensure, and to secure, a safe place for it within the human world. And the concluding phrases ('I'll reach to the very last solemn thought') contain within them a multitude of commitments: to make sure that last thoughts of the departed 'baby' are lasting ones; to insist on the intensity of such an undervalued loss; to discover in this supposedly 'insignificant' instance the type of *all* mourning and, indeed, the wrenching evidence of our own mortality. These meanings are even more hauntingly present in the original Welsh, the syntax of which allows the last line to be read, moreover, as 'before I let go my elegy in order to go' ('cyn gadael dy farwnad i fynd'). The unspoken purpose of every elegy is, after all, to fit us again, but in a new way, for life.

Even as Elfyn struggles, then, to fashion elegy anew in an effort to find appropriate forms of expression for an uniquely female experience, she clearly exposes those normally hidden ingredients of grieving that psychoanalysts have long insisted constitute the true profile of every experience of loss, regardless of gender. Resentment, anger, a mingled sense of guilt and personal betrayal – these emotions so quickly sublimated into sadness in conventional elegiac practice become nakedly apparent under circumstances that so obviously license such a reaction. If Elfyn is swept by 'a gust of longing/ in case it was I bruised it so much – / before it decomposes to the four winds' (*E*, 23), she can also recall it as 'that ugly, premature thing inside me' (*E*, 25) and confess to its having been at times 'more like an enemy, stuck tight/ to my being' (*E*, 19). And the unexpected relevance to males of this inalienably female experience is made apparent by Elfyn in her conclusion to 'Pabwyr Nos' ('Night Light'):

> Now my womb's empty, I can only
> breed a poem's
> higgledy-piggledy words
> with grief in its lap –
> the oldest epic of our history,
> the anguish baked before I was made. (*E*, 25)

The images are unequivocally female, with Elfyn taking fine, pointed advantage of the fact that *cerdd*, the Welsh word for poem, is feminine in gender; but they ultimately embrace in their purview the whole of the all-too-homely human experience of anguish and grief.

Shortly after embarking on her career as poet, Elfyn realized that she 'was out of step [with Welsh poetry]: I neither wrote in *cynghanedd* nor did I like elegies. All the poems of praise in Welsh seemed to me sickly. There was so little about human life and living.'[27] If her poems mourning her miscarriage remedied that deficiency, then so, after a different fashion, did her poetic sequence in memory of the electrifying historian Gwyn A. Williams, who had himself seemed so capable on television of magicking the Welsh past alive. In its invocation of the historian as our guide through the otherwise inaccessible regions of past time, the sequence recalls one of the greatest Welsh poems of the twentieth century, Saunders Lewis's elegy to Sir John Edward Lloyd (1861–1947), the incomparable historian of medieval Wales.[28] But whereas Lewis's stately poem, consciously modelled on passages from the *Aeneid* and the *Inferno*, was designed to convey his majestic vision of medieval Welsh culture's important place in a European Christendom that was the mighty heir of classical civilization, Elfyn's sequence offers a very different view of history. It is Williams 'the people's hero' whom she honours, with his incorrigible dream of social justice and his tempestuous, gloriously intemperate celebration of the anonymous masses' attempts, down the centuries, to realize aspects of that dream. In retrospect, his vivid recklessness as a driver comes, for her, to figure his impatient unwillingness to play safe, to play the professional historian strictly according to the rules.

In viewing Williams thus, Elfyn may be instinctively responding to him as her *alter ego* or spiritual twin, not only because she has herself been a notable political activist but also because he functions, after a fashion, as the masculine muse of her poetry. If her verbal portrait of Williams is wonderfully evocative of the man as he was – a mesmeric speaker whose fluency was always being perilously snatched from the very jaws of a stutterer – the rapid, impressionistic style she employs is both apt for her subject and intimately expressive of herself. Tony Conran's observations on that style could, in fact, apply to the historian as well as to the poet:

> Any flaws there may be in your Gwyn Alf sequence are simply the overflow of your involvement in words and in life. Words and ideas and images churn, flash, spark off one another. Sometimes I think you are only just in control; they run almost out of your grasp. It is difficult to see where they are leading you, sometimes. But this sense of words and images struggling – and you struggling with them, or flowing with them, or letting them exist, and still being you saying things, feeling things in your own particular way – that is where the excitement of your poetry comes from. (*CA*, 10)

The contrast with Saunders Lewis could scarcely be greater. His elegy is written in a style calculated to exude *gravitas* and to demonstrate the authority of the august, venerable tradition that underwrites every line of his formal composition. The unspoken message of the poem is that Lewis is as incontrovertibly the chosen heir of the great civilization being invoked as was Sir John Edward Lloyd, the historian elect of that civilization. And that civilization is constructed (as much by the magisterial style as by the exclusively male allusions) in terms so adamantly masculine that women literally never enter the picture.

However, in choosing Gwyn Alf Williams as her guide to Welsh 'tradition', Elfyn chooses an altogether different, and far less severely gendered, figure. In her elegy, immense respect is compatible with immense affection, and the blend of the two results in a companionableness, a sense of common cause and common purpose that goes deeper than gender difference. Part of the reason for this is, no doubt, that if, as a woman poet, Elfyn has been made 'conscious of the silences which have preceded her, which still surround her' (to repeat Boland's words), she has also become aware 'that these silences have been at least partly redeemed within the past expressions of other poets, most of them male'. One such 'poet' was Williams, and in paying tribute to him Elfyn is, like Gillian Clarke, affirming that her experience of her own Welshness has made it impossible for her to prioritize gender as the single most intimate determinant of her own identity. For both Elfyn and Clarke, their situation as Welsh women poets therefore seems closest to that of the Irish woman poet, as scrupulously indicated by Eavan Boland in the concluding paragraphs of *Object Lessons*:

> I am neither a separatist nor a postfeminist. I believe that the past matters, yet I do not believe we will reach the future without living through the womanly angers which shadow this present. What worries me most is that women poets may lose their touch, may shake off their opportunities because of the pressures and temptations of their present position.
>
> It seems to me, at this particular time, that women have a destiny in the form. Not because they are women; it is not as simple as that. Our suffering, our involvement in the collective silence do not – and will never – of themselves guarantee our achievements as poets. But if we set out in the light of that knowledge and that history, determined to tell the human and poetic truth, and if we avoid simplification and self-deception, then I believe we are better equipped than most to discover the deepest possibilities and subversions within poetry itself. (*OL*, 254)

7

Wales's American dreams

~

One day in 1876, Walt Whitman, one of the founders of anglophone American literature and today regarded as America's greatest poet, began to read his poems aloud in his friend Sidney Morse's sculpture studio in Philadelphia. A small crowd gathered, including the chambermaid, whose wide-eyed wonder attracted Whitman's attention. On enquiring, he discovered she had come all the way from Wales in search of the lavish wages she had been told were available at the great Centennial Exposition in Philadelphia. But she had been desperately disappointed in her expectations, and even the pittance she had been receiving as a drudge and skivvy was no longer being paid:

> 'Money, money!' exclaimed Whitman. 'All for money you came; lost your friend for money; for money are now in distress. Well, to an extent I can sympathize. But if I, like you, was well-to-do in one place, I'd not pack my duds and start for another for money.' 'Oh, no, sir; but we wanted to see the Fair, too.' '*Have* you?' 'No, not yet.' '*Will* you?' 'I don't know what I will do, sir.'[1]

Since the fabled time of Madoc, myriad Welsh men and women have gone to America for money, to see the Fair and for many other cognate reasons. Their story has been repeatedly told, as legend, as adventure, as poetry, as fiction and, of course, as history. Prominent Welsh American sites such as Bryn Mawr have been repeatedly examined; distinguished Welsh Americans have been identified (from the Philadelphia Quakers to John L. Lewis and Hubert Humphrey) or where necessary invented (the Welsh connection with the Founding Fathers seems to strengthen every year). Welsh American myths have been colourfully elaborated and later soberly disavowed. To modern tastes, some of the historical facts, particularly in the hands of Gwyn A.

Williams, have proved, if anything, stranger and more colourful than the fictions they have displaced.[2]

But this chapter is not directly concerned with any of this. Nor does it attempt to examine the wealth of materials, ever growing in mass and in richness of historical significance, that the Welsh Americans have produced over the centuries. There will therefore be no reference made here to the letters of Welsh Mormon migrants, the records of the flourishing Welsh *eisteddfodau*, or the extensive Welsh-language literature of the United States (poetry, fiction and, of course, journals and newspapers).[3] Instead, this study will limit itself simply to the descriptions of America offered by Welsh-based writers of this century – descriptions, that is, in Wallace Stevens's celebrated sense of that word:

> Description is
> Composed of a sight indifferent to the eye.
>
> It is an expectation, a desire,
> A palm that rises up beyond the sea,
>
> A little different from reality:
> The difference that we make in what we see.[4]

Rather than seeing being believing, Stevens suggested, believing is seeing, since what we see is significantly determined by our belief systems. Consequently, he added: 'Description is revelation. It is not/ The thing described, nor false facsimile.' This chapter is accordingly interested in those descriptions of America by Welsh writers that are a revelation not so much of the United States as of the Wales from which the United States is seen.

Stevens's obsessive reworking and rewording, throughout his poetic career, of the relationship between plain ocular perception and imaginative vision was itself an unorthodox version of twentieth-century America's fascination with the relationship between the European 'expectation' and 'desire' that had first caused a new country to 'arise beyond the sea', and the hard-headed realities of contemporary life in the United States. Stevens's own life seemed to offer a peculiar gloss on this situation, since he appeared to divide his time, if not his mind, between his lucrative day job as a top insurance executive and his pleasurable moonlighting as a poet. But his poetry tells its own, rather different, story. Indeed, it can be construed as a vehement denial that his life was neatly divided between serious daytime business and frivolous evening pleasure, and as a sustained affirmation that, for him, writing poetry was the most serious business of all.

This was a quixotic belief, manifestly at odds with mainstream American culture. After all, Calvin Coolidge's blunt observation that 'the chief business of the American people is business' has become a cliché the essential truth of which very few would care to dispute. But then it might also, with equal justice, be remarked that the business of America is show business – the term being here used loosely to include all aspects of the modern entertainment industry (television, film, computer games, etc.) that has for much the greater part of this century been America's most powerful means of satisfying its primal urge to represent itself to itself and to others as incarnating a dream, an ideal, a myth. Of course, that dream has, as American writers in particular have repeatedly noted, always been ambiguously related to actual historical reality. Indeed, when Scott Fitzgerald, via his character Nick Carraway, wonders, with reference to the Great Gatsby, 'what foul dust floated in the wake of his dreams',[5] the phrasing implies the tragic possibility that America's dreams may actually, disturbingly, have been the source of American foulness. A specific example of this sombre American syndrome is found in Allen Ginsberg's 'American Change': 'what visionary gleam 100 years ago on Buffalo prairie under the molten cloud-shot sky, "the same clear light 10000 miles in all directions",/ but now with all the violin music of Vienna, gone into the great slot machine of Kansas City, Reno –'.[6] Buffalo prairie – a place-name that originally accorded soberly with fact – has been distorted through the violent intervention of modern American history into a verbal mirage, purveying the illusion that 'Buffalo prairie' denotes a prairie where an abundance of buffalo may still be found. Ginsberg thus uncovers in the American language itself a hidden indictment of the American people and their murderously visionary dreams.

Buffalo prairie must surely remind many of us of Buffalo Bill, and no more arresting example can be found than he of the equivocal character of American show business – a composite term whose constituent elements (*show* and *business*) should always be borne in mind. From 1872 to 1876, Cody combined working as a cavalry scout with a career starring in Wild West melodramas on the East Coast stage. And it was from the stage that, in 1876, he announced he was heading back to the Plains to fight the savage Lakota Sioux, led by Sitting Bull, who were desperately resisting the US government's attempts to rob them of their sacred sites in the Black Hills. Very shortly afterwards, Cody's adventure took on a new, and even more colourful, complexion following the news that Custer and his men had been massacred at the Little Big Horn. And soon Cody had headline-grabbing success to report. In a skirmish with the Cheyenne on 17 July 1876, he killed a young warrior called 'Yellow Hair'; 'then, as the troopers swept toward him, [Buffalo Bill] walked to the corpse, scalped it, and waved his trophy in the air'.[7] Later, he was to repeat this histrionic gesture many times in the revenge melodrama *The Red Right Hand: or, The First Scalp for Custer.*

What is particularly worth noting, however, is that Cody was already striking an attitude, and play-acting for real, when he killed Yellow Hair. Because, anticipating what would later happen, he had deliberately dressed himself, for the skirmish with the Cheyenne, in the sort of finery that he knew would later look good on the stage. Instead of the Plainsman's ordinary functional garb, he had worn 'a brilliant Mexican *vaquero* outfit of black velvet slashed with scarlet and trimmed with silver buttons and lace' – in other words the very costume that the dime novels of the time had led their avid readers to suppose that dashing frontiersmen and Indian-fighters actually, regularly wore. It is a dizzying moment, when, instead of show business falsely glamorizing history, history, in the very making, is made obediently to conform to the glitzy requirements of show business. American life literally imitates popular American art, and with a vengeance, since it is dressed to kill. At such a moment – which in a sense serves as a parable of American culture – what exactly is the relationship between fact and fiction; between 'dream' and 'reality'? It is, I find, a disturbing question, that takes us to the treacherous heart both of America's dreams of itself and of other cultures' dreams of America.[8]

Let us begin, then, by exploring some of the ways in which modern Welsh writers have positioned themselves in relation to this complex phenomenon of an America that is always inseparable, and sometimes indistinguishable, from its own dreaming, and that has, moreover, functioned as the great dream-factory of the modern world. In his poem 'Dodge City', Gwyn Thomas (Bangor) contrasts the modern metropolis, all metal, glass and concrete, where the carbon chokes the sunshine, with the Wild West romance its name still evokes. Then, and there, in that never-never land that masquerades as the past, Dodge City still is, as it always was, and ever will be, a land fit only for heroes:

> Yno,
> Yno y mae Sitting Bull a Geronimo. Yno,
> Yno y mae Doc Halliday, Wyatt Earp, a Bill Hickok.
> Ac yno, yn y tir pell, o hyd yn oedi
> Mewn bodolaeth y mae yntau, Buffalo Bill Cody.

> [There,
> There is Sitting Bull and Geronimo. There,
> There are Doc Halliday, Wyatt Earp, and Bill Hickok.
> And there, in the far country, still lingering
> In existence, is he, Buffalo Bill Cody.][9]

These violent old heroes of the Wild West are now pacific co-inhabitants of the Elysian fields, which are 'the prairie of immortality', and as such they retain their magical power, reproduced in the ritual incantation of the verse, to carry us from the hard pavements of our age to a world where we are all eternally children. On such a view of the matter, to confuse Buffalo Bill with William Cody is to commit what philosophers would call a category error, to mis-take myth for history. William Cody was born in 1846 and died in 1917, but Buffalo Bill continues to live on exactly the same plane as Blodeuwedd, or Olwen, or Ysbaddaden Ben Cawr, or any other of the magical figures from Welsh lore and legend. What is more, Buffalo Bill Cody lives in exactly the same *place* as Blodeuwedd and the others, since all mythological figures are equidistant from history and geography, and inhabit the supra-national world of interchangeable myth. Indeed, it could be that through Buffalo Bill the modern Welsh imagination, in child and adult, may best find its way back to Twm Siôn Cati, or some other indigenous adventurer. No wonder that Gwyn Thomas, one of the most distinguished contemporary scholars of medieval Welsh literature, chose, when acting as consultant for a modern media adaptation of the *Mabinogion*, to advise that some of the characters be modelled on well-known characters from American cartoon classics. Moreover, 'Dodge City' becomes, for him, not the name of an actual grimy place but an example of how words work in poetry – of how their mundane load of referentiality is lightened, so that they experience a kind of lift-off into the verbal equivalent of cyberspace; or, to change the metaphor, of how words, under these conditions, come to acquire a magical penumbra of associations, and so turn into the very stuff that dreams are made on.

'Rwy'n mynd yn rhywle, heb wybod ym mh'le/ Ond mae enw'n fy nghlustiau – Santa Fe' ('I'm headed somewhere, not knowing where/ But there's a word in my ears – Santa Fe').[10] The sentiments may be those of Gwyn Thomas lighting out in imagination for Dodge City, but the lines are actually by a much earlier poet, T. H. Parry-Williams (1887–1975), the nearest Welsh equivalent to a poet of the open road. His poem goes on to speak of how some American place-names seem to possess the power to tap our deepest emotions, even those that lie as deep as tears: 'Yr enwau persain ar fan a lle:/ Rwy'n wylo gan enw – Santa Fe' ('The melodious names of place and locality: I am weeping with [for/ through] a word – Santa Fe'). For Parry-Williams, as for Thomas, the invincibly distant imaginary America that is *par excellence* the modern country of romance is also, therefore, by definition, the America that provides the modern poet with a rich natural habitat.

But, as Hywel Teifi Edwards has pointed out, the plangent appeal of Santa Fe for Parry-Williams derived in good part from the original Spanish meaning of the name: Holy Faith.[11] As an agnostic, Parry-Williams found in modern America a post-Christian country, ambiguously related to the religious beliefs in the name of which it had been founded. If it contained places, such as Santa Fe, that reverberated with nostalgia, it also offered another, more disturbing, kind of enchantment: the enchantment of spiritual disenchantment, which had its own mysterious aspects, not least when it assumed the form of a mystical materialism. Parry-Williams's most profound experience of this American sublime occurred when he viewed the Grand Canyon.

On that occasion, too, Parry-Williams had felt himself to have been magically summoned by a word – by the very word 'Grand

Canyon' itself; that had no equivalent in a Welsh lexicon whose range of meanings continued to be narrowly confined within the romantic discourse of faith. And Parry-Williams's poem works by repeatedly slyly subverting the key terms of this religious discourse through secularizing them. His text thus becomes the verbal equivalent of a Grand Canyon which mockingly mimics, in its geological formations, all the great temples of the world's faiths. As so often in Parry-Williams's verse, such a revelation requires a new language for its expression, and so he sums up the Grand Canyon by coining the noun *creigiogrwydd* (rockinessence?) out of the familiar adjective *creigiog* (rocky/craggy) (*CG*, 80). The coinage enacts the thrust of this new word's meaning, since it insists on acknowledging the previously unacknowledged quintessence of the world's mere, sheer, materiality; indeed, Parry-Williams's *creigiogrwydd* and the key religious concept of *euogrwydd* (guilt) are slyly homophonous, as if in coining the former he meant to displace the latter as a foundational term for man's understanding of his place in the universe. Similarly, the poem brilliantly sees, in the dirty yellow Colorado River that silently roars through the Canyon's depths, the stealthily animating, anti-spiritual principle of life. This is the Welsh equivalent of Wallace Stevens's celebrated beholding of 'nothing that is not there and the nothing that is' (*CPWS*, 10).

There is, then, in the depths of this poem, as at the bottom of the Grand Canyon, a visionary 'dreariness' such as Wordsworth associated with his own (very different) experiences of the sublime. And in 'Nebraska' Parry-Williams discloses the affinities that exist, for him, between the version of the sublime experienced when viewing the Grand Canyon and what existentialists a decade later were to call *la nausée*; the dizzying desolation that accompanies the registering of the world's meaninglessness. So, through the grammatical imperatives of his text, Parry-Williams speeds the train in which he is travelling on its way out of the terrible monotony of a *gwlad o gae*, a whole country of field (*CG*, 85).

'Description is revelation': Stevens's dictum certainly applies to Parry-Williams, whose America is the spitting image of his Wales. Spitting, that is, in the sense that through his images of America he implies a negative image of that Wales underwritten by the certainties of Nonconformist faith in which he had grown up. A negative image too, perhaps, of that powerful new Christian ideology being developed in the Wales of the 1930s by Saunders Lewis and his associates. Just as Lewis's distinctive brand of radically conservative Catholicism involved the valorizing of medieval culture and the re-Europeanization of Wales, so, maybe, Parry-Williams's agnosticism found its natural home in the modern America that Lewis found so profoundly uncongenial.

Incurably self-conscious, Parry-Williams liked to play with his reflections on the ways in which, for him, Wales and America reflected on each other; and he positioned himself repeatedly in his poems and essays at the various intersections of this interminable process of multiple cross-referencing. In particular, he was fascinated by arbitrary coincidence and the light it could throw on the purely contingent structure both of personal identity and of the universe itself. So, in his essay on travelling the Santa Fe Line, as in the related poem about visiting Chicago, he speculates on the possibility that he may be unwittingly treading in the footsteps of those (including his brother) who had passed this way before him. It is out of just such chance convergences (of atoms, or elements, as of human lives), he implies, that the universe has been generated. And America is, for him, the place for such insights, that so strikingly contrast with the Welsh Nonconformist concept of providential design.[12]

In writing thus in the 1930s about his self-disorientating and self-reorientating encounters with America, Parry-Williams was, I would suggest, very much a pathfinder, blazing a trail for several of the most interesting Welsh writers of our own time. But before we turn to those correspondences, we need to return to showbiz America, and to Buffalo Bill.

*   *   *   *

As we have seen, Gwyn Thomas (Bangor) has been inclined, in such poems as 'Dodge City', to offer Buffalo Bill and his kind asylum in myth, and to grant them immunity from prosecution by history. For him, the universal language of the human imagination has been most compellingly spoken, in modern times, with an American accent. But is it not dangerous to regard myth as universal and to disregard the way in which it cunningly mediates the values, and the ideology, of a specific culture? Has not myth,

221

down the centuries, demonstrably been the tool of empire? Did
not Barthes, in recent times, memorably argue that the very
purpose of myth, today as ever, is to stop humanity from attending responsibly to history, and to conceal the real pattern of
distribution of economic, social and political power? Is not
American showbiz itself perhaps the most powerful current
instrument of American cultural imperialism, which in turn is the
veritable screen image of American consumer capitalism?[13] Such
questions as these were already implicit in e. e. cummings's celebrated 1920 elegy for Buffalo Bill himself:

> Buffalo Bill's
> defunct
>   who used to
>   ride a watersmooth-silver
>   stallion
> and break onetwothreefourfive pigeonjustlikethat
>   Jesus
> he was a handsome man
>   and what i want to know is
> how do you like your blueyed boy
> Mister Death.[14]

The substitution of the word 'defunct' for 'dead' is cummings's
way of registering the historical fact that the passing of William
Cody coincided with the passing of the socio-economic conditions that had given rise to the myth of Buffalo Bill. Hence, in the
poem's title cummings turns the singular noun phrase 'Buffalo
Bill' into the adjectival phrase 'Buffalo Bill's' – which makes
Buffalo Bill part of a specific ideological package, by connecting
him irrevocably to the place, the time, the people whose defining
image he was, and on whom he placed his mythic stamp.

Ed Thomas's recent *House of America* is only the latest in a
series of Welsh texts which have pointed out that Wales may be
sleepwalking to its death in the grip of its American dreams,
having failed to grasp that every nation can survive only by
dreaming the dreams of its own place and time, in its own way.
The gods of China may indeed always be Chinese, as Wallace
Stevens remarked, but the gods of the derelict, post-industrial
south Wales valleys are American. 'He didn't have to think of
going to America', says the Mother in *House of America* of her
former husband,

you don't have to go to the Wild West to find America, they've built a Wild West up the valley – you can go there and be a cowboy for a day. You can dress in your cowboy outfit, have a drink in the saloon, and they've got Country and Western singers every Friday and Saturday night ... The bloke who told me is a cowboy, he thinks he's a cowboy anyway.[15]

In their industrial heyday, there may, or so Dai Smith has suggested, have been substantial social and economic reasons for dubbing the south Wales valleys American Wales,[16] and that was the very period when Buffalo Bill brought a trainful of his Wild West troupe, complete with real live Indian chiefs, to perform their swaggering lie of a show in Cardiff. But Thomas's layabout family of the desperately unemployed, living their incestuously inbred lives in a rickety house almost literally undermined by open cast, represents a very different present-day Wales, where there are only 'Mickey Mouse' jobs, in more senses than one. This Wales's impotent Americanness consists only of its eunuch dreams of accessing the power and glamour radiated by the American media industry.

For Thomas, the collapse of Wales's industrial base has resulted in a collapse of the confidence needed by a society to image itself positively, and to reproduce itself ideologically. Elvis was the king, says Sid in *House of America*, 'but look at Wales, where's its kings, where's our heroes? – one answer, mate, we haven't got any. I mean let's face it, Boyo, Harry Secombe isn't a bloke I'd stand in the rain for, is he?' 'Harry Secombe never said he was a hero', Boyo protests. 'No, and he's fucking right too', is Sid's last, telling word on a Wales supposedly unable to produce contemporary heroes, and a Wales whose previously self-empowering myths have wilted like the daffodil clutched by the insane mother in *House of America* (*HA*, 46–7). Her insanity comes from knowing the nightmare truth about her family; but her children's insanity comes from their wholesale flight into the world of fantasy – of Frank Sinatra, Elvis Presley, Clint Eastwood, Marlon Brando and, above all, Jack Kerouac. The mad logic of such obsessions is tracked throughout the play with wild, grim wit.

Throughout this century, Wales has dreamt of America in different ways, at different times, and in different places, so that this complex collective fantasia reveals a lot about Wales's biculturalism, regionalism and modern history.[17] Indeed, since

Thomas is only the latest of several writers to explore aspects of anglophone industrial south Wales's American dreams; *House of America* can be read as a cultural palimpsest, a text superimposed on others by Dai Smith, Jack Jones and Gwyn Thomas (Porth). In Gwyn Thomas's play *The Keep*, the Morton family live the lie of cosy family unity in desolate post-war Rhondda by cultivating the pious legend of a beloved mother killed in a train accident in Pennsylvania. Not altogether surprisingly, they and we learn by the end a very different truth – that Mam took off to the States with a fancy man, and has been living a joyously liberated life ever since.[18]

This plot represents a complex psychological variation on the facts of Gwyn Thomas's own early life, since he lost his beloved mother when he was only six, and his paternal grandfather had emigrated to Youngstown, Ohio, in the late 1860s, only to return to Wales on discovering America to be different from its promise.[19] By contrast, the mother in *The Keep* has fled to the United States to get away from a family tyrannized by egotistical, scheming, overbearingly garrulous males, and from a decaying society mired in pointless intrigue and materialism. Here is a post-war Rhondda whose noble proletarian vision of social justice has imploded. *The Keep* is Thomas's despairing elegy for the Rhondda of his youth, and his satire of the Rhondda of his manhood. But the medium used is humour, humour being, as Thomas once noted, 'a nervous condition. Listen to laughter. It has a strange, sinister sound; the yelping of an uneasy pack.'[20] In her flight to the United States the mother has the last laugh – her frank hedonism having, in Thomas's opinion, become infinitely preferable to the social humbug of a morally bankrupt Rhondda that has sold out to consumer capitalism. The tragic, personal irony secreted in the plot of *The Keep* is, therefore, that the mother reverses the route taken by Thomas's grandfather, who had returned from America to find a better home for body and soul in nineteenth-century Rhondda.

His must, however, have been a fairly unusual case. When the father of the Joseph Parry who was later to compose 'Aberystwyth', 'Myfanwy', and 'Hywel and Blodwen' took his family from mid-nineteenth-century Merthyr to Danville, Pennsylvania, he was emigrating for life. In 1947, his story, along with that of his celebrated son's triumphant return to Wales, was given the colourful Jack Jones treatment in *Off to Philadelphia in the Morning*, a bestseller that may not have been great fiction but was certainly a fascinating ideological construct. Through its treatment of America the novel offers us insights into the Wales of two very different yet interconnected periods – the later nineteenth century in which the action is set, and during which Jack Jones was growing up, and the later 1940s, when the novel was written. Jones brings out the felt parallels in the late nineteenth century between precociously industrial south Wales and the rapidly industrializing United States. Danville is a smaller version of vibrantly cosmopolitan Merthyr, though thankfully lacking the feudal overlordship of those English-born iron barons, the Guests and Crawshays. But America's is a completely philistine society – the only musically gifted elements in its vast population, according to Jones's Joseph Parry, being the Blacks and the Welsh. Thus *Off to Philadelphia* perpetuates the important nineteenth-century Welsh myth, that whereas the Anglo-Saxon peoples were the soul-less potentates of science, industry and empire, it was the impotent Celtic Welsh who were sensitive to religion and culture. Whereas Joseph Parry the American becomes a mechanically efficient ironworker in Danville, his Welsh soul continues to dream of music, a dream that can be fully realized only through his return to a Wales partly symbolized by Myfanwy, the girl he has left behind him.

That Joseph Parry did return to Wales, and subsequently commuted between there and the United States, is very important to a Jack Jones who had lived through the great exodus of Welsh talent in the Depression 1930s. It is surely in the light of that massive loss, so vividly apparent by the 1940s, that in *Off to Philadelphia* Jones resentfully views America as draining his country of 'tidy families . . . breadwinners[,] the best workmen we had . . . what was Wales's loss was America's gain'.[21] As important as that return of Parry's to Wales, however, is his repeated commuting between there and the United States, because such physical to-ing and fro-ing neatly dramatizes his divided allegiance; and by exploiting this psychological division, Jones is able to register his own ambivalent feelings about Wales. Parry is a hero of Welsh-language culture, yet speaks only English at home to his Welsh-American wife, a state of affairs Jones half regrets, because he is very aware of the plight of the Welsh language he believes to be an essential ingredient of Welshness, and yet half approves because, as a Merthyr boy, he knows that industrialism has made English a Welsh language. Likewise, Parry is the great hymn-writer of the Welsh Nonconformist culture sentimentally admired by Jones, but his American experience has so widened his mind that he has become critical of that culture in ways the novelist enthusiastically endorses. Hence, Jones is able to use the American connection in *Off to Philadelphia* as a means of exploring several sensitive aspects both of nineteenth-century and of twentieth-century Welsh culture.

In that novel, the greatest fear of Betty Parry, Joseph's mother, is that in America her children will lose their Welsh and turn to English. This is the great, recurrent, American nightmare of Welsh-language culture, and it has resulted in the United States being demonized as the evil empire, as the monstrously powerful partner of England in an Anglo-American combination Hell-bent on world-wide cultural hegemony. American popular culture is seen as intent on winning the hearts and minds of the whole world, while the American military–industrial complex backs up such soft persuasion with hard muscle. In this reading, Korea and Vietnam, are seen as crude examples of an imperialism that threatens Wales in subtler ways. This myth of America took strong root in Wales in the immediate aftermath of World War II, when the bombing of Hiroshima signalled the emergence of a military, economic and political superpower without rival on the world stage, and in 1958 Pennar Davies gave interesting textual expression to it in his novel *Anadl o'r Uchelder* (*A Breath from on High*), imagining a future when Wales would be a miniscule province in the vast, totalitarian empire of Anglo-Saxonia, run from Washington.[22] The parallel implicitly drawn in the novel is with the situation of the Jews in the Roman Empire at the time of John the Baptist. In a sense, therefore, Davies is recycling a myth of Wales that has been current since the nineteenth century, and that is present in *Off to Philadelphia*: namely, a belief in its potential to be the spiritual heart of the heartless world ruled by the militaristic Mammon of the United States.

The threat posed to Wales by the creep of a greedy consumerist culture by which America secretly consumes the world was powerfully explored, during the 1970s and 1980s, in Nigel Jenkins's poetry, particularly through a satiric dissection of the

Anglo-American idiolect he regarded as the lingua franca of the world-wide empire of capitalism. Its power as a moral and cultural corrosive is shown in 'Colonial', a poem based on Jenkins's experience of roughing it in Europe and North Africa. He remembers the hip Brooklyn slang out of which young Moroccan pimps proudly fashioned the pidgin English they used for barter, and the contempt of these mimic-men for their traditionalist fathers: '*They old, no good. Me/ No Moroccan, me/ English, me American freak.*'[23] But the whole Moroccan episode is recalled as a point of comparison with another native scene, unidentified yet unmistakable: 'Yes, sometimes, David bach,/ sometimes Morocco springs to mind.' Here the Welsh word *bach* functions as a double synecdoche: it stands first for the whole of the Welsh language, and then for that relationship of Welsh to English in Wales which Jenkins sees as the linguistic evidence of the colonial (or 'Moroccan') mentality of a Welsh people ultimately in thrall to Anglo-American capitalism.

In the mid-1970s Jenkins spent a period in the United States working in a travelling circus as rigger, barker and fast buckmaker. His long poem 'Circus', in eighteen short, punchy sections, is based on that experience and offers a linguistically vivid picture of a greedy, cynical life in the immediate post-Vietnam period, when several of the circus-hands were returned veterans who treated the animals the same way they had treated the gooks. In the opening lines of the sequence, the words are held in soft focus, sardonically used to suggest a clichéd view of the magic and enchantment of circus life: 'Comes by night – not a word! – comes/ the circus by night,/ raised through dew, through moonlight' (*AU*, 51). Much of the rest of the poem consists of a demolition of this oneiric vision through a violent 'wording' of this ruthless world of endlessly resourceful exploitation: '*Sno-cones! Popcorn! Cotton candy here!/* You catch em in the midway, you tell em/ what to want./ *Ice-cold sno-cones! Red-hot corn!* Hit em/ with your accent: you're English, tell em,/ English – who the fuck's heard of Wales?' (*AU*, 53) The utter contemptible uselessness of Wales judged by the standards of a world totally obsessed with the value of money – that is clearly what Jenkins is getting at. On the other hand an *English* accent has a cachet, is a cashable asset, and is therefore a power to be reckoned with. Jenkins thus dramatizes the temptation to sell one's weak and negligible Welshness for a profitable place in the macho materialistic culture of aggressive Anglo-Americanism.

The coarse accents of this culture are chillingly caught by the poetry: the cynical sweet-talking ('The seal is conveniently addicted to fish', *AU*, 55); the pious bigotry ('A clean town, this, a family town –/ you get me, son? No fags, no niggers,/ no mother-fuckin reds', *AU*, 54); the terrifying rapacity ('We dry the fuckers out/ then we hit em with the sno-cones –/ and watch those sweet-assed dollars fly', *AU*, 60); the sexist sadism, symbolised by the treatment of an elephant ('Cute Baby Lisa's cute no more./ ... She's got a date between shows with the boys/ from Nam, big screaming ex-fighters/ with a war to keep em wise.// Sticks, chains, electric prods; she/ sweating, pissing, trumpeting rage/ as the circle of pain winds her in', *AU*, 62). This, then, is the American circus that is coming to town here in Wales. But even as we register the ideological message – the outspoken anti-Americanism – of the sequence, we might usefully note how much Jenkins has actually learnt, and how much he has directly benefited, from American poetry. The rawness and abrasiveness of this writing infuse new life into a Welsh culture that has always tended to be polite and genteel. As a writer, Jenkins is a beneficiary of the very culture he is attacking: an ambivalent situation that, I think, typifies modern Wales's complex relations to America.

The self-contempt and self-alienation bred in the Welsh by the seeming wimpishness of their culture compared with that of macho America is savagely satirized by Jenkins in another sequence, 'Never forget your Welsh': 'Yankee GIs/ get drunk and screw/ ... they/ Country & Western/ in Welsh too// "and after the revelling there was silence"// finalising light/ USA genocide stations' (*AU*, 93). The parenthetical allusion ('and after the revelling there was silence') is to celebrated lines from an ancient Welsh war epic ('a gwedi elwch tawelwch fu'). *Y Gododdin* is the *ur*-poem of Welsh literature, a sixth-century work elegizing a small war-band that heroically set out to meet certain death at the hands of an infinitely more powerful foe. By paraphrasing lines from the poem in English and scattering them throughout his sequence, Jenkins produces a complex exercise in intertextuality which turns on a telling juxtaposition of discourses – the demotic style of debased popular culture, and the high style of ancient heroic poetry. Obviously, he is inclined to favour the latter, but he avoids simplistic contrasts. At the very outset, for instance, he draws an ironic parallel between the Welsh bitter in which Welsh people of today drown not only their sorrows but also all authentic memory of their past, and the 'yellow mead' that the warriors were given to drink for a full year before going to battle. If that mead was in one sense a token of the heroic immoderateness of their courage – a courage conspicuously lacking in modern Wales – it was also a symbol of the intoxicated self-delusion that made them the precursors of the media-drunk escapists of the present day. But although Jenkins implicitly recognizes the dangerous appeal to the Welsh character, irrespective of period or language, of flattering indigenous fantasy the politics of his writing is based on what he sees as the oppositional power of Welsh – the way in which it embodies alternatives to an occupying Anglo-American culture which it in the process defines as foreign, degrading and destructive.

Strong though Jenkins's sequences are, the Welsh text that conducts the most sustained and subtle enquiry into the dubious character of modern America as viewed through Welsh eyes is undoubtedly Emyr Humphreys's novel *The Anchor Tree* (1980). Given the high-mindedness that has been instilled into Welsh culture over the centuries by Nonconformity, it is not surprising, perhaps, that so much of Humphreys's best fiction takes the form of an intense meditation on the ambivalent character of ideals, and the equivocal nature of dreams. In the plot of *The Anchor Tree* he takes the rough diamond of the United States and, like an expert cutter, shapes it so as to bring out the coldly glittering multifacetedness of that fascinating society's relationship to its founding dreams. Morgan Rees Dale, a young Welsh historian, sets out to research, excavate and, if possible, restore the physical remains of the ideal Christian community established in Pennsylvania by his ancestor, Robert Morgan Reece, in 1795. Reece's Cambria Nova turns out, however, to have been long supplanted by the small town of Idrisburg, established by his fellow-countryman, and rival, Oliver Lloyd. 'Idrisburg flourished on the hilltop, nourished by aggressive commerce, industry, healthy greed, competition, compromise and original sin. The ruins of the second City of Brotherly Love were lost in the silent forest.'[24] Lloyd had been a hard-headed Calvinist, whereas Reece had been a Christian perfectibilist. There seems little doubt as to which of them has been sourly vindicated by the course of American history.

Humphreys's tragi-comic novel is full of vignettes, etched in acid, of modern American society. Its complacent self-absorption and habit of rewriting history in its own image is instanced in the character of the bigoted patriot Wallace, who as good as believes that the letters BC stands for Before the American Civil War, the terrible conflict in which he is convinced his ancestors gloriously served, and through which, he believes, America was founded. The physical and moral grossness of America is repeatedly displayed, most repulsively in the figure of the smart lawyer 'with a voice like a knife scraping metal and a double chin that wobbled like a turkey's' (*AT*, 144). America's savage, property-based ethic of individualism is shown at its most seedy and sinister in the character of the violent, shotgun-touting redneck Heber S. Hayes, the scavenging owner of the wrecked-car dump under which Cambria Nova is buried:

> Well let me tell you somethin'. Every fuckin' inch of this land is mine and I ain't intendin' no fancy societies treadin' all over it. I didn't get shot in that war just to have a load of Jews and Germans crawlin' all over my land. So you get the hell out of here right this goddamn'd minute. The whole damn lot of you. (*AT*, 71)

But something of the incorrigible idealism of America – magnetic, naive, vulnerable, yet deadly – is embodied in the beautiful young Judith, with whom Morgan Dale becomes dangerously infatuated. As one who was, when a baby, plucked to safety by American troops from the ruins of wartime Germany, Judith is a figure that emblematizes the ambiguous relationship between America and Europe. The American forces that undoubtedly saved Europe were also the forces responsible for the evil inferno of Dresden, and in the very act of liberating Europe they were also, with good-natured egotism, appropriating it for their own purposes. The more intensely involved Morgan Dale becomes with Judith, Cambria Nova, Idrisburg and America, the more morally uncertain and equivocal become those characteristics of his that mark him out as Welsh. Could the idealism on which he prides himself be no more than a suspect sublimation of his sexuality? Is his belief in the primacy of art and culture not just a symptom of his failure to function effectively in the real world of power and business? His fixation on the contribution to American history of a tiny, insignificant ethnic group (the Welsh) – is it not a pathetic flight from the present and a turning of his back on the future? Has 'history' not always belonged to the winners, and are the Welsh not chronic losers? Is this not the brutal truth being conveyed to Morgan by the chairman of his university's History department, 'the Shogun of Historical Studies. The Tycoon of Historiography' (8), whose blunt motto is 'All history matters but my history matters more'? (12).

*   *   *   *

The Anchor Tree brings us back, then, to the enigma of the American dream, the bipolar aspects of which – as inspirational fiction and as historical lie – I should again like to consider by looking briefly at two contrasting poems by Gwyn Thomas (Bangor). 'Wmgawa', he tells us in the poem of that name, was the single Orphic word by uttering which Johnny Weissmuller, when playing Tarzan, could tame all the wild beasts of the jungle.[25] As such, it represents the Pentecostal power possessed by many American films to transcend all languages and cultures and to speak in the universal human tongue of myth. In the poem 'Wmgawa', therefore, one is offered (albeit with a hint of irony, when Thomas describes 'Wmgawa' as the handiest of *African* words) a largely sympathetic vision of mythopoeic America. But 'Parrot Carrie Watson' tells a different story – the story of the first parrot in history to turn pimp, a perversion of the Welsh convention of using a bird as *llatai*, or love-messenger. Carrie Watson's parrot was used in the 1893 Chicago World's Fair to entice white men, with its 'Come on, gentlemen', into a bordello serviced entirely by nubile black girls, and as such it invites us, too, to view the sordid truth that lies concealed behind the American dream.[26]

Welsh-language culture, and those writers in both languages who have been most closely associated with it, has, understandably, long tended to identify not with the dominant WASP society in the United States, but with the Blacks and other socially marginalized ethnic and gender groups. Just as Paul

Robeson had been an inspiration to the working class of south Wales in the 1930s and 1940s, so the Civil Rights marches of the American South moved a later generation of Welsh-language demonstrators, and influenced the campaigns of Cymdeithas yr Iaith Gymraeg in the 1960s. It was, therefore, natural for Gwyn Thomas (Bangor) to mourn the assassination of Martin Luther King in a multi-media presentation for television, *Cadwynau yn y Meddwl* (*Shackles in the Mind*). He produced an ambitious poetic script that ranged freely across forms derived from jazz, blues, Negro spirituals and the rhythms of black preaching, turning the martyrdom of King into an occasion for recalling the many ways in which, from the Middle Passage to Harlem, Blacks had been brutalized, and the many spirited forms, from the controlled physical aggression of the great black boxers to the courageous moral protest of Rosa Parks in Montgomery, Alabama, that their resistance had taken. But, admirably innovative though it is in its attempts to adopt black modes of cultural expression, *Cadwynau yn y Meddwl* is strongly reminiscent, in its moral and religious fervour, of a Welsh Revivalist meeting.

What Thomas, moved by the death of Martin Luther King, has attempted to revive in his text, however, is not the fiery practice of proclaiming the Gospel but the crusading spirit of social reform that characterized radical Welsh Nonconformity in the last century wherever it was to be seen at its heroic best, as it was in the tireless campaigning by the likes of SR (Samuel Roberts, Llanbrynmair, 1800–85) for the abolition of slavery. At the climax of *Cadwynau yn y Meddwl* there is, therefore, an interesting convergence of cultures, as the *hwyl* of Welsh preaching merges with that of the Southern Baptist tradition; as the cries for freedom from the black Churches are echoingly answered by Welsh hymns; and as the haunting rhythms of Martin Luther King's famous public announcement of his dream are revealed to be clearly consonant with the rhythms of the Welsh Bible. *Cadwynau yn y Meddwl* pointedly ends by using the medium of TV film (morally stiffened by documentary clips) to redeem the American dream which had, for decades, been cheapened and falsified by popular American cinema. The Welsh words sung are a version of King's: 'Mae gen i freuddwyd am y wlad/ Lle bydd pawb yn bobol' ('I have a dream of the country/ Where everyone shall be accounted a person').[27]

To this issue of race has been added, over the last two decades, the issue of gender, and during that period several Welsh women writers have been liberatingly brought face to face with their own buried selves in the act of reading work by American counterparts much more precocious than they in exploring the politics of gender identity. Menna Elfyn therefore spoke for her own gener-ation, as well as for herself, when, in 'Byw, Menywod, Byw', she celebrated the costly victory won by Anne Sexton and Sylvia Plath through their suicide. Thanks to them, 'Chwyrlïodd sêr ein hanes/ fel sylwon crog/ uwch crud bydasawd' ('The stars of our history/ have whirled, like mobiles/ round the cradle of the world/ . . . From the live woman a live language/ is loosed, a revolution of poetry').[28]

Elfyn's response to America has, however, been ambivalent in a way that perfectly encapsulates the two starkly contrasting ways in which the United States have for some time impacted on Welsh-language culture. Indeed, during her time as a militant Welsh-language activist in the late 1960s and early 1970s, Elfyn registered through her own actions both the positive and the negative aspects of American influence. On the one hand, she bravely resisted the serious threat to the Welsh language that was posed by Anglo-American capitalism. While attempting to counter the direct threat from this quarter to the traditional rural economy (and hence the social structure) that underpinned the language, she also responded to the indirect threat from a ruth-lessly functionalist ideology that treated Wales's ancient, economically powerless culture as if it were hopelessly super-annuated. But, on the other hand, the very weapons she used to mount her counter-attack against American suzerainty were themselves made in America! Like other members of Cymdeithas yr Iaith Gymraeg, she was consciously indebted to such figures as Henry David Thoreau and Martin Luther King for their exem-plary philosophy and practice of civil disobedience.

Moreover, the ambivalence towards the United States felt by Elfyn and many other Welsh-speakers on the political level is paralleled by their equivocal psychological response to American culture, which appears both liberatingly permissive and danger-ously anarchic; and Elfyn repeatedly registers this ambivalence in gendered terms, as a yearning for and a fear of the freedom that America offers from that confining/confirming concept of the 'feminine' that is inscribed in Welsh-language culture. So, for instance, 'Bron â Boddi' ('Nearly Drowning') turns on a contrast between two bathing-scenes. The first is a scene from childhood, as Elfyn recalls a holiday in Gower, her mother standing guard on the beach to prevent her venturing beyond her depth, her father later playfully teaching his wife how to swim. The second scene sees her swimming alone, 'far from home/ in a sea called Pacific', when she is overwhelmed by a wave that panics her into terror at finding herself 'fragile as flotsam/ in the tempo of the tide'.[29] But if America represents the perilously unbounded, it also represents the exhilarating transgressing of limits, the escape from set, traditional roles, the shedding of unhealthy inhibitions. This appeals to Elfyn, irked as she sometimes is by the moral strait-jacket of a Welsh Nonconformity she nevertheless continues to admire, and exasperated as she often is by the timid submissiveness instilled into the Welsh psyche by centuries of English domination. She imputes these Welsh failings wryly to herself in 'Cot law yn Asheville' ('A Raincoat in Asheville'), as she recalls her timid packing of a mac when setting out for American climes that are eternally sunny. Before the poem's end, however, she has forgetfully left the mac behind, a mere heap of nylon melting on some seat in the sun, while she travels home to Wales ready to relish being soaked recklessly to the skin. America has awakened in her a wish to undress her tribe, to strip them layer by layer, and to leave them dancing in the rain, adventuring in the puddles, lightly prancing in a champagne shower.[30]

Elfyn is one of many who have cautiously revelled in the endless opportunities for self-remaking offered by the United States. And the deconstructing of traditional gender definitions that the culture has come to allow naturally appeals not only to feminists but also to gays and lesbians. Mihangel Morgan pays typically playful tribute to this in his camp confession 'I'm a Fan of Elizabeth Taylor'. The poem can be read as a straightforward satire on the mindless mentality of an ordinary fan who insists, in the very teeth of the self-evident, on feeling 'fairly sure/ In my heart/ That we're basically alike/ Elizabeth Taylor and me'.[31] But hidden in the text is an identification with Taylor that implicitly involves the breaking-down of gender distinctions and the association of personal identity with role-playing in the endless theatre of performative selfhood. Morgan's male persona models himself in imagination on the outrageous Taylor of the two marriages to Burton, the vulgarly expensive ring and the sometimes podgy figure, because she outrages decorum and flouts convention by shamelessly flaunting her difference. Her life is one long burlesque of invention and reinvention of the self, and it is this Taylor's expressed intention of being buried in Pont-rhyd-y-fen that makes the speaker particularly, and slyly, proud. That interment will be the crowning glory, so to speak, of a career devoutly dedicated to the incongruous and outrageous, and it will be a last laugh at the expense of a cautious, conventional Wales.

And finally, to complete the holy trinity of issues that have for some time formed the agenda of progressivist American politics, there is ethnicity, which has again provided Welsh writers more or less hostile to the dominant ethos of the United States with a means of connecting with an oppositional culture there. The Native American peoples have, for instance, been selectively regarded as having affinities with the Welsh, and in the summer of 1989 the intercultural theatre company Taliesin mounted an ambitious production. It featured the multi-racial population of South Cardiff, and was based on John Evans's celebrated journey, at the close of the eighteenth century, in search of Indians of Welsh descent. The text for *Madog: Wales Discovers America* was by Menna Elfyn, who reinterpreted Evans's search as an endeavour to evolve a richer concept of Welshness by exploring affinities with other cultures. Such an attempt had, for Elfyn, a twofold relevance for her own time. First, it offered a paradigm for what needed to happen in late twentieth-century Wales, as the racially mixed communities of Grangetown, Butetown and Riverside exchanged experiences with the longer-established white population, and in the process 'redefin[ed] what Welshness meant to them, and assert[ed] their right to be every bit as Welsh as Welsh-speaking people. It is a question of translating our identities.' Secondly, Evans's journey in search of the Mandans was an effort to make common cause between the Welsh and other disempowered peoples, an attempt Elfyn has herself repeatedly made in and through her poetry:

The experience of opening up my work from the original Welsh language to other languages demonstrate [*sic*] a wish to identify with other communities that are not Welsh-speaking but face the same situations. Transcreation is a path to the edge of my own self-questioning and, hopefully, a source of mutual enrichment.[32]

R. S. Thomas prominently argued the case for such sympathetic identification with the 'Indians' in his 1978 review of Dee Brown's *Bury My Heart at Wounded Knee*: 'I chose to write about this book . . . because of its particular appeal to us, the Welsh-speaking Welsh.'[33] In the way in which Welsh-language culture had fallen victim to the aggressive advance of English industrialization Thomas discovered a broad parallel with the Indian experience of being by turns seduced and ruthlessly coerced into accepting the destructive world of the endlessly dissembling Whites. Thomas's anger at the treatment of the Indians was all the deeper because it included his anger at himself for having, when a boy, been such a gullible fan of American westerns, such a sucker for the white American's dream:

> Many of my generation will remember going to the cinema as children to see exciting battles with the Indians. But as far as I can remember, it was always the Cowboys, the pioneers, who were the heroes. The Indians were savages, launching unprovoked attacks on the white men. We sympathised with the tough, honest cowboy, who referred to them as 'savage varmits' as he decided to avenge some awful, barbaric unprovoked attack. It was the point of view of the white man, the American pioneer, which was put before us most often, and looking back I must confess that I too accepted that point of view. Nevertheless, I can remember how I used to identify secretly with the Indians. They were the expert horsemen. They were the ones who were free and lived closest to nature. (*SP*, 177)

Implicit in these closing lines is the connection, explicitly made elsewhere, between this Native American dream and Thomas's Welsh dream:

> When I was younger, I used to dream of a different society in Wales. The population was comparatively small; there was a distinctive language; there was space. Most of the country had not yet been built on; most of the inhabitants worked on the land – except for the industrial monster in the south. Language is important; it partly reflects the personality of a people and it partly

moulds it. Would it not be possible, by means of Welsh, to avoid the over industrialisation that had taken place in England, the bottomless pit into which so many western countries were rushing? (*SP*, 180)

Enfolded in Thomas's 'description' of the Indians, therefore, is his 'revelation' (to recall Stevens's useful terms) of Wales; a vision that accepts south Wales's myth of itself as Wales's America only to reverse the implications of that myth. South Wales is seen as the country of cowboys, in more than one sense. Who would have thought that the two Thomases, Ed and R. S., could, by these means, have shared a symbolic discourse, even if the socio-political visions they thus respectively communicated differed from each other rather significantly in emphasis?

There is, moreover, a sense in which Iago Prytherch could, in the context of Thomas's remarks, be accounted an honorary Indian; because it was by developing the figure of Prytherch in his poetry, and then prowling ceaselessly around him in baffled imagination for the best part of a quarter of a century, that R. S. Thomas cross-examined his Welsh 'dream'. There is something of his attitude towards Prytherch evident in his description of Indian history:

> Here was yet another of the primitive peoples of the world who had followed a particular way of life since time immemorial; a way of life which was beautiful and in keeping with nature itself. It was confronted by the mechanised way of life, a money-gathering life based on the machine and the gun, and like every other culture, it collapsed before this soul-less Leviathan. (*SP*, 179)

But Thomas has never actually addressed a poem to the Indians, whereas other Welsh poets have. When Iwan Llwyd set out to film the Pueblo Native Americans near Los Alamos, he immediately empathized with their resistance to being caught on camera, and readily agreed to abandon the scheme: 'their words were not taken/ into another language's captivity:/ their little secret is safe' (*MPT*, 110). And although in 'Jemez' he turned the incident into a parable of the meeting between a Western consumer culture greedy for exotic throwaway images and a 'primitive' people safe-guarding 'their pictureless paradise', it is obvious that in this encounter between himself and the Pueblos, Llwyd saw mirrored aspects of the relationship between Welsh-language culture and the world-wide empire of English.

John Davies, likewise, made the Native Americans the subject of 'The White Buffalo', a subtle, eleven-poem sequence in his volume *The Visitor's Book*. In its sympathy for the dispossessed Indians of modern Washington State, its ambivalent feelings about the epic journeys of the pioneers on the Oregon Trail ('with wagons like white/ buffalo rumbling west')[34] and its morally bewildered response to the great American city named after Chief Seattle, the sequence registers Davies's complex awareness of traversing what, in a resonantly multiple pun, he calls 'unsettled ground' (*VB*, 56). This unsettled ground is that both of Washington State and of his homeground of Wales. As an anglophone native of an industrial south Wales that has been thoroughly undermined, and as one now 'settled' with his Welsh-speaking wife on the North Wales coast, John Davies feels his own identity to be a site of conflicting claims, incapable of ever being finally, definitively settled.

His sequence is all the more impressive for the scrupulous way it balances the moral account. Yes, Davies does see shades of the Welsh in the disinherited Native Americans. Looking at Turner's painting of 'SNOW/ on the welsh/ MOUNTAINS/ with an army on the march', he is reminded of his visit to the Lumni reservation, and the young liquor-store Indian stoically resigned to the 'dust and the cars blown/ west across America' (*VB*, 60). Similarly, his visit to the Salish-speaking Joe Washington leads to the wry conclusion that 'This singing in another tongue old anthems/ in a shared redoubt, I've no part in./ But am not apart. I have been here before/ elsewhere' (*VB*, 67). However, such identification does not blind him to his own responsibility as a white man, Welsh or not, for the Indians' sorry condition. Indeed, 'The White Buffalo' is a kind of tone poem on the several moral shades of whiteness – the white waggons, the snow, Robert Bly's 'all white/ hair on scandinavian overdrive' (*VB*, 57), the treacherous disregard of an Indian's white flag, the "managerial white" of an officious sign, the first white settlers whose lives were saved by the Natives, white floats wobbling on the water 'in the milky morning' (*VB*, 66).

'[F]rom reflected heat I learn my own temperature', Davies observes in *The Visitor's Book* (*VB*, 37), and his three most recent collections have been constructed on this principle, with America functioning as his primary means of gauging the current temperature of Wales. His poetry is peppered with the Frostean aphorisms suggested by his travels: 'isn't the point of travel to keep/ going?',[35] 'I think going measures what returning/ is for' (*FP*, *28*), 'connection is accident, that's all' (*FP*, 30), 'West was a verb . . . /there's no way back again' (*FP*, 37). These are the concentrate of his adventures into the American mind (via monologue), among the descendants of Welsh emigrants, in the company of Vietnam veterans. And they all throw light on the Wales that is always at the back of his mind.

'What if, I wonder sometimes,/ I'd opened some other door?' is the question asked in 'Motel' (*FP*, 26), and the idea of a life always being shadowed, or ghosted, by what might have been and the places it might then have occupied (Frost's 'The Road Not Taken') is one repeatedly explored by Davies in his American poems. This obsession arises in part, I suspect, out of Davies's relationship with Wales, figured through his relationship with his father and brother. His father's first language was Welsh, and hearing his wife and daughter speaking it is, for Davies, 'like hearing what might have been' (*VB*, 13). Also his father was a man single-mindedly identified with his locality and rooted to the spot, whereas Davies is acutely conscious of not being 'like my father:/ knowing just where he was, . . . / . . . and Well, he'd say,/ just where d'you think you're going anyway?' (*VB*, 15) Davies's brother, to whom he has addressed many poems, is the exact opposite of his father and took the road Davies had spurned. Having once upped sticks and moved to the United States, not only has he not returned but he has remained in permanent transit, and Davies accordingly regards him with something of the wistful envy with which he recalls his similarly single-minded father. As for Davies himself, he seems doomed, in his own eyes, to be forever caught in two minds, between going and staying. This, his poetry implies, is the modern Welsh condition, since contemporary Wales survives by striking an uneasy, unstable equilibrium between what it once solidly was and the many bewildering, 'foreign' possibilities that now beckon it into being. America provides Davies with occasions and metaphors for reflecting on this complex Welsh condition, just as the speaking in puns that characterizes his poetry is the mode of expression most natural to the Welsh mind of today. Such a forked tongue contrasts not only with yesterday's plain-speaking preferred by his mother ('Why can't poems be clearer?', *VB*, 12) but also with the forthright American idiom that his brother has adroitly mastered: 'At home/ in foreign parts ("Shalom, y'all!") his sights/ locked on what's Now like a keen astronaut,/ he can never stand repeats' (*VB*, 10).

★ ★ ★ ★

As has already been intimated, 'unsettled ground' is one of John Davies's most probingly thoughtful and far-reaching puns, and it is on such ground that Wales has repeatedly met America in the work of recent Welsh writers.[36] One's familiar self can, of course, be unsettled to exhilarating creative effect, and in Gwyneth Lewis's corruscating sequence of 'Illinois Idylls', the United States is associated with exactly such an experience, a kind of transport of imaginative vertigo.[37] She is nevertheless perfectly aware of the ambiguous status of such a state of psychic intoxication, and of the questionable allure of the American dream. The sequence's opening poem frames the waiting plane in an allusion to *Hamlet*, as 'The Boeing dreams its boarding passengers/ which are poured, like poison, through its weeping ear' (*PF*, 14). In like jaundiced mood, she imagines the transatlantic jets 'staining the skies above the glacier' while 'drunk on whisky and on altitude' a woman 'addicted to the "over there"' seems 'contracted to vertiginous air' (*PF*, 14).

But as the plane touches down, 'the runway's shattered shear/ shall make her walk out the shining shards of here', a feminized image which, in context, suggests the breaking of a virginal intactness of sensibility, and exposure to conflictual experience. And this is what in significant part entering the United States means to Gwyneth Lewis: the country becomes the objective correlative of her own multiply divided consciousness. So, in the sixth poem of the sequence, she goes vainly in search of the whip-poor-will whose call comes seductively out of 'the dark and deciduous paradise/ of night' (*PF*, 19). She is doomed to failure, however, since 'whip-poor-wills are ventriloquists/ of distance'. So she is left standing 'alone/ and the tracer atoms of the fireflies/ prickled my skin' (*PF*, 19).

Such moments are quintessentially American and, for Lewis, definitively Welsh. Identity is conceived, in a fashion analogous to the paradigms offered by poststructuralism and postmodernism, not as essentially unitary but as a fugitive function of the dynamic of internal and external relationships that constitute the self. This conception of selfhood is consistent with Lewis's sense of herself as constitutionally bilingual, as existing in or through the interplay between two languages – a self-dividing self-perception the implications of which she works out in another poem from *Parables and Faxes*. There a girl is described as growing up in a home where 'Welsh was the mother tongue, English was his [i.e. the father's]'. The daughter is taught her daddy's language on the sly, so that she becomes flesh of its (his) flesh in an almost salaciously intimate way: 'Was it such a bad thing to be Daddy's girl?' (*PF*, 42). Lewis feels that her identity, both personal and national, voices itself as a ventriloquism of distance, in that, speaking Welsh over here she hears herself/ her *self* speaking English over there, and vice versa. Whip her poor will as much as she likes, she can never will herself to speak with one voice. Lewis therefore sees her bilingualism as a symptom of her hybridity, of what Bakhtin would call the heteroglossia not only of her nation but also of her national and personal identity. And in America she finds the very language (whip-poor-will) and tropes for her situation.

She is thus made aware of the lightness of all being, including her own, and accordingly seems to acquire a new 'buoyancy' – one of the key recurrent words in 'Illinois Idylls', another being 'reformed'. 'We are reformed of our rectitude', she punningly records, following a visit to a building lavishly decorated with bevelled glass; and later she playfully chides herself for having failed, in spite of rising with the dawn, to catch objects re-collecting themselves, 'reforming themselves to integrity', after being disintegrated by the dark. For many of the best Welsh poets of our time, America has been the ambivalent means to re-formation, offering as it does a whole wide Continent of unsettled ground. This vision of the United States has accumulated great power in the poetry of Leslie Norris, now seventy-seven years of age, who has spent most of the last quarter-century in an America that is, for him, the compelling opposite of the pre-war Merthyr in which he felt so much at home as a boy: 'It was a known world then./ We

241

lived in it, we made it/ with our voices// . . . we walked a world/ sound to its very core.'[38] Later experience has eroded such a reassuringly simple concept of 'belonging'. In the poem of that name, Norris wryly recalls an occasion, following a reading in the United States, when an old man eagerly pressed on him evidence of Welsh descent, evidence that in fact seemed clearly to suggest the contrary. But Norris had not the heart to argue, since 'Belonging//After all, is mostly matter of belief' (*CPLN*, 142).

In Norris's work, America becomes a site for exploring the complex issue of 'placing' one's identity, and juxtaposition is the means by which he brings out the intricacy of the matter. An old woman, profiled against the restlessly shifting Maine coastline ('Each tide piles higher the granite/ Pebbles'), suddenly 'sits up, lifts one hand in pride,/ "My grandfather was a full-blooded Englishman"' (*CPLN*, 146). A 'mad boy', met at the same location, tells this stranger, Norris, that he would quickly leave if only he knew what the locals were like; and then moves away, 'was a stone, a/ Post, a shape among shifting/ Shapes, a slow uncertainty' (*CPLN*, 145). Confessing to being an inveterate border-crosser, Norris crouches with feet and palms each in a different state at a point where four states meet, and feels himself to be 'Restless as dust, scattered'; but behind him are the Navajo and Zuni Indians, 'old tribes, hardy and skilled./ They stood behind their work in the flat wind' (*CPLN*, 210).

That flat wind is expressive of the chill sublime of the natural landscape of America, so very different from the comfortable, cherishing greenness of Wales. At Christmas-time in Utah, 'Rough cold out of Idaho/ bundles irrational tumbleweed/ the length of Main Street' (*CPLN*, 180). Over all tower the distant snowpeaks that Norris elsewhere sees as being as deathly white as human bone. America is, for him, the country of the bleak reality principle of the post-war, post-Christian and, in a sense, post-communal world. Appreciative though he is of the new grandeur and beauty to be discovered in a vast world of nature totally impervious to anthropomorphic sentiments, Norris simultaneously sees it as the desolate and desolating country of an annihilating death. This forms an intimate, integral part of his response to America. Reading in Seattle, he cannot help being haunted by the memory that here Vernon Watkins died and Dylan Thomas read: '[A]fter twenty years/ Of famous death/ . . .

the bars are/ Empty of his stories/ And only the downtown Indians/ Are drunk as his memory' (*CPLN*, 141–2).

Norris's deep ambivalences about America are shared by Tony Curtis, whose aggressive delight in the country's raunchy, punchy vulgarity is darkly shadowed by an equivocal fascination with the United States' culture of violence. In 'Veteran: South Dakota 1978' he balances the Vietnam veteran's claim that he had mown down three officers who had ordered him to shoot women and children against the chilling possibility that the ex-soldier may simply have been fantasizing in order to avoid admitting even to himself that he had actually massacred 'those peasants'. If the latter is indeed the case, Curtis concludes, 'then this party is flaking off/ from your head like used skin/ and I'm far from home/ and reason and the neat confusions/ that make poetry'.[39] For both Curtis and Norris, America is indeed 'far from home' in a disturbingly radical sense – it is the place that has the disintegrative potential to make one homeless for ever, eternally unable to make one's way back to the relative stability of Welsh values. And I agree with Tony Conran, that Tony Curtis's outstanding achievement in this respect is his superb sequence 'The Deerslayers', a series of meditations on twenty-four photographs by Les Krims of hunters posing with their dead does limply adorning their Continentals, and their dead bucks peeping out of the trunks of their Buicks. In the pictorial organization of these 'shots', Curtis sees a hidden image, the true composition of a culture: 'Behind you, the land is ploughed and flat. No cover./ This buck's antlers close around you like claws.'[40] But those antlers reach out as far as Wales and close clawingly around Curtis the observer, who realizes that he, too, is figured in this scene: 'Stone-face of a movie G.I./ . . . Wide-eyed, the buck draping your roof/ testifies we use you for our killing' (*TC*, 68).

It is likewise the violence of the American collective imagination, but this time differently evident in the lawless way it violates every conceivable inherited propriety, that excites Robert Minhinnick's interest in several essays in the collection appropriately entitled *Badlands*. Hence his unlikely admiration for the aggressively reactionary Russ Limbaugh, coast-to-coast superstar host of radio talkshow: 'There is about [him] a fascinating aura of menace, rarely achieved by the rotund . . . Somewhere in Limbaugh's politics are the obscene chords of "Street Fighting

Man". There is also James Last and a leavening of country &
western wisdom.'[41] As this passage suggests, America is for
Minhinnick the land not only where anything goes but where
anything goes with anything else. In the way it turns the language
of every culture into alphabet soup, mixing everything up indis-
criminately, the country offers the writer the same kind of
stimulus to new, transgressive insights as the Surrealists used to
find in the materials of the unconscious. America hits Minhinnick
with a punch that disorders all his senses, socking it to him in the
middle of his brain and rearranging his emotions in the way that
a puncher rearranges his opponent's face. Dazed, exhilarated,
angered, outraged, amused, bewildered – Minhinnick is all these,
and sometimes all at once, as he finds himself playing Kurt
Cobain's song 'Rape Me' while 'crossing the Golden Gate
Bridge, turned fire-engine red in the morning light' (B, 133), or
is lost in 'Greyhound time' on the endless prairies in the company
of 'Mars' Barlow, a 280-pound sweet addict whose other passion
is 'running an electronic anthology of [poetic] dross' (B, 54) on
the Internet.

That interminable journey by Greyhound carried Minhinnick
mentally back to the time he went searching in Dakota for the
town of Wales, but failed to find it:

> There is nothing, said the girl at the Grey Goose terminal. There
> is nothing there at all. I pointed to the map but she said no there
> is nothing. Do you know anyone who could take you there? But I
> knew no-one in Wales, and anyway, the girl said, perhaps it isn't
> there anymore. Places disappear you know. That's why there are
> no buses. (B, 56–7)

Back on the bus, Minhinnick squints at the TV monitor tuned in
to the Oscars, at which *Hedd Wyn* had been nominated for an
award. Anthony Hopkins's compèring reminds him of *The Silence
of the Lambs* and the escape, at the end, of the mass murderer
Hannibal Lecter 'to wander anywhere in the world' (B, 57).

Hopkins brings Hannibal Lecter home to Minhinnick, in more
senses than one, and one of the serious possibilities kept in play
throughout *Badlands* is that Wales, like the rest of the world, is
just as bad, just as crazy, just as anarchically violent as the United
States. But there are also balancing possibilities, hinted at elsewhere in a description of Hopkins paying tribute to 'a film from

his native land. He was solicitous and gentle but when I looked in his eyes he wasn't there. Travelling. That's what did it. Unravelling the world. Airport influenza. Caffeine trance. The ceaseless blind migrations' (*B*, 109). For Minhinnick, America's is a culture unravelling as it restlessly, ceaselessly travels. Part of him delights in travelling and unravelling along with it, letting his imagination run riot, even in the violent meaning of that phrase; allowing the United States to reform him of his rectitude, to recall Gwyneth Lewis's expression. But another part of him holds its Welsh ground, keeping its distance, eyeing America warily, viewing it as a warning of how bad things might get. 'How bad does it have to get?', Mars wheezes as he struggles up a hillside in the badlands: 'But it is impossible to answer a demand like that. At least, not if you don't know how bad it was supposed to be in the first place' (*B*, 196). Visiting America is one way Minhinnick provides himself, and us, with an inkling of what might be in store for Wales, unless it puts itself back on the map.

Given the climate of violence with which America tends to be associated, it is appropriate that it is in Vermont that Curtis is brought tinglingly alive by his fear at being caught in a fierce electrical storm (*TC*, 80); and it is the unpredictable, uninhibited ferocity of America that also communicates itself, in all its ambivalent force, to the Welsh-language poet Iwan Llwyd. He has repeatedly drawn on the unrefined energy of American popular culture, a process both instanced and symbolized by his poem on 'Hurricane Bob', in which he uses the celebrated *Twin Peaks* series as his inspiration for imaging the churning tempest as the counterpart of the libidinous energy of creation in human beings.[42] Elsewhere he finds this dangerous energy embodied by Jack Nicholson in the film *Easy Rider*, and by Peter Fonda as he bestrides his narrow Harley-Davidson like a colossus and heads for the open road, 'cyn i'r dyfodol dyfu i fyny – cyn i'r gorwel gau' ('before the future grows up – before the horizon closes') (*DNg*, 19).

Like Curtis, Minhinnick, and others, Iwan Llwyd represents a generation of Welsh writers for whom America (thanks largely to its popular culture) is in the very blood, a fire in the veins.[43] But constant though the (ambiguous) appeal of America may have been for these writers, the inviting features of that America have varied according to the decade in which the author happened to come of impressionable age, as is evident from the recent contrasting collections of poetry published by Llwyd and by Duncan Bush, both of which pivot on their respective preoccupations with the United States. The 1960s is Llwyd's decade, his icons ranging from Elvis, JFK and Martin Luther King to Woodstock, Bob Dylan and the Americanized David Hockney and John Lennon – images full of the treacherous promise of liberation to which his poetry responds so equivocally. As the title of his collection, *Dan Ddylanwad* (*Under the Influence*) ruefully suggests, America retains a sobering power to intoxicate an ageing Welsh romantic who yearns to remain at heart a child of the 1960s even though his head urges wiser counsel. But Bush, by contrast, is a child of the 1950s, his America discovered through the glamour of Hollywood cinema, brash Yankee comics, Frankie Laine records on old 78s, and other seductive images of energy and abundance vividly superimposed on the drabness of an exhausted, belt-tightening post-war Britain.[44]

Bush's Welshness is, in fact, very much that of one who feels himself to be a West Briton. And although he announces 'I'm no patriot, and I'm proud of it', his concept of America obviously originates in his angry identification with the class-ridden, ethnically divided West Britain (south Wales) of his childhood and youth in the Llandaff area of Cardiff. Now pausing *Midway* through his own life, as the title of his volume suggests, he positions an autobiographical essay at the very axial centre of his poetry collection, and in that essay he explores the pivotal role America has played in his development as a person and as a poet. In the intermingling of Welsh and West Country ancestry in his own family background, Bush identifies the kind of meld that the melting-pot culture of the United States has helped him see as the process that also brought modern Britain into existence. Further, in the egalitarianism of the United States he discerns the lineaments of that classless society which, he believes, the British working class vainly dreamt of establishing at the end of the Second World War. But beyond all this, America is ultimately associated in Bush's mind with libertarian dreams of a much more individualistic, militantly anti-collectivist kind, in keeping with the independent line he himself likes to adopt (though he sometimes paradoxically invokes the fiercely English version of it, famously instanced by Cobbett and Orwell): 'And when (from the usual distance of their own ignorance and several thousand miles) people admire America, that is mostly what they are admiring: the famous possibility of becoming what – and who – you choose to be' (*M*, 40). Deploring the consumerist version of this ethic, enthusiastically adopted by 'the spoiled brats of consumerism, born twenty years later, out of the self-indulgence of the late Sixties, and reaching adulthood under Thatcherism thrice-returned' (*M*, 40), Bush insists that his is an entirely different brand of individualism, involving 'a choice not so much existential as imaginative'. America he therefore sees as symbolizing, in his own case, that realm of imaginative possibilities which is the native land of all artists, 'those auto-fantasists who become the compulsive fabricators of other selves' (*M*, 40). America is for Duncan Bush, the wannabe internationalist, what Abercuawg is for the confirmed nationalist R. S. Thomas.

But for Iwan Llwyd, America *is* Abercuawg. He visits the United States knowing that all its open roads start (and end) in Bangor, Gwynedd – which is where *Dan Ddylanwad* pointedly begins, with Llwyd entering a carriage full of giggling young local girls off to Manchester for the day in the same spirit of excited expectation, ancient as Madog's, that propels him to the United States. Very conscious of following imaginatively in the footsteps of T. Gwynn Jones, and literally in those of T. H. Parry-Williams, poets whose words repeatedly echo through his own, Llwyd is also highly aware that since their day the interrelationship between Wales and America has become ever more complex. This he brings out in a poem about waiting at Manchester airport and listening, through a Sony Walkman, to the music of Bob Delyn. Having cavalierly adopted and Americanised the name of Wales's most famous poet, Bob Dylan himself now suffers a like fate, as contemporary Wales's maverick troubadour of pop, Twm Morys, not only (re)appropriates that name but (re-)Welshifies it by modifying it to resemble the Welsh noun *telyn* (harp). The result is an intercultural exercise that wittily brings into play a number of problematical issues concerning the relationship between American and Welsh-language culture. Should the latter keep its distance from the former, for fear of falling victim to Anglo-American cultural imperialism? Or will Welsh culture simply become enervated and impoverished if it fails to expose itself to the urgent and inventive energies of US popular culture?

If it does so, will Welsh culture become merely derivative? Or are there ways by which it can assimilate American cultural materials on its own, renovative, terms?

These are questions that implicitly concern Llwyd throughout *Dan Ddylanwad* (indeed, the very title invites Wales seriously to consider what it means to live 'under the influence' of America), and they are worked out partly in terms of the several contrasting aspects of America with which Wales may choose to identify. Should it be exclusively the America of the ethnic minorities, particularly the Blacks and the Indians, both of them groups that Llwyd features prominently? Should it be the America of the plangent music of the blues and country and western? Or should it be the decaying 'Welsh America' of post-industrial communities in Philadelphia, of the national Gymanfa Ganu and of Welsh inscriptions on old New Orleans tombstones? The answer to these questions is, in turn, inscribed in Llwyd's very manner of writing. Shunning ghettoization of any kind, and particularly loathing the defeatism of sentimentality, Llwyd writes the American section of *Dan Ddylanwad* in the spirit of 'Bob Delyn': that is, as a defiant demonstration that it *is* possible to use America to stimulate and re-energize Welsh culture, because the Welsh language continues to have the resilience to reform itself after the shock of the initial encounter. Accelerating away from the faded, defeated Welshness of Bala Cynwyd, Philadelphia, Llwyd formulates his counter-assertive credo. He celebrates the continuing adventure of being a Welsh-language poet, and does so in the spirited terms of an American open-road movie:

> ac wrth i mi roi nhroed lawr
> ar y Freeway am y de,
> mae'r iaith yn cadw cwmni,
> yn stopio i gael coffi 'to-go',
> yn gyrru drwy'r nos:
> wneith hi ddim aros yn llonydd
> a'i phen yn ei phlu: mae hi berchen y lôn,
> yn ei hawlio hi,
> ac yn gadael hen eiriau fel hiraeth a Chymry-ar-wasgar
> yng nghanol y sbwriel siopa ym Mala Cynwyd. (*DDd*, 25)

> [and as I put my foot down
> on the Freeway for the south

the language keeps me company,
stopping to have coffee 'to-go',
driving all night:
she won't stay still
and down in the dumps: she owns the road,
she claims the road,
and she leaves old phrases like 'hiraeth' and 'Welsh exiles'
in the middle of the rubble of shopping in Bala Cynwyd.]

Llwyd's attitudes in this connection contrast revealingly with those of Gwyn Thomas (Bangor), a poet of an older generation, who included in his 1976 collection *Cadwynau yn y Meddwl* a poem that succinctly suggested the ambiguous relationship between the Welsh language and American English, and between their respective poetic 'traditions'. Most of this poem, 'Wele Di yn Deg, "Baby"' consists of a pastiche of the decorative, poeticized, heavily alliterative style favoured by conservative elements in Welsh culture: 'Lili lawen, beraidd gangen,/ Loyw, luniaidd, lân' (*CM*, 59). Then, into this decorous world of artifice there erupts a crude, invigorating but dismissive American voice: '*Hold it, buster, your tongue twister/ Just don't turn me on;/ In short,/ Baby, what the bloody 'ell are you nattering about?*' (*CM*, 59). In the comedy of that moment of intervention there lies concealed a number of other questions of urgent relevance to Gwyn Thomas and others of his generation. Could that raucously irreverent American voice be translated into Welsh? Should the language even try to capture it? And if it could, and should, then at what cost to itself could that be done? The answers to these questions were, I suspect, by no means clear to Thomas at the time he was writing. But a generation or so later, the answer could seem much clearer to Iwan Llwyd and some of his contemporaries. And with the importation into Welsh of those American accents there came a new realism, a toughness of sensibility and a new empowerment to cope with an abrasively anti-poetic contemporary world. There also came a zany appreciation of the randomness of the multiple, contradictory fictions by which modern man tries to make sense of the irrepressible serendipitousness of things. The film-buff narrator of Mihangel Morgan's important novel *Dirgel Ddyn* (*Secret Man*) revels in the 1933 version of *King Kong*, whose crude special effects turn the film into a kind of unintentional metafiction.

In recalling the famous scene where King Kong, attacked by tiny buzzing planes, scales a scyscraper while clutching a wriggling Fay Wray in his massive hand, the narrator of *Dirgel Ddyn* playfully quotes T. H. Parry-Williams's description of the Empire State Building as 'rocking with height, like a ship on water'.[45] And that prompts me to recall the suggestion I made earlier, that in his 1937 sequence of poems about travelling in the United States, Parry-Williams had anticipated the profoundest response produced by America in Welsh writers of our time. In the landscape (both man-made and natural) of America he found troubling confirmation of the radical instability, and mere contingency, not only of all human order but also of the individual personality itself. As he noted when his customary self had been rendered deaf and dumb by the thundering power of Niagara: 'Ysigol yw gwyrthiau'r ddaear ar ddyn/ Pan fo hwnnw ar daith gydag ef ei hun' ('How unnerved by the wonders of earth is a traveller/ When his companion's himself, without any other') (*CG*, 77). As a result Parry-Williams adopted what might be called the windswept skyscraper's strategy for survival. Instead of trying to maintain the rigid integrity of an unitary personality, he built pliable psychic and verbal structures that allowed for free play, in more than one sense.

And in our time writers have found in America an analogous model for a modern Wales, and a modern Welshness, whose terms of existence are not fixed but chronically uncertain and permanently open to negotiation. This is the perception that comes to John Davies in Utah, as he seeks out the descendants of the Welsh Mormons. To realize that they have virtually lost sight of their family's origins is to accept that 'Flight paths converge,/ fade out, as sky measures gain and loss' (*FP*, 39);[46] and then to return, with a new thoughtfulness, to a Wales 'that must keep/ changing and not changing to stay intact'. This obviously entails a perilous balancing act, and through his American poems Davies has most movingly explored its implications. So, in 'Sources', he is briefly drawn to the idea of cutting free, striking out, relocating himself in a United States that is the image of unencumbered mobility: 'To locate is to limit glittering lines of contact./ Best open yourself, not haunt abandoned yards.'[47] And in 'My Brother Keeps Moving' he wistfully approves of his brother, happily expatriated, who, having years ago left Wales for the

United States, still refuses to commit himself to any one place. But against all this Davies balances a different view, or a view of a different movement – the movement it takes to stay in one place. This is powerfully expressed in 'Reading the Country', a sequence in which every English sonnet is in dialogue with a specifically identified Welsh-language 'original'. And it is with this dialogue between Wales's past and its present, and between its linguistic cultures, that I want to end this chapter and this book, because inscribed in this last poem in the sequence there seems to me to be a dialogue with the United States too – that dialogue with America that has actually made possible the creative dialogue John Davies has with his own country, and that has enabled him to find a correspondence between its two cultures:

> Why speak of such things? Because, under news
> of the airports' pearly culture eased
> through opalescent screens, plain voices say
> what joins-up hills is more than just the view.
> Because hills blur. Now eyes can't see the trees
> for Hollywood, crammed ears turn the way
> of the jogger soundproofed against spring.
>
> Dead poets, tracks of the quarrymen, lakes
> mining silver – why dabble in such things?
> Because the living river of them slakes
> now with then. Strongest in ground fractured,
> it can flow speechless underground, go slack,
> and mistrusts most the fluorescent sea.
> But it runs on, pulling-in the country. (DR, 62)[48]

Notes

~

Notes to Introduction

1 Essay by Roland Mathias in Meic Stephens (ed.), *Artists in Wales* (Llandysul: Gomer, 1971), 168.
2 Robert Crawford, 'Dedefining Scotland', in Susan Bassnett (ed.), *Studying British Cultures: An Introduction* (London: Routledge, 1997), (hereafter *SBC*) 91.
3 M. Wynn Thomas, *Internal Difference: Twentieth-Century Writing in Wales* (Cardiff: University of Wales Press, 1992); (ed.), *DiFfinio Dwy Lenyddiaeth Cymru* (Cardiff: University of Wales Press, 1995).
4 Robert Crawford, *Talkies* (London: Chatto & Windus, 1992) (hereafter *T*).
5 Robert Crawford, 'Identifying Poets', in James A. Davies and Glyn A. Pursglove (eds.), *Writing Region and Nation: Proceedings of the Fourth International Conference on the Literature of Region and Nation* (Swansea: Department of English, University of Wales, Swansea, 1994), 168. See also two other studies by Crawford: *Devolving English Literature* (Oxford: Oxford University Press, 1992); *Identifying Poets: Self and Territory in Twentieth-Century Poetry* (Edinburgh: Edinburgh University Press, 1993).

Notes to Chapter 1: '*In Occidentem & tenebras*': putting Henry Vaughan on the map of Wales

1 All quotations are taken from L. C. Martin (ed.), *Henry Vaughan's Poetry and Selected Prose* (London: Oxford University Press, 1963).
2 'Westering', in Seamus Heaney, *Wintering Out* (London: Faber & Faber, 1972), 79–80.
3 Lois Potter, *Secret Rites and Secret Writing: Royalist Literature, 1641–1660* (Cambridge: Cambridge University Press, 1989), 133.
4 All the views attributed to Jorie Graham were expressed in private conversation. For the significance of her trilingualism, see Helen Vendler, 'Jorie Graham: the Nameless and the Material', in *The Given and the Made: Recent American Poets* (London: Faber & Faber, 1995), 91–130.
5 Roland Mathias, 'Address for the Henry Vaughan Service, 1977', in

A Ride through the Wood: Essays on Anglo-Welsh Literature (Bridgend: Poetry Wales Press, 1985), 237–49. His comment is a simplified version of his densely argued and scrupulously documented account of Vaughan's position in the culture of his day, 'In Search of the Silurist', in a special Vaughan issue of *Poetry Wales*, 11:2 (1975), 6–35: his later researches are summarized in 'The Silurist Re-Examined', *Scintilla*, 2 (Cardiff: Usk Valley Vaughan Association, 1997), 62–77. For Vaughan and the Breconshire of his period, see also Eluned Brown, 'Learned Friend and Loyal Fellow-Prisoner: Thomas Powell and Welsh Royalists', *National Library of Wales Journal*, 18:4 (1974), 374–82. Important studies of Vaughan include F. E. Hutchinson, *Henry Vaughan: A Life and Interpretation* (Oxford: Clarendon Press, 1947); Alan Rudrum, *Henry Vaughan* (Cardiff: University of Wales Press, 1981); Alan Rudrum (ed.), *Essential Articles for the Study of Henry Vaughan* (Hamden, Conn.: Archon Books, 1987); *Swansea Review*, 15 (1995) (special Henry Vaughan issue).

6 Raymond Garlick, *An Introduction to Anglo-Welsh Literature* (Cardiff: University of Wales Press, 1970); Roland Mathias, *Anglo-Welsh Literature: An Illustrated History* (Bridgend: Poetry Wales Press, 1987).

7 This is Meyer Wolfsheim's mistaken, hilariously reverend, description of Jay Gatsby, who 'went to Oggsford College in England. You know Oggsford College?', *The Great Gatsby* (1925; Harmondsworth: Penguin, 1962), 78.

8 The influence of classical culture on Wales is definitively explored in Ceri Davies, *Welsh Literature and the Classical Tradition* (Cardiff: University of Wales Press, 1995).

9 For the British myth of the Welsh, see, for example, T. D. Kendrick, *British Antiquity* (London: Methuen, 1950); Pennar Davies, *Cymru yn Llenyddiaeth Cymru* (Swansea: National Eisteddfod, 1982).

10 For the ideological construction of the English nation-state, see Richard Helgerson, *Forms of Nationhood: The Elizabethan Writing of England* (Chicago, Ill.: University of Chicago Press, 1994); the Welsh contribution to the work of building an English empire is intriguingly examined in Gwyn A. Williams, *Welsh Wizard and British Empire: Dr John Dee and a Welsh Identity* (Cardiff: University College Cardiff Press, 1980).

11 Homi K. Bhaba, *The Location of Culture* (London: Routledge, 1994), 21; Fanon quotation ibid., 35.

12 For Puritan Wales, see Thomas Richards, *A History of the Puritan Movement in Wales, 1639–53* (London: National Eisteddfod Association, 1920); Geraint H. Jenkins, *The Foundations of Modern Wales: Wales, 1642–1780* (Oxford and Cardiff: Oxford University Press, 1987).

13 For English-language studies, see M. Wynn Thomas, *Morgan Llwyd* (Cardiff: University of Wales Press, 1984) and the same author's 'Seventeenth-Century Puritan Writers: Morgan Llwyd and Charles Edwards', in R. Geraint Gruffydd (ed.), *A Guide to Welsh Literature: c.1530–1700* (Cardiff: University of Wales Press, 1997), 190–219; also Geoffrey Nuttall, *The Welsh Saints, 1640–1660: Walter Cradock, Vavasour Powell, Morgan Llwyd* (Cardiff: University of Wales Press, 1957). An important new view of Llwyd is offered, in Welsh, by Goronwy Wyn Owen, *Morgan Llwyd* (Caernarfon: Pantycelyn, 1992).

14 John H. Davies (ed.), *Gweithiau Morgan Llwyd o Wynedd*, vol. II (Bangor and London: Jarvis & Foster/Dent, 1907), 262. Hereafter *GMLl2*.

15 A quotation from Thomas Richards, in Geraint H. Jenkins, *Protestant Dissenters in Wales, 1639–1689* (Cardiff: University of Wales Press, 1992), 17.

16 *Gwaedd yng Nghymru yn Wyneb Pob Cydwybod* (1653), in P. J. Donovan (ed.), *Ysgrifeniadau Byrion Morgan Llwyd* (Cardiff: University of Wales Press, 1985), 7; my translation.

17 Christopher Hill, 'Puritans and the "Dark Corners of the Land"', *Transactions of the Royal Historical Society*, 13 (1963); 'The North and the West', in Christopher Hill, *The World Turned Upside Down: Political Ideas during the English Revolution* (London: Temple Smith, 1972), 59–69.

18 Nigel Smith, *Literature and Revolution in England, 1640–1660* (New Haven and London: Yale University Press, 1994). This includes an interesting comparison of Vaughan and Llwyd (267–73).

19 See Nigel Smith, *Perfection Proclaimed: Language and Literature in English Radical Religion, 1640–60* (Oxford: Oxford University Press, 1988); see also Geoffrey Nuttall, *The Holy Spirit in Puritan Faith and Experience* (Oxford: Blackwell, 1947).

20 Smith, *Perfection Proclaimed*, and M. Wynn Thomas, *Morgan Llwyd: ei Gyfeillion a'i Gyfnod* (Cardiff: University of Wales Press, 1991); see also R. Tudur Jones, 'The Healing Herb and the Rose of Love', in R. B. Knox (ed.), *Reformation, Continuity and Dissent: Essays in Honour of Geoffrey Nuttall* (London: Epworth Press, 1977), 154–79.

21 B. S. Capp, *The Fifth Monarchy Men* (London: Faber & Faber, 1972); P. G. Rogers, *The Fifth Monarchy Men* (London: Oxford University Press, 1966).

22 '1648', in T. E. Ellis (ed.), *Gweithiau Morgan Llwyd o Wynedd*, vol. I (Bangor and London: Jarvis & Foster/Dent, 1899), 22.

23 See Thomas, *Morgan Llwyd* (1991), ch. 6; N. L. Matar, 'Peter Sterry and Morgan Llwyd', *Journal of the United Reformed Church History Society*, 2 (1981), 275–9; Goronwy Wyn Owen, 'Morgan Llwyd a Peter Sterry', *Traethodydd*, 141 (1986), 128–32; Sterry's letters to Llwyd can be found in J. Graham Jones and Goronwy Wyn Owen

(eds.), *Gweithiau Morgan Llwyd o Wynedd*, vol. III (Cardiff: University of Wales Press, 1994), 166–80.

24 Louis L. Martz, *The Poetry of Meditation* (New Haven, Conn.: Yale University Press, 1954), and *The Paradise Within* (New Haven and London: Yale University Press, 1964).

25 Thomas O. Calhoun has even argued that 'Vaughan diverges from the authority of the Anglican Prayer Book in a most interesting way. His tendency toward new combinations and distillations of biblical phrase and voice is typical of the volatile rhetoric, the headlong, seemingly endless glosses upon urgent passions uttered by Independents like Cradock and Vavasour Powell' (*Henry Vaughan: The Achievement of 'Silex Scintillans'* (Newark, NJ: University of Delaware Press, 1981)), 55. Both Cradock and Powell were, of course, Welsh, and comrades of Llwyd's. Vaughan's hermeticism receives extended attention in Ross Garner, *Henry Vaughan: Experience and Tradition* (Chicago, Ill.: University of Chicago Press, 1959); and E. C. Pettet, *Of Paradise and Light* (Cambridge: Cambridge University Press, 1960).

26 Goronwy Wyn Owen, 'Morgan Llwyd and Jakob Böhme', *Traethodydd*, 139 (1984), 72–80; E. Lewis Evans, 'Morgan Llwyd and Jacob Boehme', *Jacob Boehme Society Quarterly*, 1 (1953), 11–16.

27 See J. S. P. Tatlock, *The Legendary History of Britain* (Berkeley: University of California Press, 1974).

28 See the chapter on the seventeenth century in Thomas Parry, *A History of Welsh Literature*, tr. H. Idris Bell (Oxford: Clarendon Press, 1955). A succinct summary of the decline of the *beirdd* is found in R. Geraint Gruffydd, *Llenyddiaeth y Cymry: Cyflwyniad Darluniadol*, vol. II (Llandysul: Gomer, 1989), 55–60. Gruffydd suggests: 'it could be said that Gruffydd Phylip, who died in 1666, was the last of the old *beirdd*' (56–7).

29 See Kendrick, *British Antiquity*, 112–13.

30 Glanmor Williams, 'Some Protestant Views of Early British Church History', in *Welsh Reformation Essays* (Cardiff: University of Wales Press, 1967), 207–19.

31 Glanmor Williams, 'Bishop Richard Davies', in *Welsh Reformation Essays*, 155–90.

32 'The British Church', in F. E. Hutchinson (ed.), *The Works of George Herbert* (Oxford: Clarendon Press, 1970), 109; Vaughan's interest in the British Church is briefly considered in Jonathan F. S. Post, *Henry Vaughan: The Unfolding Vision* (Princeton, NJ: Princeton University Press, 1982), 124–5.

33 M. Wynn Thomas (ed.), Morgan Llwyd, *Llyfr y Tri Aderyn* (Cardiff: University of Wales Press, 1988), 28, and discussion in Thomas, *Morgan Llwyd* (1991), 23–4; see also Donovan (ed.), *Ysgrifeniadau Byrion*, 8.

34 For Vaughan's interest in the past, see particularly Calhoun, *Henry Vaughan*.

35 See Stevie Davies, *Henry Vaughan* (Bridgend: Poetry Wales Press, 1995).

36 Letter dated 9 October 1694, in Martin (ed.), *Vaughan's Works* (Oxford: Clarendon Press, 1957), 696. It is interesting to speculate how far Vaughan's apparent reluctance to co-operate with Aubrey (noted by Mathias) was due to reservations he felt about Aubrey's modern, revisionist approach to the old pseudo-historical lore. For Aubrey's place in the new progressivist antiquarianism of the seventeenth century, see Graham Parry, *The Seventeenth Century: the Intellectual Context of English Literature, 1603–1700* (London: Longman, 1989), ch. 7.

37 See Anne Cluysenaar's poetry on this subject: sections 11, 12 and 13 of 'Henry Vaughan Variations', in her *Timeslips* (Manchester: Carcanet, 1997), 142–5.

38 R. Geraint Gruffydd, 'Dr John Davies, "the old man of Brecknock"', *Archaeologia Cambrensis*, 141 (1992), 1–13.

39 Vaughan draws the distinction between the two scholars to the attention of Anthony Wood in a letter dated 25 April 1689 (Martin (ed.), *Vaughan's Works*, 695). For John Davies of Mallwyd, see the entry in Meic Stephens (ed.), *The Oxford Companion to the Literature of Wales* (Oxford: Oxford University Press, 1986).

40 There is an excellent study of Welsh Humanism in R. Geraint Gruffydd, 'The Renaissance and Welsh Literature', in G. Williams and R. O. Jones (eds.), *The Celts and the Renaissance* (Cardiff: University of Wales Press, 1990), 17–39.

41 Siôn Dafydd Rhys's view of the *beirdd*, as expressed in his letter to the poets (1597, but unpublished) is discussed by Branwen Jarvis in *Llên Cymru*, 12 (1972), 45–56.

42 Quoted in Hutchinson, *Henry Vaughan*, 26. For the relationship between the (identical?) twins, see Stevie Davies, *Henry Vaughan*, passim. See also Eluned Crawshaw, 'The Relationship between the Works of Thomas and Henry Vaughan', *Poetry Wales*, 11:2, (1975), 73–97.

43 Ralph Maud (ed.), Dylan Thomas, *The Broadcasts* (London: Dent, 1991). The work of Thomas is directly compared to that of Vaughan (and Donne) in E. Glyn Lewis, 'Some Aspects of Anglo-Welsh Literature', *Welsh Review* 5:3 (1946), 176–86. This is a fascinating period study, an attempt – which rather poignantly betrays a colonial mentality – to argue that a distinctively Welsh, 'regional' contribution has been made to English literature whenever sophisticated, mainstream English culture has been in need of reinvigoration from 'primitive', 'barbarian' sources (179). Lewis identifies three periods when this happened: the seventeenth century (hence the

significance of Vaughan), the Romantic period, and the 1930s and 1940s (with the appearance of 'the surrealists in painting and verse' (182), among whom Dylan Thomas and Alun Lewis figure prominently).

44 Saunders Lewis, *Is there an Anglo-Welsh Literature?* (Cardiff: Guild of Graduates of the University of Wales, Cardiff Branch, 1939).

45 T. H. Jones, 'The Imagery of the Metaphysical Poem of the Seventeenth Century', (Univ. of Wales, Aberystwyth, MA thesis, 1949). For Jones's poetry, see Julian Croft and Don Dale-Jones (eds.), *The Collected Poems of T. Harri Jones* (Llandysul: Gomer, 1977). (hereafter *THJ*).

46 'Harri Webb to Harri Vaughan', in *A Crown for Branwen* (Llandysul: Gomer, 194), 25.

47 Roland Mathias, 'Man on those Hills of Myrrh and Flowers: A glimpse of Henry Vaughan's Breconshire', *Dock Leaves*, 3:7 (1952) (hereafter *DL*), 20–31. For a contrasting view of Vaughan's treatment of landscape, see Eluned Brown, 'Henry Vaughan and Biblical Landscape', *Essays and Studies*, 30 (1977), 50–60.

48 'Brechfa Chapel', in Roland Mathias, *Snipe's Castle* (Llandysul: Gomer, 1979) (hereafter *SC*), 46–7.

49 Meic Stephens, *Artists in Wales* (Llandysul: Gomer, 1971) (hereafter *AW*), 161–8.

50 'Address for the Henry Vaughan Service 1977', in Roland Mathias, *A Ride through The Wood* (Bridgend: Poetry Wales Press, 1985) (hereafter *RW*), 237–49.

51 An interview with Roland Mathias, in Susan Butler (ed.), *Common Ground* (Bridgend: Poetry Wales Press, 1985) (hereafter *CG*), 181–93.

52 'On the Grave of Henry Vaughan at Llansaintffraed', in Roland Mathias, *The Roses of Tretower* (Llandysul: Dock Leaves Press, 1952), 25. For extended discussion of Mathias's poetry, see particularly 'Roland Mathias: "the strong remembered word"', in Jeremy Hooker, *The Presence of the Past: Essays on Modern British and American Poetry* (Bridgend: Poetry Wales Press, 1987), 141–50; 'Roland Mathias: Headmaster, Critic and Poet', in Tony Conran, *Frontiers in Anglo-Welsh Poetry* (Cardiff: University of Wales Press, 1997), 200–15; M. Wynn Thomas, '"All lenient muscles tensed": The Poetry of Roland Mathias', *Poetry Wales* 33:3 (1998), 21–6.

53 '"Ye Brittish Poets . . .": Some Observations on Early Anglo-Welsh Poetry', *Anglo-Welsh Review*, 84 (1986) (hereafter *YBP*), 8–18. This sentence actually refers to the *beginning* of this process, when Welsh-language panegyric was addressed, after Bosworth, not as previously to the *uchelwyr* but to the new, Anglicized gentry class. Glyn Lewis, 'Some aspects of Anglo-Welsh literature', also features a discussion of Vaughan.

54 Davies Aberpennar, 'God and the World in Henry Vaughan', *Wales*, 5: 8/9 (1945), 62–8.

55 Ibid., 65; and see, for instance, Pennar Davies, *Meibion Darogan* (Llandybïe: Llyfrau'r Dryw, 1968), 34.

56 For Alun Llywelyn-Williams, see Elwyn Evans, *Alun Llywelyn-Williams*, Writers of Wales (Cardiff: University of Wales Press, 1991); also 'The Two Aluns', in M. Wynn Thomas, *Internal Difference* (Cardiff: University of Wales Press, 1992), 49–67. The translations that follow are my own, but a substantial selection of Llywelyn-Williams's poetry and prose in English translation is available in Joseph P. Clancy (tr.), *The Light in the Gloom* (Denbigh: Gee, 1998).

57 'Dyffryn Wysg ac Ystrad Yw', in Alun Llywelyn-Williams, *Crwydro Brycheiniog* (Llandybïe: Llyfrau'r Dryw, 1964), 32–61. There is a poem ('Llansantffraid') addressed to Henry Vaughan in L. Haydn Lewis, *Cerddi'r Cyfnod* (Carnarvon: Llyfrfa'r Methodistiaid Calfinaidd, no date), 27.

58 Alun Llywelyn-Williams, autobiographical essay in Meic Stephens (ed.), *Artists in Wales 2* (Llandysul: Gomer, 1973), 166–80.

59 Quoted in Joseph P. Clancy, *Twentieth Century Welsh Poems* (Llandysul: Gomer, 1992), 246; the English translation of 'Pont y Caniedydd' may be found on pp. 172–6.

60 Although this essay has concentrated on Anglo-Welsh poets who directly address Vaughan, it could also be revealing to consider not admitted interest and influence but rather parallels between Vaughan and certain modern Welsh poets writing in English. For a pioneer study of this kind, see W. Moelwyn Merchant, 'The Sense of Place in the Poetry of Henry Vaughan and R. S. Thomas', *Transactions of the Honourable Society of Cymmrodorion* (1983), 69–80.

Notes to Chapter 2: Hidden Attachments

1 Homi K. Bhabha, *The Location of Culture* (London: Routledge, 1994) (hereafter *LC*), 148.

2 For alternative views of the beginnings of modern Welsh writing in English, see the first chapter of M. Wynn Thomas, *Internal Difference: Twentieth-Century Writing in Wales* (Cardiff: University of Wales Press, 1992), and the case made out for Allen Raine in John Harris, 'Queen of the Rushes', *Planet* (Feb./Mar. 1993), 64–72; Sally Jones, *Allen Raine* (Cardiff: University of Wales Press, 1979); and the Introduction by Katie Gramich to Allen Raine, *Queen of the Rushes* (Dinas Powys: Honno, 1998).

3 See John Harris (introd.), *My People*, by Caradoc Evans (Bridgend: Poetry Wales Press, 1987), 7–47. As is now well known, Evans was in part concerned to debunk the cult of the *gwerin*, an integral part of the ideology of Nonconformist and Liberal Wales. For this cult, see Prys

Morgan, 'The *Gwerin* of Wales – Myth and Reality', in I. Hume and W. T. Pryce (eds.), *The Welsh and Their Country* (Llandysul: Gomer, 1986), 134–52.

4 Dylan Thomas, *Portrait of the Artist as a Young Dog* (1940; London: Guild Books, 1956), 14.

5 Dylan Thomas, *Collected Poems: 1934–1953*, ed. Walford Davies and Ralph Maud (London: Dent, 1988), 73–4.

6 T. Gwynn Jones, 'Argoed', in Tony Conran (tr.), *Welsh Verse*, (Bridgend: Poetry Wales Press, 1986), 260–6.

7 Saunders Lewis, 'The Deluge', in *Twentieth Century Welsh Poems*, tr. Joseph Clancy (Llandysul: Gomer, 1982), 75–7.

8 Saunders Lewis, *Is There an Anglo-Welsh Literature?* (Cardiff: Guild of Graduates of the University of Wales, Cardiff Branch, 1939), 14, 5. An excellent selection of Lewis's work in translation can be found in Alun R. Jones and Gwyn Thomas (eds.), *Presenting Saunders Lewis* (Cardiff: University of Wales Press, 1973); and Harri Prichard Jones (ed.), *Saunders Lewis: A Presentation of His Work* (Springfield, Ill.: Templegate, 1990).

9 Tony Conran (introd.), *Common Ground*, ed. Susan Butler (Bridgend: Poetry Wales Press, 1985), 13.

10 I am indebted to my friend Dr Tony Brown for some of the ideas and phrasing in this paragraph. There is a fine discussion of Dylan Thomas and Welsh praise poetry in Anthony Conran, *The Cost of Strangeness* (Llandysul: Gomer, 1982), 180–7.

11 Kwame Anthony Appiah, 'The Hybrid Age?' (review of *The Location of Culture*, by Homi K. Bhabha), *Times Literary Supplement*, 27 May 1994, 5.

12 R. Williams Parry, 'The Fox', in Conran (tr.) *Welsh Verse*, 269.

13 See, for instance, Tony Conran, *Frontiers in Anglo-Welsh Poetry* (Cardiff: University of Wales Press, 1997), passim.

14 Glyn Jones, *The Dragon Has Two Tongues* (London: Dent, 1968).

15 M. Wynn Thomas, 'Llenyddiaeth a'r fam iaith', *Golwg*, 9 May 1993, 20–1.

16 The arguments in the above paragraph are worked out more fully in Thomas, *Internal Difference*.

17 See, for example, Gerwyn Wiliams, 'Options and Allegiances: Emyr Humphreys and Welsh Literature', *Planet*, 71 (1988), 30–6; Jason Walford Davies, '"Thick Ambush of Shadows": Allusions to Welsh Literature in the Writing of R. S. Thomas', in Tony Brown (ed.), *Welsh Writing in English: A Yearbook of Critical Essays*, 1 (1995), 75–127.

18 Translations of poems by Alun Llywelyn-Williams can be found in Clancy, *Twentieth Century Welsh Poems*, 165–79, and the same author's *The Light in the Gloom: Poems and Prose by Alun Llywelyn-Williams* (Denbigh: Gee, 1998). For translations of Gwyn Thomas's

poetry, see Gwyn Thomas, *Living a Life: Selected Poems, 1962–82*, trans. Joseph P. Clancy and Gwyn Thomas (Amsterdam: Bridges Books, 1982).

19 M. Wynn Thomas, '"Keeping his pen clean": R. S. Thomas and Wales', in William V. Davis (ed.), *Miraculous Simplicity* (Fayetteville: University of Arkansas Press, 1993), 61–79.

20 However, Saunders Lewis did revise his view of Anglo-Welsh Literature in the post-war years. See Harri Prichard Jones, 'Saunders Lewis a'r Eingl-Gymry', in M. Wynn Thomas (ed.), *DiFfinio Dwy Lenyddiaeth Cymru* (Cardiff: University of Wales Press, 1995), 145–69.

21 'Posfyd y Bobieurosiaid', in Alan Llwyd, *Barddoniaeth y Chwedegau* (Felindre: Barddas, 1986), 43–76.

22 The influence of the *bardd gwlad* model on W. H. Davies, Idris Davies and others is considered in Conran, *Frontiers in Anglo-Welsh Poetry*.

23 See, for instance, Waldo Williams, *Dail Pren* (Llandysul: Gomer, 1956). The collection includes a notable poem of praise of, in the form of an elegy for, 'Yr Hen Fardd Gwlad' ('The Old Bardd Gwlad').

24 Harri Webb, *Collected Poems*, ed. Meic Stephens (Llandysul: Gomer 1995) (hereafter *WCP*).

25 See, for instance, *A Dissident Voice* (Bridgend: Seren, 1990); *Graffiti Narratives* (Llandysul: Gomer, 1994); *This House My Ghetto* (Bridgend: Seren, 1995); *Waiting to Belong* (Bridgend: Seren, 1997).

26 Nigel Jenkins, *Acts of Union* (Llandysul: Gomer, 1990), and *Ambush* (Llandysul: Gomer, 1998).

27 *Diawl y Wenallt* (Talybont: Y Lolfa, 1990) (hereafter *DW*); my translations.

28 See Hywel Teifi Edwards, 'O'r Pentre Gwyn i Llaregyb', in Thomas (ed.), *DiFfinio Dwy Lenyddiaeth Cymru*, 7–41.

29 A useful selection of Bobi Jones's poems can be found in Bobi Jones, *Selected Poems*, tr. Joseph P. Clancy (Swansea: Davies, 1987).

30 See Jones, *The Dragon Has Two Tongues*; Conran, *Frontiers in Anglo-Welsh Poetry*.

31 *Skevington's Daughter* (London: Faber & Faber, 1985) (hereafter *SD*).

32 Peter Finch, *Poems for Ghosts* (Bridgend: Seren, 1991), 41–3.

33 Peter Finch, *Selected Poems* (Bridgend: Poetry Wales Press, 1987), 103–4 (hereafter *SP*).

34 See, for instance, Dai Smith, 'A Novel History', in Tony Curtis (ed.), *Wales: The Imagined Nation* (Bridgend: Poetry Wales Press, 1986), 131–58. For criticism of this point of view, see D. Hywel Davies, 'South Wales History Which Almost Excludes the Welsh', *New Welsh Review*, 26 (1994), 8–13.

35 Rural Wales's obsession with respectability, following the Treachery of the Blue Books, has been devastatingly anatomized in, for instance,

Hywel Teifi Edwards, 'Cymru Lân, Cymru Lonydd', in *Codi'r Hen Wlad yn ei Hôl, 1850–1914* (Llandysul: Gomer, 1989), 1–26.

36 Conran (tr.), *Welsh Verse*, Introduction.

37 Joseph P. Clancy (tr.), *The World of Kate Roberts: Selected Stories, 1925–1981* (Philadelphia, Pa.: Temple University Press, 1991).

38 For the treatment of industrial experience by Welsh-language writers, see a number of studies by Hywel Teifi Edwards, including *Arwr Glew Erwa:'r Glo* (Llandysul: Gomer, 1994); 'The Welsh Collier as Hero, 1850–1950', in Tony Brown (ed.), *Welsh Writing in English: A Yearbook of Critical Essays*, 2 (1996), 22–48. Also invaluable are the volumes in *Cyfres y Cymoedd* (The Valleys Series), edited by the same author; these include *Cwm Tawe* (Llandysul: Gomer, 1993); *Cwm Rhondda* (Llandysul: Gomer, 1995); *Cwm Aman* (Llandysul: Gomer, 1996); *Cwm Cynon* (Llandysul: Gomer, 1997).

39 In a letter to Vernon Watkins (28 May 1941) Thomas referred to himself as 'good old 3-adjectives-a-penny belly-churning Thomas, the Rimbaud of Cwmdonkin Drive': Dylan Thomas, *The Collected Letters*, ed. Paul Ferris (London: Dent, 1985), 487.

40 'Dylan Thomas', in Euros Bowen, *Detholion* (Llandysul: Gomer, 1984), 19.

41 Dafydd Elis Thomas, 'The Poetry of Euros Bowen', *Poetry Wales*, 5:3 (1970), 5–12; Cynthia Davies and Saunders Davies (tr.), *Euros Bowen: Priest and Poet* (Cardiff: Church in Wales, 1993).

42 For useful discussion of Symbolism, see Charles Chadwick, *Symbolism* (London: Methuen, 1971); Henri Peyre, *La Littérature Symboliste* (Paris: Presses Universitaires de France, 1976); Laurence M. Porter, *The Crisis of French Symbolism* (Ithaca, NY: Cornell University Press, 1990).

43 Euros Bowen, 'Trafod Cerddi', *Taliesin*, 9 (n.d.) 31–2, and 'Barddoniaeth Dywyll', *Taliesin*, 10 (1965), 37. Bowen discusses his poetry in 'Presenting Euros Bowen', *Mabon*, 2 (1969–70), 192–200.

44 Bowen, *Detholion*, 5; my translation. For a complete English version of the poem, see Conran (tr.), *Welsh Verse*, 287, and Clancy, *Twentieth Century Welsh Poems*, 140.

45 Anthony Hurley (ed.), *The Penguin Book of French Verse*, vol. III (Harmondsworth: Penguin, 1967), 197.

46 Euros Bowen, *Beirdd Simbolaidd Ffrainc* (Cardiff: University of Wales Press, 1980), 41–2.

47 My translation.

48 Roland Mathias, *Vernon Watkins* (Cardiff: University of Wales Press, 1975); Gwen Watkins, *Portrait of a Friend* (Llandysul: Gomer, 1983).

49 Vernon Watkins, *Collected Poems*, ed. Ruth Pryor (Ipswich: Golgonooza, 1986) (hereafter *VWCP*), 103.

50 Kathleen Raine, 'Vernon Watkins: Poet of Tradition', *Anglo-Welsh*

Review, 33 (1964), 25; Roberto Sanesi, 'Vernon Watkins', *Temenos*, 8 (1987), 102–25.

51 *Listener*, 30 Apr. 1964, 721.

52 'Neffertiti', in Bowen, *Detholion*, 108; my translation.

53 Reply to questionnaire, *Wales*, 6:3 (1946), 23–4.

54 Vernon Watkins, *Selected Verse Translations* (London: Enitharmon, 1977), 15; Ian Hilton, 'Vernon Watkins and Hölderlin', *Poetry Wales*, 12:4 (1977), 101–17; H. M. Waidson, 'Vernon Watkins and German Literature', *Anglo-Welsh Review*, 21 (1972), 124–37; Ian Hilton, 'Vernon Watkins as Translator', in Leslie Norris (ed.), *Vernon Watkins, 1906–1967* (London: Faber & Faber, 1970), 74–89.

55 Vernon Watkins, *Selected Verse Translations*, 73.

56 'Marmor Carrara', in Bowen, *Detholion*, 122.

57 Bowen, 'Barddoniaeth Dywyll', 29.

58 Edmund Wilson, *Axel's Castle: A Study in the Imaginative Literature of 1870–1930* (1931; London: Collins Fontana, 1967), 26–7.

59 Susan Bassnett, *Comparative Literature: A Critical Introduction* (Oxford: Blackwell, 1993), 82.

Notes to Chapter 3: Portraits of the artist as a young Welshman

1 Replying to a research student's questionnaire in 1952, Thomas wrote: 'As you know, the name given to innumerable portrait paintings by their artists is, "Portrait of the Artist as a Young Man" – a perfectly straightforward title. Joyce used the painting title for the first time as the title of a literary work. I myself made a bit of doggish fun of the *painting*-title and, of course, intended no possible reference to Joyce': Walford Davies (ed.), *Dylan Thomas: Early Prose Writings* (London: Dent, 1971) (hereafter *EPW*), 157. However, Warren French does argue for parallels between the two *Portrait*s, in 'Two Portraits of the Artist: James Joyce's *Young Man*; Dylan Thomas's *Young Dog*', *University Review of Kansas City* (June 1967), 261–6. I am very grateful to my friend and colleague Dr James A. Davies for bringing this essay to my attention.

2 John Fletcher and Malcolm Bradbury, 'The Introverted Novel', in Malcolm Bradbury and James McFarlane (eds.), *Modernism: A Guide to European Literature, 1890–1930* (Harmondsworth: Penguin, 1976), 404–5.

3 Thomas's comments on *Portrait*, scattered throughout his letters, include the claim, in writing to Vernon Watkins: 'I've kept the flippant title for – as the publishers advised – moneymaking reasons': Paul Ferris (ed.), *The Collected Letters of Dylan Thomas* (London: Dent, 1985) (hereafter *CL*), 437.

4 Richard Kearney, 'A Crisis of Imagination: An Analysis of a Counter-Tradition in the Irish Novel', in M. P. Herdman and R. Kearney

(eds.), *The Crane Bag Book of Irish Studies (1977–1981)* (Dublin: Blackwater Press, 1982) (hereafter *CB*), 390.

5 Dylan Thomas, *Portrait of the Artist as a Young Dog* (1940; London: Guild Books, 1956) (hereafter *PYD*), 97.

6 Richard Kearney sees Joyce's *Portrait* as initiating 'a counter-tradition in the Irish novel' that could be traced through two subsequent generations of Irish writers, including Samuel Beckett, Flann O'Brien, John McGahern, John Banville and Francis Stuart (*CB*, 390).

7 See Homi K. Bhabha, *The Location of Culture* (London: Routledge, 1994). Paul Ferris attributes to Dylan Thomas a description of *Portrait* as 'a provincial autobiography' (*CL*, 277n.).

8 There is a useful outline of the life and work of both Pennar Davies and Glyn Jones in John Rowlands and Glyn Jones (eds.), *Profiles* (Llandysul: Gomer 1980).

9 Pennar Davies's father spoke Welsh, and Davies explains how he himself came to learn the language in 'A Disservice to Welsh Scholarship', in Oliver Davies and Fiona Bowie (eds.), *Discovering Welshness* (Llandysul: Gomer, 1992), 40–3. Both Glyn Jones's parents spoke the language.

10 Reply to questionnaire, *Wales* (1946), 26–7.

11 Keidrych Rhys, *Modern Welsh Poetry* (London: Faber & Faber, 1944), includes seven poems by 'Davies Aberpennar' (13–17) and five by Glyn Jones (77–9).

12 Davies's review appeared in *Wales*, 11 (1939–40), and may be found in *Wales: Numbers One to Eleven* (London: Frank Cass, 1969) (hereafter *W*), 306–8. Glyn Jones's review appeared in *Welsh Review*, 2 (1939), 179–80.

13 'Prologue to an Adventure', in *Wales*, 1 (1937), found in *W*, 1–6. The lines quoted here also appeared on the contents page of the first issue of *Wales*.

14 The culmination of his interest in Thomas's work was his study *Dylan: Druid of the Broken Body* (London: Dent, 1964).

15 First editorial, 'Front populaire', *Heddiw*, 1 (1936–7), no pagination. Aneirin Talfan Davies recalled the launching of *Heddiw* in 'Gwyliau', *Gyda Gwawr y Bore* (Llandybïe: Llyfrau'r Dryw, 1970), 122–8.

16 *Heddiw*, 5 (1939), 417–20.

17 Alun Llywelyn-Williams discussed the founding of *Tir Newydd* in his autobiography, *Gwanwyn yn y Ddinas* (Denbigh: Gee, 1975), 99–110. See also his autobiographical essay in Meic Stephens (ed.), *Artists in Wales* (Llandysul: Gomer, 1973) (hereafter *AW*), 165–80.

18 Cathrin Huws, 'Y Diffiniad Cymraeg o Artist', *Tir Newydd*, 1 (1935) 9–11.

19 Alun Llywelyn-Williams, 'Y Bywyd Dinesig a'r Gymraeg', *Tir Newydd*, 3 (1935) 12–16.

20 Alun Llywelyn-Williams, 'Rhai Sylwadau ar Farddoniaeth Gyfoes Cymru', *Tir Newydd*, 8 (1937) 19–25.

21 Glyn Jones, 'Nodiadau ar Surrealistiaeth', *Tir Newydd*, 10 (1937) 11–14. Compare Jones's comments with those of Dylan Thomas in 1951 (*EPW*, 159–60).

22 W. T. Davies, 'Ein Hamddifadrwydd Llenyddol', *Tir Newydd*, 17 (1939) 6–7.

23 Autobiographical essay by Pennar Davies (*AW*, 124–5).

24 'Sketch of the Author', first published in Glyn Jones, *Poems* (Fortune Press, 1939). The extract quoted is reprinted in Meic Stephens (ed.), *The Collected Poems of Glyn Jones* (Cardiff: University of Wales Press, 1996) (hereafter *CP*), 135–6.

25 Dylan Thomas, *The Map of Love* (London: Dent, 1939) (hereafter *ML*), 106–7.

26 For useful discussions of Thomas's fiction, see Annis Pratt, *Dylan Thomas's Early Prose: A Study in Creative Mythology* (Pittsburgh; Pa.: University of Pittsburgh, 1970); Linden Peach, *The Prose Writings of Dylan Thomas* (London: Macmillan, 1988).

27 See Rhys Davies, *Print of a Hare's Foot* (London: Heinemann, 1969), ch. 3.

28 Pennar Davies, *Meibion Darogan* (Llandybïe: Llyfrau'r Dryw, 1968).

29 Gareth Alban Davies (ed.), *Cerddi Cadwgan* (Dinbych: Gee, 1964). The Cadwgan group was also later to have close connections with another influential periodical, *Fflam* (1946–52), which published the work of R. S. Thomas, Euros Bowen and Bobi Jones, among others.

30 Kate Bosse-Griffiths, *Anesmwyth Hoen* (Llandybïe: Llyfrau'r Dryw, 1941); *Fy Chwaer Efa* (Denbigh: Gee, 1944).

31 For an account of Cylch Cadwgan, see particularly '*Meibion Darogan*, Pennar Davies a Chylch Cadwgan', in J. Gwyn Griffiths, *I Ganol y Frwydr: Efrydiau Llenyddol* (Llandybïe: Gwasg Y Dryw, 1970), 213–22.

32 Rhydwen Williams, *Adar Y Gwanwyn* (Abertawe: Davies, 1972).

33 See, for instance, *Cudd fy Meiau* (*Hide My Faults*) (Abertawe: Penry, 1957), a complex confessional work which is partly a personal diary and partly a meditation on the confessional form itself. Public confession, of a kind, was practised in the Cadwgan group, and this practice is reflected in *Meibion Darogan*: see the essay by Griffiths cited in n. 31 above.

34 Søren Kierkegaard, *The Concept of Irony*, tr. Lee M. Capel (London: Collins, 1966).

35 *Anadl o'r Uchelder* (*A Breath from on High*) (Abertawe: John Penry, 1966); *Mabinogi Mwys* (*Ambiguous Youth*) (Abertawe: Penry, 1979); *Gwas y Gwaredwr* (*Servant of the Saviour*) (Abertawe: Penry, 1991).

36 This model of the artist provides the foundation for Pennar Davies's autobiographical essay in *Artists in Wales*.

37 Two strikingly opposed readings of Davies's fiction in relation to his working class background are Gareth Alban Davies, 'Pennar Davies', in D. Ben Rees (ed.), *Dyrnaid o Awduron Cyfoes* (Pontypridd a Lerpwl: Cyhoeddiadau Modern Cymreig, 1975), 48–62, and John Rowlands, 'Pennar Davies: Y Llenor Enigmatic', *Ysgrifau ar y Nofel* (Cardiff: University of Wales Press, 1992), 219–40. See also M. Wynn Thomas, 'Yr Efrydd a'r Almonwydden: Pennar Davies, Y Llenor o Gwm Cynon', in Hywel Teifi Edwards (ed.), *Cwm Cynon (Cyfres y Cymoedd)* (Llandysul: Gomer, 1997), 309–28.

38 See John Pikoulis, 'The Wounded Bard: The Welsh Novel in English: Lewis Jones, Glyn Jones, Emyr Humphreys', *New Welsh Review*, 26 (1994), 22–34. See also Glyn Jones's discussion of the alienated artist in his introduction to the Welsh section of Stefan Schimanski (ed.), *A New Romantic Anthology* (London: Grey Walls Press, 1949), 167–9. Tony Brown considers Jones's isolation in 'Tones of Loneliness', *New Welsh Review*, 39 (1997), 43–7.

39 *The Valley, the City, the Village* (London: Dent, 1956); quotations from Severn House reprint, 1980 (hereafter *VCV*).

40 See Tony Brown, 'Shock, Strangeness, Wonder: Glyn Jones and the Art of Fiction', *New Welsh Review*, 23 (1993–4), 43–53. In 'Seven Keys to Shaderdom', Shader comes to terms with the appalling images he has seen on television by concluding that 'when in the guise of mother, I, childless, heard/ The screeches of my burning child, meaninglessness itself was then/ Without all meaning, was become vain, barren, dead and meaningless' (*CP*, 116).

41 Jones records his unhappiness at Cheltenham College and while working as a young teacher in Cardiff in *Goodbye What Were You? Selected Writings* (Llandysul: Gomer, 1994), Foreword.

42 Glyn Jones, *The Dragon Has Two Tongues* (London: Dent, 1968).

43 For Welsh-language Modernism, see Dafydd Johnston, 'Moderniaeth a Thraddodiad', *Taliesin*, 80 (1993), 13–24.

44 A room is also used by Glyn Jones for these symbolic purposes in 'Seven Keys to Shaderdom' (1988) (*CP*, 111–12).

Notes to Chapter 4: The good thieves? Translating Welsh literature into English

1 'The Good Thief', in Tony Conran, *Castles*, Variation xx (Llandysul: Gomer, 1993), 46.

2 *Poetry Wales*, 22:4 (1987), 79–81. George Steiner, *After Babel: Aspects of Language and Translation* (London: Athlone Press, 1975). For translation as betrayal, see Milan Kundera, *Testament Betrayed*, tr. Linda Asher (London: Faber & Faber, 1995).

3 Tony Conran, *Castles: A Commentary and Meditation on the Poem*,

(printed privately and circulated by the author; finished 26 August 1991); not paginated.

4 Susan Bassnett and André Lefevere (eds.), *Translation, History and Culture* (London: Cassell, 1995), 7 (hereafter *THC*).

5 Key works include Susan Bassnett, *Translation Studies* (London: Routledge, 1980; revised 1991) (hereafter *TS*); Rosanna Warren (ed.), *The Art of Translation: Voices from the Field* (Boston, Mass.: Northeastern University Press, 1989) (hereafter *AT*); Daniel Weissbort (ed.), *Translating Poetry: The Double Labyrinth* (Iowa City: University of Iowa Press, 1989); Joseph F. Graham (ed.), *Difference in Translation* (Ithaca and London: Cornell University Press, 1985); Theo Hermas (ed.), *The Manipulation of Literature* (Sussex: Croom Helm, 1985); A. Lefevere (ed.), *Translation, Rewriting and the Manipulation of Literary Fame* (London: Routledge, 1992); P. Zlateva, *Translation in Social Action* (London: Routledge, 1993); André Lefevere, *Translating Literature* (New York: Modern Language Association of America, 1992). There have been two important issues of the *Times Literary Supplement* devoted to translation: 18 Sept. 1970; 6 Sept. 1996. In Wales, see the two special numbers of *Llais Llyfrau/Books in Wales*: 3:95 (1995), 4:97 (1997); *2ieithrwydd/cyfiei-thu*, a special issue of *tu chwith* 8 (1997); Angharad Price, 'Cyfoeth Cyfieithu', *Taliesin*, 100 (1997), 11–39; and the Welsh section of *Comparative Criticism*, 19 (special issue, ed. E. S. Shaffer) (1997). An outstanding example of the decision-making, at the level of language, that constitutes literary translation, is found in John Felstiner, *Paul Celan: Poet, Survivor, Jew* (New Haven, Conn.: Yale University Press, 1995); and the emergence of poetry through translation is brilliantly demonstrated in Charles Tomlinson, *Poetry and Metamorphosis* (Cambridge: Cambridge University Press, 1983).

6 Seamus Heaney, 'Earning a Rhyme: Notes on Translating *Baile Suibhne*' (*AT*, 13–20); Michael Cronin, *Translating Ireland* (Cork: Cork University Press, 1986) (hereafter *TI*), 200. See also Thomas Kinsella, *The Dual Tradition: An Essay on Poetry and Politics in Ireland* (Manchester: Carcanet, 1995).

7 The only listings of Welsh–English translations known to me are those useful, preliminary surveys found, for instance, in Meic Stephens (ed.), *Literature in Twentieth-Century Wales: A Selected Bibliography* (London: British Council, 1995).

8 'Preface', in Tony Conran (tr.), *Welsh Verse* (Bridgend: Poetry Wales Press, 1986), 16 (hereafter *WV*).

9 Lady Charlotte Guest (tr.), *The Mabinogion*, 3 vols. (London: 1838–49); single volume edition, London, 1877. The many transla-tions and adaptations that followed would constitute a different study. The standard recent translations are Patrick F. Ford (tr.), *The Mabinogi and other Medieval Tales* (Berkeley: University of California

Press, 1977) and Jeffrey Gantz (tr.), *The Mabinogion* (Harmondsworth: Penguin, 1976). Rolfe Humphries, *Nine Thorny Thickets: Selected Poems by Dafydd ap Gwilym, with 4 translations by Jon Roush* (Ohio: Kent State University Press, 1969).

10 Prys Morgan, *The Eighteenth-Century Renaissance* (Llandybïe: Davies, 1981), 81; Emyr Humphreys, *The Taliesin Tradition* (London: Black Raven Press, 1983), 81.

11 See, for example, Chapter 4, 'The Romantic Image', in Stuart Piggott, *The Druids* (Harmondsworth: Penguin, 1968).

12 Linda Colley, *Britons: Forging the Nation* (New Haven and London: Yale University Press, 1992).

13 Trevor Herbert and Gareth Elwyn Jones, *The Remaking of Wales in the Eighteenth Century* (Cardiff: University of Wales Press, 1988), 159.

14 For Pughe, see Glenda Carr, *William Owen Pughe* (Caernarfon: Pantycelyn, 1993).

15 The term 'contributionism' is employed in Ned Thomas, 'Images of Ourselves', in John Osmond (ed.), *The National Question Again: Welsh Political Identity in the 1980s* (Llandysul: Gomer, 1985), 307–19.

16 Pughe's manuscripts include a translation of the *Mabinogion*, completed in 1800 (Aberystwyth, National library of Wales, MS13243B). Other early, historically important attempts to translate Welsh materials into English include John Walters (ed.), *Translated Specimens of Welsh Poetry* (1782); English versions of *Canu Llywarch Hen*, in William Warrington's *The History of Wales* (1788); Edward Jones (Bardd y Brenin), *The Musical and Poetical Relicks of the Welsh Bards* (1784), *The Bardic Museum* (1802), and *Hen Ganiadau Cymru* (1820); Felicia Hemans, *Welsh Melodies* (1821).

17 John Jenkins, *The Poetry of Wales* (London: Houlston; Llanidloes: Pryse, 1873), Preface (unpaginated).

18 Prys Morgan (ed.), *Brad y Llyfrau Gleision* (Llandysul: Gomer, 1991).

19 F. J. W. Harding, 'Matthew Arnold and Wales', *Transactions of the Honourable Society of Cymmrodorion* (1963), 251–72; Rachel Bromwich, *Matthew Arnold and Celtic Literature in Retrospect, 1865–1965*, O'Donnell Lectures (Oxford: 1965); Nicholas Murray, *A Life of Matthew Arnold* (London: Hodder & Stoughton, 1996).

20 For nineteenth-century condescension towards Wales, frequently tinged with racist prejudice, see Hywel Teifi Edwards, *Codi'r Hen Wlad yn ei Hôl: 1850–1914* (Llandysul: Gomer, 1989).

21 See Hywel Teifi Edwards, *Gŵyl Gwalia: Yr Eisteddfod Genedlaethol yn Oes Victoria, 1858–1868* (Llandysul: Gomer, 1980); *The Eisteddfod* (Cardiff: University of Wales Press, 1990).

22 William Watson, 'Wales: A Greeting', *Cyfansoddiadau Eisteddfod Genedlaethol 1912* (Wrexham), 170–2.

23 Hywel Teifi Edwards discusses Watson in *Codi'r Hen Wlad*, 279–80.

24 Alfred Perceval Graves, *Welsh Poetry Old and New in English Verse*

(London: Longman, Green, 1912). Graves went on to publish *English Verse Translations of the Welsh Poems of Ceiriog Hughes* (Wrexham: no publisher: 1926).

25 H. Idris Bell, *Poems from the Welsh* (Carnarvon: Welsh Publishing Co., 1913), 15 (hereafter *PW*).

26 H. I. Bell and C. C. Bell, *Welsh Poems of the Twentieth Century in English Verse* (Wrexham: Hughes & Son, 1925) (hereafter *WPEV*).

27 John Carey, *The Intellectuals and the Masses* (London: Faber & Faber, 1992).

28 Kate Roberts, *A Summer Day*, tr. Dafydd Jenkins et al. (Cardiff: Penmark Press, 1946) (hereafter *SD*). For English versions of her work, see Ioan Williams, 'Kate Roberts in Translation', *Planet*, 42 (1978), 19–26.

29 For a brief discussion of the interest shown in Wales by artists during the Second World War, see M. Wynn Thomas, *John Ormond* (Cardiff: University of Wales Press, 1997), 9.

30 Hugh Evans, *The Gorse Glen*, tr. E. Morgan Humphreys (Liverpool: Brython Press, 1948). In *Ymyl y Ddalen* (Wrexham: Hughes & Son, 1957), 175–89, R. T. Jenkins draws attention to the way in which Humphreys found echoes in Evans's book of his own upbringing in a disappeared rural Wales.

31 Robert Ruck translated the following novels by T. Rowland Hughes: *From Hand to Hand* (London: Methuen, 1950); *William Jones* (Aberystwyth: Gwasg Aberystwyth, 1953); *Out of Their Night* (Aberystwyth: Gwasg Aberystwyth, 1954); *The Story of Joseph of Arimathea* (Aberystwyth: Gwasg Aberystwyth, 1961); *The Beginning* (Llandysul: Gomer, 1969).

32 John Rowlands, *A Taste of Apples*, tr. Richard Ruck (London: Library 33/Tandem Books, 1961).

33 D. J. Williams, *The Old Farmhouse*, tr. Waldo Williams (London: Harrap, 1961). Similarly important is D. M. Lloyd's translation of W. J. Gruffydd, *The Years of the Locust* (Llandysul: Gomer, 1976). In his Introduction, Lloyd writes: '[Gruffydd's] world is now a closed book to the young generations in Wales today, whether they be Welsh-speaking or English-speaking. Many of them will know more of the remoter and more resplendent periods of Welsh culture, and will feel more affinity with them, but many young Welshmen, fervent though they may be in their patriotism, lack all feeling for a period so much nearer to them in time and therefore far more influential in governing the responses of the mass of the people even today. However much the younger generation may react against Gruffydd, they often need to learn what his memories can teach them – how so many of their fellow-countrymen "tick"' (10–11).

34 Cynthia and Saunders Davies (tr.), *Euros Bowen: Priest-Poet/Bardd-Offeiriad* (Penarth: Church in Wales, 1993), 9, 23–4.

35 R. L. Davies, *Cambrian Lyrics* (Merthyr: Welsh Educational Publishing Co., 1905). Some twenty years later Ernest Rhys produced his series of *Readings in Welsh Literature* (Wrexham: Hughes & Son, 1924) for the schools market; these volumes included snippets of translation.

36 Francis Edwards, *Translations from the Welsh* (privately printed at the Chiswick Press, 1913).

37 For instance, *Welsh Outlook* (March 1914) contains a review of translations from the Welsh, 132–3; and T. Gwynn Jones's intriguing attempt to reproduce Welsh *cynghanedd* in English while translating Dafydd ap Gwilym appears on p. 392.

38 A. G. Prys-Jones (ed.), *Welsh Poets: A Representative English Selection from Contemporary Writers* (London: Erskine MacDonald, 1917).

39 Caradoc Evans, *My People* (London: Melrose, 1915).

40 Other translations by Idris Bell include *Dafydd ap Gwilym: 50 Poems* (with David Bell) (London: Honorable Society of Cymmrodorion, 1942); his version of Welsh *penillion* for *Caseg Broadsheet 2* (Llanllechid: Caseg Press), with wood engravings by John Petts and Brenda Chamberlain; a version of Saunders Lewis, *Amis and Amile*, in *Welsh Review*, 7:4 (1948); and his English version of Thomas Parry's important survey, *A History of Welsh Literature* (Oxford: Clarendon Press, 1955). See also his *Thoughts on Translation* (1943).

41 *Wales*, first series (Summer 1937–Winter 1939/40); second series (July 1943–October 1949); third series (September 1958–New Year 1960). *Welsh Review*, 1939–48, with interruption during the War. This practice of including translations from the Welsh in leading Anglo-Welsh journals was continued by *Dock Leaves* (later *Anglo-Welsh Review*): most notably, a 1954 issue featured a translation, by Dyfnallt Morgan, of his important *pryddest*, *Y Llen*, an evocation of the industrial culture of Merthyr in that town's own distinctive Welsh dialect.

42 Gwyn Jones and Thomas Jones (tr.), *The Mabinogion* (London: Dent, 1949); the text was based on the limited edition, *The Golden Cockerel Mabinogion* (London: Golden Cockerel, 1948).

43 D. M. and E. M. Lloyd (eds.), *A Book of Wales* (London: Collins, 1953); Meic Stephens (ed.), (London: Dent, 1987); James A. Davies, *The Heart of Wales* (Bridgend: Seren, 1994). See also John Davies and Melvyn Jones (eds.), *The Streets and the Stars: An Anthology of Writing from Wales* (Bridgend: Seren, 1992).

44 John Davies and Mike Jenkins (eds.), *The Valleys: An Anthology of Writing from and about the Valleys of Glamorgan and Gwent* (Bridgend: Poetry Wales Press, 1984); Meic Stephens (ed.), *A Cardiff Anthology* (Bridgend: Seren, 1987); James A. Davies (ed.), *A Swansea Anthology* (Bridgend: Seren, 1997). See also Dewi Roberts (ed.), *A Clwyd Anthology* (Bridgend: Seren, 1995).

45 Short-story anthologies with translations from the Welsh include *Welsh Short Stories* (London: Faber & Faber, 1937); Gwyn Jones

(ed.), *Welsh Short Stories* (Harmondsworth: Penguin, 1940); Gwyn Jones (ed.), *Welsh Short Stories*, World's Classics (Oxford: Oxford University Press, 1956); George Ewart Evans (ed.), *Welsh Short Stories* (London: Faber & Faber, 1959); Gwyn Jones and Islwyn Ffowc Elis (eds.), *Twenty-Five Welsh Short Stories* (Oxford: Oxford University Press, 1971); Alun Richards (ed.), *The Penguin Book of Welsh Short Stories* (Harmondsworth: Penguin, 1976); Gwyn Jones and Islwyn Ffowc Elis (eds.), *Classic Welsh Short Stories* (Oxford: Oxford University Press, 1992); Alun Richards (ed.), *The New Penguin Book of Welsh Short Stories* (Harmondsworth: Penguin, 1993).

46 Gwyn Jones (ed.), *The Oxford Book of Welsh Verse in English* (Oxford: Oxford University Press, 1977). The following list of the translators who contributed to the volume gives some idea of the extent of the area with which we are dealing: I. C. Bell and David Bell, George Borrow, Euros Bowen, Joseph P. Clancy, Tony Conran, Kenneth H. Jackson, Glyn Jones, Gwyn Jones, R. Gerallt Jones, Saunders Lewis, Aneirin Talfan, T. Glynne Davies, Rolfe Humphries, Dyfnallt Morgan, R. S. Thomas, Ifor Williams, Mary C. Llewelyn, D. Myrddin Lloyd, Richard Llwyd, Gwyn Thomas, Gwyn Williams. The main translators are Clancy (36), Idris Bell (16), Gwyn Jones (16), Conran (15), Williams (14), Jackson (10).

47 Gwyn Williams, *The Rent That's Due to Love* (London: Editions Poetry London, 1950), 8–9.

48 Gwyn Williams (tr.), *Presenting Welsh Poetry* (London: Faber & Faber, 1959) (hereafter *PWP*), and *The Burning Tree* (London: Faber & Faber, 1956). See also Gwyn Williams, *To Look for a Word: Collected Translations from Welsh Poetry* (Llandysul: Gomer, 1976).

49 Anthony Conran (tr.), *The Penguin Book of Welsh Verse* (Harmondsworth: Penguin, 1967), 13. For a full discussion of Conran's work as a translator, see R. Gerallt Jones, 'The Poet as Translator', in Nigel Jenkins (ed.), *Thirteen Ways of Looking at Tony Conran* (Cardiff: Welsh Union of Writers, 1995), 29–53. Conran's most recent work is *The Peacemakers: Selected Poems by Waldo Williams* (Llandysul: Gomer, 1997).

50 'The Woods of Cynon', in *Harri Webb, Collected Poems*, ed. Meic Stephens (Llandysul: Gomer, 1995), 213–14.

51 There is a brief discussion of Thomas's translations from the Welsh in Jason Walford Davies, 'Allusions to Welsh Literature in the Writing of R. S. Thomas', in Tony Brown (ed.), *Welsh Writing in English: A Yearbook of Critical Essays*, 1 (Cardiff: New Welsh Review, 1995), 88–90. Emyr Humphreys's translations range from adaptations of poetry (e.g. 'Old Man Complaining . . . adapted from *Canu Llywarch Hen*', and 'Branwen's Starling . . . adapted from R. Williams Parry's *Drudwy Branwen*', in *Penguin Modern Poets 27: John Ormond, Emyr Humphreys, John Tripp* (Harmondsworth: Penguin, 1979),

99–101, 117–20), to complete plays (e.g. *Siwan*, in Alun R. Jones and Gwyn Thomas (eds.), *Presenting Saunders Lewis* (Cardiff: University of Wales Press, 1973), 251–300). Humphreys has chosen to include translations from Welsh poetry in his *Collected Poems* (Cardiff: University of Wales Press, 1999).

52 'The Hall of Cynddylan', in John Ormond, *Selected Poems* (Bridgend: Poetry Wales Press, 1987), 36–7.

53 'The Dead', in Leslie Norris, *Collected Poems* (Bridgend: Seren, 1996), 78–9. There is a fine discussion of the poem in Tony Conran, *Frontiers in Anglo-Welsh Poetry* (Cardiff: University of Wales Press, 1997), 230–3 (hereafter *FAWP*).

54 Meic Stephens (ed.), *The Collected Poems of Glyn Jones* (Cardiff: University of Wales Press, 1996), 136. Jones's translations of the old *penillion* have been edited by Dafydd Johnston, *A People's Poetry: Hen Benillion* (Bridgend: Seren, 1997). For a further discussion of the significance of this poetry for Jones, see Chapter 3 ('Portraits of the Artist as a Young Welshman') of the present study.

55 Glyn Jones with T. J. Morgan (tr.), *The Saga of Llywarch the Old* (London: Golden Cockerel Press, 1955).

56 'And good translation like this is not merely translation, for the translator is giving the original through himself, and finding himself through the original': T. S. Eliot, Introduction to Ezra Pound, *Selected Poems* (1928; London: Faber & Faber, 1964), 13.

57 Apart from those mentioned below, other important Welsh–English translations by Joseph P. Clancy include *The Earliest Welsh Poetry* (London: Macmillan, 1970) (hereafter *EPW*); *Medieval Welsh Lyrics* (London: Macmillan, 1965); *Twentieth Century Welsh Poems* (Llandysul: Gomer, 1982). Also there is the privately printed translation of *Hen Benillion* (Northgate Books, PO Box, 106), and his striking renderings, which were included in a public lecture, of some of Ann Griffiths's work into English verse closely modelled on Emily Dickinson's poetry. His most recent publication is *The Light in the Gloom: Poems and Prose by Alun Llywelyn-Williams* (Denbigh: Gee, 1998).

58 Bobi Jones, *Selected Poems*, tr. Joseph P. Clancy (Swansea: Davies, 1987), 11.

59 'Through Welsh-Tinted Glasses', *New Welsh Review*, 32 (1996) (hereafter *TWTG*), 45.

60 Clancy's own volumes of poetry include *The Significance of Flesh* (Llandysul: Gomer, 1984); *here and there, poems 1984–1993* (Clwyd and Wirral: Headland, 1994).

61 Edmund O. Jones, *Welsh Lyrics of the Nineteenth Century* (London: Simpkin, Marshall & Co.; Bangor: Jarvis & Foster, 1896). See also Edmund O. Jones, *Welsh Poets of Today and Yesterday* (Llanidloes: Ellis, 1901).

62 Conran reflects on his hybrid parentage in *Castles*; in *Visions and Praying Mantids* (Llandysul: Gomer, 1997); and in *Suite of Trumps: A Tarot Symphony* (privately produced and circulated, 1997).

63 'Wales England Wed', in Raymond Garlick and Roland Mathias (eds.), *Anglo-Welsh Poetry, 1480–1980* (Bridgend: Poetry Wales Press, 1984), 125.

64 Ernest Rhys, *Welsh Poems and Ballads* (London: Nutt; Carmarthen: Spurrell; Bangor: Jarvis & Foster, 1898). For an account of his life and work, see J. Kimberley Roberts, *Ernest Rhys*, Writers of Wales (Cardiff: University of Wales Press, 1983). Conran pays tribute to Rhys as translator in *FAWP*, and also in *The Cost of Strangeness: Essays on the English Poets of Wales* (Llandysul: Gomer, 1982).

65 R. Gerallt Jones (tr.), *Poetry of Wales 1930–1970* (Llandysul: Gomer, 1974). Removal from Wales was also an important incentive to translate in the case of Gwyn Williams: 'Living abroad and teaching English literature in universities of the Near East sometimes induced nostalgia which I found to be assuaged by reading more and more Welsh poetry and by translating some of it into the language I was paid to use in my work': *To Look for a Word* (Llandysul: Gomer, 1976), Introduction.

66 Kate Roberts, *Feet in Chains*, tr. Idwal Walters and John Idris Jones (Cardiff: Jones, 1972; London: Corgi, 1980). For a sample of the controversy surrounding the translation, see the letters by Walters in *New Welsh Review*, 36 (1997), 102–3, and in *BWA*. See also Wyn Griffith (tr.), *Tea in the Heather* (Cardiff: Jones, 1968); Wyn Griffith (tr.), *The Living Sleep* (Cardiff: Jones, 1976); Elan Closs Stephens and Wyn Griffith (tr.), *Two Old Men* (Gregynog: Gregynog Press, 1981).

67 Dafydd Johnston (tr.), *Canu Maswedd yr Oesoedd Canol/Medieval Welsh Erotic Poetry* (Cardiff: Tafol, 1991); *Galar y Beirdd/ Poets' Grief* (Cardiff: Tafol, 1993).

68 To construct an inventory, let alone an analytical survey, of the scholarly, academic editions of classic Welsh-language literature in English translation – not to mention more unorthodox treatments of the same materials – would be a considerable undertaking. Take, for instance, the following range of treatments of the *Gododdin*: a nineteenth-century translation was produced by the Reverend John Williams (Ab Ithel), while Sir Edward Anwyl's version came out at the beginning of the twentieth-century in *Transactions of the Honorable Society of Cymmrodorion* (1909–10), 95–136; Sir John Morris-Jones tried his hand at it, and so did T. Gwynn Jones, who attempted a verse translation (*Y Cymmrodor*, vol. XXXII); important scholarly translations have been produced by A. O. H. Jarman, *Aneirin: Y Gododdin; The Earliest British Heroic Poem*, Welsh Classics Parallel Text (Llandysul: Gomer, 1988), Kenneth H. Jackson *The Gododdin: The Oldest Scottish*

Poem (Edinburgh: Edinburgh University Press, 1969), and by Joseph P. Clancy in Thomas Owen Clancy, Joseph P. Clancy, Gilbert Márkus and Paul Bibire, *The Early Poetry of Scotland* (Edinburgh: Canongate, 1998); but there has also been a notable attempt by Steve Short to turn the Welsh poem into effective English poetry (Felinfach: Llanerch, 1994).

69 Helen Fulton (tr.), *Selections from the Dafydd ap Gwilym Apocrypha* (Llandysul: Gomer, 1996). Thomas Parry (ed.), *Gwaith Dafydd ap Gwilym* (Cardiff: University of Wales Press, 1952). A full survey of translations of Dafydd ap Gwilym's poetry would require a separate essay. Even confining oneself, for instance, to publications in recent decades would involve not only a consideration of scholarly editions by Rachel Bromwich, *Dafydd ap Gwilym: A Selection of Poems*, Welsh Classics Parallel Texts (Llandysul: Gomer, 1982), and Richard Morgan Loomis, *Dafydd ap Gwilym: The Poems* (Binghamton, NY: State University of New York, 1982), but also many altogether freer versions such as Rolfe Humphries, *Nine Thorny Thickets*; Nigel Heseltine, *Twenty-Five Poems by Dafydd ap Gwilym* (1944; Banbury: Piers Press, 1968); Bryan Walters, *Translations and Original Poetry from the Welsh* (Aberystwyth: Celtion, 1977); David Rowe, *A House of Leaves: Selected Poems of Dafydd ap Gwilym* (Newcastle Emlyn: Gweithdy'r Gair, 1995). Add to this the work of Williams, Jackson, Clancy and Conran, occasional translations by poets such as Norris and Jones, and materials included, for instance, in Robert Gurney, *Bardic Heritage* (London: Chatto & Windus, 1969), and the complexity of the picture begins to become apparent.

70 Menna Elfyn, *Eucalyptus: Selected Poems, 1978–1994* (Llandysul: Gomer, 1995); Gwyn Thomas, *Living a Life: Selected Poems, 1962–1982* (Amsterdam: Bridges Books, 1982); Euros Bowen, *Poems* (Llandysul: Gomer, 1974). See also Rhydwen Williams, *Rhondda Poems* (Swansea: Davies, 1984).

71 T. James Jones and Jon Dressel, *Cerddi Ianws Poems* (Llandysul: Gomer, 1979). See also the sequel, published following the September 1997 referendum, *Wyneb Yn Wyneb/Face To Face* (Llandysul: Gomer, 1997).

72 Menna Elfyn, *Cell Angel* (Newcastle: Bloodaxe, 1996); Nuala Ní Dhomhnaill, *Pharaoh's Daughter* (Loughcrew: Gallery Press, 1994); *Selected Poems*, tr. Michael Hartnett (Dublin: Raven Arts Press, 1993). For the multi-faceted cultural policy adopted by the Irish Arts Council to facilitate such translations, see *TI*, 167ff.

73 Susan Bassnett, *Comparative Literature: A Critical Introduction* (Oxford: Blackwell, 1993), 156.

74 *Poetry Wales,* 11.3 (1976) (special issue on translation).

75 Joseph P. Clancy (tr.), *The Plays of Saunders Lewis*, 4 vols. (Llandybïe: Davies, 1985); Joseph P. Clancy (tr.), *The World of Kate Roberts:*

Selected Stories, 1925–1981 (Philadelphia, Pa.: Temple University Press, 1981). Czeslaw Milosz, 'Bringing a Great Poet Back to Life' (a review of Jan Kochanowski, *Laments*, tr. Stanislaw Baranczak and Seamus Heaney, in *New York Review of Books* (15 Feb. 1996), 26.

76 Harri Pritchard Jones (tr. and ed.), *Saunders Lewis: A Presentation of His Work* (Springfield, Ill.: Templegate, 1990); Jones and Thomas, *Presenting Saunders Lewis*. See also Saunders Lewis, *Selected Poems*, tr. Joseph P. Clancy (Cardiff: University of Wales Press, 1993); and Saunders Lewis, *Monica*, tr. Meic Stephens (Bridgend: Seren, 1997).

77 Roy Harris, 'The Ephemerality of Translation', *Times Literary Supplement*, 28 Aug. 1987, 924, 933.

78 Wiliam Owen Roberts, *Pestilence*, tr. Elizabeth Roberts (London: Hamish Hamilton, 1991); Robin Llywelyn (tr.), *From Empty Harbour to White Ocean* (Cardiff: Parthian Books, 1996); the Rowlands quotation appears on the back cover.

79 Menna Gallie (tr.), *Full Moon* (London: Hodder & Stoughton, 1973); Phillip Mitchell (tr.), *One Moonlit Night* (Edinburgh: Canongate, 1995). It was reprinted in 1999 as a Penguin Modern Classic.

80 Daniel Owen, *Gwen Tomos*, tr. T. Ceiriog Williams and E. R. Harries (Wrexham: Hughes & Son, 1963). Other translations of Owen's work include James Harris (tr.), *Rhys Lewis, Minister of Bethel: An Autobiography* (Wrexham: Hughes & Co., 1888; revised 1915); Claude Vivian (tr.), *Enoc Huws* (1895).

81 Marion Eames, *The Secret Room*, tr. Margaret Phillips (Llandybïe: Davies, 1975); Elin Garlick (tr.), *The Fair Wilderness* (Llandybïe: Davies, 1976); Marion Eames (tr.), *The Golden Road* (Llandysul: Gomer, 1990); E. Tegla Davies, *The Master of Penybryn*, tr. Nina Watkins (Llandybïe: Christopher Davies, 1975).

82 Eifion Evans (tr.), *Pursued by God* (Bridgend: Evangelical Press, 1996); Bethan Lloyd-Jones (tr.), *The Experience Meeting: An Introduction to the Welsh Societies of Evangelical Awakening* (Bridgend: Evangelical Movement of Wales, 1973). See also Robert Jones (tr.), *A View of the Kingdom of Christ* (London: Clowes, 1878); Mrs Richard Llewellyn (tr.), *William Williams, Pantycelyn: Hymns Translated from the Welsh* (London: William Pickering, 1850); R. R. Williams (tr.), *Popular Hymns of Pantycelyn* (Liverpool: Hugh Evans, 1948). Another essay would be required to examine all the translations of classic Welsh religious literature, which include the following: a translation of the verse of Vicar Prichard (London: Longman, 1815); George Borrow (tr.), *The Sleeping Bard . . . from the Cambrian-Welsh* (1860); a translation of the same text by Robert Gwyneddon Davies (1897); T. Gwynn Jones (tr.), *The Visions of the Sleeping Bard* (Gregynog: Gregynog Press, 1940); John Ryan (tr.), *The Hymns of Ann Griffiths* (Carnarvon: Tŷ ar y Graig, 1980); John Ryan (ed.), *Homage to Ann Griffiths* (1976). Morgan Llwyd, *The Book*

of the Three Birds, tr. L. J. Parry in E. Vincent Evans (ed.), *Winning Compositions in the Llandudno Eisteddfod, 1896* (Liverpool, 1898), 195–274.

83 Heaney and Hughes (eds.), *The School Bag.* A similar catholicity of spirit is demonstrated in Simon Armitage and Robert Crawford (eds.), *The Penguin Book of Poetry from Britain and Ireland since 1945* (London: Viking, 1998); but their protestations that they found it difficult to unearth translations from the Welsh language is continuing sad confirmation of the invisibility of Welsh culture (in both languages) beyond (as, indeed, all too often within) the boundaries of the country itself.

84 *Modern Poetry in Translation,* 7 (1995) (special Welsh issue, ed. Dafydd Johnston) (hereafter *MPT*).

85 For instance, there is a need to explore the different *kinds* of work translated: important period pieces such as Gwilym Hiraethog, *Gwen and Gwladys,* tr. W. Rees Evans (London: Paternoster Row, 1896); politically significant works, such as T. E. Nicholas, *Prison Sonnets,* tr. Daniel Hughes et. al. (Griffiths, 1948); popular verse, such as I. D. Hooson, *Poems* and *The Wine,* tr. Blodwen Edwards (Denbigh: Gee, 1980); the genre of the *ysgrif*/essay, as in Meic Stephens (tr.), *The White Stone: Six Essays by T. H. Parry-Williams* (Llandysul: Gomer, 1987), and *Illuminations: An Anthology of Welsh Short Prose* published by the same translator (Cardiff: Welsh Academic Press, 1998); popular classics, exemplified by Meic Stephens (tr.), Islwyn Ffowe Elis, *Shadow of the Sickle* (Llandysul: Gomer, 1998). In addition, there is the fascinating subject of the uncollected translations scattered through many literary and cultural journals.

86 Robert Welch, *Changing States: Transformations in Modern Irish Writing* (London: Routledge, 1973), xi.

87 For consideration of translation along these lines, see Lawrence Venuti, *The Translator's Invisibility* (London: Routledge, 1995). One advantage of multi-authored translations, such as those in *Eucalyptus* and *Cell Angel,* is that they highlight the ways in which the work of the original author is differently refracted by different translators.

88 See the understandable resistance of some contemporary Irish-language writers to English translation, described by Pol O Muiri as deriving from 'a desire to scavenge rather than a desire to propagate. It is patronage and pity' (*TI*, 175).

89 W. H. Auden, *Selected Essays* (London: Faber & Faber, 1964), 32–3.

Notes to Chapter 5: 'Shaman of shifting form': Tony Conran and Welsh *barddas*

1 Parts of this chapter first appeared in Nigel Jenkins (ed.), *Thirteen Ways of Looking at Tony Conran* (Llandysul: Gomer, 1995). The

volume contains important discussions by other contributors of several of the issues touched upon here.

2 Autobiographical essay by Antony Conran in Meic Stephens (ed.), *Artists in Wales 2* (Llandysul: Gomer, 1973), 111–23 (hereafter *AW*). The quotation is from pp. 116–17.

3 Tony Conran, *Castles: Variations on an Original Theme: A Poem* (Llandysul: Gomer, 1993) (hereafter *C*).

4 P. P. Howe (ed.), *The Complete Works of William Hazlitt* (London: Dent, 1930), V, 347.

5 'The Windhover', in W. H. Gardner and N. H. Mackenzie (eds.), *The Poems of Gerard Manley Hopkins* (London: Oxford University Press, 1967), 69.

6 'Anglo-Welsh manqué: On the Selected Poems of Bobi Jones', *Planet*, 76 (1989), 68 (hereafter *BJ*).

7 'The Uncommitted Persona: A Review of *Selected Poems* by Leslie Norris', *Planet*, 62 (1987), 94.

8 T. S. Eliot, 'Introduction' (1928) to the *Selected Poems of Ezra Pound* (London: Faber & Faber, 1969) (hereafter *EP*), 11.

9 'An Invocation of Angels', in Tony Conran, *Formal Poems* (Denbigh: Gee, 1960) (hereafter *FP*), 24.

10 'The Blade', in Tony Conran, *Spirit Level* (Llandybïe: Davies, 1974) (hereafter *SL*), 15.

11 'Elegy for Brenda Chamberlain', in Tony Conran, *Life Fund* (Llandysul: Gomer, 1979) (hereafter *LF*), 51.

12 'My poem pictures the scientist's desire to *know* as a kind of greed in which the ego wants to swallow the whole world' (note on 'Space', in *SL*, 136).

13 Wolfgang Iser, 'On Translatability: Variables of Interpretation', in *European English Messenger*, 4:1 (1995) (hereafter *WI*), 30, 32, 33.

14 'Tony Conran Interview', in *Materion Dwyieithog/Bilingual Matters*, 3 (1991) (hereafter *BM*), 11–12.

15 'Blodeuwedd', in Tony Conran, *Blodeuwedd and Other Poems* (Bridgend: Poetry Wales Press, 1988) (hereafter *B*), 60.

16 See Ian Gregson, 'Tony Conran's Gift Poems in Context', in Jenkins (ed.), *Thirteen Ways*, 119–35; and R. Gerallt Jones, 'The Poet as Translator', ibid., 29–53.

17 Tony Conran, 'Gerard Manley Hopkins as an Anglo-Welsh Poet', in William Tydeman (ed.), *The Welsh Connection* (Llandysul: Gomer, 1986), 118.

18 'A Pregnant Woman', in Bobi Jones, *Selected Poems*, tr. Joseph Clancy (Swansea: Davies, 1987) (hereafter *SP*), 47.

19 Tony Conran, 'Tribal Poetry and the Gogynfeirdd', *Planet*, 99 (1993), 47–58. See also his poem 'Ebyevugo' (*LF*, 67–9).

20 Introduction to Tony Conran (tr.), *Welsh Verse* (Bridgend: Poetry Wales Press, 1986) (hereafter *WV*), 55.

21 Tony Conran, *Frontiers of Anglo-Welsh Poetry* (Cardiff: University of Wales Press, 1997) (hereafter *FP*), 73.

22 David Jones, *Epoch and Artist* (1959; London: Faber & Faber, 1973), 149 (hereafter *EA*).

23 Wallace Stevens, 'Thirteen Ways of Looking at a Blackbird', in *The Collected Poems of Wallace Stevens* (London: Faber & Faber, 1959), 92–5.

24 Review article on Rachel Bromwich, *Dafydd ap Gwilym: A Selection of Poems*, in *Anglo-Welsh Review*, 75 (1984), 85.

25 I am grateful to Dr Peredur Lynch, and to my daughter, Elin Manahan Thomas, for assistance in this analysis.

26 Quoted in Peter Brooker, *A Student's Guide to the Selected Poems of Ezra Pound* (London: Faber & Faber, 1979), 72.

27 'The Debatable Land: Tony Conran on the Tension in His Work between Lyric and Tragedy', *Planet*, 90 (1991–2), 55–65; also the interview in *Materion Dwyieithog/Bilingual Matters*, 15–16. For futher discussion of *The Gododdin* see p. 228 of the present study.

28 Conran, *Castles*, Section IV, Variation xxiv ('Sestina on sestina').

29 From Tony Conran, *A Gwynedd Symphony* (1996), commissioned by Gwynedd County Council and privately printed by the author; no page numbers.

Notes to Chapter 6: The place of gender in the poetry of Gillian Clarke and Menna Elfyn

1 All quotations here from 'Snow White and the Seven Dwarfs', originally published in *Transformations*, are taken from Helen Vendler (ed.), *The Faber Book of Contemporary American Poetry* (London: Faber & Faber, 1990), 269–73.

2 Alicia Ostriker, 'The Thieves of Language: Women Poets and Revisionist Mythmaking', in Elaine Showalter (ed.), *The New Feminist Criticism* (London: Virago, 1993), 314–38.

3 Delyth George, 'Blodeuwedd – Dymchwelydd y Drefn', in John Rowlands (ed.), *Sglefrio ar Eiriau* (Llandysul: Gomer, 1992), 100–14; Jane Aaron, 'Y Flodeuwedd Gyfoes: Llên Menywod, 1973–1993', in M. Wynn Thomas (ed.), *DiFfinio Dwy Lenyddiaeth Cymru* (Cardiff: University of Wales Press, 1995), 190–208.

4 'Blodeuwedd', in Gillian Clarke, *Selected Poems* (Manchester: Carcanet, 1985), 81 (hereafter *SP*).

5 For a useful discussion of aspects of 'Blodeuwedd', and of Clarke's view of women, see Linden Peach, *Ancestral Lines* (Bridgend: Seren, n.d.), 76–94.

6 An English-language version of Saunders Lewis's *Blodeuwedd* is *The Woman Made of Flowers*, tr. Joseph P. Clancy in *The Plays of Saunders Lewis*, vol. I (Llandybïe: Davies, 1985), 45–98.

7 A good introduction to Saunders Lewis's plays is the essay by Bruce

Griffiths on 'His Theatre', in Alun R. Jones and Gwyn Thomas (eds.), *Presenting Saunders Lewis* (Cardiff: University of Wales Press, 1973), 79–92.

8 'Gender in Poetry: A Symposium', *Planet*, 66 (1987/8); Gillian Clarke's contribution is pp. 60–1.

9 'Letter from a Far Country', in Gillian Clarke, *Letter from a Far Country* (Manchester: Carcanet, 1982), 7–18.

10 'The King of Britain's Daughter', in Gillian Clarke, *The King of Britain's Daughter* (Manchester: Carcanet, 1993) (hereafter *KBD*), 1–20.

11 Gillian Clarke has published important essays on the biographical background of 'The King of Britain's Daughter': see 'Beginning with Bendigeidfran', in Jane Aaron, Sandra Betts, Teresa Rees, Moira Vincentelli (eds.), *Our Sisters' Land* (Cardiff: University of Wales Press, 1994), 287–93, and 'The King of Britain's Daughter', in Tony Curtis (ed.), *How Poets Work* (Bridgend: Seren, 1996), 122–6. Other important discussions by Clarke of her work may be found in Susan Butler (ed.), *Common Ground: Poets in a Welsh Landscape* (Bridgend: Poetry Wales Press, 1985), 195–8; 'Interview with Gillian Clarke', in David T. Lloyd (ed.), *The Urgency of Identity: Contemporary English-Language Poetry from Wales* (Evanston, Ill.: Northwestern University Press, 1994), 25–31; introduction to her own work, in Meic Stephens (ed.), *The Bright Field: An Anthology of Contemporary Poetry from Wales* (Manchester: Carcanet, 1991), 54; 'Gillian Clarke: The Poet's Introduction', in Judith Kinsman (ed.), *Six Women Poets* (Oxford: Oxford University Press, 1992), 1.

12 See Gillian Clarke, 'Hunter-Gatherer or Madonna Mistress', *Bloodaxe Catalogue, 1986–7*, 20.

13 Diane Green, '"Making for the Open Sea", A Study of Gillian Clarke as a Female Poet' (University of Wales, Swansea, MA thesis, 1994). See also the same author's 'Gillian Clarke: Love Poet/Historian', *Swansea Review*, 16 (1996), 87–92.

14 *Planet*, 66 (1987/8), 61.

15 'Belfast', in Seamus Heaney, *Preoccupations: Selected Prose, 1966–1978* (London: Faber & Faber, 1980), 34.

16 R. Williams Parry, 'Drudwy Branwen', *Cerddi'r Gaeaf* (Denbigh: Gee, 1952; 1971 edn), 25–8; English translation, 'Branwen's Starling', in Joseph Clancy (tr.), *Twentieth Century Welsh Poems* (Llandysul: Gomer, 1982), 49–53.

17 'A Crown for Branwen', in Harri Webb, *A Crown for Branwen* (Llandysul: Gomer, 1974), 12–13.

18 For the paucity of Welsh literature by and about women, see Tony Conran, 'The Lack of the Feminine', *New Welsh Review*, 17 (1992), 28–31; Francesca Rhydderch, '"Between my tongue's borders": Contemporary Welsh women's Poetry', *Poetry Wales*, 33:4 (1998),

39–44; and the special women's issue of *Traethodydd* (1986). For discussion of women in Welsh society, see Deirde Beddoe, 'Images of Welsh Women', in Tony Curtis (ed.), *Wales: The Imagined Nation* (Bridgend: Poetry Wales Press, 1986), 225–38. For Gillian Clarke as a Welsh woman writer, see Peach, *Ancestral Lines*; also the following articles by Kenneth R. Smith: 'The Portrait Poem: reproduction of mothering', *Poetry Wales*, 24:1 (1988), 48–56, 'Poetry of Place: The Haunted Interiors', *Poetry Wales*, 24:2 (1988), 59–65; 'A Vision of the Future?', *Poetry Wales*, 24:3 (1988), 46–52; 'Praise of the Past: the Myth of Eternal Return in Welsh Writers', *Poetry Wales*, 24:4 (1989), 50–8. The issue of Clarke and gender is also considered in '"A big sea running in a shell": The Poetry of Gillian Clarke', in Jeremy Hooker, *The Presence of the Past* (Bridgend: Poetry Wales Press, 1987), 151–5; see also the same author's essay 'Ceridwen's Daughters: Welsh Women Poets and the Uses of Tradition', in Tony Brown (ed.), *Welsh Writing in English: a Yearbook of Critical Essays* 1 (*New Welsh Review*, 1995), 128–44; and M. Wynn Thomas, '"Staying to mind things": Gillian Clarke's Early Poetry', in Menna Elfyn (ed.), *Trying the Line: A Volume of Tribute to Gillian Clarke* (Llandysul: Gomer, 1997), 44–68.

19 Marilyn Reizbaum, 'Canonical Double Cross: Scottish and Irish Women's Writing', in Karen R. Lawrence (ed.), *Decolonizing Tradition: New Views of Twentieth-Century 'British' Literary Canons* (Urbana: University of Illinois Press, 1992), 165–91. I am grateful to Dr Suzanne Hagemann, University of Mainz, for drawing my attention to this essay.

20 For Clarke and Boland, see Green, '"Making for the Open Sea"'.

21 Quoted in Reizbaum, 'Canonical Double Cross', 177–8.

22 Eavan Boland, *Object Lessons* (London: Vintage, 1996) (hereafter *OL*), 237–8.

23 Menna Elfyn, *Cell Angel* (Newcastle: Bloodaxe, 1996) (hereafter *CA*), 17.

24 Menna Elfyn, *Eucalyptus* (Llandysul: Gomer, 1975) (hereafter *E*), 77.

25 'The Windhover', in W. H. Gardner and N. H. Mackenzie (eds.), *The Poems of Gerard Manley Hopkins* (London: Oxford University Press, 1967), 69.

26 Rowlands (ed.), *Sglefrio ar Eiriau*, 28.

27 Menna Elfyn, 'Beyond the Boundaries', *Planet*, 66 (1987/8), 54–5. See also 'A Poet of Industry and Difficulty: Jon Gower Profiles Menna Elfyn', *New Welsh Review*, 36 (1997), 14–16.

28 'Marwnad Syr John Edward Lloyd', in R. Geraint Gruffydd (ed.), *Cerddi Saunders Lewis* (Cardiff: University of Wales Press, 1992), 31–3; translated in Joseph P. Clancy (tr.), *Saunders Lewis: Selected Poems* (Cardiff: University of Wales Press, 1993), 31–3.

Notes to Chapter 7: Wales's American dreams

1 Sidney Morse, 'My Summer with Walt Whitman', in Horace Traubel (ed.), *In Re Walt Whitman* (?Boston, MA: D. McKay, 1893), 370.

2 Important studies of Wales and America include Hywel Teifi Edwards, *Eisteddfod Ffair y Byd, Chicago 1893* (Llandysul: Gomer, 1990); A. Conway, *The Welsh in America* (Cardiff: University of Wales Press, 1961); David Williams, *Wales and America* (Cardiff: University of Wales Press, 1948); William D. Jones, *Wales in America: Scranton and the Welsh, 1868–1928* (Cardiff: University of Wales Press, 1993); Gwyn A. Williams, *The Search for Beulah Land: the Welsh and the Atlantic Revolution* (London: Croom Helm, 1980); *New Welsh Review*, 32 (1996) (special American number: *Looking towards America (and Back)*).

3 Welsh-language literature published in America will form part of the new Longfellow Institute Series in American Languages and Literatures, edited by Marc Shell and Werner Sollors, to be jointly produced by Harvard's Longfellow Institute and the Johns Hopkins University Press. I am grateful for this information to Melinda Grey, a postgraduate student closely associated with the project.

4 Wallace Stevens, 'Description without place', in *The Collected Poems of Wallace Stevens* (London: Faber & Faber, 1959) (hereafter cited as *CPWS*) 343–4.

5 F. Scott Fitzgerald, *The Great Gatsby* (1925; Harmondsworth: Penguin, 1973), 8.

6 'American Change', in Allen Ginsberg, *Collected Poems, 1947–1980* (London: Viking, 1985), 186.

7 Richard Slotkin, 'Buffalo Bill's "Wild West" and the Mythologization of the American Empire', in Amy Kaplan and Donald E. Pease (eds.), *Cultures of United States Imperialism* (Durham, NC, and London: Duke University Press, 1993), 168.

8 The demythologizing of the American West has been a prominent feature of recent work in American history. See, for instance, Richard Slotkin, *Regeneration through Violence: The Mythology of the American Frontier, 1600–1860* (Middletown, Conn.: Wesleyan University Press, 1973); Clyde A. Milner II, Carol A. O'Connor and Martha A. Sandweiss (eds.), *The Oxford History of the American West* (Oxford: Oxford University Press, 1994); Geoffrey C. Ward (ed.), *The West: An Illustrated History* (London: Weidenfeld & Nicolson, 1996). The fiction that most strikingly illustrates this tendency is that by Cormac McCarthy, including the Border trilogy, and *Blood Meridian: or, The Evening Redness in the West* (London: Picador, 1989).

9 'Dodge City', in Gwyn Thomas, *Symud y Lliwiau* (Denbigh: Gee, 1981), 15; my translation.

10 'Santa Fe', in *Casgliad o Gerddi T. H. Parry-Williams* (Llandysul: Gomer, 1987) (hereafter *CG*), 79.

11 'Pantycelyn a Parry-Williams: Y Pererin a'r Tramp', in Hywel Teifi
Edwards, *Darlith Goffa Syr Thomas Parry-Williams, 1995*
(Aberystwyth: Canolfan Uwchefrydiau Cymreig a Cheltaidd Prifysgol
Cymru, 1996), 24. The American poems of Parry-Williams are also
considered, along with many other responses to the United States by
Welsh-language writers, in Jerry Hunter, 'O'r Ymfudwr Ffuglennol i'r
Twrist Barddol: Teithiau Llenyddol i'r Amerig', in M. Wynn Thomas
(ed.), *Cymru ac America* (Cardiff: University of Wales Press, forth-
coming).

12 'Ar y "Santa Fe"', in *Casgliad o Ysgrifau T. H. Parry-Williams*
(Llandysul: Gomer, 1984) (hereafter *THPW*), 216–18.

13 Roland Barthes, *Mythologies*, tr. Annette Lavers (St Albans: Paladin,
1973); Laurence Coupe, *Myth* (London: Routledge, 1997); K.
Ruthven, *Myth* (London: Methuen, 1976); Sacvan Bercovitch
and Myra Jehlen (eds.), *Ideology and Classic American Literature*
(Cambridge: Cambridge University Press, 1986); Sam B.
Girgus, *The American Self: Myth, Ideology and Popular Culture*
(Albuquerque: University of New Mexico Press, 1981); James Oliver
Robertson, *American Myth, American Reality* (New York: Hill &
Wang, 1980).

14 'Buffalo Bill's', in *e. e. cummings: a selection of poems* (New York:
Harcourt Brace Jovanovich, 1965), 34.

15 Edward Thomas, *Three Plays: 'House of America', 'Flowers of the Dead
Red Sea', 'East from the Gantry'*, ed. Brian Mitchell (Bridgend: Seren,
1994) (hereafter *HA*), 69–70. For Thomas's view of theatre and of
Wales, see 'Wanted: A New Welsh mythology' [interview with Hazel
Walford Davies], *New Welsh Review*, 27 (1994), 56; and Heike Roms,
'Making It New', *Planet*, 125 (1997), 10–16. Daniel Williams sets
Thomas's work in an American context in 'Harry Secombe and the
Junkshop: Nation, Myth and Invention in Edward Thomas's *House of
America* and David Mamet's *American Buffalo*', in Tony Brown (ed.),
Welsh Writing in English: A Yearbook of Critical Essays 4 (1998),
133–58.

16 For American Wales, see Dai Smith, *Wales! Wales?* (London: Allen &
Unwin, 1984).

17 Other treatments of America in recent Welsh theatre include *Dead
Man's Hat*, in Charles Way, *'Dead Man's Hat', 'Paradise Drive', 'In
the Bleak Midwinter'*, ed. Brian Mitchell (Bridgend: Seren, 1994): see
Way's introduction to that volume and his interview with Hazel
Walford Davies, 'A Journey of Exploration', *New Welsh Review*, 33
(1996), 72–81; also Eddie Ladd, *Once upon a Time in the West*,
discussed by Lizzie Eldridge in 'Theatre and Identity', *New Welsh
Review*, 34 (1996), 78–9; Duncan Bush, *Sailing to America*, in Phil
Clark (ed.), *Act One Wales* (Bridgend: Seren, 1997); Dic Edwards,
Utah Blue (1995) and *Mother Hubbard* (1991). These are discussed in

Anna-Marie Taylor (ed.), *Staging Wales: Welsh Theatre, 1979–1997* (Cardiff: University of Wales Press, 1997).

18 Gwyn Thomas, *Three Plays: 'The Keep', 'Jackie the Jumper', 'Loud Organs'*, ed. Michael Parnell (Bridgend: Seren, 1990). For a useful discussion of Ed Thomas and Gwyn Thomas, see Martin Rhys, 'Keeping It in the Family: *Change* by J. O. Francis, *The Keep* by Gwyn Thomas and *House of America* by Ed Thomas', in Katie Gramich and Andrew Hiscock (eds.), *Dangerous Diversity: The Changing Faces of Wales* (Cardiff: University of Wales Press, 1998), 150–77. Also *Opening Up the Keep* (Cardiff: BBC Wales, 1996).

19 Michael Parnell, *Laughter From the Dark: A Life of Gwyn Thomas* (London: Murray, 1988).

20 Quoted in John Ormond, 'Laughter Before Nightfall: An Entertainment culled from the Wit and Work of Gwyn Thomas' (unpublished typescript, n.d.).

21 Jack Jones, *Off to Philadelphia in the Morning* (Harmondsworth: Penguin, 1951), 144.

22 Pennar Davies, *Anadl o'r Uchelder* (Abertawe: Penry, 1966).

23 'Colonial', in Nigel Jenkins, *Acts of Union: Selected Poems, 1974–1989* (Llandysul: Gomer, 1990) (hereafter *AU*), 99.

24 Emyr Humphreys, *The Anchor Tree* (London: Hodder & Stoughton, 1980) (hereafter *AT*), 183. The novel came out of *Our American Dream* (1976), a six-part series on the history of the Welsh in America, written and co-produced by Humphreys. The Cambria settlement in the novel is named after the Welsh settlement of that name, with Beulah as its principal town, established in Pennsylvania by the minister and political activist Morgan John Rhys (1760–1804): see Williams, *The Search for Beulah Land*.

25 'Wmgawa', in Gwyn Thomas, *Wmgawa* (Denbigh: Gee, 1984), 16.

26 'Parrot Carrie Watson', in Gwyn Thomas, *Am Ryw Hyd* (Denbigh: Gee, 1986), 46–7.

27 'Cadwynau yn y Meddwl', in Gwyn Thomas, *Cadwynau yn y Meddwl* (Denbigh: Gee, 1976) (hereafter *CM*), 25.

28 'Byw, benywod, byw' ('Live, sisters, live'), in Menna Elfyn, *Eucalyptus: Detholiad o Gerddi/Selected Poems, 1978–1994* (Llandysul: Gomer, 1995), 80–1.

29 Menna Elfyn, *Cell Angel* (Newcastle upon Tyne: Bloodaxe, 1996) (hereafter *CA*), 49.

30 An unpublished poem, cited with the kind permission of the author.

31 Mihangel Morgan, 'I'm a Fan of Elizabeth Taylor', in *Modern Poetry in Translation*, 7 (1995) (special issue on Welsh literature) (hereafter *MPT*), 120. American films and film stars have regularly featured in Morgan's writings: see, for example, 'James Dean', in Mihangel Morgan, *Diflaniad Fy Fi* (Llandybïe: Barddas, 1988), 12–14.

32 Quotations are from the programme for the show, kindly provided by

Menna Elfyn. For the part played by the Madoc story in British and American history, see Gwyn A. Williams, *Madoc: The Making of a Myth* (London: Eyre & Methuen, 1979).

33 Review by R. S. Thomas of Dee Brown's *Bury My Heart at Wounded Knee*, in Sandra Anstey (ed.), *R. S. Thomas: Selected Prose* (Bridgend: Poetry Wales Press, 1983) (hereafter *SP*), 177.

34 John Davies, *The Visitor's Book* (Bridgend: Poetry Wales Press, 1985) (hereafter *VB*), 56.

35 John Davies, *Flight Patterns* (Bridgend: Seren, 1991) (hereafter *FP*), 30.

36 This aspect of recent Welsh poetry is explored further in M. Wynn Thomas, 'Prints of Wales: Contemporary Welsh Poetry in English', in Hans-Werner Ludwig and Lothar Fietz (eds.), *Poetry in the British Isles: Non-Metropolitan Perspectives* (Cardiff: University of Wales Press, 1995), 97–114.

37 Gwyneth Lewis, *Parables and Faxes* (Newcastle upon Tyne: Bloodaxe, 1995) (hereafter *PF*). See also the same poet's *Zero Gravity* (Newcastle upon Tyne: Bloodaxe, 1998).

38 'Islands', in Leslie Norris, *Collected Poems* (Bridgend: Seren, 1996) (hereafter *CPLN*), 178. The influence of the American Western on Norris's short fiction is explored in Linden Peach, 'Gunslingers and Gamblers: Law and Lawlessness in Leslie Norris's Short Fiction', in Tony Brown (ed.) *Welsh Writing in English: A Yearbook of Critical Essays*, 5 (1999), 130–49.

39 Tony Curtis, *War Voices* (Bridgend: Seren, 1995), 74.

40 Tony Curtis, *Selected Poems, 1970–1985* (Bridgend: Seren, 1986) (hereafter *TC*), 67. Conran's assessment is to be found in Tony Conran, *Frontiers in Anglo-Welsh Poetry* (Cardiff: University of Wales Press, 1997).

41 Robert Minhinnick, *Badlands* (Bridgend: Seren, 1997) (hereafter *B*), 124. See also 'Yellow Dust Journal', *New Welsh Review*, 39 (1997–8), 14–19.

42 'Corwynt Bob (Awst, 1991)', in Iwan Llwyd, *Dan fy Ngwynt* (Talybont: Lolfa, 1992) (hereafter *DNg*), 2.

43 See, for instance, Tony Curtis's 'Couples from the Fifties', in *The Last Candles* (Bridgend: Seren, 1989), 73–4, or 'Dolenni' (translated as 'Bonds'), the work of Gerwyn Wiliams, a Welsh-language poet of a younger generation (*MPT*, 162–9). There is also the interesting case of John Barnie, who has implicitly explored the Welsh context of his interest in blues in *The King of Ashes* (Llandysul: Gomer, 1989).

44 Iwan Llwyd, *Dan Ddylanwad* (Bodedern: Taf, 1997) (hereafter *DDd*); Duncan Bush, *Midway* (Bridgend: Seren, 1998) (hereafter *M*). Other interesting recent works to feature Wales in relation to America include Gary Ley, *Taking Ronnie to the Pictures* (Bridgend: Seren, 1998) and Lewis Davies, *Freeways* (Cardiff: Parthian Books, 1997).

45 Mihangel Morgan, *Dirgel Ddyn* (Llandysul: Gomer, 1993), 94. For the complete poem, see *CG*, 76. There is an illuminating discussion of Mihangel Morgan's work by John Rowlands, 'Ymyl Aur y Geiniog: Agwedd ar waith Mihangel Morgan', in Hywel Teifi Edwards (ed.), *Cwm Cynon* (Llandysul: Gomer, Cyfres y Cymoedd, 1997), 342–80.

46 See also such other poems in *Flight Patterns* as 'Utah' (34) and 'At Spanish Fork' (37).

47 John Davies, *Dirt Roads* (Bridgend: Seren, 1997) (hereafter *DR*), 35.

48 The poem is a response to 'Maniach', in Euros Bowen, *Cerddi Rhydd* (Liverpool: Gwasg y Brython, 1961), 8. Davies based his poem on the translation 'Bits and Pieces', in Joseph Clancy (tr.), *Twentieth Century Welsh Poems* (Llandysul: Gomer, 1982), 142.

Index